Jurisprudence
of
Liberty

In memory of Eugene Kamenka

Jurisprudence of Liberty

Suri Ratnapala

LLB (Colombo), LLM (Macquarie), PhD (Queensland)
Senior Lecturer in Law, University of Queensland

G A Moens

JD (Leuven), LLM (Northwestern), PhD (Sydney)
Professor of Law, University of Queensland

Butterworths

Sydney — Adelaide — Brisbane — Canberra — Melbourne — Perth
1996

AUSTRALIA BUTTERWORTHS 271-273 Lane Cove Road, North Ryde 2113
111 Gawler Place, Adelaide 5000
King George Tower, 71 Adelaide Street, Brisbane 4000
53-55 Northbourne Avenue, Canberra 2601
461 Bourke Street, Melbourne 3000
178 St Georges Terrace, Perth 6000
On the Internet at: www.butterworths.com.au

CANADA BUTTERWORTHS CANADA LTD Toronto and Vancouver

IRELAND BUTTERWORTH (IRELAND) LTD Dublin

FRANCE EDITIONS DU JURIS-CLASSEUR Paris

HONG KONG BUTTERWORTHS ASIA

MALAYSIA MALAYAN LAW JOURNAL SDN BHD Kuala Lumpur

NEW ZEALAND BUTTERWORTHS OF NEW ZEALAND LTD Wellington and Auckland

SINGAPORE BUTTERWORTHS ASIA Singapore

SOUTH AFRICA BUTTERWORTH PUBLISHERS (PTY) LTD Durban

UNITED KINGDOM BUTTERWORTH & CO (PUBLISHERS) LTD London and Edinburgh

USA MICHIE Charlottesville, Virginia

National Library of Australia Cataloguing-in-Publication entry

Ratnapala, Suri, 1947- .
Jurisprudence of liberty.
Includes index.
ISBN 0 409 30785 8 (pbk.).
1. Liberty. 2. Civil rights. 3. Civil rights — Australia. 4. Law — Philosophy.
I. Moens, Gabriël, 1948- . II. Title.
342.94085

Typeset in Berkeley and Helvetica.
Printed in Australia by Brown Prior Anderson Pty Ltd.

CONTENTS

PREFACE

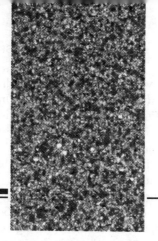

Liberty means different things to different persons. Yet, it is clear that all human beings cherish liberty in one form or another. It is also clear that law has a profound connection with liberty. People are often deprived of their liberty contrary to law. Equally people are denied liberty by force of law. Law has potential to both promote and destroy liberty.

As legal theorists we have also been inquisitive about the nexus between liberty and the abstract idea of law. Textbooks on jurisprudence tend to focus on the great debates surrounding the various definitions of law. While these debates are central to the concerns of this book, we seek to engage the reader in a discussion of the profound further question concerning the extent to which liberty is dependent on the way we understand the concept of law.

Of course, natural law theory, the oldest tradition in western jurisprudence has always maintained the inadequacy of notions of law which associate legality solely with formal validating criteria such as a ruler's express will or a judge's authoritative determination. Though not all natural lawyers subscribe to the maxim *lex injusta non est lex*, the tradition as a whole has sought to test enacted law against moral criteria. In doing so, it has erected historic barriers against governmental oppression and inspired the global recognition of fundamental human rights. The recent convictions of German borderguards, for killing on superior orders those fleeing the former East Germany, demonstrate again the timeless political force of natural law doctrine. The re-ignition of the natural law debate in these cases provided a major impetus to the compilation of this book.

There is another jurisprudential tradition which has contributed immensely to the cause of liberty but which recently has been studiously neglected in legal circles. This is the tradition which embraces the work of a diverse group of scholars who explain law as an endogenous 'bottom up' phenomenon rather than an exogenous 'top down' projection of authority. The revival of this tradition owes more to the efforts of F A Hayek than, perhaps, to any other modern thinker. Professor Hayek's work has inspired or provoked many of the contributions to this volume.

We dedicate this book to the memory of Professor Eugene Kamenka, a contributor to this book who died during its compilation, on 19 January

1994. Professor Kamenka was for many years the distinguished Professor of the History of Ideas at the Australian National University. He survived the Nazi devastation of Europe and the communist tyranny in Eastern Europe to become one of· the world's most erudite and articulate intellectual defenders of liberty. Professor Kamenka's intellectual prowess, his courage and his sincerity of purpose won him deep respect on both sides of the ideological divide in the west.

At critical phases of the production of this book Gabriël Moens was Visiting Professor of Law at the J Reuben Clark Law School, Brigham Young University and Suri Ratnapala was Senior Visiting Scholar at the Institute of Humane Studies, George Mason University. Much of the research and writing leading to the chapter entitled 'Law as a Knowledge Process' was done with the aid of the resources provided by the IHS, in particular, the treasure of classical liberal literature held at its Harper Library.

This book is the result of the work of a truly international cast of contributors who, though diverging in their theoretical and methodological approaches, share a deep interest in the complex inter-relationship between law and liberty. We are grateful for their enthusiastic commitment to this project and their outstanding contributions.

Editing a book of writings generated within diverse stylistic systems and traditions poses special problems. In this regard we must make special mention of the excellence and dedication of Anne Melano, Anna Crago and Joanne Rich, editors with Butterworths, whose efforts eased our burden and ensured that the book met the highest editorial standards.

We hope that this book will not only serve as a valuable teaching resource in jurisprudence, but will also help to generate an awareness in the wider community of the relevance of legal theory to the cause of liberty.

1 January 1996   *Suri Ratnapala*
                                                         Gabriël A Moens

CHAPTER 1

Law, Legal Theory and Liberty

Suri Ratnapala and Gabriël A Moens*

This book is about the relationship between law and liberty. That there is a connection between these two concepts is obvious. Particular laws can limit liberty or destroy liberty. Laws can also promote and protect liberty. Liberty, it appears, is ever dependent on law. This connection exists no matter how we define liberty.

There is another connection between law and liberty that is not so easily discerned. The abstract concept of law that prevails in a society may have a profound bearing on liberty in that society. The kind of liberty that is present in a society where the ruler's every whim is regarded as law is very different to the liberty found in a society where law is conceived as possessing a less arbitrary and hence more enduring quality. A concept of law under which legal rules are supplied by the private desires of law-makers will produce a society which is very different to one in which the law must bear some correlation to the morality of the community, whether such morality is determined by consulting supernatural authority or is established by public consensus. This book is chiefly concerned with the connection between liberty and the *concept* of law as opposed to the *content* of law.

The meanings of liberty

The relation between liberty and legal theory is dynamic. Not only is there no one agreed conception of law, there is also no single agreed conception of liberty. One's conception of law may be critically influenced by one's conception of liberty and *vice versa*.

In this book, the term 'liberty' is often used interchangeably with the term 'freedom'. The broadest possible meaning of freedom is the absence

---

*   Suri Ratnapala is Senior Lecturer in Law and Gabriël Moens is Professor of Law, T C Beirne School of Law, University of Queensland.

of impediment. Of course, there is no such condition in the universe. The environment always constrains possible outcomes, whether one thinks of the physical world, the biological world or the world of culture. We do not usually use the word 'freedom' in relation to purely physical phenomena; we don't say that the clouds are free to drift or that the rain is free to fall. Sometimes we speak of the freedom of animals in the wild, but generally, the words 'freedom' and 'liberty' are used to describe a particular aspect of human social life.

Everyone believes in some form of freedom. The question is: freedom from what? By one account, the terms 'liberty' and 'freedom' have been used in the history of ideas in more than 200 different senses.[1] The ideal of liberty is sometimes comprehended in the concrete sense. Many liberation struggles have been waged only to replace one oppressor with another, for example a foreign despot with a home-grown one. These are struggles for freedom from a particular oppressor, not from oppression. In this book we are concerned with the more abstract notions of liberty.

It is also true that we rarely use the term liberty to mean the absence of purely physical impediments. Gravity is an impediment to flight, but we do not say that we have no liberty to fly, only that we are unable to fly.[2] Thus, liberty is generally regarded as signifying the absence of impediments for which human agents are responsible. At this point, agreement ends. The question 'what forms of human action or inaction constitute abridgments of liberty?' throws up a spectrum of responses resulting sometimes in literally violent disagreement.

At one end of the spectrum are those who believe that liberty is measurable only in relation to deliberate actions of human agencies. At the other end are those who believe that liberty should be measured in relation to all those circumstances for which human beings, individually or collectively, directly or indirectly, are responsible or about which human beings individually or collectively can do something. According to the latter view, human inaction can also affect liberty. There are, of course, innumerable variants of these positions in between.

Negative freedom and positive freedom

There is a tendency among political philosophers to distinguish between two types of liberty under the labels *negative freedom* and *positive freedom*. Negative freedom is identified with the words 'freedom from' and positive freedom with the words 'freedom to'. Negative freedom refers to freedom from coercion by others. Positive freedom refers to the capacity to act, or as Sir Isiah Berlin puts it, the freedom 'of conceiving goals and policies of my own and realizing them', or the freedom 'which consists in being one's own master'.[3] However, when logically viewed, these two kinds of

---

1   I Berlin, *Four Essays on Liberty*, Oxford University Press, London, 1969, p 121.

2   Helvetius: '... it is not lack of freedom not to fly like an eagle or swim like a whale', in I Berlin, 1969, p 122.

3   I Berlin, 1969, note 1 above, p 131.

freedom are reducible to a common denominator, namely, the absence of impediments to actions of one's choice. Thus, the classic negative freedom from arbitrary arrest or unlawful restraint may be expressed as an aspect of the freedom to move. And the classic positive freedom to stand for parliament may be expressed as an aspect of the freedom to participate in the political process. In each case it is the absence of impediment which signifies the freedom. In a legal context, liberty whether 'positive' or 'negative' means the absence of legal impediment or legal duty to the contrary. The identification of this fairly straightforward but often overlooked proposition and its corollaries is the lasting contribution to legal theory made by Wesley Newcomb Hohfeld whose analysis of jural relations is discussed by Ben Brazil in Chapter 14. Brazil argues, in our view cogently, that Hohfeld's analysis, when logically advanced, results in a more basic dichotomy of the legal states: 'duty' and 'no duty' which in turn breaks down into the proposition: One either has a *duty to* do something or *no duty to* do something or one has a *duty not to* do something or *no duty not to* do something.

Although the notions of negative and positive freedom may be equated in logic, they have tended to diverge dramatically in their political manifestations. It is not entirely clear when negative freedom takes on the positive complexion. The idea of negative freedom finds its most celebrated expression in John Stuart Mill's principle concerning the justification of coercion. He stated:

> That principle is, that the sole end for which mankind are warranted, individually or collectively in interfering with the liberty of action of any of their number, is self-protection. That the only purpose for which power can be rightfully exercised over any member of a civilised community, against his will, is to prevent harm to others. His own good, either physical or moral, is not a sufficient warrant. He cannot rightfully be compelled to do or forebear because it will make him happier, because, in the opinions of others, to do so would be wise, or even right ... The only part of the conduct of any one, for which he is amenable to society, is that which concerns others. In the part which merely concerns himself, his independence is, of right, absolute.[4]

The idea of liberty which Mill sought to convey by these words has since been undermined, often by persons claiming passionate allegiance to Mill's ideal. The subversion has occurred in two principal ways.

Inflation of the notion of harm

Mill's principle of liberty is that a person's freedom ought to be limited only for the purpose of preventing harm to others, and never to stop that person harming themselves. The principle leaves two crucial questions unanswered. First, what is meant by 'harm'? In any society, there will be widespread consensus with respect to a set of individual interests which are thought to be worthy of protection from harm. They are likely to include

---

4   J S Mill, *On Liberty*, Prometheus Books, Buffalo, New York, 1986, p 16.

the person, the property, and the basic autonomy of individuals. However, there will always be contentious issues. To what extent should one's reputation be protected? And, what about one's moral wellbeing? Should we be screened from pornography, for instance?

Second, there is the question of responsibility for harm. When is a person responsible for harm to another? According to Mill's harm principle, the state should not seek to prevent persons from harming themselves. But is it possible to argue that the providers of harmful products are causing harm to the consumers? Excessive consumption of alcohol will make a person very sick and may even kill him or her. Gambling may impoverish a family. Who is responsible for this kind of harm? Are capitalists causing harm to the proletariat by owning the means of production? Are employers harming workers by their bargaining power? Are producers harming consumers by excessive profit taking?

The extension of positive freedom

The tension between negative and positive freedoms is not immediately apparent, for they complement each other to a considerable degree: I can better secure my negative freedom if I also have positive freedom. My freedom from arbitrary arrest, expropriation or discrimination would be more secure if I had the freedom to express opinions, to associate and to elect my rulers, in short, if I had the freedom of political action. However the freedom of political action has its limits. At a certain point, the exercise of my freedom to act will violate some other person's freedom from coercion — my so-called positive freedom will collide with another's so-called negative freedom. Thus, there appears to be an inherent and unavoidable limit to positive freedom, in the form of the negative freedom of others.

However, we know that often this barrier is breached and negative freedom drastically curtailed. We are not surprised when tyrants do this, but when democratically elected governments and legislatures coerce citizens in the name of freedom, we are curious about their justification. As Berlin revealed in his seminal essay, 'Two Concepts of Liberty', the key to this puzzle is to understand the effect of rationalism in politics.

The rationalist argument for coercion goes like this. A man who is forcibly prevented from entering a mine field because there is no time to warn him of the imminent danger is not having his freedom curtailed, because he would not have wanted to get blown up anyway. A child who is restrained by her parents is usually not said to be enslaved by the parents. The child is being made to behave the way she would, if she had the wisdom of her parents. Compulsory primary education is not an abridgment of freedom because education has an emancipating effect. Generally, there is little argument against examples similar to those above. However issues become more complex. It is argued by some that restricting alcohol and tobacco consumption is not an assault on freedom, as it is in a person's own interest to abstain. Recently these bans have also been defended on the grounds that they concern actions which harm the health of others and cost the community more by way of health-care.

Banning pornography can be justified as pornography is a form of enslavement to one's (negative) passions, and so it is similarly in a person's own interest to abstain.

Whenever these coercive measures have been justified in the name of freedom (as opposed to other values such as justice, equality, compassion etc), the rationale has been, explicitly or implicitly, that the person whose life is being regulated would behave in the manner dictated if that person were rational. This rationale is founded on the idea that in each person there is a Platonic truly rational self, and a contingent heteronomous self. True freedom is the freedom of the rational self. So long as we do not coerce this rational self, we are not limiting freedom.

Often limits on freedom are said to be for the common good of society as a whole, but despite the rhetoric the justification remains the same. My individual wellbeing depends on the wellbeing of the community to which I belong and within which alone I may survive and flourish. Humans, being a social species, cannot prosper except within communities. When I am coerced 'for the common good' I am simply asked to act in my own interest.

This argument presupposes that the rational answer is always available, however complex the question. It is this brand of rationalism and paternalism which gives a ruler the confidence to claim that he or she knows what is in the subject's true interest. As Berlin put it:

> [T]he rationalist argument, with its assumption of the single true solution, has led by steps which, if not logically valid, are historically and psychologically intelligible, from an ethical doctrine of individual responsibility and individual self-perfection to an authoritarian state obedient to the directives of an *élite* of Platonic guardians.[5]

Limitation of freedom on other grounds

Mill's principle of liberty is not the only guiding principle that is followed on questions of coercion. Often there are direct appeals to ideals such as equality, fairness and justice. Liberty is not the only condition we value and compromises have to be made. The extent to which liberty is curtailed will depend on the particular notions of equality, fairness, justice etc which are pursued. For example, the goal of abstract legal equality will entail relatively small levels of coercive measures whereas the aim of substantive material equality will require large-scale and continuous programs of coercive redistribution. The ideal of securing a safety net living standard for all will involve less coercion than the goal of procuring substantially similar living conditions for all.

However, these arguments too can be reduced to the harm principle or rational self-justification. It can be argued that conditions such as inequality are forms of harm. It has also been said, for instance by Marxists, that a rational being would in fact desire the equality of everyone.

---

5   I Berlin, 1969, note 1 above, p 152.

The concept of law and the abridgment of liberty

Liberty is often affected by illegal acts of governments and individuals. Protecting liberty from unlawful acts is the task of substantive public and private law. The primary concern of this book is not with illegal attacks on liberty. It is with the licence which the very concept of law may grant to rulers to abrogate freedom.

As we have seen, whichever justification we adopt for limiting liberty, there are difficult questions to answer. A community answers these questions through its moral rules and ultimately through its laws. Often it is a matter of political judgment or legislative act. The answers are crucially influenced by the community's dominant conception of law.

Consider John Austin's positivist conception which regards law as the command of a determinate political superior who is habitually obeyed by the bulk of the community.[6] The great issues concerning liberty will be answered for the community by this superior. A wise superior may consult widely on these matters, but a tyrant or an oligarch may not. Even if the omnipotent political superior is an elected parliament which functions on the principles of representative democracy, liberty is not entirely secure. Majorities can be as inimical to liberty as minorities. As Berlin remarked, 'democracy as such is logically uncommitted to [the inviolability of a minimum extent of individual liberty] and historically has at times failed to protect it while remaining faithful to its own principles'.[7] Benjamin Constant put it this way:

> When you establish that the sovereignty of the people is unlimited, you create and toss at random into society a degree of power which is too large in itself, and which is bound to constitute an evil, in whatever hands it is placed. Entrust it to one man, to several, to all, you will still find that it is equally an evil. ... It is against the weapon, not against the arm holding it, that it is necessary to strike ruthlessly. There are weights too heavy for the hand of man.[8]

It should surprise no one that in unrestrained democracies, majorities founded on criteria such as race, religion, caste and socio-economic position may oppress minorities. However, despite the early warnings of liberals like Bentham, Mill and Constant, the inherently oppressive nature of crudely majoritarian democracy was not widely appreciated until recently. Democracy's tragic contradiction was exposed largely by the work of the scholars who developed modern public choice theory. This work demonstrated that unbridled democracy can, and often does, degenerate into a political game of distributional coalition building and revolving majorities in which genuine collective choices prove elusive. If democracy itself is incapable of resolving the complex issues concerning the protection of liberty, there is need for auxiliary safeguards. Two kinds

---

6   J Austin, *The Province of Jurisprudence Determined*, Weidenfeld & Nicolson, London, 1954, pp 118–26.
7   I Berlin, 1969, note 1 above, p 165.
8   B Constant, *Political Writings* (ed B Fontana), Cambridge University Press, Cambridge, 1988, p 176.

of safeguards have been prominent in the western liberal tradition. One kind consists of ideas associated with natural law and natural rights and the other kind comprises ideas associated with constitutionalism. More recently, another wave of ideas has swelled within the liberal tradition emphasising the virtue of legal decentrism.

Natural law's defence of liberty

Historically, the ideas associated with natural law and natural rights have rendered more service to the cause of liberty than, perhaps, any other intellectual tradition. The very idea of an unwilled natural law places a fetter on legislative authority. The concept of the human being as a morally responsible agent engenders the idea of a minimal province of personal autonomy which no authority may invade. Every modern charter of rights has been derived directly or indirectly from natural law and natural rights doctrines. Many constitutions, including the American, owe great debts to natural law. In Chapter 7, Professor Douglas Kmiec examines the classical tradition of natural law, particularly its Christian manifestation, and considers its impact on the US Constitution.

Yet, natural law is seen by many as a double-edged sword. By definition, natural law exists independent of the ruler's will. If so, who determines natural law's content? The utilitarian-positivist case against natural law is that it makes the law uncertain. If the law is uncertain, liberty is insecure. In Chapter 8, Professor Gabriël A Moens undertakes a discussion of this extraordinarily complex issue in the setting of the recent trials and convictions of former East German borderguards accused of the unlawful killings of citizens trying to escape to the west. The chapter discusses the wider implications of the German courts' adoption of Gustav Radbruch's proposition concerning the minimum content of natural law. Apart from the utilitarian reservations concerning these judgments, Moens raises the moral question whether the German court should have applied the ethical standards identified with western critical rationality to the East German borderguards without regard to the culture of obedience which may have dictated their behaviour.

The rise of legal decentrism: Hayek's theory of order

Theories of legal decentrism involve different methodologies and have different emphases. Yet they have in common the notion that law ought not to be regarded as something to be created and imposed from above. Rather, law should evolve spontaneously as the outcome of decisions which individuals make in furtherance of disparate ends. Hence, law constitutes considered adaptations to the highly complex and variable environments in which individuals and communities exist. The proponents of legal decentrism claim that this kind of law is more compatible with liberty than legislation, in that its very existence depends on conditions that permit individuals a high degree of autonomy to determine and pursue their own ends. They claim further that the rules of conduct that such spontaneous order generates are more suited than mere legislation to the task of resolving conflicts within the social order. This is because spontaneous laws incorporate a great deal of dispersed knowledge which no centralised legislature can hope to command.

According to the leading proponent of the evolutionary view of law, F A Hayek, the steady erosion of liberty in modern democratic states owes much to the 'constructivist rationalism' which drives public policy in such states. Hayek argues that this kind of rationalism grossly exaggerates our capacity to construct society according to our wishes by deliberately intervening in its workings. This fatal conceit results from a serious misunderstanding of the nature of the overall order of larger societies and some of their component structures such as language, moral systems, markets and law.

It is possible, in the case of an organisation deliberately created for known purposes, to direct and control its elements to achieve specific tasks in the service of a predetermined plan. There are other kinds of social orders however which have no creator and hence no purpose. They result from human actions but not from human design. The rules of such systems emerge spontaneously out of the coincident behaviour of elements acting in their own interests, according to their own plans. Human cooperation relies on both types of system but the overall order of society bears the spontaneous character. While rulers often tyrannise societies, none have succeeded in redesigning society to their liking without causing unintended consequences. There are simply too many elements to control, each driven by their private ends. If a ruler does succeed in creating a tyranny, society will have turned into an organisation in which there is little individual freedom. Moreover, a society in which individual behaviour is fully controlled is a society which functions on very limited knowledge, ie only the knowledge that is available to the central planner.

Hayek does not argue that spontaneous orders need no correction by deliberate law-making. Orders may evolve in undesirable directions owing to mistaken or corrupt decisions of judges and others responsible for law-making. These situations call for corrective measures. Again, rapid changes in the physical or cultural environment may require immediate legislative responses as the rules of the spontaneous order concerning the new situation may not be immediately clear. Hayek's point is that such correctives should proceed from immanent (as opposed to radical) criticism, and be aimed at restoring the character of the grown order. These corrections cannot be effected by decrees aimed at producing specific outcomes, but by general and abstract rules.

Hayek's critics

The power of Hayek's argument for freedom is acknowledged by many of his critics. In Chapter 7 of this book, Kmiec explains the natural law's bias in favour of individual autonomy against the power of the state. He finds powerful insights in Hayek's evolutionary theory concerning the self-serving nature of the state and important coincidences with natural law. Yet he sees Hayek's case for freedom as incomplete as it fails to reconcile 'individual liberty and the corresponding immunity from state directive' with the 'social inclination of human nature to live in society'. In the classical tradition of natural law, Kmiec points out that liberty is worthy not only because it confers immunities from coercion but also because it multiplies opportunities to do good, that is to nurture others, and thus ourselves, to proper ends. Following St Thomas Aquinas, Kmiec points out that the state is not the result of our fallen or sinful nature, or solely a human creation, but is something that is 'known to, and prefigured by God'. The state thus serves our only end: reunification with God. The interventionist welfare state not only limits freedom but also fractures the relationship between donor and donee and thereby breaks 'the bonds of the natural law community'. It is individuals who must seek God, not the state which merely facilitates their quest for reunification with God. The welfare state, by nationalising virtue creates a barrier between God and us.

Professor Neil MacCormick examines Hayek's theory from the social democratic viewpoint. In Chapter 4, he pays Hayek the highest compliment by agreeing fully with his thesis of spontaneous orders and the fallacy of radical social engineering. Yet, he argues that projects for the elimination of economic inequalities may be regarded as correctives to the workings of the social order proposed through immanent criticism, hence within the Hayekean evolutionary paradigm. (Hayek argued that the improvement of a spontaneous order is achievable only through criticism from within and not by radical redesigning). MacCormick suggests that attempts to undo these reforms in order to 'reestablish the legal conditions of spontaneous order' is open to the same Hayekean objection to constructivism, namely, that they produce unintended consequences. He asks: 'Is the conscious and deliberate creation of a market order wholly exempt from the critique of government planning, and if so why?'.

MacCormick's criticism is addressed, albeit indirectly, by Professor Viktor Vanberg who holds the Chair of Economic Policy at Freiburg University, a position which Hayek once held. In Chapter 3, Vanberg looks at the alleged contradiction between Hayek's condemnation of constructivist rationalism on the one hand and his advocacy of constitutional design on the other. He argues that no such contradiction arises when Hayek's objection is examined in relation to two different kinds of activity. First, Hayek criticises constructivist rationalism which is associated with central planning conducted under the synoptic delusion that it is possible for anyone to take 'conscious account of all the particular facts which enter into the order of society' or 'on which the overall order of the activities in a Great Society is based'. Hayek, on the contrary, acknowledges our irremediable ignorance, which compels us to rely on rules. Hayek condemns the kind of constructivist rationalism that abandons rules in favour of decrees aimed at producing particular results: such decrees have no place in spontaneous order which rests on abstract rules. Decrees cannot result from immanent criticism. Hayek's objection to wealth equalisation measures lies in the extent to which they rely on such specific decrees; in fact Hayek favours a minimum income safety net approach to social security.

Vanberg points out that Hayek does not reject outright the idea of rational institutional design and rule-making, but only the presumptuous claim 'that it is both possible and desirable to reconstruct all grown institutions in accordance with a preconceived plan'. Hayek's message was that we can improve our condition only by improving 'the rules of the game' and not by laws which are specific commands. Hayek's theory would condemn such laws whether they be conceived in aid of the market or in furtherance of redistribution.

In Chapter 5, Dr Suri Ratnapala explores the epistemological roots of legal evolutionism to discover continuities among prebiotic evolution of the universe, the emergence of life and biological evolution on earth and cultural evolution leading to complex social orders. The chapter draws on insights provided by the philosophy of science, evolutionary epistemology and work in artificial intelligence and life, to support the evolutionary view concerning the emergence of order from the free play of elements. A further rationale for rule-governed society is found in the fact that rules supply testable or falsifiable hypotheses concerning the environment whereas patternless projections of authority deprive us of opportunities to systematically develop knowledge and improve the human condition.

Legal decentrism: justification from economic analysis

In the history of ideas, the case for liberty has been made mostly on moral grounds. However, the determination of the means by which liberty is secured has always involved pragmatic considerations. We have seen that evolutionary theory commends legal decentrism on epistemological grounds. The modern 'law and economics' school opts for liberty through legal decentrism on grounds of economic efficiency. A key problem with this approach has centred on the question whether the efficiency criteria available to economic analysts are always consistent with liberty.

In Chapter 9, Dr Ian McEwin explains the imperfections of the efficiency criteria of Pareto optimality, hypothetical Pareto efficiency and wealth maximisation. Despite these imperfections, they provide useful ways to evaluate the consequences of actions more accurately than the impressionistic and anecdotal measurements which commonly guide public policy making and law reform. The trouble is that criteria of efficiency which 'assumes preferences and tries to replicate the outcome that people with those preferences would try to reach if they did not have any bargaining impediments' assume a utopian world of zero transaction costs in which liberty for everyone is a given and the initial distribution of rights and entitlements is fair. McEwin draws attention to recent attempts to directly integrate values such as liberty into economic analysis, by treating them as 'normative resources' determined prior to efficiency analysis.

Mainstream economic analyses have concentrated on measuring the efficiency of particular legal rules whether they are enacted by statute or supplied by common law precedents. Recently, however, a group of economists have been investigating the economic efficiency of the methods by which laws are made in societies. In particular, they have compared forms of legal decentrism such as contractual law-making and the spontaneous emergence of customary law with centralised legislative enactment. In Chapter 6, Professor Francesco Parisi uses game-theoretic and evolutionary models to explain that the decentralised processes by which customary rules emerge have a comparative efficiency advantage over other institutional settings. Parisi argues that since individuals and social groups have direct perception of their costs and benefits, and can express their preferences among alternative legal regimes by concurring in the formation of enforceable social norms, the courts should, whenever possible, 'rely on the capillary process of norm formation through which society creates rules for itself'.

Republicanism and constitutionalism

Liberty, however defined, exists at the mercy of those who have the power to coerce. Liberty is susceptible to destruction by private coercion as well as official coercion. However, private coercion at least on the rampant scale is unlikely to occur without official condonation, connivance, indifference or impotence. Hence, throughout history, the champions of liberty have sought to make political arrangements whereby the capacity of rulers to act in the public interest is balanced by checks on the potential abuse of official power. Their mistrust of absolute power, whether in the hands of tyrants or in elected assemblies, have engendered the political theories of republicanism and constitutionalism.

In Chapter 2, Professor Mortimer Sellers traces the turbulent history of classical republicanism to argue that the republican ideal is the parent of modern liberalism. Sellers demonstrates that their overriding concern that government exists solely for the realisation of the common good (*res publica*), made republicans reject majoritarianism in its cruder forms in favour of systems of mixed government. They found that the common good was unachievable without liberty ie, liberty not in the sense of licence — which inevitably impinges on the liberty of others — but in the sense of freedom tempered by the rule of law. In this chapter, Sellers examines the subtle interconnection between liberty and civic virtue and the means by which republican theory sought to promote virtue without harm to liberty. Supplementing Sellers' account of republican liberty is Professor Raoul Van Caenegam's outline of the historical tradition in jurisprudence in Chapter 15.

The theme of the balance between authority and restraint is further explored by Professor Geoffrey de Q Walker in Chapter 13. Walker finds a fundamental antinomy between power and law, ie between the arbitrary unchecked might which power connotes and the restraints which law provides. He points out that neither law nor power in their pure form can lead to stable government. Absolute power is unpredictable and absolute legalism is inflexible; each contains the seeds of its own destruction. Walker argues that the necessary balance is provided by the rule of law doctrine. This doctrine should be understood as the subjection of individuals and governments to a kind of law which possesses properties that not only enable people to obey it, but also make them usually want to obey it. He identifies 12 such properties, some of which concern the normative quality of the law and others which concern the effective and fair implementation of the law.

One of the perennial issues in discussions of law-governed societies concerns the role of the judge. The issue is livelier in common law countries where judges are regarded as the final arbiters of the law, having authority to change incrementally the law in the process of adjudicating specific disputes. Is the rule of law compromised when judges decide 'hard cases' that are not governed by clear precedents? Positivist theory holds that judges legislate in such cases. If judicial discretion is unfettered as some positivists hold, the rule of law is in jeopardy. In Chapter 10, Professor Alan Fogg considers the 'declaratory counter revolution' represented by the body of opinion which maintains that judges do not decide hard cases in a normative vacuum but that they are constrained (at least when they properly conceive their role), by principles and norms generated by the political or social system. Fogg examines the approaches of two of the leading modern declaratory theorists, Ronald Dworkin and F A Hayek, in order to evaluate their liberal credentials.

Law as oppression

Liberal legal theorists hold that law in some sense is necessary for liberty, or, at least, is not inconsistent with liberty. There are others who argue that law by definition is oppressive. The most prominent critic of the abstract notion of law is Karl Marx.

According to Marxist historicism, humans initially live in a classless, stateless egalitarian condition where there is no surplus production. With the generation of surplus, there arises unequal distribution. Those who have more use their power to maintain their shares, and the arrangements they enforce constitute the state. The state and its laws, then, form the *superstructure* reflecting the *base* which consists of the real world of economic relations. When economic relations change, the superstructure changes. However, the superstructure is always oppressive as it represents the enforcement of unequal relations. Finally, the class struggle leads to the revolution in which the proletariat triumphs and sets up a transitional dictatorship. The dictatorship brings about egalitarian conditions governed by the principle 'from each according to his means and to each according to his needs'. The economic conditions that cause exploitation are removed, class conflict is terminated and the redundant state together with its laws simply withers away.

Marx's historicism has not been vindicated by history, at least thus far. Where revolutions occurred and dictatorships were established in the name of the proletariat, they failed to usher in the promised utopia. The state and its laws persisted often in their most brutal forms. Elsewhere, in the industrialised world, the predicted revolutions failed to materialise, and the Marxist theory of law had to be revised in each context. In Chapter 12, Professor Igor Grazin examines the contradictions in Marxist legal theory which emerged in the eastern European communist states and the revisionary processes that accompanied the collapse of communism. In

Chapter 11 Professor Alice Erh-Soon Tay and the late Professor Eugene Kamenka survey the revisionism that occurred in the west as capitalism refused to yield as foreshadowed by classical Marxism.

The 'law as oppression' theme also permeates some strands of post-modern critical theory. This view of law emanates from postmodernism's wider assault on disciplines that claim to be rationally objective. Postmodernists revive the ancient philosophical scepticism about the possibility of objective knowledge. Finding no demonstrable foundation for such knowledge, some postmodernists conclude that knowledge claims are essentially claims that are legitimated by convention or by an epistemic authority which has power to dictate the criteria by which truth claims are evaluated. Thus, knowledge is seen as a form of power. This view radically undermines the idea of law as rules capable of being objectively determined and impartially applied to ascertainable facts. In Chapter 5, Dr Ratnapala examines the implications of this approach for liberal legalism and for the notions of liberty and argues that an alternative approach to the central problem concerning the irremediable limitations of human knowledge is provided by recent work in evolutionary epistemology. Unlike postmodern critiques, this approach assigns to law a positive cognitive function and holds law to be an indispensable condition of liberty.

CHAPTER 2

Republican Liberty

M N S Sellers*

When George Washington gave his inaugural speech as first President of the United States under the new Federal Constitution, he asserted that the 'preservation of the sacred fire of liberty, and the destiny of the republican model of government' were 'deeply' and perhaps 'finally' dependent on 'the experiment entrusted to the hands of the American people'.[1] My aim in this chapter will be to identify the nature and origins of the sacred flame Washington sought to preserve, and its association with republican government. I will briefly review the history of 'republican liberty' and examine the arguments of its leading supporters, to identify the origins and central elements of the republican ideology that animated the revolutionary era, and inspired the United States Constitution. My purpose here will not be to analyse American republicanism on its own, or in its totality, which I have done at length elsewhere,[2] but rather to review the broader republican tradition as it relates to the concept of liberty. I will present the history and evolution of a pattern of thought to reveal republican liberty as the parent of liberalism in modern law and politics.

The republican conception of liberty, like the words 'republic' and 'liberty' themselves, originated in Rome and developed much of its modern meaning in the partisan rancour and class conflict that culminated in the principate of Augustus. The patrician nostalgia of Roman historians under the early empire perpetuated a sense of *libertas* that associated Roman liberty with annual elections, the rule of law, and

---

* Professor of Law, Director, Center for International and Comparative Law, University of Baltimore School of Law.

1 G Washington, 'The First Inaugural Speech' (30 April 1789) in *George Washington: A Collection* (ed W B Allen), Liberty Classics, Indianapolis, 1988, p 462.
2 M N S Sellers, *American Republicanism: Roman Ideology in the United States Constitution*, Macmillan, Basingstoke, and New York University Press, New York, 1994.

other central elements of the Roman Constitution instituted by Lucius Junius Brutus in 509 BC.[3] This Constitution came to an end, and Roman 'servitude' (*servitium*) began 500 years later, when Caesar and Augustus ended government by the senate and people of Rome, and usurped for themselves the functions of the senate, the magistracy and the laws. At this point, Roman historians agreed, equality was gone, and with it the *res publica*.[4] Roman liberty and the republic were born together in the ouster of the kings and died together in Rome's final factious struggles to divide the spoils of empire.[5]

This destroyed the state that subsequent 'republicans' still hoped to revive when they adopted the word 'liberty' to describe their political agenda. Donato Giannotti put it clearly in a passage adopted by James Harrington in England in 1656 and again by the American John Adams in 1787. Giannotti divided the history of government into two periods — the 'ancient prudence', or government *de jure* ending with the liberty of Rome, and the 'modern prudence', or government *de facto*, beginning 'with the arms of Caesar' which 'extinguish[ed] liberty' and 'deformed the whole face of the world' with the 'ill features' of despotic government.[6] The translation of this passage from Italy to England, and finally to America illustrates the modern history of republican liberty, and its three major triumphs in the political institutions of western government, each inspired by Rome. Republicanism enjoyed a fourth (and somewhat anomalous) victory in France, where Camille Desmoulins attributed the French Revolution to the influence of Cicero's ideal of the Roman republic.[7] I will briefly examine the history of liberty in each of the five chief seats of republican thought, aiming to discover the common thread that republicanism contributed to modern jurisprudence and why republican liberty remained so successful a manifesto of revolution on two continents over 2000 years.

---

3   Livy, *Ab urbe condita* 2.1: '*Liberi iam hinc populi Romani res pace belloque gestas, annuos magistratus, imperiaque legum potentiora quam hominum peragam*'; Tacitus, *Annals*, l.1: '*liberatatem et consulatum L Brutus instituit*'.

4   Tacitus, *Annals*, 1.2; *Histories*, 1.50.

5   For the strong connections between the concepts of *libertas* and *res publica* and a bibliography of Roman sources, see J Hellegouarc'h, *Le vocabulaire latin des relations et des partis politiques sous la république*, 2nd ed, Les Belles Lettres, Paris, 1972, p 545; P A Brunt, *The Fall of the Roman Republic and Other Essays*, Clarendon Press, Oxford, 1988, p 299; L R Lind, 'The Idea of the Republic and the Foundations of Roman Political Liberty' in *Studies in Latin Literature and Roman History*, vol IV (ed C Deroux), Latomus, Brussels, 1986, pp 48–9; C Wirszubski, *Libertas as a Political Idea at Rome during the Late Republic and Early Principate*, Cambridge University Press, Cambridge, 1950, pp 5–6.

6   J Harrington, *The Political Works of James Harrington* (ed J G A Pocock), Cambridge University Press, Cambridge, 1977, p 161, quoting D Gianotti, *Libro della repubblica de' Viniziani* in *Opere*, I, Pisa, 1819, p 15.

7   C Desmoulins, 'Fragment de l'histoire secrète de la Revolution' (1793) in *Oeuvres*, vol I (ed J Claretie), Paris, 1874, p 309.

Roman liberty

The essential and original meaning of *libertas* was status in the political community as a free or *liber* person (not a slave). The word derives from the Indo–European root **leudheros*, and is related to the German and Lithuanian words for 'the people' (*leute*, *liáudis*) and the Greek ἐλεύθερος.[8] This original meaning of the term gradually developed into a broader understanding of liberty that embraced the essential attributes of membership in the political community — what it meant to be a free Roman and not a slave — which explains the close association between *libertas* and the *res publica*. *Libertas* embraced the rights one could expect to exercise simply by virtue of being a Roman citizen.[9]

Popular sovereignty and the rule of law were the first and fundamental attributes of Rome's republican liberty, protected by popular elections and the limited terms in office of Rome's governing magistrates. This required the expulsion of the kings, and Livy described the first act of Rome's new consuls as the imposition of an oath on the people that they would never tolerate a monarch again.[10] The spirit of monarchy for Livy was the licence (*licentia*) of the elite, while the essence of republican government was to give the people equal rights (*aequare ius*). He viewed republican laws as blind and inexorable, while the justice of kings was partial, and subject to personal influence.[11] Rome's first consuls, Lucius Junius Brutus and Publius Valerius Publicola demonstrated their dedication to equal laws and popular sovereignty by executing Brutus' own sons for treason, and lowering the symbols of sovereignty (*imperium*) to the people, in recognition of the superiority and power of the *populus*.

Livy's semi-mythical history of early Rome confirmed the importance of elected magistrates, impartial laws, and the sovereignty of the people. However he also made it clear that not everyone is capable of republican government. The Romans only achieved liberty after they had developed a society and sense of community. Premature liberty would have launched them on a course of self-interest, class warfare, and destruction.[12] Livy illustrated the Roman sense of community with Menenius Agrippa's parable of the human body — the head, the hands, and the belly must cooperate to survive.[13] So too the magistrates, the senate, and the people, all had different and complementary roles in government, without which true liberty could not continue. A *populus* which did not defer to the

---

8   A Walde and J B Hofmann, *Lateinisches etymologisches Wörterbuch*, vol I, 4th ed, Winter, Heidelberg, 1965, sub verbo 'Liber', p 791.

9   For the meaning, history, and development of the Roman term '*libertas*', see also J Bleicken, *Staatliche Ordnung und Freiheit in der römischen Republik*, M Lassleben, Kallmünz, 1972; C Meier, *Res publica amissa. Eine Studie zur Verfassung und Geschichte der späten römischen Republik*, Steiner, Wiesbaden, 1966.

10 Livy, note 3 above, 2.1.9.

11 Livy, 2.3.4–5.

12 Livy, 2.1.3–6.

13 Livy, 2.32.8–12.

moral authority (*auctoritas*) of the senate lost its liberty in the *licentia* of the mob.[14]

The history of the Roman republic, as it was understood by the Romans, and described by Livy, was the working out of the proper balance between the *magistratus*, *senatus* and *populus*, and the demarcation of the political boundary between *libertas* and *licentia*. For most of Roman history, after the fall of the kings, concern with this boundary led to a conflict between the *auctoritas senatus* and the *imperium* (sovereignty) or *potestas* (power) of the *populus*. How much senatorial authority was appropriate to preserve liberty without compromising the sovereignty and equality of the people? In theory all power rested ultimately with the *populus Romanus*, but in practice it was subject to considerable senatorial control, and magistrates acted in the name of *senatus populusque Romanus* (the senate and the people of Rome).[15]

At first the consuls, though annually elected, had all the rights and powers of the kings they had replaced, and laws passed by the people could take effect only with the approval of the senate. But Publicola constrained the magistrates by instituting a right of appeal to the people, and the *lex Publilia* of 339 BC obliged the senate to approve all legislation in advance, before voting began. Even so, no law could come before the people without being proposed to them by a magistrate, and voting in the popular assemblies was carefully controlled to guarantee the dominance of the richest citizens.[16]

Livy's account put particular emphasis on the importance of codification, which took place in 450 BC. Unwritten laws left the magistrates with excessive discretion which should have been 'intolerable in a *libera civitas*'.[17] Written laws would make liberty more equal by equalising civil rights under an impartial code. Before the new laws were approved, they were published for public discussion, so that the final code could be promulgated by *consensus omnium*, the universal consent.[18] *Aequa libertas*, *aequum ius* and *aequae leges* were almost synonymous terms, signifying a republic in which known laws were equally binding on all citizens, regardless of class.[19]

---

14   For popular measures as a threat to *libertas*, constrained by the *auctoritas senatus*, see Livy, 2.41.2–4 and 23.2.1. On *licentia*, see J Hellegouarc'h, 1972, note 5 above, pp 558–9; C Wirszubski, 1950, note 5 above, pp 7–9; P A Brunt, 1988, note 5 above, pp 320–2.
15   Livy, 7.31.10; 24.37.7. Compare Cicero, *Philippicae*, 6.2.4.
16   The Romans voted in the *comitia centuriata* according to their wealth. Those with property valued at 100,000 *asses* or more had 80 centuries, those with 75,000–100,000 had 20 centuries, 50,000–75,000 another 20 centuries, 25,000–50,000 another 20 centuries, those with 11,000–25,000, 30 centuries, and one extra century was allowed for citizens who owned less than 11,000 *asses* worth of property. Livy, 1.42.4–43.13. Compare Dionysius of Halicarnassus, 4.16–21, 7.59.2–8; Cicero, *De Republica*, 2.39–40.
17   Livy, 3.9.2.
18   Livy, 3.34.5.
19   C Wirszubski, 1950, note 5 above, pp 9–15; P A Brunt, 1988, note 5 above, pp 334–8.

Roman *libertas* implied equality before the law and government for the common good, but not full political equality, or at least not initially. The same reforms that produced Rome's first written code guaranteed that only patricians could propose new laws to the people. The central dispute between Rome's conflicting factions throughout the republic was how far political equality and direct popular legislation could go before they degenerated into *licentia*, and began to threaten the rule of law and legal equality which they were intended to serve. This was not an idle dispute. Numerous plebeian leaders were accused of aspiring to monarchical power, and were assassinated when they proposed measures that catered to popular *licentia*. Their supporters would have said that they were simply vindicating the rights of the people. To prevent demagogues, the senate established that no magistrate could succeed himself in office.[20]

After the institution of annual elections, and a written code of laws, the progress of liberty in Rome concerned the privileges of the patricians, and the property of the plebs. First the right of appeal to the people was re-established as the ultimate protection (*praesidium*) of liberty and equality before the law. Then plebeians obtained the right to stand for the consulship. Finally it was agreed that votes of the tribal assembly (*plebiscita*) should have the same effect as laws passed in the old *comitia centuriata*, which had voted by wealth.[21]

All these innovations were opposed by the patricians, who argued that liberty and equal laws for all citizens depended for their survival on the rights, deliberations, and influence of the senate. But although everything was denied to the plebeians at first, they obtained what they wanted in the end, even admission to the patrician priesthoods. This meant that when the Roman republic finally fell, the question for posterity was not which rights were missing to make Roman liberty complete, but which power of the *populus* or lost privilege of senate finally crossed the line between liberty and licence, and ruined the republic.

Romans generally agreed that the height of their republic lasted from the Second Punic War to the tribunate of Tiberius Gracchus.[22] This made Gracchan agitation for land reform the central event in the decline of Roman liberty, and elicited two possible explanations for the fall of the republic. Either the arrogance of the senate provoked the Gracchan conflicts or the Gracchi destroyed themselves and the state with their excessive demands on behalf of the people.[23] Tiberius and Gaius Gracchus had argued that the people's share in the *res publica* should be tangible, and thus extended to embrace not only political rights but a share in the public land and treasure. They encouraged the people to exercise their sovereignty directly, by deposing magistrates who stood in the way of agrarian reform and the exercise of the popular will.

---

20 Livy, note 3 above, 3.21.2.
21 Livy, 8.12.14–15 and 3.55.3; P A Brunt, 1988, note 5 above, pp 343–5; L R Taylor, *Roman Voting Assemblies from the Hannibalic War to the Dictatorship of Caesar*, University of Michigan Press, Ann Arbor, 1966, pp 6, 16–17, 60–1.
22 C Wirszubski, 1950, note 5 above, pp 31–2, with citations.
23 On the Gracchi, see D Stockton, *The Gracchi*, Clarendon Press, Oxford, 1979.

The senate accused the Gracchi of aiming at monarchy and killed them, as senators had killed Spurius Cassius, Spurius Maelius, and Marcus Manlius before them and would kill Lucius Sergius Catilina and Gaius Julius Caesar afterwards. These judicial and extra-judicial murders were supported by Publicola's oath that no king would ever be allowed in Rome.

Roman historians agreed that republican liberty and Roman glory ended with the principate of Augustus, but there was no consensus about how this catastrophe might have been averted. Livy blamed wealth and luxury for the loss of the republic.[24] Sallust thought that victory over Carthage left Romans without an enemy to unite them,[25] and Tacitus attributed the monarchy to a desire for peace and order after the terrible dissensions of the civil wars.[26] The basic desiderata of republican liberty were known and agreed upon by all: elected magistrates, rotation in office, the rule of law, equal justice, and popular sovereignty subject to the moral authority of a deliberative senate. However, it was not clear that liberty was always appropriate. Livy was glad that the Romans did not obtain their liberty before they were ready for it[27] and Tacitus thought that republican government was commendable but evanescent, unobtainable in an age without virtue, like his own.[28] The central fact about Roman liberty under the empire was that it was gone, and had died in an orgy of violence and misery. Rome's republican glory was a wonderful inspiration to all who came afterwards, but Rome's fate also presented a terrible warning to would-be successors.

The Roman conception of republican liberty reached its canonical form in the last years of the republic, when Cato, Brutus, Cassius and Cicero fought their losing battle against Caesar, Mark Antony and finally Octavian (Augustus) in the name of *libertas* and the *res publica*. Their careers were preserved for posterity by subsequent historians, and particularly in the *Lives* of L Mestrius Plutarchus. But one of the last defenders of republican liberty, Cicero, also wrote extensively himself about the rights and the constitution he was struggling to preserve. The best surviving Roman arguments in favour of liberty and the republic appear in the speeches and philosophical books of Cicero, particularly his writings *On the Laws* and *De Republica*. These constitute the basic texts for evaluating the Roman conception of republican liberty.

Italian liberty

The next great exponents of republican liberty after Augustus' victory in Rome were the turbulent city-states of the Italian Renaissance and late Middle Ages. The Roman Caesars had given way to German emperors to the north of Italy, and imperial Popes in Latium and Romagna. Tuscany fell between the two and was the constant battleground in which

---

24   Livy, *Praefatio*, 11–12.
25   Sallust, *Bellum Catilinae*, 10.1–2; *Bellum Jugurthinum*, 41.
26   Tacitus, *Histories*, 1.1; *Annals*, 1.2.
27   Livy, note 3 above, 2.1.3–6.
28   Tacitus, *Annals*, 4.33 and 3.28; C Wirszubski, 1950, note 5 above, pp 160–7.

ecclesiastics and emperors pursued their despotic claims to universal empire. At first no one sought or offered liberty in the republican sense of the word. However, cities slowly began to assert their civic liberty or independence from outside domination. This led gradually to claims of internal liberty by citizens within the Tuscan republics, and particularly in Florence, which had led the Italian resistance to imperial pretensions, and benefited from the weakness of the city's nominal allies in the papacy.[29]

By 1375 the commune of Florence had sent a red banner marked 'Libertà' in white letters to other Italian cities, to encourage their independence from the Pope. The people of Bologna greeted their liberators with the shout 'vivat populus et libertà' in conscious imitation of ancient Rome. 'Libertà, popolo e Guelfo' had long been a recurrent expression in the Florentine propaganda, and medieval Italians were well aware of Sallust's observation that Rome only began to flourish when it became a republic and gained its liberty. But Florentine self-consciousness about the republican nature of civil liberty developed most fully after the city's lone opposition to the Milanese tyrant Giangaleazzo Visconti in 1400–1402,[30] and the subsequent writings of Leonardo Bruni, particularly his *Laudatio Florentinae Urbis* (1403–1404) and *Histories* of the people of Florence (1415–1421).

Bruni expressed a new Florentine consensus rejecting the city's supposed founding by Caesar's veterans, and attributing Florence instead to the age of Sulla, before the emperors destroyed the republic and deprived the people of their liberty.[31] Bruni claimed that Florence had always fought for liberty against tyrants, and always hated the destroyers of the Roman republic. Florence had inherited Rome's virtue and preserved civic liberty through a carefully mixed and balanced constitution. Bruni thought that Florentine liberty depended on justice and the universal application of the laws,[32] under the ultimate sovereignty of the people.[33] Laws were made prudently in Florence, for the common good, and rich and poor received equal treatment because of their common citizenship.

Bruni had spoken of Florence's Constitution as finely tuned and balanced, like the strings of a harp, but in fact the city's most striking attribute was its constant discord, as was readily apparent in Bruni's own

---

29 See N Rubinstein, 'Florentina Libertas', 1986, XXVI *Rinascimento* 3–26; R Witt, 'The Rebirth of the Concept of Republican Liberty in Italy' in *Renaissance: Studies in Honor of Hans Baron* (eds A Molho and J A Tedeschi), Northern Illinois University Press, De Kalb, Illinois, 1971, pp 173–9; Q Skinner, 'Machiavelli's *Discorsi* and the pre-humanist origins of republican ideas' in *Machiavelli and Republicanism* (eds G Bock, Q Skinner and M Viroli), Cambridge University Press, Cambridge, 1990, pp 121–31.

30 H Baron, *The Crisis of the Italian Renaissance: Civic Humanism and Republican Liberty in an Age of Classicism and Tyranny*, rev ed, Princeton University Press, Princeton, pp 12–46; N Rubinstein, 1986, note 29 above, pp 8–17.

31 L Bruni, 'Laudatio Florentinae Urbis' in *From Petrarch to Leonardo Bruni: Studies in Humanistic and Political Literature* (ed H Baron), University of Chicago Press, Chicago, 1968, p 245.

32 L Bruni, 1968, pp 258–259.

33 L Bruni, 1968, p 260: '*Ita in omni re populus libertasque dominatur*'.

Histories. Guelfs fought with Ghibellines, then turned on each other in 'Black' and 'White' parties, then divided into 'nobles' and 'commons', and again into 'commons' and 'plebs' in a constant turmoil that led every victorious party to split in turn into violent new factions, and then turn upon itself.[34]

The man most responsible for reminding Florentines of their Constitution's instability was Niccolò Machiavelli, whose *Istorie Florentine* (1532) paid particular attention to Florence's civil discords, and the importance for republics of maintaining internal unity. Florence thrived despite internal dissensions, but Machiavelli speculated that a united Florence might have surpassed all other republics — ancient and modern.[35] One need not go into all the plots and parties that distracted Florence to agree with Machiavelli's widely accepted observation that Italy's 'republican' constitutions were inadequate.

Machiavelli's study of Livy's first ten books led him to doubt that Florence had ever been a true republic, because its government was never organised to serve the public good, and he grudgingly praised Venice as more successful in the impartial application of its laws.[36] Other Florentines also increasingly turned to Venice as the best modern example of ancient republican institutions.[37] Although the citizens of Florence had long claimed to be a free people, it was only after Bruni began to call their state a republic that they looked to the desiderata of republican liberty in detail as a basis for constitutional reform.

Rome's republican Constitution had rested on nominal popular sovereignty, mediated in practice by a division of power between the senate, magistrates and *populus Romanus*. Early conceptions of Florentine liberty concentrated on equality before the law and sovereignty of the people, as in Rome, but overlooked the actual structure of the Roman government. As stability became increasingly an issue in the course of the fifteenth century, politicians turned more and more to Rome, and to the tranquil Venetian government, now interpreted as perpetuating Rome's mixed Constitution in its Doge, Senate, and *Consiglio Maggiore*.[38] When King Charles of France interrupted Medici domination in 1494, Florence adopted a new republican constitution that mimicked Venice and Rome

---

34 For a useful chronology of Florence's confusing factional history, see D S Fanti, 'Indice cronologica' in *Leonardo Bruni, Historiarum Florentini Populi* (ed E Santini), Tipi della casa editrice S Lapi, Città di Castello, 1927, pp 377–402.

35 Niccolò Machiavelli, 'Istorie Florentine' in *Opere* (ed E Raimondi), U Mursia, Milano, 1966, p 464.

36 N Machiavelli, 1966, p 211.

37 See J G A Pocock, *The Machiavellian Moment: Florentine Political Thought and the Atlantic Republican Tradition*, Princeton University Press, Princeton, 1975, pp 272–333.

38 J G A Pocock, 1975, p 103; F Gilbert, 'The Venetian Constitution in Florentine Political Thought' in *Florentine Studies: Politics and Society in Renaissance Florence* (ed N Rubinstein), Northwestern University Press, Evanston, Illinois, 1968, p 468; F Gilbert, *Machiavelli and Guicciardini*, Princeton University Press, Princeton, 1965, pp 7–9.

by instituting a *Consiglio Maggiore* or Assembly of the People along with the Signoria and a Gonfalonier. This introduced an elective element into Florentine politics, in place of the corrupt (but supposedly more democratic) sortition by lot.

Francesco Guicciardini described the incidents that led to the adoption of Florence's new Constitution of 1494 in his *History of Florence* (1508–1509). The departure of the Medici family was welcomed at once with cries of 'long live the people and liberty'.[39] But the decisive influence on the city's new constitution was the Dominican monk Girolamo Savonarola, who proposed to restore popular government in the Venetian manner, with a right of appeal from the magistrates to the people, as represented in the new *Consiglio Maggiore*.[40]

Savonarola's conception of republican government was far more democratic than the traditional understanding of Roman or Venetian institutions would support, and very much at variance with the ideas of the aristocratic party that had first encouraged republican constitutionalism in Florence. The Florentine party of *ottimati* (named for Cicero's senatorial faction in Rome) continued to agitate for the creation of a senate, through which they might guide the magistrates and people, and institute a more aristocratic mixture in their city's balance of power. The law that finally established their Florentine Senate in September 1512 referred to the model of 'ancient and modern republics' which maintained senates to preserve their political stability and *libertà*.[41] The Florentine Senate differed from the Venetian *Pregadi* in serving for life, as at Rome, and conceding some fiscal authority to the *Consiglio Maggiore* whose approval was necessary for all financial legislation.[42]

This system lasted barely three months before the return of the Medici family in December 1512, and the revival of the old regime. But an idealised Venice and the Roman republic remained central inspirations for opposition politics.[43] This Florentine attitude towards Venice as a modern Rome was reinforced in 1527 by Giannotti's discourse *Della Repubblica dé Viniziani*,[44] which recalled the corruption of the Roman state since Caesar and praised Venice for resurrecting and even surpassing Rome's ancient virtue. Giannotti observed that Venice had less power than the old Roman republic, but superior tranquillity.[45] He thought Venice's stability had taught all Italy how to preserve its liberty, and avert the oppression of tyrants. Giannotti identified the secret of republican liberty as the maintenance of a balance of power, so that no faction or individual could exploit public laws for private advantage.

---

39   F Guicciardini, 'Storie Florentine' in *Opere* (ed E L Scarano), Unione Tipograficoeditrice Torinese, Torino, 1970, p 123.
40   F Guicciardini, 1970, p 136.
41   F Gilbert, 1965, note 38 above, pp 77–8.
42   F Gilbert, 1968, note 38 above, p 485.
43   F Gilbert, 1968, pp 487–8.
44   D Giannotti, *Opere,* vol 2 (ed F L Polidori), F Le Monnier, Florence, 1850, pp 1–174.
45   D Giannotti, 1850, p 14.

Giannotti's expertise on Venetian institutions brought him to the forefront of Florentine public affairs in 1527, when Florence ousted the Medici family for the final time, and began its last doomed attempt at republican government. The new Gonfalonier, Niccolò Capponi, requested that Giannotti prepare a paper to explain which constitutional arrange-ments would be most advantageous for Florence.[46] Giannotti proposed a mixed government of the one, the few, and the many.[47] He identified liberty with the popular assembly, which should be sovereign, pass the laws, and vote on magistrates. He also thought that Florence needed a senate elected by the popular assembly to govern foreign affairs, and a Gonfalonier for life, to direct the public administration.[48] The state would rise, like a pyramid, on the basis of the people, who would decide in the *Consiglio Grande* how to advance public good (*utile della repubblica*). The senate would advise the people, and magistrates would execute the popular will.[49] In Giannotti's Florence, as in Venice and all Italian republics, the number who would count as citizens and participate in the popular assembly remained quite small.

Florentine liberty began as a fight for civic independence and self-determination. This came to imply certain internal rights for citizens, and eventually a specific form of government, which averted tyranny and protected the public interest. *Libertà* entailed popular sovereignty and the rule of law, but not necessarily a senate in Florence, despite appeals to Venice and Rome. The *ottimati* who fought for senatorial authority were only briefly successful, and Giannotti's constitution was never implemented. Instead in 1528, as in 1494, the city fell under the unchecked domination of the radical middle classes, ruling through the *Consiglio Maggiore*. The dominant spirit was Christian, Guelf and democratic, rather than Roman and republican. Partisans of balanced government began to share Tacitus' doubts that republican liberty under popular sovereignty could ever last very long and indeed the Medici soon imposed themselves again as perpetual Gonfaloniers and hereditary Dukes of the Florentine republic under a stronger and more despotic principate. This was the end of republican liberty in Florence.

Venice survived to confirm the superiority of mixed government. But the conception of republican liberty that Venice preserved was a Florentine creation, and somewhat at variance with Venice's own tradition of untrammelled aristocracy. The citizens or *gentiluomini* of Venice in the *Consiglio Maggiore* excluded many residents of the city, and ruled in their own interest. The very stability of the Venetian state precluded the development of detailed political theory in the manner of turbulent Florence, and Venice only emerged as a self-conscious Renaissance republic in the sixteenth century, as Florence fell back into Medicean despotism. The long Venetian history of selfish and unscrupulous foreign

---

46   D Giannotti, '*Discorso sopra il fermare il governo di Firenze*', in *Opere*, 1850, note 44 above, pp 3–42.
47   D Giannotti, 1850, note 44 above, p 3.
48   D Giannotti, 1850, note 44 above, pp 4–5.
49   D Giannotti, 1850, note 44 above, p 6.

relations also acted to limit the city's direct political influence on other Italian cities,[50] although the Venetian author, Gasparo Contarini, did play a significant role in preserving and disseminating Renaissance republican ideas in his work *De Magistratibus et Republica Venetorum* (1543).[51] Venice declined and became increasingly oligarchical after the papal interdict of 1607, but the republic's mere survival was an argument in favour of republican liberty, and an inspiration to opponents of despotism and theocracy throughout Europe.[52]

Despite its hollow afterlife in Venice, and Florence's own troubled and discouraging constitutional history, the Italian conception of republican liberty revived the 'ancient prudence' in Europe. These new Florentine ideas received their most sophisticated and influential elaboration in the works of Niccolò Machiavelli, particularly his *Discorsi sopra la prima deca di Tito Livio*. Machiavelli wrote this work, as Cicero wrote his books on the *Laws* and the *Republic*, during a period of political quiescence enforced by an emerging prince. When the Medici returned to power in 1512 Machiavelli lost his public positions and was driven to his country estate. This was a decisive moment in Florentine history. Machiavelli still hoped when he began the *Discourses* that the Medici would establish a quasi-republican regime, and accept a limited role as the dominant figures in a balanced government.[53] Later, as Florentine politics came down to a conflict between democrats and despots, republicans lost heart. Florence's troubled history became an embarrassment to the republican cause, and later republican authors such as John Adams repudiated the 'series of alternate tragedy, comedy, and farce, which was called the liberty of Florence'.[54] But they still read Machiavelli carefully, as 'the great restorer of true politics',[55] despite his partiality to popular government.

English liberty

When Adams set out in his *Defence of the Constitutions of the United States of America* to give examples of the 'kind of reading and reasoning' that produced the American republics he began with Cicero and Rome[56] and devoted most of the second volume of his work to Machiavelli and the Italians.[57] His third volume came at last to England whose 'theory of

---

50 W J Bouwsma, *Venice and the Defense of Republican Liberty: Renaissance Values in the Age of the Counter Reformation*, University of California Press, Berkeley, 1968, p 57.

51 On his influence, see Z S Fink, *The Classical Republicans: An Essay in the Recovery of a Pattern of Thought in Seventeenth Century England*, 2nd ed, Northwestern University Press, Evanston, Illinois, 1961.

52 W J Bouwsma, 1968, note 50 above, pp 624–8.

53 F Gilbert, 1965, note 38 above, pp 154–6.

54 J Adams, *A Defence of the Constitutions of the United States of America*, vol II, C Dilly, London, 1787, p 25.

55 J Adams, 1788, vol III, p 210.

56 J Adams, 1787, vol I, pp xix–xxii.

57 J Adams, 1787, vol II, especially pp 10–134 on N Machiavelli's *Histories*, and pp 241–50 on 'Machiavelli's Plan of a perfect Commonwealth'.

government' and 'present liberties' had 'more merit with the human race than any other among the moderns'.[58] Adams identified three periods in the history of England that had produced very valuable writings and inspired the American republics: first the Reformation, which generated John Ponet's *Shorte Treatise of Politicke Power* (1556); then the whole interval between 1640 and 1660, which produced Harrington, Milton and the *Vindiciae contra Tyrannos*, and finally, the Revolution in 1688, which led to the writings of Sidney, Locke, Hoadley, Trenchard, Gordon, and Plato Redivivus.[59]

The history of republican liberty in England comprises a strange and fragmented evolution, in which the words 'liberty' and 'republic' became separated, without losing their mutual imprint and related ideological foundations. Regal government managed to survive in Britain, but only by adopting many republican institutions, and embracing (or at least tolerating) a largely republican conception of liberty, with its implied condemnation of hereditary honours and nobility. The modern history of British jurisprudence, from Hobbes and Hume through to Austin and Hart, is deeply influenced by the natural conflict between ideas of liberty and regal authority. However, British monarchy under the Tudors had already begun to adopt a rhetoric of liberty and balanced government, and Charles I lost his life and crown when he repudiated the rule of law and challenged the ultimate sovereignty of the people.

Ponet, the Bishop of Winchester under Edward VI, was exiled from England in the reign of Queen Mary and wrote his *Shorte Treatise of Politicke Power* in Strassburg, where many leaders of the English reformation had gathered, among them most of Ponet's humanist friends from his undergraduate days at Cambridge. Ponet recognised a law of nature 'grafted . . . in the mind of man'[60] but translated into positive rules by those granted such authority at the 'discretion of the people'.[61] He described the best system for maintaining such a 'common-wealth' as a mixed state of monarchy, aristocracy and democracy (or king, nobility and commons). But Ponet insisted that the primary aim of this, as of every other state, should be the maintenance of justice.[62] To this end commonwealths balanced their executive officers with ephors (in Sparta), tribunes (in Rome), or parliaments (in England) 'to defend and maintain the liberty of the people', lest tyrants step in 'to suppress the good orders of the commonwealth'.[63]

---

58 J Adams, 1788, vol III, pp 209–10.

59 J Adams, 1788, vol III, pp 210–11.

60 J Ponet, *A Shorte Treatise of Politike Power, and of the true Obedience which subjects owe to Kynges and other civile Governours, with an Exhortacion to all true naturall Englishe men*, Strassburg, 1556, p 4, reproduced in facsimile in W S Hudson, *John Ponet (1516?–1556): Advocate of Limited Monarchy*, University of Chicago Press, Chicago, 1942.

61 J Ponet, 1942, p 8.

62 J Ponet, 1942, p 9.

63 J Ponet, 1942, pp 11–12.

Ponet condemned courts and parliaments that failed to conserve 'the liberties and commonwealth of their country', and specifically the popish Queen and 'brutish commons' of England.[64] Magistrates should obey the law of nature, and the positive laws and customs of their countries. But kings and princes could not legitimately make any laws without the consent of the people.[65] Those like Caligula and Nero who acted against the common good to satisfy their own lusts were evil men. But Ponet blamed the senate and people of Rome as much as the emperors, because they 'might have bridled [their magistrates] and did not'.

Ponet adopted the republican viewpoint that the proper end of all authority is the maintenance of justice and the common good. Political power used to any other end is tyrannical, and not to be tolerated. This meant that the prince must be subject to the laws,[66] since equality before law is the foundation of republican government.[67] Ponet made the radical observation that 'commonwealths may stand well enough and flourish, albeit there be no kings'[68] and reminded his English readers of 'the manifold and continual examples' in history 'of the deposing of kings, and killing of tyrants' which 'most certainly confirm[s] it to be most true, just, and consonant to God's judgement' to remove any magistrate who 'seek[s] too much his own will, and not the wealth of the whole body'.[69]

Elizabeth's accession to the throne of England rehabilitated the Marian exiles, without necessarily endorsing their conception of liberty. Her ambassador to France, (later Secretary of State) Thomas Smith, who had been a close associate of Ponet's at Queen's College, Cambridge wrote a treatise *De Republica Anglorum* that presented many of the same views without conceding the superfluity of the monarch. Smith distinguished monarchy, aristocracy and democracy, and advocated a mixture of the three.[70]

According to Smith, tyrants were rulers who ignored the advice of the people, the standing laws or the common good. Smith thought absolute power was dangerous to king and subjects, because it led to tyranny. There could be no commonwealth without free citizens. Thus, in its broadest sense he took the Latin *res publica* to mean 'the rule of the multitude'.[71] But when he identified Parliament as the 'most high and absolute power of the realm of England', Smith meant the consensus of the king, lords and commons. He was very clear that as things currently stood the monarch was 'the life, the head, and the authority of all things that be done' in the commonwealth of England.[72]

---

64   J Ponet, 1942, pp 19–20.
65   J Ponet, 1942, p 28.
66   J Ponet, 1942, p 43.
67   J Ponet, 1942, p 44.
68   J Ponet, 1942, p 61.
69   J Ponet, 1942, p 61. Compare p 107.
70   T Smith, *De Republica Anglorum*, first published 1583 (ed M Dewar), Cambridge University Press, Cambridge, 1982, p 52.
71   T Smith, 1982, p 62.
72   T Smith, 1982, p 88.

The conflict between the concept of a republic or commonwealth and the presence of a king became increasingly sharp in England as the Stuart monarchs sought to establish a firmer grasp on government. While Elizabeth staunchly opposed Spain and the Roman Catholic powers in Europe, it had been plausible for the sovereign to assert that her own exercise of power preserved liberty by protecting the kingdom from foreign subjugation.[73] But even then free English citizens expected a certain measure of personal and political liberty by simple virtue of their non-servile status.[74] The Stuart monarchs' tendency to flirt with continental powers raised fears that they would adopt the arbitrary policies of the European Counter-Reformation. Under intense pressure from Parliament, Charles I found it expedient to formally concede the mixed and balanced nature of the English government, the desirability of the aristocratic and democratic portions of the constitution, Parliament's joint responsibility for approving laws, and even the special role of the House of Commons as 'Conservor of Liberty', so long as the monarch remained as sole executive holding the actual reins of government.[75] James I had also unambiguously conceded that a king became a tyrant when he ceased to rule by law for the common good of his people.[76]

The gradual development of a republican balance in England's constitution, and the idea of ordered liberty, received a sudden impetus with the execution of Charles I in 1649. For the first time in its history, England could be accurately considered a commonwealth or republic, and was so described on the Great Seals of State. Parliament marked official documents by the years since which 'freedom' was 'by God's blessing restored'. Yet the removal of the king created a curious dilemma for English advocates of republican liberty. Where was the balance in the new constitution? The Commons of England in Parliament assembled declared themselves 'the supreme power in this nation', and the sole source of law. But the purged parliament was an oligarchy and hardly representative of the nation as a whole.

The pre-eminent and subsequently most influential political theorist of this second period in which the 'principles of government [were] anxiously studied' by the English was James Harrington. Harrington had been educated at Trinity College, Oxford, and attended Charles I after May 1647 at the direction of Parliament, prior to the king's execution. He published his most famous work, *The Commonwealth of Oceana* in 1656

---

73 See Elizabeth's 'Golden Speech' of 1601 discussed by D H Sacks, 'Parliament, Liberty, and the Commonweal' in *Parliament and Liberty from the Reign of Elizabeth to the English Civil War* (ed J H Hexter), Stanford University Press, Stanford, 1992, p 85.

74 D H Sacks, 1992, pp 98–101.

75 See 'His Majesties Answer to the XIX Propositions of both Houses of Parliament' excerpted in C C Weston, *English Constitutional Theory and the House of Lords, 1556–1832*, Columbia University Press, New York, 1965, pp 263–5.

76 See his speeches to Parliament in 1603 and 1609, quoted by J Locke, *Two Treatises on Government* (ed P Laslett), Cambridge University Press, Cambridge, 1960, Second Treatise, § 200, pp 417–18.

and dedicated it to Oliver Cromwell during the period in which the Lord Protector was contemplating a final constitutional settlement for the Commonwealth of England, Scotland and Ireland. Harrington recalled 'the liberty of Rome' and sought to recreate a civil society based on 'common right or interest' and 'the empire of laws and not of men'.[77] Since in his view monarchy, aristocracy and democracy all tend to degenerate, Harrington proposed a mixture of them all, according to the 'doctrine of the ancients'.[78] He praised the example of the Roman republic where the senate proposed the laws and the people passed them, *censuere patres, jussit populus*.[79] For Harrington, 'the liberty of a commonwealth consisteth in the empire of her laws, the absence whereof would betray her unto the lusts of tyrants'.[80] He proposed that an elected senate and people (or popular assembly) should constitute the sovereign power in the commonwealth, making all laws, with an executive consisting of a 'strategus' and 'orator' corresponding to the two consuls in Rome, and perhaps an 'archon' like the Protector Oliver Cromwell.[81]

The central aim of Harrington's proposal for a mixed and balanced republican constitution was the *libertas* that Romans enjoyed before Caesar. But Harrington was well aware of the first republic's failure, which he attributed to its internal divisions. He proposed two solutions to forestall Rome's fate: frequent rotation among the magistrates, and an agrarian law to preserve the widespread distribution of landed property. Harrington attributed the first to Sparta and the second to Venice, which he preferred in this respect to Rome.[82] The Venetian influence may also be seen in Harrington's desire for limited suffrage.[83] Other commonwealth authors such as Milton went even further in their advocacy of oligarchic government, dispensing with balance altogether in the interests of a ruling elite. This reflected support for a reconstituted Long Parliament and drove a wedge between the conception of a commonwealth and the republic. The English conception of a commonwealth came to be associated with oligarchic unicameralism.[84] Adams blamed the unicameral ideas of the 'divine immortal Milton' and his associates for the Stuart restoration. Milton's constitution would have created another Venice, and 'stripped the English people of every shadow of liberty'.[85]

The collapse of the English commonwealth, first into Cromwell's protectorate and finally into Stuart monarchy discouraged British advocates of popular or oligarchic government; however it strengthened

---

77   J G A Pocock, *The Political Works of James Harrington,* Cambridge University Press, Cambridge, 1977, p 161.

78   J G A Pocock, 1977, p 162.

79   J G A Pocock, 1977, p 166. Compare p 338.

80   J G A Pocock, 1977, p 170.

81   J G A Pocock, 1977, pp 245, 247–8, 346.

82   J G A Pocock, 1977, pp 276–7. For rotation and the agrarian law, see also pp 333–4.

83   J G A Pocock, 1977, pp 212–13.

84   J Adams, 1788, note 54 above, vol III, pp 160–1.

85   J Adams, 1788, vol I, p 368; vol III, p 371. Adams only excused Milton as having written under duress: see vol III, pp 212, 371.

supporters of a republican mixture. Even Charles II was prepared to concede the value of a free parliament and a balanced constitution, provided the king presided in its execution. Most of the English could support this arrangement, and would do so permanently, after the Glorious Revolution of 1688. But the Stuarts insisted on their regal prerogatives, and provoked a spirited opposition, including Algernon Sidney, England's last and greatest openly republican author.

Sidney was a violent opponent of the Stuart monarchy; he had fought at Marston Moor under Cromwell, and sat as a member of the Long Parliament. But his subsequent fame and status as a republican martyr derived from his unfinished *Discourses Concerning Government*, which were introduced as the decisive evidence against him in his trial for treason under Charles II, resulting in Sidney's decapitation on 7 December 1683.[86] John Toland printed the *Discourses* posthumously in London in 1698.[87] Sidney intended his treatise as a refutation of Sir Robert Filmer's *Patriarcha*, concerning the 'universal and undistinguished right of all kings', but also as a vindication of 'the best and wisest of men' who 'constituted commonwealths' by balancing the powers of the magistrates so 'that they might all concur in producing the publick good' or, as Cicero says, obtaining justice, which is the same thing.[88]

Sidney considered liberty a natural attribute of humanity, subject to the 'just ordinances of man' but not to the will of a king, unless the people consented.[89] To depend upon the will of another is slavery, and for Sidney the only free nations were those under the empire of laws and not men, where *potentiora erant legum quam hominum imperia*. The people 'were and would be governed only by laws of their own making'.[90] This doctrine of Livy and Tacitus rested on the ultimate sovereignty of the people, but for Sidney the wisest and best part of mankind had always framed mixed governments, combining attributes of democracy, aristocracy, and monarchy.[91] The Romans had such a government, deplored by Filmer for its liberty. Sidney observed that even though Roman kings were not born, but elected by the senate and people, the Romans themselves never flourished until they recovered their liberty and dispensed with kings altogether. Ultimate sovereignty rested in the people, always guided by the advice of the senate so that the style of *senatus censuit, populus jussit* was never altered while liberty persisted at Rome. Like Tacitus, Livy, Giannotti and Harrington, Sidney traced the origin of liberty to Lucius Brutus, Rome's first consul, and dated the end of Roman liberty from Julius Caesar, who overthrew Rome's balanced Constitution, and put himself above the law.

---

86   For a good brief biographical sketch of Sidney, see A C Houston, *Algernon Sidney and the Republican Heritage in England and America*, Princeton University Press, Princeton, 1991, pp 15–67.

87   A Sidney, *Discourses Concerning Government* (ed T G West), Liberty Classics, Indianapolis, 1990.

88   A Sidney, 1990, pp 5–6.

89   A Sidney, 1990, pp 8–10.

90   A Sidney, 1990, p 17.

91   A Sidney, 1990, p 31. Compare pp 166–70.

Sidney was first in Adams' list of writers 'who will convince any candid mind, that there is no good government but what is republican', by which he meant a balanced government, sharply distinguished from the unicameral and democratic tendencies of the English and Italian commonwealths.[92] Sidney made no secret that he preferred the form of government constituted at Rome 'from the expulsion of Tarquin to the setting up of Caesar' to any other that the world had ever seen.[93] Future English authors would be much more circumspect. Out of deference to the re-emerging monarchy, they spoke of what was practicable rather than what was best. Locke, Sidney's close contemporary and ally in the plots against Charles II, was a partisan of the Prince of Orange and defined 'republic' to encompass monarchies.[94] He studiously avoided constitutional prescriptions, except in his much reviled plan of legislation for Carolina[95] and his work was understood by subsequent republicans as useful for the *principles*, but never for the *forms* of government.[96]

After the Glorious Revolution of 1688 even conservative and established lawyers, such as William Blackstone, the Vinerian professor of English Law at Oxford University, conceded that the society at large could displace and discipline magistrates (including kings) who abused or exceeded their public powers.[97] But Blackstone thought regular elections of monarchs ('the perfection of liberty') would lead to tumult and anarchy.[98] Even the strongest advocates of English liberty such as John Trenchard and Thomas Gordon now hotly denied that they were republicans. Yet they still embraced almost all of Sidney's republican *Discourses* as 'eternally true' and 'agreeable to our own constitution'.[99] Sidney was a 'martyr for that liberty which he so nobly defended', and his book made some amends for the loss of Cicero's *de Republica*.[100] For Trenchard and Gordon, England's Constitution was 'a thousand degrees nearer akin' to Sidney's republic than to absolute monarchy. The English Cato praised England as 'the best republic in the world, with a prince at the head of it'.[101]

---

92   J Adams, 1787, note 54 above, vol I, pp 148–52.
93   A Sidney, 1990, note 87 above, p 194.
94   J Locke, 1960, note 76 above, *Second Treatise*, § 205, p 420. Compare *Second Treatise*, § 133, p 373 for 'commonwealth'.
95   On which see J Adams, 1787, note 54 above, vol I, p 365. Locke's plan of legislation 'astonish[ed] the world with a signal absurdity' despite his devotion to 'the principles of liberty and the rights of mankind'.
96   See also B Rush, *The Selected Writings of Benjamin Rush* (ed D Runes), The Philosophical Library, New York, 1947, p 78, discussed by G Stourzh, *Alexander Hamilton and the Idea of Republican Government*, Stanford University Press, Stanford, 1970, p 4.
97   W Blackstone, *Commentaries on the Laws of England*, vol I, Clarendon Press, Oxford, 1765, p 207.
98   W Blackstone, 1765, p 211.
99   J Trenchard and T Gordon, *Cato's Letters: Essays on Liberty, Civil and Religious, and Other Important Subjects,* vol II, 6th ed, printed for J Walthoe et al, London, 1755, p 28.
100 J Trenchard and T Gordon, 1755, vol I, pp 195–6.
101 J Trenchard and T Gordon, 1755, vol II, p 28.

The history of English liberty and balanced government is the history of the gradual integration of republican ideals into a state which, by retaining a monarch, denied itself legitimate use of the name 'republic'. Although it was widely accepted that the 'same principle[s] of nature and reason' that supported liberty at Rome 'must support it here and everywhere',[102] very few political thinkers after Sidney openly advocated a republic in England, believed it possible, or even wished for one. Following Trenchard, the most radical English apostles of liberty thought themselves better off than any practicable constitutional change could make them. English lawyers such as Blackstone boasted that the spirit of liberty was deeply planted in the English Constitution, and flourished best 'in these kingdoms'.[103] But the root of English liberty was in the Civil War and Interregnum. The purest and frankest advocates of republican liberty in England were Harrington and Sidney, who wrote without hope of royal favour, in the expectation of a revived republic and the unadulterated rule of law.

American liberty

The United States began its political history as an English colony, and participated in the development of the English sense of liberty through the legal disagreements and civil wars that did so much to shape the British Constitution. Many Americans, particularly in Pennsylvania and the northern colonies, traced their ancestry to the old commonwealth armies, and supporters of the English Reformation. On the eve of their Revolution, Americans shared in the English conception of liberty, but with greater conviction and personal commitment than most of their British cousins. The development of American constitutional ideas after the Revolution reflects a gradual (and chronologically inverted) progression from Trenchard and Gordon through Locke to Sidney, Harrington and the Italian and Roman republicans who stand as an example of the largest and most successful previous experiments in government without a king.

The beginnings of the conflict between America and England took place in the context of traditional common law disputation, in which Americans referred to Locke rather than Sidney in order to avoid the cry of rebellion. James Otis and others constructed elaborate arguments in the years prior to 1776, construing the powers of Parliament, with references to Coke, the Magna Carta, and other English precedents.[104] Only after 1776, with the repudiation of King George III and the institution of the new state constitutions could Americans finally begin openly to embrace

---

102 J Trenchard and T Gordon, 1755, vol I, p xxviii.

103 W Blackstone, 1765, note 97 above, vol I, pp 122–32.

104 B Bailyn, *Ideological Origins of the American Revolution, 1750–1765*, Harvard University Press, Cambridge, Massachusetts, 1967, pp 176 ff; *Pamphlets of the American Revolution 1750–1765* (ed B Bailyn), Harvard University Press, Cambridge, Massachusetts, 1965, contains several good examples of this sort of reasoning, including J Otis, 'The Rights of the British Colonies Asserted and Proved' (1764), pp 408 ff and 'A Vindication of the British Colonies against the Aspersions of the Halifax Gentlemen' (1765), pp 545 ff.

republican liberty, and to frame their institutions accordingly. The best and most influential example of the new republican constitutional ideas was Adams' *Thoughts on Government*, written to help Richard Henry Lee in shaping Virginia's new frame of government, and published in Boston in 1776.[105]

Adams cited Sidney, Harrington and other English theorists of the Glorious Revolution and interregnum for the proposition that there is no good government but what is republican. The 'only valuable part of the British constitution' derived from adopting republican principles, and particularly the maxim that free governments must be 'empire[s] of laws, and not of men'.[106] Adams did not believe that any people could long remain free or happy under the government of a unicameral assembly because of human passion, avarice and ambition. He cited the corruption of the English Long Parliament and commonwealth. Instead Adams proposed to create an upper chamber in the legislature, with a veto over the House of Representatives, and an elected governor to hold the balance between them. The judicial power would be distinct from both the legislature and executive, and general education liberally funded, to inspire the people with the 'conscious dignity befitting free men'. Adams cited 'the known rules of ancient liberty' to support the notion of 'the wisest and happiest government that human wisdom can contrive'.

Adams' proposals and prevailing republican ideals were reflected in the state constitutions approved in the years following the Declaration of Independence. At first, these represented temporary expedients 'to continue during the present unhappy and unnatural contest with Great Britain' (Constitution of New Hampshire 1776) and until an accommodation of the 'unhappy differences' between Great Britain and America could be obtained (Constitution of South Carolina 1776). But eventually the states made more permanent arrangements, beginning with the Virginia Constitution of 29 June 1776. The new Commonwealth of Virginia, was governed by a Senate and House of Delegates in the legislature, and an executive governor (without a veto). The Virginia Bill of Rights recognised a natural right to free government for the common benefit and public weal, a government that would secure the 'blessings of liberty' by firm adherence to justice and virtue, and a 'frequent recurrence to fundamental principles'. New Jersey also instituted a single executive and bicameral legislature during 1776, as did Delaware, Maryland, and North Carolina. These all chose to be states or colonies rather than commonwealths, while recognising that the right of the people to participate in the legislature 'is the best security of liberty, and the foundation of all free government'.[107]

---

105 *American Political Writings in the Founding Era, 1760–1805* (eds C S Hyneman and D S Lutz) Liberty Press, Indianapolis, 1983, pp 402–9.

106 C S Hyneman and D S Lutz, 1983, p 403.

107 'The Declaration of Rights of Maryland' in F N Thorpe, *Federal and State Constitutions, Colonial Charters and Other Organic Laws*, Government Printing Office, Washington, 1909, p 1687. Compare the North Carolina list of rights in Thorpe, pp 2787–8.

The only other 'commonwealth' of 1776 was Pennsylvania, which followed the example of the English commonwealth and Long Parliament by vesting all legislative power in a single house of representatives. The conflict between the Roman form of commonwealth (with a Senate) and the English form (without one) soon became the central disagreement among American advocates of constitutional government, who all agreed on the importance of liberty and government for the public weal.[108] Georgia and the Commonwealth of Vermont adopted the Pennsylvania model. New York, South Carolina and the Commonwealth of Massachusetts all followed Virginia in instituting senates. Adams noted that the very name of 'commonwealth' had been discredited by the House of Commons' 'unsuccessful and injudicious' attempts at unicameral government during the English Civil War.[109] A 'Republican' party sprang up at once in Pennsylvania to oppose the unicameral constitution, and to fight for independent judges and a legislative senate.[110]

The battle between the Pennsylvania Republicans and their opponents (the 'Constitutionalists') set the tone for constitutional debates throughout the colonies in the decade following independence, leading to the United States Constitutional Convention held at Philadelphia in 1787.[111] The Republican Society's open letter 'To the Citizens of Pennsylvania' in the *Pennsylvania Packet* of 23 March 1779, laid out their party's basic principles. They claimed the 'Liberty and Happiness of Pennsylvania' as their primary aims, in opposition to the faction and tyranny that threatened to emerge from Pennsylvania's new Constitution. The Republicans' first and principal objection to the Pennsylvania Constitution was that it vested the 'whole legislative authority in a single body, without any controul'. They advocated two legislative chambers, both elected by the people, who were seen as 'the fountain of all authority'. There need not be, as in Rome and Venice, 'two distinct orders of men' but rather as in 'all the most celebrated free Governments of antiquity' and all the other American states except Georgia, two distinct branches or bodies in the legislature, to preserve the liberty and tranquillity of the commonwealth. The Republicans also objected to Pennsylvania's judiciary, because the judges held their offices for limited terms. They should serve for life, to secure the impartial administration of law and justice. This alone would

---

108 W P Adams, *The First American Constitutions: Republican Ideology and the Making of the State Constitutions in the Revolutionary Era* (trans R and R Kimber), University of North Carolina Press, Chapel Hill, 1980, pp 256–66.

109 J Adams, 1787, note 54 above, vol I, p 208.

110 On the Pennsylvania Republicans, see D M Arnold, *A Republican Revolution: Ideology and Politics in Pennsylvania*, Garland, New York, 1989; R L Brunhouse, *The Counter-Revolution in Pennsylvania, 1776–1790*, Octagon Books, New York, 1971; R A Ryerson, 'Republican Theory and Partisan Reality in Revolutionary Pennsylvania: Toward a New View of the Constitutionalists' in *Sovereign States in an Age of Uncertainty* (eds R Hoffman and P J Albert), University Press of Virginia, Charlottesville, 1981, pp 95–133.

111 See M N S Sellers, 1994, note 2 above, Chapter 8.

protect the public good — provided that no citizen or body of citizens ever enjoyed 'uncontrouled power' in the state.[112]

Leading Pennsylvania Republicans such as Benjamin Rush, had rested their arguments on Adams' *Thoughts on Government*, as well as the example of antiquity. Their advocacy of bicameralism depended on the belief that mixed and balanced government was the form 'best contrived to support an impartial and exact execution of the laws'.[113] All power should be *derived* from the people, not *seated* in them. Unicameral assemblies had led to Caesar in Rome, and Cromwell in Great Britain.[114] For Republicans, the liberty of the whole world rested on the efforts of the United States.[115] They prevailed in Georgia with the inauguration of a bicameral legislature and independent judiciary in 1789, in the United States as a whole with the implementation of a bicameral federal government in March 1790, and finally in Pennsylvania itself in November 1790, with the approval of a new constitution vesting the legislative power of this commonwealth in a Senate and House of Representatives.

The Constitution of the United States is the single most important document in the modern history of republican liberty, and was perceived as such by the men who wrote and ratified it.[116] When it became apparent that a convention would be held in Philadelphia to prepare a new constitution, the Pennsylvania Republicans began immediately to repeat their old arguments for republican government to a new and broader audience. Rush's 'Address to the People of the United States' reiterated his party's insistence that republican 'principles of liberty' required protection against popular ignorance and licentiousness,[117] and a division of the United States legislature into two distinct, independent branches.[118] He repeated that national power, like state power, should be derived *from* the people, not seated *in* them. The people possess power only on the days of their elections. 'Nor can they exercise or resume it, unless it is abused.'[119]

Rush thought that the Americans had begun their revolution 'ignorant of the forms and combinations of power in republics'.[120] But by the time of the constitutional convention virtually no American politician outside Pennsylvania questioned the importance of balancing three branches of

---

112 Republican Society, 'To the Citizens of Pennsylvania' in the *Pennsylvania Packet*, 23 March 1779, first and last pages.

113 B Rush, *Observations upon the Present Government of Pennsylvania in Four Letters to the People of Pennsylvania*, Styner and Cist, Philadelphia, 1777, title page (quoting J Adams) and *passim*.

114 B Rush, 1777, Letter III, p 15.

115 B Rush, 1777, Letter IV, p 21.

116 Eg, George Washington's inaugural speech. See note 1 and accompanying text.

117 B Rush, 'Address to the People of the United States', 1787, reprinted in *The Documentary History of the Ratification of the Constitution,* vol XIII (eds J P Kaminski and G J Saladino), State Historical Society of Wisconsin, Madison, 1981, p 46.

118 B Rush, 1777, p 47.

119 B Rush, 1777, p 47.

120 B Rush, 1777, p 47.

government in a divided legislature to protect liberty and justice as in England and Rome. If anything, opponents of the Constitution thought the checks insufficient and the balance too weak.[121] The central question was not the proper structure of republics, but whether the federal union should be treated as a republic at all. Adams, the great proponent of traditional republicanism, doubted at first that its requirements were applicable to the United States in their federal capacity, because Congress was only a 'diplomatic' assembly.[122] But he later endorsed the United States Constitution as 'the greatest single effort of national deliberation that the world has ever seen'.[123] If the United States was to be a republic, its liberty would need the protection of fully republican institutions.

The most detailed and prolific defence of the new United States Constitution appeared in the *Federal Essays* of Publius (the collective pseudonym of John Jay, James Madison and Alexander Hamilton). Publius' very name reflected a commitment to liberty and republican principles. The original Publius Valerius Publicola had been Brutus' colleague as founder and first consul of the Roman republic. The American Publius wrote his letters to establish the 'conformity of the proposed Constitution to the true principles of republican government'[124] and to confirm the example of those 'stupendous fabrics reared on the basis of liberty', which had 'flourished for ages' proving the value of 'free government' against the 'gloomy sophisms' of self-interested despots.[125] The 'genius of republican liberty' demanded that all power should be derived from the people.[126] But it was also essential to the preservation of liberty that power be separated among several departments of government. Publius insisted that '[a]mbition must be made to counteract ambition' and protect the public liberty through a division of the legislature.[127]

Adams provided the best description of the ideas and sources that shaped the idea of republican liberty in the United States; Jay, Madison and Hamilton as Publius supplied the clearest arguments in the debate that endorsed it. But the best evidence for the triumph of republican liberty in England's American colonies is the United States Constitution itself, which set out to 'secure the Blessings of Liberty to ourselves and our Posterity'[128] through the creation of a senate in the legislature,[129] and

---

121 Eg, James Monroe in the Virginia Convention, 10 June 1788. See J P Kaminski and G J Saladino, 1990, note 117 above, vol IX, pp 1112–13. 'There was a composition of Aristocracy, Democracy, and Monarchy, each of which had a repellent quality, which enabled it to preserve itself from being destroyed by the other two — so that the balance was continually maintained.'

122 J Adams, 1787, note 54 above, vol I, p 362.

123 J Adams, 1788, vol III, p 506.

124 Publius, 'Federalist No 1' in *The Federalist Papers* (ed I Kramnick), Penguin, London, 1987, p 89.

125 Publius, 'Federalist No 9', p 118.

126 Publius, 'Federalist No 37', p 243.

127 Publius, 'Federalist No 51', p 319. Compare 'Federalist No 47', p 303.

128 *Constitution of the United States*, Preamble.

129 Article I, Section 1.

independent judges, holding their offices for life 'during good Behavior'.[130] The Constitution guaranteed 'to every State in this Union a Republican Form of Government'[131] and rested its authority on the ratification and consent of the people.[132]

French liberty

Adams drew a sharp distinction between the 'true' definition of a republic, and the 'peculiar sense' in which the words 'republic, [and] commonwealth' are used by some English and French writers to mean a representative democracy or government by a single assembly, invested with the whole sovereignty.[133] This was the doctrine of Marchamont Needham and the English commonwealth, adopted and elaborated by the Pennsylvania Constitutionalists, and finally carried to France by men such as Anne Robert Jacques Turgot and Gabriel Bonnot de Mably, who (wrongly) attributed the Pennsylvania Constitution of 1776 to Benjamin Franklin. Adams wrote his *Defence* to refute Turgot's endorsement of unicameral government that 'collect[ed] all authority in one center'. For Adams this amounted to democracy, and there never was 'freedom nor justice in a simple democracy for any but the majority'.[134] The main distinction between French ideas and American republicanism in the eyes of the Americans was that the French too readily disregarded the principles of balance and the separation of powers, promoting unicameral ideas 'unworthy of so great a cause as that of liberty and republican government'.[135]

Not all French authors opposed balanced government. The Baron de Montesquieu advocated the creation of a senate for life (or at least long terms)[136] to maintain a balance of power in the legislature, as in Rome and England.[137] Montesquieu became the favourite author of those who opposed the United States Constitution, because of his strong strictures against large republics, which he said could not be governed on the principles of freedom.[138] Montesquieu also suggested confederation as the solution to this difficulty, which was acceptable to both sides of the

---

130 Article III, Section 1.
131 Article IV, Section 4.
132 Article VII.
133 J Adams, 1788, note 54 above, vol III, pp 160–1.
134 J Adams, 1788, vol III, p 355.
135 J Adams, 1788, vol III, p 390. On republican liberty in France, see C Nicolet, *L'idée républicaine en France (1789–1924)*, Gallimard, Paris, 1982; *L'esprit républicain* (ed J Viard), Klincksieck, Paris, 1972; *Liberty/Liberté: The American and French Experiences* (eds J Klaits and M Haltzel), Johns Hopkins University Press, Baltimore, 1991; P Higonnet, *Sister Republics: The Origin of French and American Republicanism*, Harvard University Press, Cambridge, Massachusetts, 1988; H T Parker, *The Cult of Antiquity and the French Revolutionaries*, University of Chicago, Chicago, 1937.
136 Baron de Montesquieu, *De l'Espirit des lois*, Barillot & Fils, Geneva, 1748, I.v.7; *Spirit of the Laws* (trans T Nugent), Hafner, New York, 1949, p 47.
137 Baron de Montesquieu, I.xi.6; Nugent, 1949, p 160.
138 Baron de Montesquieu, I.viii.6; Nugent, 1949, pp 120–1.

American constitutional debate, although they put very different interpretations on what the word 'confederation' meant.[139] But although he was very much influenced by the examples of England and Rome, Montesquieu's use of the term 'republic' remained broad, encompassing any state in which the people, or any part of the people possessed supreme power.[140] This meant that oligarchies would count as republics[141] and that a state could be a republic without being free.[142] Adams considered Montesquieu 'scarcely ... a republican writer' because of his loose definition of liberty. For Adams, true liberty required not only *equal laws* by *common consent* but also that all legislation serve the *general interest*, or the *public good*, which Montesquieu had neglected to mention explicitly.[143]

Jean-Jacques Rousseau also spoke confusedly of liberty and the public good in terms that appalled more orthodox republicans. Americans remembered Rousseau for his dictum that 'a society of Gods would govern themselves democratically'. But Rousseau himself defined a republic as any state under the rule of law, whatever its form of government. (*Tout gouvernement légitime est républicain.*) Only through law could the public interest govern, and *la chose publique* or *res publica* exist. Rousseau was very clear that monarchies, aristocracies, and democracies could all be republics, provided they served the general will, which is the law (*la volonté générale, qui est la loi*).[144] He believed that citizens must transfer all individual rights to the community (the *moi commun* or *république*) to enjoy social liberty.[145] But like Montesquieu, Rousseau insisted that republican government was only appropriate for small intimate cantons.[146] This followed from his assumption that law must be an expression of the general will, and therefore that no law can exist without formal ratification by the people as a whole (not their representatives, as in England and the United States).[147]

Rousseau frequently referred to the example of Rome. No law was sanctioned there, and no magistrate elected, except by vote of the Roman people, who were truly sovereign both in law and in fact.[148] But Rousseau also admired the strength of Rome's senate and preferred the *comitia centuriata* to the *comitia tributa* because it preserved the senate's influence and participation.[149] The senate should administer the democratically adopted laws of the republic. Rousseau considered an elective aristocracy of 'venerable senators' the best of all governments, provided the executive

---

139 Baron de Montesquieu, I.ix.1–2, Nugent, 1949, pp 126–8.
140 Baron de Montesquieu, I.ii.1, Nugent, 1949, p 8.
141 Baron de Montesquieu, I.ii.2, Nugent, 1949, p 8.
142 Baron de Montesquieu, I.xi.6, Nugent, 1949, p 152.
143 J Adams, 1787, note 54 above, vol I, pp 123–4. Also see Baron de Montesquieu, note 136 above, I.xi.3.
144 J-J Rousseau, *Du contrat social* (ed J-P Simelon), Editions du Seuil, Paris, 1977, II.6, pp 205–6.
145 J-J Rousseau, 1977, I.6, pp 183–4.
146 J-J Rousseau, 1977, III.1, p 227; III.15, p 268.
147 J-J Rousseau, 1977, III.15, p 266.
148 J-J Rousseau, 1977, IV.4, p 288–9.
149 J-J Rousseau, 1977, IV.4, p 292.

power recognised the sovereignty of law, ratified by a popular assembly.[150] Like Livy and Montesquieu (whom he cited to support this assertion), Rousseau did not believe that all peoples were capable of liberty. He suggested that warm climates encouraged despotism, cold climates encouraged barbarism, and that a 'good polity' may only be possible in the temperate zone.[151] In any case, there could be no liberty without assemblies of the people, and therefore republics may only exist in separate, independent towns.[152]

Neither Montesquieu nor Rousseau publicly identified himself as an advocate of republican government, nor did anyone else in France before 1790, when François Robert published *Le républicanisme adapté à la France*, arguing that liberty would not be possible without a republic. Previous French writers, like authors in England and pre-revolutionary America had been constrained by the existence of a king, and the general assumption (challenged by Rousseau) that monarchy and republicanism were incompatible systems. Robert observed that the logic of the Revolution made the king superfluous. But his initiative provoked immediate opposition. The *Journal des Clubs* argued that republican government in France must either be unitary — treating France as one large republic — or federative, breaking the nation up into small allied republics. A unitary republic would lead to despotism and civil war under a modern Nero, Domitian, Sulla or Catiline. But federation would also lead to subjugation, either by France's own local aristocracy or by foreign powers. The primary argument against republicanism in France, as in England, was not that it was undesirable, but that it was impracticable. The French were too ignorant, corrupt and poor to support a republic. Republics might be the best of governments, but the cost of establishing and maintaining them was too high.

Although no one openly endorsed republicanism before 1790, the republican sensibility had been pervasive in France for many years prior to the Revolution, and republican conceptions of liberty were widely praised by important members of the governing classes. Desmoulins, writing in 1793, attributed French republicanism to the reading of Cicero in schools, which had inculcated a 'passion for liberty' among the educated French. Desmoulins himself, like most of his compatriots prior to Varennes, had been reconciled to the principate of Louis XVI, whom he compared to the 'good prince' Trajan. But he already thought of France as a republic in 1790, and wished to subject the king to republican guidance.[153] The sources of French republican attitudes are also evident in Germaine de Staël's notes for her discussion of the circumstances and principles of French republicanism. Madame de Staël prepared for her treatise on French institutions by reading about Greece, England, America, and pre-eminently Rome, whose republican foundation always

---

150 J-J Rousseau, 1977, III.5, pp 238–9.
151 J-J Rousseau, 1977, III.8, p 249.
152 J-J Rousseau, 1977, III.12, p 262.
153 A Aulard, *Histoire Politique de la Revolution Française*, 4th ed, Librairie A Colin, Paris, 1909, pp 5, 85.

remained *le vote général du peuple*, under the direction of an elected Roman senate.[154] As early as 1730, Voltaire had written a popular play, *Brutus*, which glorified the founder and principles of the Roman republic, and classical virtues and ideas were widely admired and imitated by many who never imagined or sought for a revolution in France.[155]

The word 'republican' was often used loosely in this period to refer to supporters of liberty in general.[156] D'Argenson wrote before 1735 that the monarchy would benefit from an infusion of republican institutions. This remained the program of most reformers during the early years of the French Revolution — to develop free institutions without necessarily displacing the monarch. The first reforms of the Constituent Assembly following the fall of the Bastille consisted in restricting feudal privileges and establishing a common law for all French citizens, without trespassing on the executive power of the king, who was recognised as the 'Restorer of French Liberty'. The *Declaration of the Rights of Man and Citizen*, promulgated on 27 August 1789, asserted that 'men are born and remain free and equal in rights' but also that 'social distinctions' may be established, based upon 'general usefulness'. The *Declaration* defined liberty as the power to do 'whatever is not injurious to others' within limits set by law through the expression of the general will (applied equally to all). Government must pursue the advantage of all and not the interests of particular persons or groups. The Assembly's *Decree on the Fundamental Principles of Government* confirmed that 'all powers emanate essentially from the nation', but added that 'the French government is monarchical' and 'the crown is hereditary in the reigning family, from male to male, by order of primogeniture'.

The new French politics adopted republican principles in its respect for popular sovereignty, an independent judiciary, and the rule of law.[157] But France differed significantly from the classical republics in its hereditary monarchy and unicameral assembly. French unicameralism may be traced to the peculiarities of French politics and the history of the Third Estate. But it also gained considerable support from the Pennsylvania Constitution and the example of the Greek republics. The French tendency to look to the Greek city-states for political inspiration was evident already in Montesquieu's praise for Lacedaemonian institutions (which he compared to Pennsylvania's) and Rousseau's admiration for the 'perfect' egalitarian liberty of Sparta, even though it depended on the absolute subjection of Sparta's Helot serfs. Citizen equality did not extend to all of the French

---

154 A L G de Staël-Holstein, *Des circonstances actuelles qui peuvent terminer la révolution et des principies qui doivent fonder la république en France* (ed L Omacini), Librairie Droz, Geneva, 1979 (first published 1798), pp 383–5.

155 H T Parker, 1937, note 135 above, pp 62–72.

156 A Aulard, 1909, note 153 above, p 6, note 1.

157 For the 'Decree on the Fundamental Principles of Government' (5 October 1789), see J H Stewart, *A Documentary Survey of the French Revolution*, Macmillan, New York, 1951, p 115.

either, only 'active' (moderately wealthy) citizens would be allowed to vote in elections for the new National Assembly.[158]

The first French form of representative government, united with hereditary monarchy, reflected the Constitution of England more closely than that of any other nation, despite the absence of a House of Peers. This was the period in which Montesquieu and the English Revolution of 1688 were most closely studied. The French Constitution completed by the Constituent Assembly in September 1791, and approved by the king, provided for liberty, equality of rights and the rule of law.[159] Liberty was defined to exclude injury to the rights of others, or to public security, as determined by laws 'common to the entire kingdom'.[160] Such laws would be made by a unicameral National Assembly, selected indirectly by electors chosen by the 'active' (propertied) members of local assemblies. The king would rule by law only,[161] but could postpone the enactment of laws for four years by refusing his consent to proposed legislation. He retained the sole executive power, including primary control over foreign affairs, and formally declared himself dedicated to the liberty of the nation.[162]

Despite the moderation of the Constitution of 1791, France soon found itself at war with its neighbours and supporters of the old regime. This undermined the king's position and created a popular movement against the monarchy that resulted in the election of a new National Convention, without reference to the property restrictions in the Constitution of 1791. The Convention tried the king for his collaboration with foreign powers, condemned him to death, and on 20 January 1793, executed 'Louis Capet' amidst cries for liberty and a republic. The Convention also established special revolutionary tribunals and a Committee of Public Safety to facilitate the public defences and maintain the executive functions of government during wartime. Finally the Convention purged itself of its moderate members, and completed a new constitution, which reflected the policies of its dominant (Jacobin) party.

In the early years of the French Revolution, as in America after 1776, the 'republicans' often found themselves at odds with 'democrats', or citizens who professed a doctrine of more complete equality. Robespierre and even Desmoulins criticised 'determined republicans' like Brissot and Boisguyon for seeking to establish an 'aristocratical republic' on the American model under their own 'Washington' or 'Cromwell' — Lafayette.[163] Robespierre would rather have seen a representative popular assembly 'with citizens free and respected' under a king, than an 'enslaved, degraded people under the yoke of an aristocratic senate and a

---

158 'Decree Establishing Electoral and Administrative Assemblies' (22 December 1789), J H Stewart, p 129.
159 See J H Stewart, Preamble to the Constitution of 1791, 1951, p 231.
160 See J H Stewart, Title I of the Constitution of 1791, 1951, p 232.
161 See J H Stewart, 1951, Title III.2.1.3, p 240.
162 J H Stewart, Royal Proclamation, 28 September 1791, p 263.
163 A Aulard, 1909, note 153 above, pp 179–84; C Desmoulins in the first edition of *La Tribune des patriotes*, 30 April 1792.

dictator'.[164] The republican debate at this point was still primarily over the presence or absence of a king, which seemed secondary to Robespierre and his Jacobin allies (who used as their historical reference Sparta, which had retained its kings throughout its history). Later, when the King was gone, Robespierre embraced republicanism and used the word 'republic' to describe his revolutionary government. He prescribed death for anyone who sought to alter the republican form of government, introduce corruption into the republic, subvert the public spirit, or 'assassinate' liberty. To resist the *gouvernement révolutionnaire et républicain* was to attack the *liberté publique*, and deserved the ultimate punishment.[165]

Robespierre and his colleagues had identified 'public liberty' with the reign of the National Convention, which would usher in a 'democratic republic' and an era of public virtue. But his opponents saw him acting as a Catiline or a Cromwell. As the French armies became more successful, and the republic more secure, Robespierre lost his influence, and soon afterwards his life. He died at the guillotine amid cries of 'Down with the Tyrant' and '*Vive la République*'.[166] This still left the problem of constructing a French republic, purged of Jacobin democracy. The Convention prepared a new frame of government, which finally rejected the unicameralism of France's previous republican constitutions, and many of their most egregiously egalitarian features.

The French Constitution of 1795 began like its predecessors with a Declaration of Rights, defining liberty as freedom to do anything 'not injurious to the rights of others'. Equality meant equality before the law, and law itself the general will, expressed by the majority of the citizens or their representatives (not the Jacobin minority). But the new Declaration of Rights now included a list of 'Duties' to protect the laws and serve the *Patrie*.[167] Property qualifications for the vote were restored, along with the old indirect election of the magistrates. The primary innovation of the new frame of government was a bicameral legislature, divided into the Council of Elders and the Council of Five Hundred. The Council of Five Hundred was to propose the laws, and the Council of Elders to approve or reject them, according to its own judgment. The Council of Elders would also elect an Executive Directory of five members from a list of 50 prepared by the lower chamber. No member of the Directory could share in the legislative power.

Advocates of the new Constitution compared it to American institutions, which all now maintained bicameral legislatures and property qualifications for elected officials. It was noted that the *sages Américains* had never called any state in their union a 'democratic republic'.[168] On the contrary, not a single American constitution supported the idea of universal suffrage. Boissy d'Anglas explained that

---

164 M Robespierre "Exposition de mes principes" in the first number of *Defenseur de la constitution* (19 May 1792), quoted in A Aulard, 1909, p 182.

165 A Aulard, 1909, Loi de 23 ventôse an II, p 365.

166 A Aulard, 1909, p 509.

167 A Aulard, 1909, p 574.

168 A Aulard, 1909, p 550.

while the larger assembly would be the 'imagination' of the French republic, the Council of Elders would be its 'reason'. Nearly all the American states, according to d'Anglas, 'our seniors in the career of liberty', had achieved public tranquility by maintaining senates. Only Pennsylvania had for a time a single chamber which (despite their 'purity of manners', 'simplicity', and 'private virtues') caused dissension among Pennsylvania's citizens, so that eventually they were forced to adopt a bicameral system.[169] The same was true of Rome and England.

The new French regime under the Directory was ostentatiously devoted to the liberty suspended by Robespierre's revolutionary dictatorship. All its early proclamations begin with the resolution 'to maintain liberty or to perish'. Its program was 'republican and conservative', and firmly opposed to Robespierre's Terror, which had 'plunged a dagger in the heart of the young Republic'.[170] So opponents of the Directory self-consciously assumed the mantle of the Roman *populares*. Led by the *soi-disant* 'Gracchus' Babeuf, they advocated equality and an agrarian law on the model of Sparta and the Roman Gracchi.[171] The Babouvist journal, *Tribun du peuple*, claimed the authority of the Roman tribunes, and advocated equality over concord, and 'chaos' over hierarchy.[172] But public opinion was moving away from Gracchan equality towards a more 'optimate' republicanism. When the Directory finally fell, the victorious French armies installed their own general, Napoléon Bonaparte as commander of Paris and first consul of the French republic, to preserve the liberty of France.

The subsequent history of republicanism in France is the history of the principles of the French Revolution, as adapted by subsequent generations. However a review of the revolutionary constitutions has shown that these principles were contested and confused. Lafayette saw himself as Cincinnatus, Robespierre imitated Lycurgus, Babeuf followed Gracchus, and Bonaparte wanted to become another Caesar or Augustus. The history of the French Revolution is that of the Roman republic in miniature, moving from Lucius Brutus to Augustus in a decade. The most striking feature of the era was the Terror, and its greatest innovation was egalitarian democracy, as advocated by Robespierre and Babeuf. Subsequent autocrats blackened French republicanism with the excesses of Jacobin equality, and to some extent the terminology stuck, so that later French republicans looked as much to Athens and Sparta for inspiration as to Rome.

The strongest French advocates of Roman institutions, and optimate republicanism in its original sense, were the leaders of 1789, such as Lafayette and his successors under the Directory, who supported the Constitution of 1795. But Bonaparte's 'republican' Constitution of 1799 tended to discredit Roman institutions, and his rapid rise to tyranny seemed to vindicate the criticism that republicanism could never survive in a country as large as France. The effect of the French Revolution was to

169 Boissy d'Anglas is quoted at length by A Aulard with citations to other contemporary authors: see A Aulard, 1909, p 559.
170 A Aulard, 1909, p 626.
171 A Aulard, 1909, pp 628–9. Compare J H Stewart, note 157 above, pp 656–7.
172 A Aulard, 1909, p 630.

separate 'liberty' from 'republicanism' in the French imagination. Disciples of the *véritable républicain* Lafayette such as Madame de Staël, resigned themselves to constitutional monarchy on the English model, and adopted ideas of free government which included *des monarchies limitées* in large states, where *républiques indépendantes* were impractical.[173] Benjamin Constant carefully distinguished the liberty of the ancients, a 'kind of liberty for which we are no longer fitted' from the liberty of the moderns, better suited to France's fallen state, which consisted in the security to pursue one's private pleasures.[174]

Constant's distinction between 'the liberty of the ancients' and 'the liberty of the moderns' represents the final separation of liberalism from republicanism in France, just as liberty and the republic had divided in England after the Glorious Revolution of 1688. After the excesses of Robespierre and Bonaparte, men such as Constant hesitated to call themselves 'republicans' at all. Constant conceded that 'the kind of liberty offered to men at the end of the last century' was borrowed from the ancient republics.[175] But he worried that Rousseau, Mably and many others had mistaken authority for liberty, and embraced Sparta's 'monastic barracks' as their ideal of a free republic.[176] They treated despotism as the foundation of freedom, and gave France 'prisons, scaffolds' and countless persecutions, all in the name of liberty.[177] This for Constant was the error of the ancients, such as the Spartan Therpandrus who could not add a string to his lyre without causing offense to the ephors.[178] Constant preferred the 'modern liberty' of England and the United States, which meant being subject only to the laws, and able to 'come and go without permission'.[179] Constant could not read the 'beautiful pages of antiquity' without 'feeling an indefinable and special emotion' which 'nothing modern can possibly arouse'. However 2000 years had seriously altered the dispositions of mankind. By transposing ancient institutions to the modern age, Rousseau furnished 'deadly pretexts' for a multitude of tyrannies.[180]

Constant blamed Rousseau, Mably and even the 'less excitable' Montesquieu for the excesses of the French Revolution, due to their admiration and emulation of Sparta, which combined the republican forms of popular sovereignty with enslavement of individuals through the tyranny of the collective.[181] Constant believed that even Rome in its golden centuries

---

173 A L G de Staël-Holstein, *Considérations sur la Révolution Française* (ed J Godechot), Tallandier, Paris, 1983, p 600.

174 B Constant, 'The Liberty of the Ancients compared with that of the Moderns' (1819), in *Political Writings* (ed B Fontana), Cambridge University Press, Cambridge, 1988, p 317.

175 B Constant, 1988, p 102.

176 B Constant, 1988, p 108.

177 B Constant, 1988, p 113.

178 B Constant, 1988, p 311.

179 B Constant, 1988, pp 310–11.

180 B Constant, 1988, p 318.

181 B Constant, 1988, p 319.

lost the individual in the nation, and the citizen in the city.[182] This was possible because all ancient republics were restricted to a narrow territory. France was not, which is why the 'restored edifice of the ancients' collapsed, despite many efforts, and 'many heroic acts' which 'call for our admiration'.[183] By the early nineteenth century the word 'republic' was so closely associated with material equality, Robespierre's Terror, and the Constitution of 1793 that orthodox supporters of liberty preferred not to use it. Constant believed representative government to have been unknown to the free nations of antiquity. Its presence in France made direct citizen sovereignty impossible (and undesirable). The French were not ready for Robespierre's empire of Virtue.[184] Instead Constant embraced the principles of France's 'most illustrious' defender of liberty — Lafayette.[185]

After Napoleon, self-styled French republicans had their own tradition, separated from republican history and older conceptions of republican liberty. When they called themselves republicans, French politicians usually meant that they embraced the French Revolution (or some aspect of it) and not necessarily the classical republicanism of Cicero or Livy. Often they meant the 'democratic' republicanism of 1793, or Robespierrist or Babouvist ideas, which rejected bicameralism, the separation of powers, and even the rule of law, in as much as these protected property or social stability.[186] No new political stance on which all republicans could agree emerged from the French Revolution, except perhaps the Declaration of Rights of 1789. Instead, French republicans continued to read the *Social Contract* and the *Spirit of the Laws*, and to debate the same political issues that Montesquieu and Rousseau had raised and made famous under the monarchy, issues the Revolution had done nothing to resolve. The most influential and coherent French contributions to republican thought preceded the Revolution, and concerned the general principles of political science, rather than the specifics of civic organisation, or the constitution of liberty.[187]

Republican liberty

The history of republican liberty and the arguments of its leading advocates show the gradual development of a comprehensive, compelling and immensely influential doctrine. The concepts of republic and liberty arose from the republican institutions of early Rome, and only gradually diverged in the course of more than two millennia. For some, the connection was severed by Constant's sharp distinction between the 'liberty of the ancients' and 'liberty of the moderns', in the wake of France's catastrophic revolution. However Constant had narrowed the scope of ancient liberty without altering its substance. The purpose of liberty remained independence

---

182 B Constant, 1988, p 312.
183 B Constant, 1988, p 320.
184 B Constant, 1988, p 320.
185 B Constant, 1988, p 327.
186 C Nicolet, 1982, note 135 above, pp 111, 172.
187 For a fascinating recent contribution to French republican thought, see C Nicolet, *La République en France, Etat des lieux*, Editions du Seuil, Paris, 1992.

from another's will, and security from private depredations. Constant and his followers simply abandoned liberty's traditional connection with citizen participation in the balanced republican government that had been the political defence of ancient liberty in Rome.

These five great centres of republican thought — Rome, Italy, England, America, and France — all took their inspiration and conception of liberty from the same brief period in Roman life between 509 and 133 BC. However the history of republican liberty before the French Revolution was less a natural progression than a series of variations on the same Roman material and themes. Rome's republic recognised popular sovereignty, the election of magistrates, and equality before the law. It ended in a civil war over the spoils of empire, and relative power of the people and senate to distribute booty. This left modern republics with the question of how to re-establish Roman liberty without suffering Rome's fate or that of other modern republics. Italy revived the Roman idea of liberty, without resolving its proper boundaries or acceptable controls on popular sovereignty. England settled for the rule of law and a balanced government under an hereditary monarch. America sought to strengthen the senate against the excesses of popular enthusiasm, and France hoped that republican virtue would preserve public liberty. All shared a commitment to popular sovereignty in pursuit of the common good, with governmental protection against the arbitrary exercise of any individual or collective will.

This dual dedication to political participation and personal security remained the essence of republican liberty, derived from Roman ideas of what it is to be a free citizen and not a slave. Opponents of republican liberty denied the connection of these two elements. But republican writers since Cicero have sought to explain why neither is possible without the other. Leading theorists of republican liberty all agreed that liberty requires popular sovereignty, the rule of law, and government in the public interest. Cicero had defined *libertas* as life without a master. For magistrates to act on any other basis than service to the *res publica* would be tyranny, treating citizens like slaves. The rule of law holds magistrates to their duties, and prevents arbitrary government. But none of this need require popular sovereignty unless one accepts that popular elections will yield just laws and magistrates. Cicero believed that they would, if the republic maintained a balanced constitution and the senate's proper authority. Machiavelli proposed rotation in office to secure virtuous citizens and magistrates. Harrington suggested an equal agrarian law. But Sidney and Adams simply reiterated Cicero's old republican assumption that the people deserve to vote because they are best judges of public virtue. Madison added that they should not vote directly, as in Rome. Harrington, Sidney, Adams and Madison all agreed that the people should vote indirectly through their representatives, as in the American colonial assemblies. The people are the best judges of other citizens, but not of legislation. Republicans insisted that they defer to their chosen magistrates or senate in deciding about public affairs.

Republican liberty linked *libertas* with the *res publica* by identifying popular suffrage as the best technique for finding the common good. Subsequent authors would separate political equality from the liberty of being subject to no one's will. But republicans saw the two as united.

Laws are needed to protect us from each other. Unless laws serve the common good they are arbitrary and we are not free. So proponents of liberty must offer a constitution and legal theory to support it. Republicans suggest that the best test of a law's justice is its wide acceptance by the people, after due deliberation under a mixed constitution. Montesquieu put greater faith in the moderating influence of a monarch and hereditary aristocracy. Rousseau preferred to rely on popular virtue (in small, temperate cantons). Constant simply asked his rulers for personal security. Republicans, however, sought to protect everyone from the unfettered will of others, and proposed a constitution to do so, by balancing the powers of private avarice and ambition.

Republican liberty was a theory of law, which understood the purpose of law as the preservation of liberty, in pursuit of the common good. For republicans since Cicero there could be no liberty without law, and no valid law or legal system, when liberty was disregarded. Liberty in this sense is both negative and positive, to use more recent terminology. It is negative because the essence of liberty is independence from the will of another. It is positive because law must guarantee this independence. Republican liberty required certain protections (liberties), including the right to vote, because voting best determines the scope of the common good. Republican writers argued that simply doing what one wants without legal restraint is not liberty, but licence, because this inevitably invades the liberty of others. Legal restraints are not legitimate unless they serve the common good, determined by public deliberation, and ratified by popular elections. Popular sovereignty, the rule of law, and pursuit of the common good together constitute the 'sacred flame' George Washington embraced in his inaugural address, which was guaranteed to Americans by the United States Constitution. The mixed and balanced structures of the Constitution, particularly the senate, reflect republican ideals of government as old as Cicero and Rome. Republicans could not imagine liberty without its ancient safeguards.

CHAPTER 3

Hayek's Theory of Rules and the Modern State

Viktor Vanberg*

Introduction

Hayek has a highly sceptical view of the modern state, if by 'modern state' we mean the kinds of government that are usually subsumed under the rubric 'western democracies'. The 'particular set of institutions which today prevails in all Western democracies', he tells us in his study on *Law, Legislation and Liberty*, 'produces an aggregate of measures that not only is not wanted by anybody, but that could not as a whole be approved by any rational mind because it is inherently contradictory'.[1] There are, Hayek claims, 'certain deeply entrenched defects of construction of the generally accepted type of 'democratic' government'[2] that 'lead us away from the ideals it was intended to serve,' that let us drift 'towards a system which nobody wanted'.[3] And it is his diagnosis of these defects that made him, as he notes, 'think through alternative arrangements' and led him to come up with 'a proposal of basic alteration of the structure of democratic government'[4] and 'a suggestion for a radical departure from established tradition'.[5]

Hayek's critique of western democratic institutions and his proposals for reform — as detailed, in particular, in the chapter on 'A Model Constitution' in volume 3 of *Law, Legislation and Liberty*[6] — are well

---

*   Professor of Economic Policy, Freiburg University.
1   F A Hayek, *Law Legislation and Liberty*, vol 3, Routledge & Kegan Paul, London, 1979, pp 1, 6.
2   F A Hayek, 1979, p xiii.
3   F A Hayek, *Law Legislation and Liberty*, vol 1, Routledge & Kegan Paul, London, 1973, p 3.
4   F A Hayek, 1979, note 1 above, p xiii.
5   F A Hayek, 1973, note 3 above, p 4.
6   F A Hayek, 1979, note 1 above, pp 105–27.

known. What is, however, less well understood is how they fit into his overall approach. In fact, a number of commentators have pointed to the discrepancy that they see between, on the one side, the rationalistic flavour of his argument on the reform of democratic institutions and, on the other side, his critique of what he calls *constructivist rationalism* (or *rationalist constructivism*), a critique that plays a fundamental role in his system of thought. While the thrust of this critique is to warn us against jeopardising the implicit wisdom of traditional institutions through rationalistic reconstruction, it seems as if Hayek ignores his own warnings when, with regard to the institutions of western democracies, he calls 'for a radical departure from established tradition',[7] for 'institutional invention'[8] and 'constitutional design'.[9]

My purpose in this chapter is to show how the two components of his work, despite their seeming inconsistency, can be understood as constituting a coherent argument. More specifically, I want to argue that Hayek's critique of the institutions of western democracies, and his suggestions for their reform, are consistent with and systematically connected to core assumptions of his work, in particular, the *theory of rules* that informs his critique of constructivist rationalism.

Constructivist rationalism and the role of rules

Closer inspection shows that Hayek's critique of constructivist rationalism is directed against two distinguishable notions which I propose to call *constructivist rationalism I* and *constructivist rationalism II*.

The critique of *constructivist rationalism I* is central to Hayek's rejection of the notion of central planning, ie his rejection of the 'claim that man can achieve a desirable order of society by concretely arranging all its parts in full knowledge of all the relevant facts'.[10] Such a claim, Hayek argues, 'ignores the limitations that are set to the powers of reason'[11] and involves 'a colossal presumption concerning our intellectual powers'.[12] Not only is it, according to Hayek, impossible for a single person to coordinate 'his activities successfully through a full explicit evaluation of the consequences of all possible alternatives of action, and in full knowledge of all possible circumstances', it is *a fortiori* impossible to coordinate innumerable individual actions in such manner.[13] It is impossible for anyone to take 'conscious account of all the particular facts which enter into the order of society',[14] or 'on which the overall order of

---

7   F A Hayek, 1973, note 3 above, p 4.
8   F A Hayek, 1979, p 3.
9   F A Hayek, 1979, p 4.
10   F A Hayek, *Studies in Philosophy, Politics and Economics*, University of Chicago Press, Chicago, 1967, p 88.
11   F A Hayek, 1967, p 88.
12   F A Hayek, 1967, p 90.
13   F A Hayek, 1967, p 90.
14   F A Hayek, 1973, note 3 above, p 13.

the activities in a Great Society is based'.[15] The limits of our knowledge and reason make it necessary for us, Hayek asserts, to *rely on rules*, both in our personal affairs and even more so in the social realm. The rationalist-constructivist claim 'that conscious reason ought to determine every particular action'[16] ignores the need for rules. It fails to see that the 'whole rationale of the phenomenon of rule-guided action', the fact that 'makes rules necessary', lies in our 'inescapable ignorance of most of the particular circumstances which determine the effects of our actions'.[17] Whereas the constructivist approach denies that it can be rational to observe such rules, Hayek contends that 'most of the rules of conduct which govern our actions, and most of the institutions which arise out of this regularity, are adaptations to the impossibility of anyone taking conscious account of all the particular facts which enter into the order of society'.[18]

Hayek's critique of what I classify here as *constructivist rationalism I* is, in summary, directed against the claim that we can create a desirable social order by discretionary planning and particular commands, by centrally directing the 'activities of all ... according to a single plan laid down by a central authority'.[19] The alternative view that he advocates emphasises the notion 'of a self-generating or spontaneous order in social affairs', a notion that was espoused by Adam Smith and other authors in the classical liberal tradition.[20] It is the notion of an order that is not the product of deliberate design but instead emerges as an unintended outcome from the mutual adjustments of individuals who are left free to pursue their own purposes, based on their own knowledge, within the constraints of a framework of general rules of conduct, rules that typically specify what they *may not do*, instead of telling them what they have to do. Hayek's familiar argument in favour of such spontaneously formed order is that it makes possible the utilisation of far more knowledge than a deliberately arranged and centrally planned order could ever do.[21] To be

---

15 F A Hayek, *Law Legislation and Liberty*, vol 2, Routledge & Kegan Paul, London, 1976, p 8.
16 F A Hayek, 1973, note 3 above, p 29.
17 F A Hayek, 1976, note 15 above, p 20.
18 F A Hayek, 1973, note 3 above, p 13.
19 F A Hayek, 1967, note 10 above, p 82.
20 As Hayek notes: 'Adam Smith's decisive contribution was the account of a self-generating order which formed itself spontaneously if the individuals were restrained by appropriate rules of law. His *Inquiry into the Nature and Causes of the Wealth of Nations* marks perhaps more than any other single work the beginning of the development of modern liberalism': F A Hayek, *New Studies in Philosophy, Politics, Economics and the History of Ideas*, The University of Chicago Press, Chicago, 1978, pp 124 ff.
21 'The great advantage of such a self-generating order was thought to be, not only that it left the individuals free to pursue their own purposes ... It was also that it made possible the ... utilisation of more knowledge of particular facts than would be possible under any system of central direction of economic activity': F A Hayek, 1978, p 136. Also: 'The chief reason why we cannot hope by central direction to achieve anything like the efficiency in the use of resources which the market makes possible is that the economic order of any large society rests on a utilisation of the knowledge of

sure, Hayek acknowledges that deliberate organisation and central direction can be an efficient principle of coordination for limited purposes, such as the coordination within firms, or in organisations more generally. What he disputes is that it can be successfully extended to an entire economy or society. In Hayek's view this is simply not feasible and, if tried, can only result in an *undesirable* order.[22]

Because it is based on general rules, the nature of a spontaneous order depends on the nature of these rules. There is, as Hayek puts it, a systematic connection between the *order of rules* and the *order of actions* that results from these rules, a connection that is illustrated, for instance, by the manner in which the resulting pattern of actions in a game of sport is dependent on the rules of the game. The freedom of individual choice within a framework of general rules allows, as noted before, for the utilisation of more knowledge in a rule-based spontaneous order, and it accounts for the potential superiority of spontaneous over centrally planned orders. Yet, this does not *per se* assure that the resulting order of actions is 'desirable' from the perspective of the persons involved. Whether this is the case or not will depend on the *nature of the rules*.[23] For a desirable or beneficial order to result, rules are required that are suitable or appropriate to that task, a fact which, as Hayek notes, the classical liberal advocates of the spontaneous market order were well aware of, but

---

particular circumstances widely dispersed among thousands or millions of individuals': F A Hayek, 1978, p 236. And: 'The central concept of liberalism is that under the enforcement of universal rules of just conduct, protecting a recognizable private domain of individuals, a spontaneous order of human activities of much greater complexity will form itself than could ever be produced by deliberate arrangement': F A Hayek, 1967, note 10 above, p 162.

22　'We shall see that it is impossible, not only to replace the spontaneous order by organisation and at the same time to utilize as much of the dispersed knowledge of all its members as possible, but also to improve or correct this order by interfering in it by direct commands': F A Hayek, 1973, note 3 above, p 51.

23　'But, if our main conclusion is that an individualist order must rest on the enforcement of abstract principles rather than on the enforcement of specific orders, this still leaves open the question of the kind of general rules which we want ... it still allows almost unlimited scope to human ingenuity in the designing of the most effective set of rules ... there is a good deal ... we can learn ... with regard to the desirable nature and contents of these rules': F A Hayek, *Individualism and Economic Order*, University of Chicago Press, Chicago, 1948, pp 19 ff. Also: 'The relation between the character of the legal order and the functioning of the market system has received comparatively little study ... How well the market will function depends on the character of the particular rules. The decision to rely on voluntary contracts as the main instrument for organizing the relations between individuals does not determine what the specific content of the law of contract ought to be; and the recognition of the right of private property does not determine what exactly should be the content of this right in order that the market mechanism will work as effectively and beneficially as possible': F A Hayek, *The Constitution of Liberty*, University of Chicago Press, Chicago, 1960, p 229.

which some of their later successors in the liberal tradition did not always sufficiently appreciate.[24]

This raises, of course, the issue of how we can expect suitable and appropriate rules to come about, and how we can hope to achieve improvements in these rules.[25] It is with regard to this issue that Hayek's critique of constructivist rationalism becomes relevant to what I propose to call *constructivist rationalism II*. Hayek's critique of constructivist rationalism in the realm of rules is not an outright rejection of the idea of rational institutional design; it is a rejection of the presumptuous rationalist claim 'that it is both possible and desirable to reconstruct all grown institutions in accordance with a preconceived plan'.[26] It is a critique of a mind-set that ignores the extent to which, in our efforts to improve our rules and institutions, we need to rely on past experience that has been transmitted to us in our cultural traditions.[27]

It should be noted that Hayek does not explicitly distinguish between the two versions of *constructivist rationalism*. Though the two are clearly concerned with different issues, he occasionally fails to differentiate between them, for instance when he refers to 'a particular conception of the formation of social institutions, which I shall call "constructivist rationalism" — a conception which assumes that all social institutions are, and ought to be, the product of deliberate design'. He then observes that 'this intellectual tradition can be shown to be false both in its factual and in its normative conclusions, because the existing institutions are not all products of design, neither would it be possible to make the social order wholly dependent on design without at the same time greatly restricting the utilisation of available knowledge'.[28] With this latter remark, Hayek apparently refers to the issue of central planning, ie the issue that I call *constructivist rationalism I*. Yet, as Hayek has explicitly acknowledged elsewhere, the question whether an order is spontaneously formed or is the product of deliberate design, and the question whether

---

24 'That a functioning market presupposes not only prevention of violence and fraud but the protection of certain rights, such as property, and the enforcement of contract, is always taken for granted. Where the traditional discussion becomes so unsatisfactory is where it is suggested that, with the recognition of the principles of private property and freedom of contract, which indeed every liberal must recognize, all the issues were settled, as if the law of property and contract were given once and for all in its final and most appropriate form, ie, in the form which will make the market economy work at its best. It is only after we have agreed on these principles that the real problem begins': F A Hayek, 1948, pp 110 ff. See also F A Hayek, *Freedom and the Economic System*, University of Chicago Press, Chicago, 1939, p 11.

25 'The question which is of central importance both for social theory and social policy is what rules the individuals must follow so that an order will result ... [and] that this order will be of a beneficent character': F A Hayek, 'Kinds of Order in Society', (1964) 3 *New Individualist Review* 8.

26 F A Hayek, 1967, note 10 above, p 161.

27 F A Hayek, 1967, p 88.

28 F A Hayek, 1967, p 88.

the rules on which an order is based have evolved or have been deliberately chosen, are two different issues.[29]

Not only does Hayek fail to deny the role of deliberate institutional reform, he explicitly argues that such efforts are our principal means of improving our social condition. His critique dealing with the issues raised by *constructivist rationalism I* implies that it is impossible for us to create a desirable social order by deliberate arrangement, and that it is, for the same reasons, also impossible to improve the order of society by specific interventions. As we need, in his account, to rely on rules as coordinating devices in order to achieve a desirable social order, we need to rely on *improvements in these rules* in order to improve the order of actions. The principal means for improving our social condition is, therefore, to improve the 'rules of the game'. Hayek states:

> [A]lthough we can endeavour to improve a spontaneous order by revising the general rules on which it rests, and can supplement its results by the efforts of various organizations, we cannot improve the results by specific commands that deprive its members of the possibility of using their knowledge for their purposes.[30]

In fact, he notes that his rejection of central planning is not about 'whether we ought to choose intelligently between the various possible organizations of society'[31] and he explicitly contrasts that kind of 'central planning' with what he calls the 'liberal plan', the deliberate reform of the framework of rules and institutions.[32] Hayek insists, though, that such efforts in institutional reform can only aim at 'piecemeal change'[33] as opposed to total reconstruction. As Hayek puts it, 'although we must always strive to improve our institutions, we can never aim to remake them as a whole'.[34] Furthermore, our efforts towards deliberate reform ought to be carried out with an awareness of the fallibility of our design, and with a recognition that the process of institutional change can only be an experimental process of trial and error. '[A]ll we can hope for will be a

---

29 'Although undoubtedly an order originally formed itself spontaneously because the individuals followed rules which had not been deliberately made but had arisen spontaneously, people gradually learned to improve those rules; and it is at least conceivable that the formation of a spontaneous order relies entirely on rules that were deliberately made. The spontaneous character of the resulting order must therefore be distinguished from the spontaneous origin of the rules on which it rests, and it is possible that an order which would still have to be described as spontaneous rests on rules which are entirely the result of deliberate design': F A Hayek, 1973, note 3 above, pp 45 ff.

30 F A Hayek, 1973, note 3 above, p 51.

31 F A Hayek, 1978, note 15 above, p 234.

32 'According to the modern planners ... it is not sufficient to design the most rational permanent framework within which the various activities would be conducted by different persons according to their individual plans. This liberal plan, according to them, is no plan ... What our planners demand is a central direction of all economic activity according to a single plan': F A Hayek, 1978, note 20 above, p 234.

33 F A Hayek, 1960, note 23 above, p 114.

34 F A Hayek, 1960, p 63.

slow experimental process of gradual improvement rather than any opportunity for drastic change'.[35] Hayek adds, however, that '[a]lthough probably all beneficial improvement must be piecemeal', the separate steps need nonetheless be 'guided by a body of coherent principles'.[36]

It is in the context of his criticism of what I have called *constructivist rationalism II* that Hayek introduces the notion of 'cultural evolution' by which he primarily means the decentralised process in which, *within* a society or polity, different individuals or groups of persons experiment with alternative practices. From these competing practices the ones that are perceived as more advantageous become widely adopted, while others are abandoned as less successful. Interpreted in this sense, cultural evolution is, in contrast to *legislation*, a mechanism for *deliberate* rule-change through the political process of collective choice.[37] Note however that as indicated above, Hayek's criticism of *constructivist rationalism II* is *not* an argument against legislation *per se*, even if its general thrust favours the decentralised evolutionary process in which customs and traditions develop, or which is exemplified by the common law process. Yet, Hayek explicitly acknowledges that such spontaneous evolution may not work for all kinds of rules on which the order of society is based and notes that 'the important question of which of these rules of individual action can be deliberately and profitably altered, and which are likely to evolve gradually with or without such deliberate collective decisions as legislation involves, is rarely systematically considered'.[38] He does not believe that the spontaneous order can be expected to work beneficially under all circumstances and notes in relation to the common law:

> For a variety of reasons the spontaneous process of growth may lead into an impasse from which it cannot extricate itself by its own forces or which it will at least not correct quickly enough ... The fact that law that has evolved this way has certain desirable properties does not prove that it will always be good law or even that some of its rules may not be very bad. It therefore does not mean that we can altogether dispense with legislation.[39]

---

35   F A Hayek, 1967, note 10 above, p 92.
36   F A Hayek, 1973, note 3 above, p 56.
37   I said that this is how Hayek 'primarily' understands the notion of cultural evolution, because he uses this notion also in a second, more inclusive sense. In the first and more narrow sense, cultural evolution can be contrasted with legislation as a deliberate process of rule-change. In this sense, cultural evolution and legislation can meaningfully be distinguished as the principal alternative mechanisms by which rules may be changed within a defined group or jurisdiction, namely: either by a decentralised spontaneous process or by explicit collective legislative choice. Yet Hayek uses the notion of cultural evolution also in a more inclusive sense in which it is not an alternative to, but may comprise legislation. I am referring here, of course, to his argument on group-selection by which he suggests an evolutionary process of competitive selection among groups, a process in which rules come into competition as attributes of groups, whether they were adopted by deliberate legislation, or whether they came to prevail in a spontaneous process.
38   F A Hayek, 1967, note 10 above, p 72.
39   F A Hayek, 1973, note 3 above, p 88.

Hayek emphasises the special role of the *rules of law* 'which, because we can deliberately alter them, become the chief instrument whereby we can affect the resulting order'.[40] There is, as he argues, 'ample scope for experimentation and improvement within that permanent legal framework which makes it possible for a free society to operate most efficiently', and he adds: '[w]e can probably at no point be certain that we have already found the best arrangements or institutions'.[41]

Notwithstanding his emphasis on the spontaneous evolution of rules and institutions, Hayek expressly recognises the role of legislation as one of deliberate institutional reform through political, collective choice. Both cultural evolution and legislation have their place in his understanding of how the institutional-constitutional framework of society changes over time. For the purposes of this chapter I shall set aside the issues raised by Hayek's notion of cultural evolution, and concentrate exclusively on his view of the role of legislation.[42] In the following analysis, I shall examine Hayek's understanding of legislation as part of the political process, and his understanding of the relation between the institutional framework of politics, in particular the institutional framework of western democracies, and the working properties of the legislative process.

The rules of government and the order of politics

As noted earlier, the social order that we call 'society' is, in Hayek's account, necessarily a spontaneous order. It comprises, however, many organisations, one of which is the special organisation called 'state', which Hayek defines as 'the organisation of the people of a territory under a single government'.[43]

Hayek sees the principal task of government as the creating and maintaining of a suitable framework of rules within which individuals, separately and in groups, can successfully pursue their purposes. This task includes, as its most essential part, the enforcement of the 'body of abstract rules which are required to secure the formation of the spontaneous overall order'.[44] He states that 'although it is conceivable that the spontaneous order which we call society may exist without government, if the minimum of rule required for the formation of such order is observed without an

---

40   F A Hayek, 1973, p 45.
41   F A Hayek, 1960, note 23 above, p 231.
42   I have examined Hayek's concept of cultural evolution in some detail elsewhere. See V Vanberg, 'Spontaneous Market Order and Social Rules', (1986) 2 *Economics and Philosophy* 75–100.
43   F A Hayek, 1979, note 1 above, p 140. In this definition the terms 'state' and 'government' have different meanings. The 'state' is defined as the inclusive political organisation, including the citizens as its members, while the 'government' is more narrowly defined as the organised apparatus that acts on behalf of the citizenry. In my discussion here I shall, however, use the two terms without regard to this distinction.
44   F A Hayek, 1964, note 25 above, p 10.

organised apparatus for their enforcement, in most circumstances the organisation which we call government becomes indispensable in order to assure that those rules are obeyed'.[45] Hayek also acknowledges that the task of improving and further developing the framework of rules as circumstances change 'may also, though it need not, be the object of organised effort'.[46] Hayek sees a secondary task of governments to be what he calls their 'service functions', ie the rendering of 'other services which the spontaneous order cannot produce adequately'.[47] How well government performs its functions will depend on its organisational structure. It is in this context that Hayek's critique of prevailing forms of western democracy and his proposals for reform must be evaluated.

Hayek describes the task of enforcing and maintaining the framework of rules as the 'coercive functions' of a government, in order to indicate that it is only for these functions, and not for its service functions, that a government needs its coercive powers and monopoly role.[48] He states:

> The task of government is to create a framework within which individuals and groups can successfully pursue their respective aims, and sometimes to use its coercive powers of raising revenue to provide services which for one reason or other the market cannot supply. But coercion is justified only in order to provide such a framework within which all can use their abilities and knowledge for their own ends so long as they do not interfere with the equally protected individual domains of others.[49]

In distinguishing 'two kinds of social order',[50] Hayek contrasts *spontaneous order* and *organisation* which he sees as 'rule-based' and 'command-based' orders. A *spontaneous* social order results from the mutual adaptation of separate individual choices made within a framework of general rules of conduct. In *organisational* order, by contrast, a central authority gives instructions or commands to participating actors. As Hayek points out, however, an organisation with even a minimal level of complexity cannot entirely operate on specific commands, but has to also use rules as coordinating devices.[51] In this sense, organisations are also 'rule-based'

---

45   F A Hayek, 1973, note 3 above, p 47.

46   F A Hayek, 1964, note 25 above, p 8.

47   F A Hayek, 1978, note 20 above, p 111.

48   F A Hayek, 1973, note 3 above, p 48.

49   F A Hayek, 1979, note 1 above, p 138. Also: 'The central concept of liberalism is that under the enforcement of universal rules of just conduct, protecting a recognizable private domain of individuals, a spontaneous order of human activities of much greater complexity will form itself than could ever be produced by deliberate arrangement, and that in consequence the coercive activities of government should be limited to the enforcement of such rules': F A Hayek, 1967, note 10 above, p 162.

50   F A Hayek, 1964, note 25 above, pp 36 ff.

51   'To some extent every organisation must rely also on rules and not only on specific commands. The reason here is the same as that which makes it necessary for a spontaneous order to rely solely on rules: namely that by guiding the actions of individuals by rules rather than specific commands it is possible to make use of knowledge which nobody possesses as a whole': F A Hayek, 1973, note 3 above, pp 48 ff.

orders, though, as Hayek explains, there are 'important differences between the kinds of rules which the two kinds of order require'.[52] In contrast with the *general rules of conduct* on which *spontaneous* orders are based, *organisational* rules are 'rules for the performance of assigned tasks', and they are 'different for the different members of the organisation according to the different roles which have been assigned to them'.[53] In so far as organisations are themselves based on rules, we can speak of the connection between the *order of rules* and the *order of actions* with regard to an organisation, even though the nature of the rules, and the nature of the connection between rules and the resulting order, are critically different between spontaneous and organisational-based orders. In the case of spontaneous orders, general rules of conduct are the principal coordinating devices. Within the general constraints that they define, individuals are left free to pursue their own purposes. Within organisations, not only are the relevant rules different in nature, but individuals are placed within a hierarchy of authority, and specific commands issued within that hierarchy are the principal instrument of coordination.[54]

What is true for organisations in general is also true for the special organisation that we call *government*, namely that 'beyond its simplest and most primitive forms, [it] also cannot be conducted exclusively by *ad hoc* commands of the ruler' but 'will require distinct rules of its own which determine its structure, aims, and functions'.[55] The rules which 'determine the organisation of government' make up what we can call, in a broad sense, the *constitution* of a state. More specifically, the rules that are commonly subsumed under this label can themselves be divided into two categories, namely into *constituting* and *limiting* rules of government. The *constituting* rules are *organisational* rules in the strict sense,[56] they are 'chiefly concerned with the organisation of government and the allocation of the different powers to the various parts of this organisation'.[57] Or, in other words, they define the procedures that allow the multitude of persons who make up a polity to engage in organised collective action. They *constitute* government in the sense of enabling it to operate as an organised unit: Hayek speaks of constitutions as 'formal documents "constituting" the organisation of the state'.[58] The *limiting* rules, by contrast, are more like 'rules of conduct' in the sense that they define general constraints on what the organisation called 'government' or its

---

52   F A Hayek, 1973, p 48.
53   F A Hayek, 1973, p 49.
54   'Yet these rules governing the apparatus of government will necessarily possess a character different from that of the universal rules of just conduct which form the basis of the spontaneous order of society at large. They will be rules of organisation ... [a]nd they will have to establish a hierarchy of command determining the responsibilities and the range of discretion of the different agents': F A Hayek, 1973, p 124 ff.
55   F A Hayek, 1973, p 123.
56   F A Hayek, 1973, p 134.
57   F A Hayek, 1979, note 1 above, p 37.
58   F A Hayek, 1979, p 37 ff.

agents may do, similar to the way in which the general rules of conduct (on which the spontaneous order of society is based) define limits on what individuals are allowed to do in their private capacities. As Hayek notes, the general rules of just conduct 'restrict the range of permitted actions for any member of the society', while the limiting rules of the constitution impose constraints 'on the members of the organisation we call government'[59] and 'regulate the powers of the agents of government over the material and personal resources entrusted to them'.[60] In fact, what we mean by 'government under the law' is a government that is subject to the specific limits defined for it in the constitution, as well as to the (applicable) general rules of conduct that constrain its citizens.[61]

What has been said earlier about the connection between the order of rules and the order of actions can be applied, with the above qualifications, to the connection between the *constitutional order of rules* and the *order of political actions* that emerges under these rules. As Hayek notes, the distinction between the rules which determine the organisation of government and the rules which 'form the basis of the spontaneous order of society at large' corresponds to the familiar distinction between public law and private law. We can accordingly distinguish between, on the one side, the connection between the general rules of conduct of the private law and the resulting order of society and, on the other side, the connection between the organisational rules of public law and the resulting order of the governmental apparatus.[62] To be sure, what the political process generates will critically depend on what particular policies are chosen within the constraints that the constitutional rules define. Yet the nature of these rules will affect the general nature of the political order that results, similar to the ways in which the general rules of conduct affect the general nature of the spontaneous order of actions that emerges from these rules. As the suitability of the latter rules is, in Hayek's account, to be judged in terms of the quality of the spontaneous order that they help to form, the suitability of the rules of politics are to be judged in terms of the quality of the overall political order, or the pattern of political outcomes, that they generate. The rules of politics determine the general working properties of the political process. Though political outcomes can surely be 'improved' by the selection of 'better' politicians and the choice of 'better' policies, the overall order of politics will critically depend on the order of constitutional rules, and it is through an improvement in these rules that we can hope to achieve a systematic

---

59   F A Hayek, 1973, note 3 above, p 127.

60   F A Hayek, 1973, p 125.

61   F A Hayek, 1979, note 1 above, p 123. For a more detailed discussion of Hayek's concept of constitutional rules in the context of his various distinctions between different kinds of rules, see V Vanberg, 'Cultural Evolution, Collective Learning, and Constitutional Design' in *Economic Thought and Political Theory* (ed D Reisman), Kluwer Academic Publishers, Boston, Dordrecht and London, 1994, pp 171–204.

62   F A Hayek, *Freiburger Studien*, J C B Mohr (Paul Siebeck), Tübingen, 1969, pp 116 ff, 178.

improvement in the order of politics, similar to the sense in which the principal means of improving the spontaneous order of society is an improvement in its framework of rules.[63]

It is in the context of this notion of the interrelation between the order of constitutional rules and the order of politics that Hayek's critique of the prevailing form of western democracy and his proposals for constitutional reform have to be seen. As Hayek emphasises, the deficiencies in this form of government are 'not due to a failure of the principle of democracy as such'[64] but result from the 'particular set of institutions'[65] that have been adopted. In his view, it is because of its particular institutional structure that the democratic process tends to 'produce aggregate results that few people have either wanted or foreseen'. He observes: 'It appears that the particular process which we have chosen to ascertain what we call the will of the people brings about results which have little to do with anything deserving the name of the common will of any substantial part of the population'.[66] And it is only through a correction of the defects in the constitutional framework that he sees a prospect for systematic improvement in the resulting pattern of political outcomes.

The constitutional defects of majoritarian democracy

As noted earlier, Hayek sees the principal task of government as lying in maintaining an 'appropriate' framework of rules, ie a framework that allows for a spontaneous order of society with desirable characteristics, a task that includes the effective enforcement of existing rules as well as their adaptation and improvement over time. Hayek believes that government should be evaluated on its capacity to fulfil this task, and it is in this regard that Hayek finds fault with 'the particular set of institutions which today prevails in all Western democracies, and in which a majority of a representative body lays down the law *and* directs government'.[67]

Hayek's critique of the 'present structure of democratic government' is focused on what he considers its principal defect, namely the 'fact that we

---

63   A similar view is adopted in J M Buchanan's constitutional economics approach: 'How does one "improve" a market? One does so by facilitating the exchange process, by reorganizing the rules of trade, contract, or agreement. One does not "improve" or "reform" a market-like exchange process by arbitrary rearrangement of final outcomes ... To improve politics it is necessary to improve or reform the rules, the framework within which the game of politics is played. There is no suggestion that improvement lies in the selection of morally superior agents, who will use their powers in some "public interest". A game is described by its rules, and a better game is produced only by changing the rules.' J M Buchanan, *Liberty, Market and State: Political Economy in the 1980s*, New York University Press, New York, 1986, p 22.

64   F A Hayek, 1979, note 1 above, p 98.

65   F A Hayek, 1979, p 1.

66   F A Hayek, 1979, p 1.

67   F A Hayek, 1979, p 1.

have charged the representative assemblies with two altogether different tasks': on the one side, 'the articulation and approval of general rules of conduct' and on the other side, 'the direction of the measures of government concerning particular matters'.[68] When he speaks of the 'deeply entrenched defects of construction of the generally accepted type of "democratic" government',[69] Hayek has in mind the combination of these two different functions within the same body, 'legislature'. Due to this combination, 'the task of stating rules of just conduct and the task of directing particular activities of government to specific ends would come to be hopelessly confounded'.[70] This has, in Hayek's account, lead to a situation in which 'we have not only forgotten that government is different from legislation but have come to think that an instruction to government to take particular actions is the normal content of an act of law-giving'.[71]

In Hayek's view, the most serious consequence that has resulted from this misconstruction is that it critically undermines the capacity of the democratic legislature to go about its principal assignment, namely to deal with 'the grave and difficult questions of the improvement of the legal framework, or of the framework of rules within which the struggle of divergent interests ought to be conducted'.[72] Consequently, he argues, the legislative role has become subservient to the administrative role, such 'that the very structure and organisation of the representative assemblies has been determined by the needs of their governmental tasks but is unfavourable to wise rule-making'.[73] The main reason for this is that, while rules should be chosen for their long-term effects, there is too great a temptation for a governmental assembly that has legislative powers to define or alter rules according to its current administrative expediencies, in particular rules that impose constraints on what it may do.[74] As Hayek puts it:

---

68 F A Hayek, 1979, p 22.
69 F A Hayek, 1979, p xiii.
70 F A Hayek, 1979, p 105.
71 F A Hayek, 1979, p 22. Also: 'Let us recall once more how different the task of government proper is from that of laying down the universally applicable rules of just conduct. Government is to act on concrete matters, the allocation of particular means to particular purposes. Even so far as its aim is merely to enforce a set of rules of just conduct given to it, this requires the maintenance of an apparatus of courts, police, penal institutions, etc, and the application of particular means to particular purposes.' F A Hayek, 1979, p 23.
72 F A Hayek, 1979, p 27.
73 F A Hayek, 1979, p 22. Also: 'It is, however, by no means true that a body organised chiefly for the purpose of directing government is also suited for the task of legislation in the strict sense, ie to determine the permanent framework of rules under which it has to move its daily tasks.' F A Hayek, 1979, p 23.
74 '[T]rue legislation is thus essentially a task requiring the long view ... it must be a continuous task, a persistent effort to improve the law gradually and to adapt it to new conditions ... Though it may require formal decisions only at long intervals, it demands constant application and study of the kind for which politicians busy wooing their supporters and fully occupied with pressing matters demanding rapid solutions will not really have time.' F A Hayek, 1979, p 37.

> An assembly whose chief task is to decide what particular things should be done, and which in a parliamentary democracy supervises its executive committee (called government) in the carrying out of a general programme of action approved by it, has no inducement or interest to tie itself by general rules.[75]

We cannot, he argues, trust such an assembly to be fit to define the rules that bind its own choices, no more than we would expect an individual person to be fit to make practical choices and at the same time to choose the moral rules that he or she is supposed to obey in making these choices.[76] As Hayek charges, such an arrangement means in effect that there are no limits on the power of the democratic legislature. It leads to 'the unlimited power of the democratically elected assembly',[77] which is the cause of 'many of the gravest defects of contemporary government'.[78]

While he emphasises that it 'is not democracy or representative government as such, but the particular institutions, chosen by us' that are to blame for the problems which he identifies, Hayek sees a systematic connection between the rise of the ideal of democracy and the lessened appreciation for the role of constitutional limits on governmental power. As Hayek notes, constitutionalism, ie the ideal of limited government, long preceded the rise of democracy. Efforts to limit the power of government extended over centuries, and they were 'the great aim of the founders of constitutional government in the seventeenth and eighteenth century'.[79] Yet with the 'victory of the democratic ideal' the concern for constitutional limits on government seemed to have faded away, fuelled, presumably, by the implicit assumption that such limits are expendable where government is under democratic control, an assumption that Hayek characterises as a 'tragic illusion'.[80]

The belief that the democratic control of government 'would adequately replace the traditional limitations',[81] or that the 'democratic control of the exercise of power provided a sufficient safeguard against its excessive growth'[82] is, in Hayek's eyes, an illusion because it fails to appreciate that

---

75 F A Hayek, 1979, p 26.
76 'Eine einzige "Legislative" kann dieser doppelten Aufgabe aber ebensowenig gerecht werden, wie ein einzelner imstande waere, gleichzeitig praktische Entscheidungen zu treffen und die Moralregeln festzusetzen, die er in diesen Entscheidungen befolgen soll': F A Hayek, 1969, note 62 above, p 53.
77 F A Hayek, 1979, note 1 above, p 20.
78 F A Hayek, 1979, p 143.
79 F A Hayek, 1973, note 3 above, p 128.
80 F A Hayek, 1979, note 1 above, p 3. Also: 'For centuries efforts had been directed towards limiting the powers of government; and the gradual development of constitutions served no other purpose than this. Suddenly it was believed that the control of government by elected representatives of the majority made any other checks on the powers of government unnecessary, so that all the various constitutional safeguards which had been developed in the course of time could be dispensed with': F A Hayek, 1978, note 20 above, pp 152 ff. For similar statements see F A Hayek, 1960, note 23 above, p 403 and F A Hayek, 1978, note 20 above, p 109.
81 F A Hayek, 1979, p 3.
82 F A Hayek, 1979, p 128.

the 'ideal of a democratic control of government and that of the limitation of government by law' are *different* ideals, ideals that are compatible and complementary, but cannot be substituted for each other.[83] While the latter ideal, *liberalism*, is concerned with the functions of government, and particularly with the extent and limits of its power, the former ideal, *democracy*, 'is concerned with the question of who is to direct government'.[84] Another factor that, according to Hayek, further contributes to the rise of *unlimited democracy* is an erroneous concept of 'popular sovereignty'. This confuses the correct notion that, in a democracy, the people are the ultimate sovereign and as such are not subject to any other power, with the erroneous notion that the power of the people should not be subject to any limitations. As Hayek notes, the error in this concept of popular sovereignty 'lies not in the belief that whatever power there is should be in the hands of the people, and that their wishes will have to be expressed by majority decisions, but in the belief that this ultimate source of power must be unlimited'.[85]

Because of the absence of effective limitations on the authority of democratic legislatures, 'western democracy' can be taken to mean *unlimited democracy*, a fact that has two interrelated detrimental consequences. First, an unlimited legislature, not prevented from decreeing discriminatory measures, cannot avoid acting in an 'unprincipled manner'.[86] Lacking the guidance that only a genuine commitment to general principles can provide, unlimited democracy will tend to generate an aggregate of incoherent and contradictory outcomes that leaves almost everybody unsatisfied. Hayek finds it 'not really surprising that the consequence of modern democratic legislation which disdains submitting to general rules and attempts to solve each problem as it comes on its specific merits, is probably the most irrational and disorderly arrangement of affairs ever produced by the deliberate decisions of men'.[87] Second, paradoxically, the very fact of its *unlimited power* makes democratic government in the end a very weak government, because 'a government with unlimited powers will be forced to secure the continued support of a majority, to use its unlimited powers in the service of special interests — such groups as particular trades, the inhabitants of particular regions, etc'.[88] Hayek asserts:

> [A]n omnipotent democratic government ... will be forced to bring
> together and keep together a majority by satisfying the demands of
> a multitude of special interests, each of which will consent to the

83 F A Hayek, 1979, p 26.
84 F A Hayek, 1978, note 20 above, p 143. Also: 'Liberalism and democracy, although compatible, are not the same. The first is concerned with the extent of governmental power, the second with who holds this power. The difference is best seen if we consider their opposites: the opposite of liberalism is totalitarianism, while the opposite of democracy is authoritarianism': F A Hayek, 1967, note 10 above, p 161. See also F A Hayek, 1960, note 23 above, p 103.
85 F A Hayek, 1979, note 1 above, p 33.
86 F A Hayek, 1978, note 20 above, p 157.
87 F A Hayek, 1964, note 25 above, p 12.
88 F A Hayek, 1978, note 20 above, p 107. See also p 156 ff.

special benefits granted to other groups only at the price of their own special interests being equally considered. Such a bargaining democracy has nothing to do with the conceptions used to justify the principle of democracy.[89]

The 'domination of government by coalitions of organised interests' is, as Hayek suggests, the 'inescapable result of a system in which government has unlimited powers to take whatever measures are required to satisfy the wishes of those on whose support it relies'.[90]

Invoking a theme that modern public choice theory discusses under the rubric of *rent-seeking*[91] Hayek argues that the presence of an 'omnipotent and omnicompetent single democratic assembly' necessarily invites rent-seeking by special interests, ie efforts to secure privileges of some sort.[92] In consequence, 'an ever larger part of human activity is diverted from production into political efforts'[93] seeking wealth not by providing services for others in the market place but instead through redistribution via the political mechanism. And, at the same time, the 'arbitrariness and partiality' that the discriminatory granting of special benefits implies, undermines the fundamental working principles of the spontaneous order of society and the market.[94]

Like public choice theorists, Hayek insists that the deficiencies of such political regimes have their principal roots in a defective institutional structure, ie in the rules of the game, and not in personality defects of politicians who operate under these rules. Given the rules as they are, Hayek notes, 'even a statesman wholly devoted to the common interest of all the citizens will be under the constant necessity of satisfying special interests'.[95] Therefore, appeals to politicians to more steadfastly resist pressures from special interest groups will not solve the problem; a cure can only come from a reform of the institutional structure itself. The

---

89   F A Hayek, 1979, note 1 above, p 99.
90   F A Hayek, 1979, p 15. Also: 'If no superior judiciary authority can prevent the legislature from granting privileges to particular groups there is no limit to blackmail to which government will be subject': F A Hayek, 1979, p 11; '[T]he very omnipotence conferred on democratic representative assemblies exposes them to irresistible pressures to use their power for the benefit of special interests, a pressure a majority cannot resist if it is to remain a majority': F A Hayek, 1979, p 128; 'The root of the trouble is, of course, to sum up, that in an unlimited democracy the holders of discretionary powers are forced to use them, whether they wish it or not, to favour particular groups on whose swing-votes their power depends': F A Hayek, 1979, p 139.
91   *Toward a Theory of the Rent-Seeking Society* (eds J M Buchanan, R D Tollison, and G Tullock), Texas A & M University, College Station, 1980.
92   F A Hayek, 1979, note 1 above, p 138.
93   F A Hayek, 1979, p 138.
94   About the 'general rules of the game' on which a spontaneous order rests, Hayek states: '*Was sie ausschliessen, ist jede Art vom Staate gefoerderter Privilegien oder von Diskriminierung. Sie wuerden ein fuer alle gleiches Rahmenwerk bieten, innerhalb dessen jeder weiss, dass er das gleiche tun darf wie jeder andere*'. F A Hayek, 1969, note 62 above, p 50.
95   F A Hayek, 1978, note 20 above, p 108.

issue, as Buchanan puts it, is: '[h]ow can constitutions be designed so that politicians who seek to serve "public interest" can survive and prosper?'[96]

Constitutional reform

As Hayek sees it, the malfunctioning of the common form of modern democratic government is 'not due to a failure of the principle of democracy as such but to our having tried it the wrong way', and he declares: 'It is because I am anxious to rescue the true ideal ... that I am trying to find out the mistake we made and how we can prevent the bad consequences of the democratic procedure we have observed'.[97]

According to Hayek, the predominant model of liberal democratic institutions is derived from the limiting conception of a constitution that was formed in England[98] and that inspired, in particular, the framework of the American Constitution. Though acknowledging the achievements of American constitutionalism,[99] Hayek suggests that its method of limiting government through the separation of powers must, from today's perspective, be regarded as a failure, in the sense that it did not, in the long run, achieve what it was meant to accomplish, namely 'to provide institutional safeguards of individual freedom'.[100] That the western model of constitutionally limited democratic government worked fairly well in its original setting over a significant period of time must, in Hayek's assessment, be attributed to 'unwritten traditions and beliefs, which ... had for a long time restrained the abuse of the majority power'.[101] Yet, with the erosion of these informal constraints, and with the 'export' of the western model into different cultural environments, it became, as he

---

96   J M Buchanan, 'How can constitutions be designed so that politicians who seek to serve "public interest" can survive and prosper?', (1993) 4 *Constitutional Political Economy* 1–6. Also: 'The challenge to us is one of constructing, or re-constructing, a political order that will channel the self-serving behaviour of participants towards the common good in a manner that comes as close as possible to that described for us by Adam Smith with respect to the economic order.' J M Buchanan, 'From private preferences to public philosophy: the development of public choice', in *The Economics of Politics*, Institute of Economic Affairs, London, 1978, p 17.
97   F A Hayek, 1979, note 1 above, p 98.
98   F A Hayek, 1973, note 3 above, p 1.
99   F A Hayek, 1960, note 23 above, p 191.
100 F A Hayek, 1973, note 3 above, p 1. Also: 'In the form in which we know the division of power between the legislature, the judiciary, and the administration, it has not achieved what it was meant to achieve. Governments everywhere have obtained by constitutional means powers which those men had meant to deny them. The first attempt to secure individual liberty by constitutions has evidently failed': F A Hayek, 1973, note 3 above, p 1. Elsewhere, Hayek characterises 'the American attempts to limit in their Constitution the powers of the legislature' more mildly as a 'limited success': F A Hayek, 1973, p 21. On a still more positive note he had commented earlier: 'Incredibly successful as the American experiment in constitutionalism has been ... it is still an experiment in a new way of ordering government, and we must not regard it as containing all wisdom in this field': F A Hayek, 1960, note 23 above, pp 91 ff.
101 F A Hayek, 1979, note 1 above, p 108.

suggests, apparent that the formal constitutional framework in itself does not provide a sufficient safeguard against a continuous expansion of the power of democratic government.[102]

Hayek's conclusion from the above diagnosis is that a new attempt needs to be made at solving 'the problem in which the founders of liberal constitutionalism failed'. What is needed is a genuine revival of the constitutionalist ideal 'that the power of all authorities exercising governmental functions ought to be limited by long run rules which nobody has the power to alter or abrogate in the service of particular ends'.[103] We need, as he puts it, to ask what the 'founders of liberal constitutionalism would do today if, pursuing the aims they did, they could command all the experience we have gained in the meantime'.[104] An understanding of past failures is necessary in order to come up with a 'new institutional invention' and 'constitutional design'; a replacement of 'the tottering structure by some better edifice'.[105] If this sounds like a project in 'rational construction' this is because it is in the nature of things. As Hayek notes, '[g]overnment is necessarily the product of intellectual design',[106] and the rules of the organisation of government, ie constitutional rules, have always been a matter of deliberate design.[107] When, with regard to the rules of government or constitutional rules, Hayek speaks of constructivist rationalism, what he criticises is not the notion of deliberate design in constitutional matters, but instead a view that one may call 'anti-constitutionalism', ie the refusal to bind governmental powers by general rules.[108] Whatever some of his arguments on cultural evolution may suggest with regard to general rules of conduct, as far as the constitutional rules of government are concerned, Hayek clearly does not assume that we can wait for an 'invisible hand' to generate a beneficial constitutional order for us.

Since Hayek sees the principal defect of the existing forms of democratic government as their insufficient separation of rule-making authority from administrative power, his suggestions for constitutional reform focus naturally on the issue of how a more effective division

---

102 '[T]he particular institutions which for a time worked tolerably in the West presuppose the tacit acceptance of certain other principles which were in some measure observed there but which, where they are not yet recognized, must be made as much a part of the written constitution as the rest': F A Hayek, 1979, p 108. See also F A Hayek, 1969, note 62 above, p 56.

103 F A Hayek, 1979, p 129.

104 F A Hayek, 1973, note 3 above, pp 1 ff. Also: 'What can we do today, in the light of the experience gained, to accomplish the aims which, nearly two hundred years ago, the fathers of the Constitution of the United States of America for the first time attempted to secure by a deliberate construction? Though our aims may still be the same, there is much that we ought to have learnt from the great experiment and its numerous limitations. We know now why the hope of the authors of those documents, that through them they could effectively limit the powers of government, has been disappointed.' F A Hayek, 1979, note 1 above, p 105.

105 F A Hayek, 1979, note 1 above, p 152.

106 F A Hayek, 1979, p 152.

107 F A Hayek, 1973, note 3 above, pp 90, 124.

108 F A Hayek, 1973, p 34; F A Hayek, 1979, note 1 above, p 129.

between these two functions might be achieved. The core element of his proposal for 'A Model Constitution' is the idea of an arrangement 'which would secure a real separation of powers between two distinct representative bodies whereby law-making in the narrow sense as well as government proper would be conducted democratically, but by different and mutually independent agencies'.[109]

In a refined 'constitutional model' which takes account of the difference in nature between the general rules of conduct on which the spontaneous order of society is based and the constitutional rules on which the organisation of government rests, Hayek has proposed 'a three-tiered system of representative bodies ... of which one would be concerned with the semi-permanent framework of the constitution, ... another with the continuous task of gradual improvement of the general rules of just conduct, and a third with the current conduct of government, that is, the administration of the resources entrusted to it'.[110] With regard to their respective functions, Hayek explains:

> The function of the Legislative Assembly must not be confused with that of a body set up to enact or amend the Constitution ... [W]hile the Constitution allocates and restricts powers, it should not prescribe positively how these powers are to be used. The substantive law in the sense of rules of just conduct would be developed by the Legislative Assembly ... The Governmental Assembly and its government as its executive organ on the other hand would be restricted both by the rules of the Constitution and by the rules of just conduct laid down or recognized by the Legislative Assembly.[111]

Much of the discussion on Hayek's reform proposal has concentrated on his suggestions for implementing the institutional separation between the legislative and administrative representative bodies. It is not only because of space limitations that I do not enter this debate here. More importantly, it seems to me that the details of Hayek's proposal can easily distract from his principal argument, one whose validity is completely independent of the soundness of the specifics of his reform ideas. The essence of his exposition lies in a general diagnosis of the systemic defects of the standard model of democratic government, and his general argument that a remedy can only be found in a genuine revival of the ideal of constitutionally limited government. Hayek's principal argument is based on a call for an institutional arrangement that effectively insulates the rule-making authority from the short-term demands of day-to-day government, and for effective constraints that subject governmental authority to the discipline of general principles.[112] Whether these aims can

---

109 F A Hayek, 1979, note 1 above, p 107.
110 F A Hayek, 1979, p 38.
111 F A Hayek, 1979, pp 122 ff; see also p 38.
112 *'Das Ideal des 'government under the law' kann nur erreicht werden, wenn auch die Volksvertretung, die die Regierungstätigkeit dirigiert, unter Regeln steht, die sie selbst nicht ändern kann, sondern die von einer anderen demokratischen Körperschaft bestimmt werden, die gewissermassen die langfristigen Prinzipien festlegt'*: F A Hayek, 1969, note 62 above, p 53.

best be achieved with the particular institutional reforms that Hayek himself has suggested, or whether one could imagine more effective alternative structures, is a question of second order. If his principal arguments should find acceptance, the search for appropriate institutional arrangements should not be the most difficult part of the task. Should his basic argument be rejected, there would be no point in discussing the particulars of his reform proposal.

Conclusion

The purpose of this chapter has been to show how Hayek's critique of the institutional structure of western democracy, and his venture in constitutional design and institutional invention, can be systematically related to his arguments on the role of rules which are at the core of his political philosophy. His rational and constructive approach to the issue of constitutional reform in our democratic institutions is not, as one might perhaps suspect, an alien and ad hoc addendum to the main thrust of his work which is imbued by his critique of what he calls *rational constructivism*. It is, instead, a logical extension of his general argument on the interrelation between the *order of rules* and the *order of actions*, and his understanding of how we may hope to improve our 'social condition' by improving the 'rules of the game.'

A principal task of politics is, according to Hayek, to enforce and further develop a suitable framework of rules within which a beneficial social order can form itself. Whether, and to what extent, the political process is suitable for this task will depend, again, on the rules under which this process itself operates. It is primarily in terms of this criterion that Hayek finds the institutional structure of the prevailing form of democratic government wanting. His proposals for institutional reform aim at making the institutional framework more conducive to that task.

More generally, Hayek's argument is that the same principle that applies to the spontaneous order of society and the market applies to the realm of politics as well, namely: our principal means to improve the order that emerges in either realm is through our efforts to improve the framework of rules.

CHAPTER 4

Spontaneous Order and Rule of Law: Some Problems

Neil MacCormick*

Introduction

This chapter expounds a critique, albeit a genuinely respectful one, of two thinkers who have made distinctive contributions to current conservative thinking, F A Hayek and Michael Oakeshott. Its chief target is Hayek's theory of 'spontaneous order', its subordinate target Oakeshott's 'Rule of Law'. It is argued that neither theory nor any combination of them establishes an adequate case for certain claims made by their authors in respect of social justice. Since Hayek's work grows partly out of reflections on Scottish legal thought of the eighteenth century, and I have a special interest in that body of thought, I will start at the same point as Hayek. That we come to different final conclusions does not diminish my respect for his work.

The Hayekian ideal of the spontaneous order

Law, according to one rationalist definition, is the dictate of reason, whereby every rational being determines what is congruous with and convenient to its nature and condition.[1] If the definition were sound, and if no two beings had precisely the same nature and condition, law could

---

*   Regius Professor of Public Law and the Law of Nature and Nations, and Provost of the Faculty Group of Law and Social Sciences, The University of Edinburgh.
1   See J D Stair, *Institutions of the Law of Scotland* (ed D M Walker), University Presses of Edinburgh and Glasgow, Edinburgh and Glasgow, 1981, p 73. I do not in fact ascribe to Stair a belief in 'special providence' through law. See text for footnote 2.

even appear to be a matter of 'special providence', laying down a unique and particular set of ordinances for each being. Since no two beings can be in *exactly* the same condition, law must indeed be a matter of special providence in that sense. This would seem to conjure up the alarming spectacle of an ideal state issuing the most specific and particular instructions to each of its citizens, aimed at securing the maximum good for each through perfect coordination of all.

The extent to which successful economic enterprises, armies, and football teams achieve their success by means of effective planning for the activities of each unit or member and smooth coordination of each with every other may, however, make us think less coolly of the rationalist model. There is even a certain sort of individuality or individualism which fits perfectly well into or perhaps is even demanded by successfully integrated team efforts of this sort. On the one hand, firms, armies and teams do precisely aim to exploit each member's special skills; on the other hand, these special skills are never better or more advantageously displayed than when deployed as a response to some sudden and unplanned change in the environment, whether caused by natural forces or by some move made by a rival, antagonist or competitor. But, of course, the criterion of the effective use of special skills or initiatives is its utility towards the overall corporate or game plan. Individuals have a role in such activities to the extent that they identify themselves with the common or corporate effort and thus find their success within it. There is a further role for individuals where the mode of corporate government is democratic. Whether or not this is a practical recipe for success, there is no reason in principle not to have democratic planning, or democratic election of plan-makers and executive officers.

So why must that which is possible and perhaps desirable in the microcosm be judged either impossible or undesirable in the macrocosm? Why should we not wish to see societies made successful through teamwork, making optimal use of everyone's individuality and talents in pursuit of the common endeavour? Why should we not make it our ideal for law that it work towards some system of special providence which is, as far as possible, congruous with and convenient for the exact nature and condition of every individual citizen and ideally adapted to the good of the whole? Why not further re-enforce this ideal by insisting on democratic organisation of it?

To such a proposal there are objections of both principle and practice. The objections of principle address the category difference between microcosms and macrocosms. Firms, teams, armies and all sorts of voluntary associations have in their very nature common purposes. 'Societies' or 'states' do not. Society is the *context* of human endeavours, including collectively organised endeavours, and is not in itself an instance of organised endeavour. The members of a society may have some or even many shared or common goods, and it may indeed be a proper object of common or general endeavour to procure such public goods. But that is not the same as having broad common goals or objectives like maximising production or profits or winning the match.

A second, not unrelated, objection of principle depends upon a particular version of human nature, according to which a capacity for independent or autonomous action is of the essence of human beings. Associational activities, team efforts, are one mode of exercising autonomy, of realising one's self in free collaboration with another. But precisely what the collaboration must be is left open, in the sense that the opportunity of non-participation exists. This is not so in the case of the state or of 'civil society', for these are non-voluntary associations. And, however desirable democracy may be, it cannot turn the state into a voluntary association. In principle, law at the level of state or civil society ought to leave space for autonomy, for independence in action; without that, human nature is stifled. In principle, then, laws ought not even to aspire to the 'special providence' model.

The second of these objections of principle would be enthusiastically upheld by rationalists such as Hayek and Oakeshott. To be sure, a jurist such as Stair believed that it was human nature to honour and obey God, and to keep covenants with each other. But he also believed that humans were by nature free beings beyond their obligations of obedience and their own engagements. Stair saw the very nature of humans being such that their freedom ought to be secured to them by positive law, precisely in order that natural law might find its fulfilment. No doubt each person ought to do all things to the greater glory of God; but in the very nature of things this requires a free discretion in each as to how he or she should act to that greater end.

This line of thought depends on the truism that humans are not gods. Even if God knows what each person is doing and ought best to be doing at every moment, it is beyond the capacity of any individual human intelligence or process of collective deliberation to achieve such knowledge. So it is in practice necessary for human beings, especially those in authority, to abstain from and guard against any pretension to such divine perfection of knowledge. This is the great practical objection to any special providence model of human law. Again, it is an objection perfectly familiar to at least some of the rationalists, who take law to be a dictate of reason. Stair, for example, has much to say in favour of the use of experimental customary development of law — case law — over resorting to statutes. Human knowledge and foresight are limited, he points out, and yet in enacting statutes we must know and foresee much. Always we fail, and leave *casus incogitati*. Better results are usually achieved by the experimental, step by step, permanently self-correcting process of developing law from precedent to precedent.[2]

This attitude can be usefully described in terms of Hayek's distinction between 'critical rationalism' and 'constructivist rationalism'.[3] To be critically rationalist is to apply reasoned criticisms to inherited systems of thought and action on the ground that change within such systems can only be partial and incremental rather than total. We have to hold some

---

2   J D Stair, 1981, pp 85–9.

3   F A Hayek, *Law, Legislation and Liberty*, vols 1–3, Routledge & Kegan Paul, London, 1982, vol 1, pp 26–34.

principles as 'given' in order to criticise others or develop them by analogy. Whether in speculative or practical matters, we can never do more than apply the individual talent to critique and development of the tradition of thought in which we have been reared and educated. It is impossible for any of us to invent it all single-handedly. 'Constructivist rationalism' is the intellectual vice of forgetting this impossibility, and of treating systems of thought and practical action as though we were entirely in control of them and could, any of us, redesign them in their entirety to a perfectly rational pattern.

If eighteenth century writers prefigured this line of thought, nowhere was this clearer than in David Hume's reflections on justice.[4] Justice, for Hume, was on the one hand defined by the established rules and institutions of a community, and yet on the other hand was capable of ranging beyond these established institutions both in analogical extrapolations to deal with new cases, and in forming the basis for a critique of internal inconsistencies and incoherencies within the system. Hume's metaphysical anti-rationalism amounted to a critique of all claims to innate knowledge and to self-evidence in empirically testable propositions. Our claims to knowledge must always be tentative, grounded in probability rather than certainty, and provable by experimental evidence rather than by recourse to innate ideas.

However if knowledge is based on experience and if people's experience differs — and differs more greatly the further advanced division of labour is —it follows that the total stock of knowledge available to a society is greater than any individual can possess. This corollary of Hume's point is one for which we are indebted to Hayek. It brings us back to the truth that humans are not gods and cannot act as though they have divine knowledge; this Hayekian insight adds a special force to the warning to humans not to play God. For if no individual or organised group is capable of knowing for itself all that is usefully known in a community, and far less by human beings at large, it follows that no government can utilise directly or plan the use of all the knowledge that is available for the pursuit of human advantage. Conversely, a government which tries to apply the special providence model of law would always be imposing a judgment from ignorance upon subjects who have a specialised knowledge of their circumstances not available to the government. In the light of Hayek's epistemological theses, what started as a practical objection to undue governmental interference in individual lives has become an objection of principle. No government could ever know enough to be capable of rationally applying the special providence model of law. Due to their nature, governments must always know or have access to knowledge substantially less than the sum of the useful knowledge available within the governed population.[5]

---

4   D Hume, *Enquiries Concerning Human Understanding and Concerning the Principles of Morals*, 3rd ed (eds L A Selby-Bigge and P H Nidditch), Clarendon Press, Oxford, 1975, pp 154–63; see also D Hume, *A Treatise of Human Nature*, 2nd ed (ed L A Selby-Bigge), Clarendon Press, Oxford, 1978, Book 3.

5   F A Hayek, 1982, note 3 above, pp 8–11.

This of course poses a problem, to which the earliest convincing solution was put forward by Adam Smith. If there is available in society more useful information than any individual or organised collectivity can know, then it is not possible for any planning authority to direct the useful application of this information. How then does it come to be exploited? Smith's answer was in terms of an analysis of the way in which diverse individual efforts and activities can achieve coordination through markets, not however because markets were designed to achieve this nor because any single momentary coordination was designed by anybody. Open markets are places where people using information, knowledge and skills for their own purposes necessarily make these available to others for other purposes, all parties acquiring new knowledge in the process, including information about less profitable avenues to pursue. Given that markets have the curious property of rewarding best whoever can supply a given commodity at the lowest price, they tend to coordinate public and private interests, though nobody has designed that this should be so.[6]

Here, of course, one must allude to the famous metaphor of the invisible hand. The mutually advantageous coordination of private and public interest comes about in a market without any of the market traders having any intention of bringing it about. In pursuit of their own interest, they are led as by an invisible hand to favour also the general interest, so Smith tells us. 'Design after all?', one may ask. Is this the unseen hand of the great designer in the sky manipulating all to his ends? Or is it, rather, no hand at all? With Robert Nozick, I would suppose the latter. Smith has not elaborately shown how the designs of human beings can regularly and predictably produce outcomes designed by no one, only in order to fall back on the explanatory hypothesis of a superhuman designer. Even if he did, his prior explanation has rendered the hypothesis utterly redundant. Smith's explanation of the way markets function to produce public benefits dispenses with the need for such a designer. We should certainly read the text using the 'invisible hand' rather than the 'hidden hand' interpretation. As Nozick remarks, an invisible hand is no hand at all — and that is exactly the point we should take from Smith's writings.[7]

We owe also to Nozick the application of the 'invisible hand' explanation to social processes. This explanation allows us to recognise that human beings acting alone and institutional collectivities of humans are the only conscious acting subjects the social sciences need postulate, though not everything brought about by social processes is caused by a human's deliberate action aimed at causing or changing the social process. By explaining what such agencies have done and meant by their actions and by showing how others have reacted or responded, it is possible to demonstrate how social changes come about in a way which transcends human intelligence and individual or collective intentions without

---

6   A Smith, *An Inquiry into the Nature and Causes of the Wealth of Nations*, vol 1, Book IV, Chapter ii (ed R H Campbell, A S Skinner and W B Todd), Clarendon Press, Oxford, 1976, p 456; F A Hayek, 1982, vol 2, pp 107–132.

7   See R Nozick, *Anarchy, State and Utopia*, Clarendon Press, Oxford, 1974, pp 18–22; A Smith, 1976, p 456.

presupposing any guidance or manipulation other than those intelligences and intentions. Social changes result from human intelligence though often not in the way intended by human agencies.

Be that as it may, the conditions in which a market works optimally to secure public goods through the pursuit of private interests can be shown to be those in which there are the fewest possible interventions in the private judgment of the participants. Civil liberty is favourable to markets and markets are favourable to civil liberty, even if neither is strictly essential to the other.

Liberty has in turn an independent value. It is worth seeking, according to Smith and his contemporaries (especially Ferguson and Hume) and successors, regardless of economic advantage. But the way to secure liberty is to restrict the task of law-making to the enactment of what Hume called 'general inflexible rules'.[8] Modes of government which so restrict themselves are modes of free government. A task of politics and political philosophy is to help secure a continuance of the conditions of liberty through an insistence on the continuance of general inflexible rules of conduct as the exclusive vehicle of legal regulation by government of citizens. As Hayek points out, such general rules of conduct must be mainly negative in tenor, such as prohibitions on interferences with others, save in the case of rules governing such special relationships as those of parent and child. Beyond the range of the prohibitions laid down, people have freedom to act at their own discretion, and here again, quite apart from the market, arises the opportunity for individuals singly or in concert to apply their own knowledge to their own purposes.

As an ideal for society and law, this picture is clearly at the opposite pole from that of a legal order of special providence such as was envisaged at the outset of this paper. Hayek's name for such an order is 'spontaneous order' or *cosmos*, in contrast with *taxis* or directed order. His legal and political theory amounts to a root and branch defence of the ideal of society as a spontaneous order, coupled with a blistering critique of managerialism and socialism in all their forms. A special target for his criticism is the concept of 'social justice', and all political programs advanced in the name of social justice.[9]

To this argument, the 'special providence model' is directly relevant. For the substance of Hayek's thesis is that all attacks mounted in the name of social justice upon existing patterns of affluence and poverty, that is, denunciations of economic and consequential political inequalities, postulate a readiness to engage in or indeed institutionalise schemes of 'special providence'. Under such schemes we must inquire into each person's degree of fortune and misfortune and readjust their circumstances according to some *a priori* formula. Furthermore, since no precise formula for such readjustment has ever been established in theory or agreed upon in practice, the 'social justice' which is supposed to be

8   D Hume, *Essays, Moral, Political and Literary*, vol 1 (eds T H Green and T H Grose), Longman, Green & Co, London, 1907, p 96.
9   F A Hayek, 1982, note 3 above, vol 1, pp 35–54 (*cosmos/taxis*); vol 2, pp 62–100 (on social justice).

constituted by such readjustment is a bogus concept. One might add that the concept of 'substantive' justice, as against 'formula' or 'abstract' justice is much the same case — here again, the stress is on looking to the personality and needs of every individual and responding to these in all their particularity instead of dealing with human beings in the purely abstract terms of general legal categories.

The chimerical quality of 'social justice' is further exhibited, in Hayek's view, by the unintelligibility of the concept of 'social injustice' which it presupposes. Injustice, says Hayek, is properly understood as a vice of human action. To be the victim of injustice is to have some wrong done to one by some intentional or negligent action of another acting subject. Since 'societies' are not themselves acting subjects, they cannot create injustices as such. Societies cannot be held responsible, whether as a matter of blame or as one of praise, for the results of the workings of spontaneous order within societies. Humans are acting subjects and, though they can commit injustice by wilfully or neglectfully breaking the general abstract rules of the spontaneous order to others' detriment, they cannot be said to wilfully bring about any of the moment-to-moment distributions of good and bad fortune which occur in the market. Inequalities which result from nobody's act or wilful omission cannot be injustices — social injustice is as foolish an idea as genetic injustice, social justice as misconceived an ideal as eugenics.[10]

Accordingly, there are not only strong arguments in favour of *cosmos* or spontaneous order; there are also powerful arguments against all interventionist programs aimed at altering the spontaneous order in favour of some small or large element of *taxis* or special providence. These involve the exercise of power in ignorance, and depend upon a profoundly incoherent pseudo-concept of justice and injustice.

Problems with Hayek's spontaneous order

That powerful arguments can be advanced in favour of the Hayekian ideal of the spontaneous order is clear. As the title of this chapter shows, however, I see difficulties with the ideal. In summary, my difficulties are as follows; *first*, it is not clear that some of the criticisms of spontaneous order did not themselves spontaneously evolve as a result of critically rationalist extrapolation from developed ideas of justice; *second*, even if this were not so, such criticisms and associated political reforms of a socialist or social-democratic kind have brought into being a state of affairs in which Hayek's supporters have to take positive action to restore the conditions of spontaneous order — but then, it seems that political agents are after all responsible for the outcomes of the order they have assigned to establish; *third*, and further to the prior point, it seems that a deliberate and designed policy of re-establishing a spontaneous order goes against the proscription upon social planning; *fourth*, the decision to re-establish the conditions of spontaneous order, if taken, has to be justified, and must be justified by recourse to consequentialist and probably to utilitarian arguments.

10   F A Hayek, 1982, vol 2, pp 31–43, 80–4.

Spontaneous evolution of opponents of spontaneous order

One need not be a Marxist to agree with Marx's observation that only in a capitalist or market order does the idea of the equality of human beings acquire the fixity of a popular prejudice.[11] The evolution of law away from the status relationships of the feudal order and even of the *Ständestaat* is an *evolution* of the ideal of equality of all before the law. But once the principle of equality is seen to be implicit in the law of spontaneous order, and once it acquires the fixity of a popular prejudice, the principle may be applied in criticism of the institutions of the spontaneous order in other aspects of their operation. The liberties under law to be enjoyed equally by all citizens may be seen to be of greatly different worth to different groups in accordance with their economic means. The equality of all before the law may fail to be matched by equal opportunities for different groups or individuals to avail themselves of the law's facilities. The equality of status and of will presupposed by contract law may be at least partly negated in practical effect by radical inequalities of bargaining power.

Whether sound or unsound, there is no reason to envisage this criticism as being anything other than the type of immanent criticism which is allowable within the Humean or Hayekian scheme of practical reasoning. Nor will it necessarily be unintelligible if projects for equalisation of the economic inequalities allowable under pre-existing law are promoted in the name of 'social justice' by implied contrast with 'legal justice'. The concept will not be made meaningless because its users fail to agree upon positive criteria for its application. This will merely entail its membership in the well-documented class of 'essentially contested concepts'. Further, provided that reforms aimed at procuring redistribution of assets are developed as correctives to the workings of the order upon the basis of the immanent criticisms, it is not of itself clear why the resultant order should be deemed lacking in spontaneity. Certainly, the outcomes of such interventions will include unforeseen and unintended consequences, which will in turn call for further responses. But that is merely to say that evolutionary processes are continuous.

Non-spontaneous actions by supporters of spontaneous order

Certainly such opposing developments have taken place, if to different extents, by differing means and under different political conditions, in all western societies this century. Let me suppose, contrary to the preceding section, that all such developments have involved recourse to constructivist rather than critical rationalism and have resulted in the destructive superimposition of *taxis* upon *cosmos*. If this is the correct

---

11   See R Kinsey, 'Marxism and the Law', (1978) 5 *British Journal of Law and Society* 202–27, 216.

Hayekian analysis of the situation, it follows that the partisans of the 'Great Society' have to take steps to reverse the process. And some have done so. In Britain since 1979, and in the USA since 1981, determined efforts have been made to lessen state involvement in the economy. The task has been to restore the conditions of spontaneous order. Even if the steps to implementing this have been half-hearted or misguided or both, it is not to be denied that this is the task a Hayekian would and should take upon him or herself.

To the extent that restoration of a spontaneously self-regulating market order is, in these circumstances, an object of deliberate endeavour, it seems obvious that the outcomes of the working of the market must now cease to fall beyond the realms of justice. Those who seek to restore the market know that properly working markets generate considerable ranges of economic inequality. No such inequalities are or need be intended by any of the market's participants. But those who deliberately set about to restore a market-based economic order must be deemed to intend just such inequalities, for a person must intend what he or she knows to be the foreseeable outcome of his or her act. That one cannot foresee *who* will make the gains and suffer the losses is irrelevant to the issue of responsibility. If I give a hand grenade to a madman en route to the theatre and people are killed by the grenade, I cannot afterwards excuse myself by saying that I couldn't foresee who would be killed.

Hence the moment-to-moment outcomes of the working of a spontaneous order are not altogether outside the realms of justice. Those who re-establish free markets intend them to work as markets work, with the range of outcomes for individuals which that entails. Even if the case were not one of deliberately restoring free market conditions — even if it were merely a case of deliberately choosing to maintain such conditions despite awareness of an alternative — the outcome would be the same.

Social planning by supporters of a theory which opposes social planning

Abstaining for the moment from any judgment about the justice or injustice of decisions to reinstate free market conditions, we may nevertheless note that they have a somewhat paradoxical character. The Hayekian thesis implies that governmental planning is always apt to result in unintended consequences and hence that planning can never bring about exactly or even approximately what was planned. Apart from anything else the planner can never tell how other human beings will respond to the changes in the environment that he or she makes. What is not clear in Hayek's thesis is why this does not apply with equal force to those whose plan it is to re-establish the legal conditions of spontaneous order. Is the conscious and deliberate creation of a market order wholly exempt from the critique of government planning, and if so, why? Should it be seen as yet another of the possible policies which, as the Hayekian epistemological thesis warns us, is apt to turn out in execution quite differently than was intended?

The English Conservative Government, after almost 16 years of effort directed on more or less Hayekian lines has ended up with a level of public expenditure higher than that which it inherited from the previous Labour administration; similarly, the Reagan administration in the United States ran the largest budget deficit in the history of that land. With these facts in hand, one is perhaps best justified in concluding that the Hayekian epistemological thesis shines as bright a warning light towards those who plan the restitution of spontaneous order as it does towards those whose gaze is turned to the left. Working on the assumption that the welfare state is itself the product of a spontaneous process of evolution, is it not true to say that any attempt at the deliberate creation of a Hayekian spontaneous order by resort to legislative and governmental power would be a manifestation of constructivist rationalism at its worst? Certainly, the Thatcher administration has been the most rigorously centralist in its policies of any British government in the post-war years, presenting the paradox of a program continually increasing the powers of central government in order finally to let them wither away.

Justifying the spontaneous order with consequentialist arguments

When such interventionist policies are consciously and deliberately proclaimed and pursued, it is evidently necessary for them to be justified. And how should they be justified? The answer must surely be in terms of the quality of human lives lived in these legal and constitutional conditions as compared with the quality of life or lives under other orders. No doubt a powerful case can be made in terms of the arguments set out in Hayek's *Law, Legislation and Liberty*. In a spontaneous order people are free to pursue their own projects as they see fit, subject only to respecting their duties to avoid wronging others. People apply their own knowledge to their own projects and learn by their own mistakes. They take the benefit of whatever free associations they see fit to participate in. And since the system is geared to rewarding best those whose projects turn out to be the most economically advantageous, opportunities of economic wellbeing at all levels of the system are enhanced at the same time as liberty is secured. Put simply, people are certainly more free and likely to be more prosperous in spontaneous orders than in any other form of human society we can imagine.

Such an argument strikes me as extremely forceful. It does state an appealing reason for favouring that which proponents of spontaneous order propose. The trouble is, again, that it appears to be an argument which the consistent Hayekian ought to oppose. For it is nothing other than a utilitarian argument, and, according to Hayek, utilitarianism is a classical case of the errors of constructivist rationalism.[12] In our rush to exhibit the folly of any, too instrumentalist, view of legislation and government, we ought to avoid the error of supposing that all modes of

---

12   F A Hayek, 1982, note 3 above, vol 2, pp 17–24.

argument for the values constituted or secured by particular modes of legal order are all equally objectionable.

Oakeshott's rule of law

The four points discussed above seem to me to constitute a fair and substantial objection to Hayek's case. There is much of weight and value in his political philosophy, but it is not in the end acceptable in its entirety. Could we set up a stronger version of the same case?

One candidate for the job proposed is perhaps Michael Oakeshott who set out his thoughts on the representation of 'the rule of law' in his *On History: and other Essays.*[13] What he says is very relevant to our discussion of the possibility of a consequentialist justification of Hayekian spontaneous order. Oakeshott is at pains to investigate the idea that either 'prosperity' or 'freedom' should be represented as *effects* of the sustenance of a state under the rule of law or, therefore, should be proposed as consequentialist grounds favouring adoption or sustenance of such a state. As to prosperity, he acknowledges the 'inconsistency of attributing the virtue of a non-instrumental mode of association to its propensity to produce, promote or even encourage a substantive condition of things'.[14] He sees that freedom in one of its many senses is not an effect of, but an intrinsic element in, the *Rechtsstaat*; and so likewise 'peace' and 'order', in some senses of the terms. Oakeshott is absolutely clear that commendation of the rule of law can only be in terms of its intrinsic virtues, not in terms of its effects:

> The rule of law bakes no bread, it is unable to distribute loaves or fishes (it has none), and it cannot protect itself against external assault, but it remains the most civilized and least burdensome conception of a state yet to be devised.[15]

This line of thought might be a more promising basis on which to make a case for the Hayekian 'spontaneous order' or something like it. The trouble with this is that deeper probing would call into question the extent to which the Oakeshottian 'rule of law' is anything like the Hayekian spontaneous order. Indeed spontaneity has no part in Oakeshott's idea. As he characterises the rule of law, a fundamental element in it is a decidedly *gesetzespositivistisch* notion of the 'authenticity' of rules:

> The expression 'the rule of law', taken precisely, stands for a mode of moral association exclusively in terms of the recognition of authority of known, non-instrumental rules (that is, laws) which impose obligations to subscribe to adverbial conditions in the performance of the self-chosen actions of all who fall within their jurisdiction.[16]

---

13 M Oakeshott, *On History: and Other Essays*, Clarendon Press, Oxford, 1983, pp 119–164.
14 M Oakeshott, 1983, p 161.
15 M Oakeshott, 1983, p 164.
16 M Oakeshott, 1983, p 136.

When Oakeshott refers to the authority of rules he has in mind much the same concept as in Joseph Raz's *Authority of Law*,[17] namely he depends on an essentially source-based conception of the validity or authenticity of law. Quite clearly, legislative authenticity is the paradigm case — and for Oakeshott, as for Austin, case-law will only count to the extent it can be assimilated to enacted law. The idea of a legislator or legislature whose enactments fulfil procedural conditions of validity and who has authority, in that the subjects acknowledge it as obligatory to conform with any rules, is an idea central to the Oakeshottian 'rule of law'. This idea is 'a mode of moral association' among *personae*, that is, among roles which can be played by human actors as one among various of the *personae* they bear, each proper to its own mode of association. Modes of association are, like Wittgensteinian languages, forms of life; and, like them, are the deadly serious games we all play.

The Hayekian stress on the special evolutionary virtues of the common law so characteristic of his spontaneous order finds no echo in Oakeshott. For Oakeshott as for the English positivists legislative law is the paradigm, and every other sort merely the penumbral case. The great modernisations of the eighteenth and nineteenth centuries did perhaps have this characteristic, in that they required and involved a stress upon the legislature as the unifier and generaliser of law. The sweeping away of the myriad of special customs and local rights so essential to a *Ständestaat* doubtless called for acts of legislative will. France gained a common law by getting a code, and that came about due to the presence of Napoleon. Elsewhere, as in Britain, it may have been a less clear process; but in Britain Bentham was a Napoleon of the intellect, and his intellectual descendants shaped the modern fetish of the sovereignty of Parliament. For Dicey, the greatest of those descendants, the 'rule of law' was the other face of parliamentary sovereignty among the fundaments of the constitution.[18] So there is a good deal to be said historically for Oakeshott's view that law as a statute is the focal kind of law for the emerging idea of the rule of law or its German cousin the *Rechtsstaat* as these came to be received in the nineteenth and early twentieth centuries.[19]

Such a view, it may be argued, is not merely historically sound but, in the present context, also dialectically useful. For the second and third of the points taken against Hayek in the preceding section of the chapter relate specifically to the *spontaneous* character of Hayekian 'spontaneous order'. There would be no contradiction between Oakeshott's conception of the 'rule of law' and the fact of its being procured by deliberate legislative intervention. The theory says that it has always been so, wherever the rule of law as a mode of association has arisen. The *cosmos* is, after all, always also a *taxis* on this view.

17   J Raz, *The Authority of Law*, Clarendon Press, Oxford, 1979.

18   See A V Dicey, *An Introduction to the Law of the Constitution*, 10th ed (ed E C S Wade), Macmillan, London, 1964, pp 163–206.

19   Compare D N MacCormick, 'Der Rechtsstaat und die Rule of Law' (1984) 39 *Juristenzeitung* 65–70; T O'Hagan, *The End of Law?*, Basil Blackwell, Oxford, 1984, pp 116–43.

Perhaps this saves the game at too high a price, however. The enacted rules which Oakeshott's rule of law postulates are, it will be recalled, 'known, non-instrumental rules (that is, laws)'. The parallel with Hayek's 'purpose-independent rules of just conduct' is perfect here, however much our sources may diverge as to the proper origin of the rules they postulate. But what is particularly plausible in Hayek's idea of the purpose-independent character of rules, namely that they characteristically evolve through common law processes, is wholly implausible when the idea is transferred to the case of enacted laws where these are deemed to be the focal case for the rule of law. Enacted laws are not characteristically, nor ought they to be, enacted in a purpose-independent way — which was exactly why Bentham and his followers favoured that sort of law, and is exactly why Hayek is disposed to take so poor a view of legal positivism in all its more voluntaristic manifestations.[20]

There is, on the face of it, no reason other than a purely stipulative one why Oakeshott should be so insistent on the purely 'adverbial' or 'procedural' quality of legal rules as such. Certainly, one can see that laws in so far as they impose obligations have the character of setting what Nozick calls 'side-constraints' upon action.[21] Whatever we choose to do, we should do it so as to avoid infringing any obligation. But *a fortiori* we also then have to abstain from setting as our aim an objective performance of that which the law forbids, or abstention from that which it enjoins. In this sense the law is far from being purpose-independent or purpose-indifferent. Viewed from the angle of securing the prevention or performance of forbidden or obligatory acts, laws are far from being non-instrumental. In any sense in which it is 'adverbial' to have a law against murder ('whatever you do, do it so that your positive acts cause no person's death') it can be equally relevant to have a good Samaritan law ('whatever you do, do it so that you omit no reasonable act which would prevent another from falling into indigence').

It appears unnecessary to adjudicate over the issue whether or not Oakeshott's theory is 'something like' Hayek's; for the facts are that it has its own grounds of implausibility, and that those cover exactly the points on this approach differs to the Hayekian. However far one finds plausible the Hayekian protests and warnings against 'constructivist rationalism', or what I have been calling 'special providence', to that very extent one must have doubts about Oakeshott's ideal legislator. And however much one favours Oakeshott's ideal legislator, to that very extent must one have doubts about Hayek's spontaneous order. In neither case, therefore, need one take as absolute the thesis that laws either have to be or ought to be 'purpose-independent' or 'non-instrumental'; nor indeed could they be if legislation were used as the vehicle through which to restore the *cosmos* or re-establish the rule of law.

20   F A Hayek, 1982, note 3 above, pp 44–61.
21   R Nozick, 1974, note 7 above, pp 28–35.

The significance of Hayek's theory

My own view is that there is great force in Hayek's case against constructivist rationalism. There is no more powerful nor soundly stated warning to be found anywhere against giving credence to the possibility of social engineering on a grand scale. The idea that any legislature or government can redesign a whole society according to some rationally elaborated plan is indeed as fatuous as Hayek advises us, and for the very reasons he states. Whatever is carried out based on such designs, the outcome will always be different, even frighteningly different, from what was designed and intended. What we can rationally do is tinker with, extrapolate from and improve the institutions we have inherited, always being alert to the side-effects of our tinkering.

So far, however, from taking this to be a ground for abandoning confidence in the social democratic institutions of the modern western states, I take it as a warning against those grand designs of social engineering espoused by those who think a Hayekian spontaneous order can be created or recreated by simple design and decision. Social justice is a concept which has developed by immanent criticism of inherited institutions and in the light of which we have sought to amend and modify them. In reminding us of the values of liberty and the rule of law we put at risk in pressing too far the claims of social justice, Hayek has done great service; in interpreting him as though it proposed a constructivist rationalist plan for large scale social engineering, the new right has done Hayek's thought a great disservice.

What Hayek really shows is that certain aspects of planning and of state socialism, so far as they postulate perfectibility of planning, are chimerical. The human and social world are not plannable in that way. What he fails to show is that there can be no positive duties of justice — of 'social justice' — among people. As Onora O'Neill argues in her *Faces of Hunger*,[22] one can construct a Kantian kind of argument for extensive transnational positive duties to relieve hunger and starvation. In a different rhetoric one can interpret the right to life as a right not to be left to starve in a world with a food surplus. And there are other 'welfare rights', or duties to attend actively to the welfare of others, for which perfectly sound arguments can be made. An adequate conception of social justice will embrace such rights and duties. There need be nothing either conceptually absurd or practically self-defeating about them. We should not be mesmerised by arguments for either spontaneous order or rule of law into thinking that these qualities are, as Hayek and Oakeshott maintain, incapable of accommodating rights of or duties toward welfare.[23]

---

22   O O'Neill, *Faces of Hunger: an Essay on Poverty, Justice and Development*, George Allen & Unwin, London, 1986, Chapters 6–8; I think one can make more of the concept of a right in such arguments than does Dr O'Neill.

23   This paper was prepared for and presented to a Liberty Fund colloquium in Gleneagles, Scotland, convened by Professor N B Reynolds in July 1986. It has been previously published in (1986) 35 *Jahrbuch des Öffentlichen Rechts der Gegenwart* 1–13.

CHAPTER 5

Law as a Knowledge Process

Suri Ratnapala*

Introduction

Law school philosophers are a quarrelsome bunch. Yet, until recently, they appeared to be united by a common belief, namely, that lawyers deal with real people and real things in a real world. They hold very different views of the way the world and society function. Liberal theorists, for example, think that impersonal rules and negative freedoms emancipate the individual whereas critical legal scholars believe that these notions alienate individuals from society and defeat their genuine aspirations. But, these are differences about what the reality is, not about the presence of reality. In short, law school jurisprudence has been largely untouched by the perennial controversy in philosophy as to whether there is a world outside the mind and if so whether we can have knowledge of it.

I think that lawyers are right in proceeding in this way despite attracting the scorn of many philosophers. If there is no disagreement among most lawyers on this question, what is the point in addressing it? One reason is that it is no longer possible to ignore this question now that the issue of the possibility of objective knowledge and its implications for legal theory have been raised unequivocally by postmodernists in the legal academy. More importantly, it is seen that the re-examination of the epistemological basis of jurisprudence in the wake of the postmodern critique promises rich rewards in the form of the exposure of alternative theoretical approaches within the broader liberal tradition. The aim of this chapter is to discuss the prospects for one such approach.

The postmodernist challenge to traditional jurisprudence is part of a wider assault on disciplines which lay claim to objectivity. The denial of a knowable transcendent world leads postmodernists to treat all knowledge claims (whether they be in literary criticism, history, philosophy, law or

---

*   Senior Lecturer in Law and Deputy Dean, T C Beirne School of Law, University of Queensland.

even the natural sciences) as ethereal and justified by nothing more than rhetoric, convention or the dictate of an epistemic authority. Versions of postmodernism such as deconstruction posit the thesis that law is radically indeterminate, and hence see the liberal ideals of the rule of law, and justice according to law, as unachievable and fraudulent.

In this chapter I concede the impossibility of perfect knowledge but deny that knowledge is therefore purely a matter of personal taste, rhetoric, convention or authority. On the contrary, I espouse a theoretical approach modelled on the basic Darwinian theme of natural selection which, in my view, recentres the whole debate concerning the nature of knowledge in a way which exposes the inadequacy of the postmodern critique. This approach is grounded in evolutionary epistemology developed within philosophy of science by Karl Popper, Donald T Campbell, Konrad Lorenz, Peter Munz et al, and within political economy by F A Hayek. Evolutionary epistemology postulates the thesis that the growth of knowledge in human communities is continuous with biological evolution and is governed in the final analysis by the same process of blind variation and selective retention. Like postmodernist critical theory, evolutionary epistemology affirms the futility of searching for the origins or ultimate foundations of knowledge. However unlike postmodernism, evolutionary epistemology affirms the possibility of knowledge, though never perfect knowledge. It does so by redirecting the inquiry away from the origin of knowledge and towards the processes of the growth of knowledge.

Much of the effort of evolutionary epistemologists has been directed at explaining, in evolutionary terms, the growth of knowledge in the natural sciences and the epistemic status of scientific theories. However, it is evident that if the evolutionary explanation is valid for the growth of scientific knowledge, it should apply, at least presumptively, to other cultural outgrowths such as ethics and law. It will be argued that despite superficial hurdles, the case for extending the blind variation and selective retention model to socio-cultural evolution including legal evolution is compelling. As the leading philosophical proponent of legal evolutionism F A Hayek argues, our inability to command knowledge in the sphere of human actions strengthens the case for recognising and relying upon evolved social rules. Hayek's work is informed by evolutionary epistemology[1] and represents an important advancement of that approach in relation to law and political economy.

The aim of this chapter then is to suggest an alternative approach to the inquiry concerning the nature of law which addresses the fundamental philosophical questions raised by postmodern critical theory. What is proposed is not a fully developed theory of law but a research program within a nascent school of thought. Hence it represents a start rather than a consummation of a philosophical inquiry.

---

1   Hayek's debt to evolutionary epistemologists is clearly acknowledged in the epilogue to his great book *Law, Legislation and Liberty*. See F A Hayek, *Law Legislation and Liberty*, Routledge & Kegan Paul, London, 1982, vols 1–3, vol 3, pp 153–76 and notes.

The ancient problem and its postmodern twist

Lawyers are not alone in thinking that there is a real world out there. Most people go about their lives without questioning the realness of the world that they perceive with the help of their senses and their minds. When I see my neighbour's dog I think that there is a real animated object which is black, furry, four legged and tailed. However, scientists know only too well that the way we see the dog is not the way the dog really is. To begin with, what we sense is mediated by the nature of our sense organs. We live in a world of perception. Although we may have reason to think that the perceptual world is affected by, and hence bears some correspondence to the physical world, the two are very different. As the French mathematician Henri Poincaré put it, even 'perceptual space, under its triple form, visual, tactile and motor, is essentially different from geometric space'.[2] In microbiological terms the dog is a collection of cells with lives of their own. In the world of the particle physicist, it is a collection of interacting quanta. The world of our daily life is very different to the world of the scientist.

Philosophers at least from the time of the Sophists have identified an even deeper problem concerning our belief in a transcendent world.[3] The world of the scientist, though different from the world of the laity, is nonetheless built on perceptions or mental pictures of things which are assumed to exist outside the mind. Hence his or her entire enterprise presupposes the presence of a physical world. However no scientist or philosopher has shown conclusively that the perceptions of our mind have anything to do with an external reality, although no one has established the contrary either.

There are in fact two problems here. Firstly, we cannot show that a world outside the mind exists without using our minds. Every perception of a thing is mediated by the mind. If we get rid of our minds, we cannot perceive anything and hence cannot demonstrate anything. Secondly, even if there are things out there, no one has shown that the perceptions which occur in the mind reflect those things. In other words, no one has seen the bridges which connect things to our minds. As David Hume wrote, 'The mind has never anything present to it but perceptions, and cannot possibly reach any experience of their connexion with objects'.[4]

Philosophers have responded differently to these problems. Some have maintained that there is a real world outside the mind. They are called 'realists'. Some realists think that the mind, in the ultimate analysis, is a physical phenomenon. These are the thoroughgoing materialists, also known as physicalists. On the contrary there are 'idealists' who maintain

---

2   H Poincaré, 'Space and Geometry', in *The World of Physics* (ed J H Weaver), Simon & Schuster, New York, 1987, p 108.

3   Bertrand Russell reports that one of the Sophists, Gorgias, maintained that nothing exists; that if anything exists, it is unknowable; and even if it is knowable, it cannot be communicated from one to another. B Russell, *History of Western Philosophy*, George Allen & Unwin, London, 1961, p 95.

4   D Hume, *An Inquiry Concerning Human Understanding*, Liberal Arts Press, New York, 1955, p 162.

that all we know are products of the mind. Some idealists like Berkeley and Mach have denied the existence of a material world altogether. Berkeley argued that the assertion that sensible objects existed independent of perception amounts to a manifest contradiction. 'What do we perceive,' he asked, 'besides our own ideas or sensations'.[5] Other idealists, notably Immanuel Kant, have theorised that there are two worlds: (1) the world of phenomena which consists of our perceptions and (2) the world of noumena or things in themselves which exist outside our minds. According to Kant, we can only know the phenomenal world. The noumena of the outer world cause sensations in us, but these sensations are ordered by our own mental apparatus into the things which we perceive. Believers in this theory are commonly called phenomenologists.

Idealism raises a fundamental question concerning human knowledge. If all that we know are products of our own minds, is it possible that the objects we perceive are our own creations? It suggests that consciousness is not simply a passive receptacle or, as Locke envisaged, a white paper upon which the external world inscribes itself, but in fact is constitutive. If so, it may be argued, as some postmodernists do, that truth is a matter of the coherence of one's subjective beliefs or, at best, a question of conformity with the conventions of the epistemic community to which one belongs.

It is not hard to see that such a conclusion is completely at odds with the way knowledge is regarded in society. It is generally thought that on most questions there is a right view, or at least, an objectively preferable view. There are frequent disagreements among reasonable persons as to the truth, but there is a general consensus concerning the criteria by which the better view can be determined. Most of us do not doubt the evidence of our senses or question the relevance of logic in resolving disputed questions. In short, we believe in rationality and the possibility of objective knowledge. Postmodernism, on the contrary, represents a revolt against rationality and a rejection of objective reality.

The adage 'knowledge is power' has taken a new meaning in postmodern thinking. In the past, this meant that knowledge was helpful in an instrumental sense. Knowing something which your opponent did not know (eg, the knowledge of the battlefield or of the state of the coffee crop in Brazil) gave you an advantage over him or her. To the postmodernist, the claim of knowledge has a more sinister ring. Since there is no objective knowledge, what passes for knowledge are claims of truth legitimated by convention or by the authority which has power to dictate the criteria by which claims of truth are to be evaluated. What is scientifically true is determined by the norms set by the scientific community and what is legally correct is determined by the modes of reasoning of the legal fraternity. Thus knowledge is seen as a form of power. According to postmodernists, the rational subject while holding essentially subjective views 'constitutes itself as an authorized knower of that world while excluding other forms of subjectivity from having a

---

5   G Berkeley, *A Treatise Concerning the Principles of Human Knowledge*, reprint ed, Open Court, La Salle, 1950, p 31.

similar, representational voice [and] these other forms of subjectivity, for example certain feminist and non-Western types, are invalidated or marginalised to greater or lesser degrees'.[6] Rationality is seen as an indeterminate process involving standards that are 'historically contingent matters of convention, interpretation, or the imposition of power'.[7]

The postmodernist challenge to liberal legality

Postmodernism's denial of the possibility of objectivism undermines all disciplines which claim to be rational. It is not surprising that postmodernism strikes at the heart of the liberal idea of law. Central to liberalism is the idea of law as the guarantor of rights and the demarcator of the provinces of permissible and impermissible actions. It is thought that law, when it holds sway over governmental and private whim, provides the stability of expectations which defines freedom. As Lon Fuller expressed it, law 'rescue(s) man from the blind play of chance and ... put(s) him safely on the road to purposeful and creative activity'. To achieve this end, the law has to be reasonably certain. The citizen should be able to predict with some confidence, the manner in which the legal system will treat his or her claims and complaints.

However, the certainty of the law depends in a large measure on people being able to agree on its meaning. Such consensus is impossible if all knowledge is subjective. The common sense view is that law, whether it consists of inarticulate custom, judicial precedent or express enactment, is objectively ascertainable, as are the facts to which the law is applied. The postmodern thesis that all knowledge is subjective, conventional or dictated by authority radically undermines this notion. We have to make two very important distinctions here between conventional theory and postmodernism.

First, according to mainstream theory, there is a difference between the statement that the *law* is conventional or authoritarian and the statement that *knowledge* is conventional or authoritarian. Traditional jurisprudence readily accepts that law is often a matter of convention (ie, custom) or the result of authoritarian rule (as in the case of the commands of a sovereign). However, lawyers believe that the law, once established, is a matter of objective knowledge. On the contrary, according to postmodernism, nothing is objectively knowable, hence there can be no correct or privileged interpretation of the law. Every statement of knowledge, whether it concerns law or science, is an act of legislation in the most fundamental sense.[8] Second, traditional legal theory admits that there can be equally persuasive alternative interpretations of the law. Indeed, disagreements concerning the law and its applications to particular facts are the very stuff of legal practice.

6   M Poster, 'Why not to read Foucault', (1989) 3(1) *Critical Review* 155 at 159.

7   B H Smith, *Contingencies of Value*, Harvard University Press, Cambridge, Massachusetts, 1988, p 149.

8   See for example, F Lyotard, *The Postmodern Condition: A Report on Knowledge*, University of Minnesota Press, Minneapolis, 1984, p 8.

However, lawyers generally agree on the modes of reasoning that are relevant to the evaluation of legal arguments. They subscribe to the logical method and regard the hard cases as matters of information failure, ie, they attribute such cases to the inadequacy of existing rules or the lack of decisive factual evidence either way. By contrast, the postmodern denial of the possibility of a right answer is radical. The absence of a transcendent reality makes all knowledge necessarily subjective. No amount of information can help us overcome this problem for information itself is subjective. In this context the proclamation of a right view can be justified only in terms of convention or authority.

Does the postmodernist world view exclude altogether the idea of liberal legality? Certainly, Derrida's deconstructionism appears to do so. This is not the place to discuss the Derridean thesis but I have elsewhere argued that it leaves no room for the liberal concept of law.[9] The reason has to do with Derrida's metaphysics (and I use this term advisedly) according to which every case is an unsubsumable singularity and the meanings of texts including those of laws are 'undecideable'.[10] This theory of extreme indeterminacy denies law its claimed attributes of generality and impersonality.

However, while all postmodernists share Derrida's disbelief in the possibility of objective knowledge, not all of them treat knowledge purely as a matter of momentary personal taste. Language game theorists, for example, treat knowledge as something which is legitimated by the conventions of the relevant speech community. According to them, knowledge questions are not 'undecideable'. Indeed, on this question Richard Rorty, a postmodern champion of rhetoric against philosophy accuses Derrida of succumbing 'to nostalgia, to the lure of philosophical system building, and specifically that of constructing yet another transcendental idealism'.[11] According to language game theorists, knowledge, though lacking a transcendent foundation, is not a matter of unbridled subjectivism. These theorists:

> ... try to show that the standards we develop for such matters as justice and truth are the products of specific language games, conventions, shared normative understandings or community practices, due to change when new contingencies arise from whatever source, including pure happenstance.[12]

---

9   S Ratnapala, 'Review Article: *Asking the law question*', (1995) 16(3) *New Zealand Universities Law Review* 326–47.

10 See J Derrida, 'Force of Law: The Mystical Foundation of Authority' in *Deconstruction and the Possibility of Justice* (eds D Cornell, M Rosenfeld and D G Carlson), Routledge, New York, 1992, p 4.

11 R Rorty, *Consequences of Pragmatism*, University of Minnesota Press, Minneapolis, 1982, p 89.

12 A Wolfe, 'Algorithmic Justice' in *Deconstruction and the Possibility of Justice* (eds D Cornell, M Rosenfeld and D G Carlson), Routledge, New York, 1992, p 361. Compare S Fish, *Doing What Comes Naturally*, Duke University Press, Durham, North Carolina, 1989, p 323.

According to language game theory, knowledge is anchored in a contingent 'reality'. However, this 'reality' consists not of unsubsumable singularities, as Derrida alleges, but of understandings that are in harmony with the conventions of the relevant community. As François Lyotard sees it, truth is that which conforms to the 'relevant criteria ... accepted in the social circle of the "knower's" interlocutors'.[13] According to Stanley Fish, this makes the individual a 'situated subject ... who is always constrained by the local or community standards and criteria of which his judgment is an extension'.[14] Language game theory's concession to a relatively stable though contingent form of communal knowledge appears to accommodate the rule of law at least in a limited way. It means that rules can have stable meanings such that they are capable of guiding human action in the context of a given community.

However, even this type of postmodernism seriously destabilises the notion of liberal legality. The definition of the relevant community is always open to dispute. Where the epistemic communities are clearly segregated into culturally homogeneous groups, problems for the rule of law are minimised. However, this is not the situation in most technologically advanced, pluralistic and multicultural societies. Let me illustrate this point with the aid of hypothetical scenarios. Let us assume that there are two groups living their communal lives separately. One group comprises scientists and the other, artists. Let us also assume that the scientists never have a non-scientific outlook (even when they are singing or painting) and that the artists never have a non-artistic attitude (even when they are selling a painting or constructing a monument). Then, what is true according to the conventions of the scientists may not be true according to the conventions of the artists and *vice versa*. But this would not matter as knowledge claims will be valid in the relevant community. Within each community, life would be reasonably predictable.

The trouble is that real life is not like this at all. It is not possible to segregate persons into epistemic compartments in this manner. Individuals are constantly changing roles. A person may be a mathematician during the day and a music lover at night, a producer today and a consumer tomorrow. Moreover, scientists and artists interact all the time with each other as well as with lawyers, philosophers, politicians and paupers. Communal life then has a kaleidoscopic quality defying compartmentalisation except in a very momentary sense. Given these incessant interactions, there can be no rule of law unless there is a common speech community which unites the interacting individuals over a wide range of activities. Without such a common epistemic culture, sub-groups will be talking past each other all the time and the prospects for the emergence of common rules of conduct would be remote. It seems that contrary to views held by Fish et al, language game theories import more subjectivity into human discourse than the rule of law can withstand.

---

13   F Lyotard, 1984, note 8 above, p 19.
14   S Fish, 1989, note 12 above, p 323.

Is there another way?

It seems to me that there is much that is right about the philosophical stance of language game theorists. Indeed, as presently made clear, I share with postmodernists the scepticism that perfect knowledge is, or will ever be, within human grasp. I am also convinced that the knowledge that we profess is substantially grounded in convention. Having said this, I still believe that postmodernists let themselves down by either refusing to examine the nature of convention or by providing facile accounts of it.

Postmodernists who refuse to look behind the conventional basis of knowledge think that it is futile to do so. A search for a foundation results in an infinite regression or ends in the stalemate on the questions whether we can trust the evidence of our senses or whether our thoughts can be taken as referring to anything other than thoughts. Given the futility of this quest, some postmodernists throw up their arms and resign themselves to the practice of rhetoric, with their attitude to knowledge being (to use Lyotard's words): '[the] simple fact [is] that they do what they do'.[15] Rorty, perhaps more than any other, epitomises this attitude. Rorty, who held a Chair of Philosophy, repudiated philosophy, resigned his Chair and wrote a long book on the impossibility of philosophy at the end of which he concluded that truth is the 'normal result of normal discourse'.[16] If philosophers have any useful role, he wrote, it is to maintain 'the conversation of mankind which Plato began'.

Some language game theorists do make an attempt to explain convention and in an ironic twist settle for a form of positivism. According to them, conventions are forms of domination. They represent the views of the powerful. In the ultimate analysis, these postmodernists see knowledge as a case of 'right being might'. In Fish's graphic terms, 'there is always a gun at your head. Sometimes the gun is, in literal fact, a gun; sometimes it is a reason, an assertion whose weight is inseparable from some already assumed purpose'.[17] The bottom line is that 'some interpretive perspective will always rule by virtue of having won out over its competitors'.[18]

Is this all we can usefully say about conventions: that they are inscrutable or that they are crude projections of political power? I think not. Postmodernists have made an invaluable contribution to contemporary thinking by reminding us once again that human knowledge is permanently and irreparably flawed. We live our lives thinking that the world around us is real, whatever 'real' may mean. We may well be right. However, all too often we forget that even if there is a real world out there, our knowledge of it must be severely distorted, not only because of the limitations of our perceptual apparatus, but also because knowledge in a very real sense is a product of culture.

---

15   F Lyotard, 1984, note 8 above, p 23.
16   R Rorty, *Philosophy and the Mirror of Nature*, Princeton University Press, Princeton, 1979, p 377.
17   S Fish, 1989, note 12 above, p 520.
18   R Rorty, 1979, p 10.

Consequently, we lapse into unfortunate states of intellectual complacency. Thankfully, from time to time, we are awoken from this intellectual slumber, by critics such as postmodernists. However, the realisation that our knowledge of the world may be irremediably flawed does not compel us to accept the postmodern thesis. We may be entitled to think that we have a kind of knowledge which, though far from perfect, is neither entirely subjective nor completely authoritarian. Not only do I subscribe to the view that such knowledge is possible, I also think that the phenomenon of law, like much else that is culture, is a manifestation of the process by which such knowledge grows. In what follows I will explain the basis of these views

Getting to first base — acknowledging our universe

The strongest objection, though clearly not the only objection, to any claim of objective knowledge concerns the impossibility of proving the presence of a transcendent reality. If nothing can be shown to exist outside the mind, then it could be said that all knowledge is subjective.

However, there are some serious problems with this argument. Firstly, as Moritz Schlick, the instigator of the Vienna Circle pointed out, 'the denial of the existence of a transcendent external world would be just as much a metaphysical statement as its affirmation'.[19] Secondly, the argument that we can only know mind as opposed to matter presupposes that mind and matter are totally different and independent of one another — a proposition that begs a fundamental question. As Bertrand Russell observed, the one point on which idealists, materialists, and ordinary mortals are in agreement, namely that they know sufficiently what they mean by the words 'mind' and 'matter' to be able to conduct their debate intelligently, is precisely the point as to which they seem to be alike in error.[20] Philosophers such as William James, John Dewey and Russell himself have rejected the distinction between the mental event (sensation) and its object (sense datum) alleging that the distinction can be sustained only on the assumption that there is a 'self' which exists independently of experience as opposed to a 'self' which is constituted by such experiences.[21] It is not possible in this essay to discuss the

19   M Schlick, 'Positivism and Realism' in *Logical Positivism* (ed A J Ayer), Glencoe, Illinois, 1959, p 54. The Vienna Circle, a group of scientists and mathematicians who met regularly in Vienna from 1922 to 1933 to discuss philosophy, are credited with the leadership of the movement which saw the ascendancy of logical positivism in the twentieth century. Besides Schlick, the group included Herbert Feigl, Kurt Gödel, Philipp Frank, Hans Hahn, Karl Menger, Otto Neurath and Friedrich Waismann and Rudolf Carnap.

20   B Russell, *The Analysis of Mind*, George Allen & Unwin, London, 1961, p 10.

21   For an illuminating discussion of this problem see B Russell, 1961, pp 137–56. See also B Russell, *Our Knowledge of the External World*, rev ed, George Allen & Unwin, London, 1926, Lecture III.

differences between the various brands of idealism, realism and hybrid world views. Nor is such a discussion necessary for my thesis.

It seems as though, in an important sense, we cannot be wholly subjective however much we may try. I cannot conjecture the world to suit my whim. I would love to walk on water and fly over hills. Alas, I cannot make these things happen except as momentary imaginings. The point is, even if I happen to be the only person there is and the universe is wholly the product of my mind (as solipsism maintains), I cannot do as I please or change the nature of my imaginary universe. Even if I am dreaming up the world, my capacity to dream appears to be severely restricted by factors which I cannot control at all or over which I have only very limited influence. In short, it appears that the universe of my dreams obeys its own highly complex laws and is not subject to my will. In fact it appears that my dream is dictated to a very great extent by these laws, not the other way around. Many idealists acknowledge this condition. Kant pointed out that we cannot arrange our sensations in any manner we wish. The apparatus of perception is ruled by certain *a priori* conditions.[22] We cannot think of an object without involving space or time or ignore certain *a priori* conceptual categories mandated by logic.[23]

The essential point is that it does not seem to matter a jot whether the universe exists in my mind alone, or exists in the minds of many or exists transcendentally as a reality outside all minds. The 'reality' is that there is a universe which seems to be independent of my mind's momentary wishes, and from which my mind cannot escape. Most importantly, assuming that the universe is my dream, it appears that by getting to know the nature of this dream universe I can actually improve the quality of my dream. I know that I cannot walk through the wall, so I walk around it. The fly who does not have this information spends hours trying to get to the other side. The more I know of the things and processes that occur in my dreams, the better I am able to cope with my dream life and to make use of the opportunities it offers. Or at least it seems so. I may be mistaken, but I cannot think otherwise.

The next step: admitting the impossibility of perfect knowledge

The fact that there is a universe, mental or otherwise, does not mean that we can know it perfectly. Some of the difficulties we encounter in our efforts to know the world were mentioned above under the heading 'The ancient problem and its postmodern twist'. It is worth mentioning two further impediments to knowledge, one concerning the physical world and the other having to do with human action.

---

22   A proposition is *a priori* when it is seen to be valid without physical experience. For example, 2+2=4 appears *a priori* valid even though a child may first learn of it with the aid of marbles.
23   There are 12 such categories.

Even the most optimistic physicists are reconciled to the fact that we can never make absolutely certain predictions concerning physical phenomena. They include those who believe that we are at the threshold of a grand unified theory — a theory of everything which would account for all that happens in the universe. Even if such a theory is found, there are two apparently insurmountable obstacles to perfect prediction. One is the uncertainty principle in quantum theory which postulates that one cannot simultaneously and accurately measure both the position and the momentum of a particle. The more precisely we measure one, the less precisely we measure the other. Hence, at the particle level, all that we can come up with are the probabilities of different outcomes, never certainty. The other is the fact that in any given system, even the slightest change in the initial conditions brings about very exaggerated divergences at a later stage. The mathematical expositions of this aspect of nature, identified under the rubric of chaos theory, point to the fundamentally hazardous nature of predicting events even in a predetermined world. The celebrated 'butterfly effect' is a good illustration of the sort of things that the chaos theorists are talking about.[24] In answering the question 'Is everything determined?', Stephen Hawking, the Lucasian Professor of Mathematics at Cambridge University and a visionary of the grand unified theory states: 'The answer is yes, it is. But it might as well not be, because we can never know what is determined'.[25]

The problems of prediction become even more serious when we consider human affairs. Each individual brain receives countless different *stimuli* every moment of its existence and we cannot possibly monitor all of these. Even if we discover the laws which govern the human mind, scientific prediction of human action seems impossible. Ludwig von Mises observed that 'no scientific method can succeed in determining how definite external events, liable to a description by the methods of the natural sciences, produce within the human mind definite ideas, value judgments and volitions'.[26] In scientific terms, as Hawking reminds us, the problem is that it is just too hard to solve the relevant equations when more than a few particles are involved, and the human brain has a hundred million billion billion particles (10^{26}).[27]

---

24 The physicist Edward Lorenz developed a simple mathematical model which in theory came close to perfectly predicting the world weather pattern. But as Lorenz discovered the problem with the model was that it was sensitive to the slightest change in the initial condition. So sensitive was it that a butterfly flapping its wings in Hong Kong could cause hurricanes in the Gulf of Mexico. For this and other examples of 'chaotic' order, see the introductory work of J Gleick, *Chaos: Making a New Science*, Viking Penguin, New York, 1987.

25 S Hawking, *Black Holes, Baby Universes and other Essays*, Bantam Books, New York, 1994, p 139.

26 L von Mises, *The Ultimate Foundation of Economic Science*, D Van Nostrand, Princeton, 1962, p 82.

27 S Hawking, 1994, note 25 above, p 133.

Realising the hypothetical nature of knowledge

Popper, perhaps more than anyone else, is responsible for the currency of the idea that all synthetic knowledge[28] is hypothetical, hence also refutable. In retrospect, the Popperian thesis is extraordinarily simple. There is no way that we can be *certain* of the validity of any knowledge claim. The statement 'All ravens are black' appears to be true because every raven so far observed has been black. But, as Hume pointed out, it does not mean logically that the next raven will also be black. We can consider the statement verified only when we have observed every raven now living, has ever lived and will live in the future. We can limit our task by pointing out that the statement means: 'All existing ravens are black'. Verification still remains practically impossible and besides, we have drastically reduced the value of the knowledge statement. We can define a raven to exclude any specimen which is not black. Then, we almost end up with a tautology.

This fact does not mean that we cannot have knowledge, or indeed, objective knowledge. It only shows that all knowledge statements of a synthetic kind are hypothetical. It is arguable that analytic statements such as '2 + 2 = 4' are not of this nature. But, analytic knowledge does not, *by itself*, give us an idea of the external world.

Popper argued that the way in which human knowledge grows is best exemplified by the growth of scientific knowledge. Scientific knowledge, he claimed, grows by the process of bold conjectures and vigorous attempts at refutation. Scientific knowledge does not grow by the process of verification or confirmation of theories (for that is impossible) but by the process of falsification of theories.

Popper has many critics. Critics such as Imre Lakatos have engaged in immanent criticism adopting Popper's model of falsification but seeking to refine it. They leave the epistemological core of Popper's theory intact while questioning its sociology. They argue that the real life processes of knowledge growth do not easily fit the Popperian paradigm of 'instant rationality'. They point out that scientists are trying more often than not to confirm their theories, not to falsify them. Besides, most routine experiments are trivial and even when they are not, their importance is often realised in hindsight. Lakatos argues that scientific theories do not stand on their own but are parts of evolving scientific research programs. He sees science as 'a battleground of research programmes rather than of isolated theories'.[29] Moreover, he argues that the dialectic of research programs is not necessarily an alternating series of speculative conjectures and empirical refutations in that order, but that the actual pattern is often a matter of historical accident.[30]

---

28 Synthetic knowledge is negatively defined as knowledge which is not analytic. Analytic knowledge consists of propositions of mathematics or deductive logic. 2+2=4 is an analytic statement whereas 'I have four apples in my bag' or 'Apples grow only on trees' are synthetic statements. In this discussion unless otherwise indicated, knowledge means synthetic knowledge.

29 I Lakatos, 'Methodology of Scientific Research Programmes' in *Criticism and the Growth of Knowledge* (eds I Lakatos and A Musgrave), Cambridge University Press, Cambridge, 1970, p 175.

30 I Lakatos, 1970, p 151.

But, these critics adhere to Popper's insight that knowledge is hypothetical and whilst it cannot be proved, it can be falsified, although they regard the process of theorising and falsification to be more complex than what Popper appears to suggest.[31] In so far as this discussion is concerned, the importance of the falsificationist approach lies in its suggestion that our inability to prove knowledge statements does not mean that knowledge is necessarily or entirely subjective. It proclaims the objectivity of knowledge through its claim that theories (or scientific programs according to Lakatos), though they may be subjectively formulated, are criticisable and stand only so long as they remain unfalsified.

There are other critics, like Thomas Kuhn and Paul Feyerabend who accept the falsificationist approach but deny that contending theories can be compared on a purely rational basis. Their arguments are based on the belief that any new theory which departs from an existing theory to any significant or non-trivial extent would involve a change of world view which makes purely rational comparisons impossible. The main difference between Kuhn and Feyerabend concerns the frequency of the occurrence of non-trivial change in theories. Kuhn thinks that most of the time scientists are engaged in 'normal science' which consists essentially of problem solving within an established theoretical paradigm.[32] However, this activity shows up anomalies in the paradigm. A point is reached when the anomalies are observed to be so serious or so numerous that the paradigm has to be abandoned and a new paradigm adopted. At times like this there is 'revolutionary science'. But according to Kuhn, the very idea of a paradigm shift (*Gestalt*-switch) means that the old criteria of theory evaluation are replaced by a new set. Hence the new paradigm is not only incompatible but also incommensurable with the old. This makes purely rational comparisons impossible.[33]

Kuhn is not very radical; he sees the irrationality as occurring only at revolutionary times. Besides, Kuhn extols 'normal science' as 'mature science'. Its achievements are minuscule but are essential to the development of science.[34] Feyerabend, however, takes the thesis of irrational scientific growth further, alleging that not only paradigms, but theories involve changes in world view, and in the meaning of terms. Hence theories themselves (except the most trivial) are incommensurable and cannot be rationally evaluated.[35] Feyerabend argues, for this reason,

---

31 However, Lakatos thinks that Popper was aware of these complexities and that his falsificationism is more sophisticated than his critics think it is. I Lakatos, 1970, pp 180–4.

32 T Kuhn, *The Structure of Scientific Revolutions*, 2nd ed, Chicago University Press, Chicago, 1970, pp 5–39.

33 T Kuhn, 1970, p 103.

34 T Kuhn, 1970, p 24.

35 P Feyerabend, 'Consolations for the Specialist' in *Criticism and the Growth of Knowledge* (eds I Lakatos and A Musgrave), Cambridge University Press, Cambridge, 1970, pp 219–22.

that knowledge is advanced by a process of anarchic (or Dadaist) theory proliferation achieved by discarding methodological rules.[36]

Kuhn and Feyerabend have been roundly criticised on logical, sociological and normative grounds. Kuhn's linear view of the history of science, ie a period of normal science followed by a *Gestalt*-switch followed by a period of normal science, has been dismissed as unhistorical by critics including Feyerabend.[37] Popper thinks that Kuhn's treatment of non-revolutionary science as 'normal science' is positively dangerous. The 'normal scientist' who does not question his paradigm is a victim of indoctrination, an applied scientist (as opposed to a pure scientist) who is content to use techniques without asking 'why?'.[38] Feyerabend's thesis in turn has been faulted on grounds of logic and unreality by critics such as Achinstein[39] and Suppe. The ultimate problem for both Kuhn and Feyerabend is that of theory selection. Each of them believes in the possibility of scientific progress, but yet does not explain satisfactorily how we can choose one theory as against another.

The debate within the 'growth of knowledge' school of theories is very important but regrettably cannot be explored further in this chapter. However, it appears that the answers to the problems presented by the irrationality theses of Kuhn and Feyerabend may be found in evolutionary epistemology to which Popper provided a crucial stimulus. It is also through the explanatory power of evolutionary epistemology that we can make further progress towards a theory of law as a knowledge process.

Evolutionary epistemology

At the time that Popper advanced his argument that all knowledge is hypothetical and falsifiable, he was not thinking of the way nature worked through blind variation and selective retention. He was principally a philosopher of physics. It was some years later that he began to appreciate the extent to which biology lent support to his general thesis. Like the growth of knowledge, biological evolution proceeds by trial and error, by conjectures and refutations. *More accurately, biological evolution is growth of knowledge.* The emergence of the most primitive life forms and the most sophisticated scientific theories result from the same laws. From amoeba to Einstein, the same process is at work. This realisation led Popper to declare that 'the main task of the

---

36 P Feyerabend, *Against Method: An Outline of an Anarchist Theory of Knowledge*, New Left Books, London, 1975, pp 17–24.

37 P Feyerabend, 1975, pp 207–8. Popper concedes that Kuhn's 'normal science' does occur, but argues that it is not the norm but the exception and that to the extent it occurs, it reflects a dangerously uncritical attitude. K R Popper, 'Normal Science and its Dangers' in *Criticism and the Growth of Knowledge* (eds I Lakatos and A Musgrave), Cambridge University Press, Cambridge, 1970, pp 49–58.

38 K R Popper, 1970, pp 52–3.

39 P Achinstein, *Concepts of Science: A Philosophical Analysis*, Johns Hopkins Press, Baltimore, 1968, pp 3, 96.

theory of knowledge is to understand it as continuous with animal knowledge; and to understand also its discontinuity — if any — from animal knowledge'.[40]

Charles Darwin's theory postulates that species evolve by a process of blind variation and selective retention, a process which Darwin termed 'natural selection'. It is a theory of breathtaking simplicity. The basic proposition is that organisms which are not suited to their environment find it difficult to survive in that environment. Hence, their populations diminish as the numbers who survive to reproduce lessen. Conversely, organisms which are suited to the environment tend to survive to reproductive age in larger numbers. Hence their populations grow. However all is not lost for ill adapted species. Organisms do not reproduce perfect copies of themselves but owing to the influence of the environment and chance, produce offspring which differ from themselves in minor respects. Some of these differences may prove fortuitous in terms of environmental fit and the offspring may survive to reproduce others with the happy qualities. Over time, this process leads to the species adapting to its environment. Thus, we speculate that in jungles, cats with spots proliferated because the camouflage gave them an edge in hunting whereas in the grasslands, cats with tawny hides multiplied for the same reason. According to Darwinian theory the endless variety and complexity of life that we encounter today are explainable by nothing more mysterious than this process of chance variation and natural selection or, to use the more exacting terminology of Campbell, 'blind variation and selective retention'. We just have to remember that this process has been going on for four billion years. Evolutionary epistemologists argue that the very same process is at work in the growth of knowledge at every level.

Campbell and the nested hierarchy of selective retention processes.

Although Popper is regarded as the founder of evolutionary epistemology, the first uncompromising application of evolutionary theory to the problem of knowledge is, perhaps, Campbell's essay 'Evolutionary Epistemology' first published in 1974.[41] Popper described the essay as a 'treatise of prodigious historical learning' with which scarcely anything in modern epistemology (including his own work) could be compared.[42]

---

40   K R Popper, 'Replies to my critics' in *The Philosophy of Karl Popper* (ed P A Schlipp), Open Court, La Salle, 1974, p 1061.

41   D T Campbell, 'Evolutionary Epistemology' in *Philosophy of Karl Popper* (ed P A Schlipp), Open Court, La Salle, 1974, pp 413–63, reproduced in *Evolutionary Epistemology, Rationality and the Sociology of Knowledge* (eds G Radnitzky and W W Bartley III), Open Court, La Salle, 1987, pp 48–89. The references in this chapter will be to the latter book.

42   K R Popper, 'Campbell on the Evolutionary Theory of Knowledge' in G Radnitzky and W W Bartley III (eds), 1987, p 115.

In my view it is Campbell's work which enables us to see most clearly the evolutionary nature of knowledge and the continuity (and essential similarity) between the most elementary adaptive tendencies and the most sophisticated scientific theories and which shows that cultural outgrowths such as law obey the same fundamental principle which caused biological emergence as well as the pre-biotic evolution of the universe.

Campbell's thesis is that 'a blind-variation-and-selective-retention process is fundamental to all inductive achievements, to all genuine increases in knowledge, to all increases in fit of system to environment'.[43] He finds this thesis substantiated at every observed level of knowledge retention, from the non-mnemonic problem solving of unicellular organisms to the activities of scientists.

The story of knowledge could commence at the beginning of time or the big bang and proceed through the expansion of the universe, the formation of the earth by the condensation of interstellar gases some 4.6 billion years ago and the chance emergence of the first self-replicating molecules in the primordial organic soup of the earth's oceans about four billion years ago. But, that is neither feasible within the confines of this chapter nor necessary to explain Campbell's thesis. Instead we could begin with the first unicellular organisms formed by the chance combining of specialised molecules.

Campbell points out that even these unicellular organisms are endowed with hypothetical knowledge although they have no memory. For example, they are able to halt their random movements (blind variation of locomotor action) when a nourishing or non-noxious setting is found.[44] An organism which cannot move may know that the environment changes with time (temporal discontinuity) but one that moves will know that the environment is also spatially discontinuous in terms of the distribution of substances. It 'knows' that changes to its condition are brought about more rapidly when it moves than when it is sedentary.[45] This is the stage of non-mnemonic problem solving.

Campbell proceeds to examine a series of advancing levels of knowledge retention. There is the use of vicarious locomotor devices. The blind man's cane and the ship's radar are devices which lessen the need for wasteful and potentially catastrophic trial and error movement. The active-sonar devices of bats and dolphins are well known examples from the animal kingdom. But Campbell reminds us that contrary to common sense realism, vision itself is just as indirect as radar. He points to the fact that the eye in fact is a kind of multiple photocell device 'which uses the multiplicity of cells instead of the multiplicity of focusings of one cell, resulting in a search process equally blind and open-minded, equally dependent upon a selection-from-variety epistemology'.[46] Like the cane and the radar, vision provides the means of substitute trial and error

---

43 D T Campbell, 1987, note 41 above, p 56.
44 D T Campbell, 1987, p 57.
45 D T Campbell, 1987, p 58.
46 D T Campbell, 1987, p 60.

exploration. Instead of searching the actual physical environment through direct contact, the animal explores the visual representation of it.

Thought represents an astonishing breakthrough in substitute trial and error learning. Instead of physically searching the environment by overt contact or mentally searching the visual representation of it, the animal is able to explore mentally a mnemonic version of it, ie the environment as constructed by memory and previously acquired knowledge.[47] Popper regards the emergence of the mind as the third great miracle after the emergence of animal consciousness and the emergence of life itself.[48] How the mind evolved may only be speculated. Popper suggests that the mind is the result of open behavioural programs encoded in DNA. These differ from closed behavioural programs which dictate animal behaviour in great detail, thus limiting the animal's range of actions. Open programs make choices possible although the propensity for making particular choices may be genetically determined. Popper conjectures that open programs evolved due to the selection pressures of complex and irregularly changing environmental situations.[49] At the rudimentary level, animals who felt pain and fear would withdraw from sources of danger and survive while those who had no such sense would perish. From these beginnings, thinking powers grew as the more discriminating animals were selected by the harsh and unpredictable environment.[50]

Whatever caused its emergence, we know that the mind allows, on a scale previously unachieved, the substitution of imaginary trial and error for actual, wasteful and dangerous trial and error. Instead of submitting to the process of life and death winnowing of organic evolution, the human animal can construct theories and test them. As Popper notes, 'it allows us to *dissociate ourselves* from our own hypotheses, and to look upon them critically ... to let our conjectures, our theories, die in our stead'.[51]   Mind bestowed another incalculable advantage on humans which, in evolutionary terms, represents a quantum leap. It facilitated the development of syntactical language and conceptual thought (which goes hand in hand). These in turn made possible for the first time, non–genetic transmission of knowledge not just within one generation, but more importantly, from one generation to the next. Lorenz, a leader in modern ethology, estimates that conceptual thinking and language accelerated the process of evolution by some powers of ten.[52]

A great deal of knowledge is genetically transmitted. Among social animals there is also cultural transmission in the form of imitation and observational learning. Use of scouts in insect communities and the play

---

47   D T Campbell, 1987, p 62.
48   K R Popper, *The Open Universe*, Rowman and Littlefield, Totowa, New Jersey, 1982, pp 122–3.
49   K R Popper, 'Natural Selection and the Emergence of Mind' in G Radnitzky and W W Bartley III (eds), 1987, note 41 above, pp 152–3.
50   K R Popper, 1988, pp 152–3.
51   K R Popper, 1988, p 152.
52   K Lorenz, *The Foundations of Ethology*, Springer-Verlag, New York, 1981, p 343.

routines of hunting mammals are useful examples. However, the lack of language is a severe hindrance to cultural transmission within and between generations. Imitational learning requires the subject of the lesson to be immediately present, and this is not always the case. As Lorenz observes, 'a jack daw cannot convey to its progeny that cats are dangerous if there is no cat at which to discharge a "rattling attack", nor can a brown rat transmit the knowledge that a certain food is poisonous if it is not there to be urinated upon'.[53]

Language and conceptual thought alleviate this problem. Language can represent, albeit in a generalised way, the environmental hazard as well as the successful response. Thus the capacity to convey ideas and information is increased dramatically leading to exponential growth of knowledge. A child still needs to learn language by trial and error.[54] But once it has language, it gains access to a great store of knowledge which its ancestors have accumulated. The transfer of knowledge within groups and between generations makes possible tradition, culture and the evolution of social structures. At the level of socio-cultural evolution, the selective elimination of whole social organisations is very rare. Although in the past communities have lived in isolation with the risk of total elimination, that is hardly likely in the present era. Today, for the first time, the whole of the human race appears to be culturally linked, thanks to the wonders of modern communications. It is even possible to speak of an overall human culture despite innumerable local variations. Rather than being eliminated, cultures are transformed by means such as impositions by other cultures, by imitation, and by rational self-criticism. The capacities to conceptualise and communicate which facilitated socio-cultural emergence in the first instance help groups to avoid wholesale elimination.

Problems with the natural selection account of cultural evolution

The abundance of anecdotal evidence relating to 'independent invention' of cultural products makes it easy to hypothesise that culture is an evolutionary phenomenon. The independent emergence in isolated societies of headship institutions, family units, laws such as those against homicide and theft, the division of labour and the sanctity of promises strongly suggest a process of selective retention of culture.

However, when we enter the realm of culture, we confront, to use a sporting term, a whole new ball game. No longer are we observing the selective retention and elimination of whole species, but the selective retention and elimination of particular cultural products of only one species, the human, such as organisations, rules, customs and practices.

---

53   K Lorenz, 1981, p 342.
54   As Campbell reminds us language cannot be transmitted directly to the child. It has to learn to associate things with sounds through trial and error. Campbell, 1974, note 41 above, p 69.

Naturally, it is as hazardous to analogise between the biological and cultural forms of evolution as it is to analogise between biological evolution and the pre-biological development of the earth and its life sustaining ecology. However, such analogies among these stages are unnecessary for the acceptance of the blind variation and selective retention model. This model proposes the abstract principles of an evolutionary process which is fundamental to inorganic, organic and cultural forms of evolution and of which they are but instances. Yet, the application of the model to cultural evolution poses certain superficial difficulties which have to be explained away.

For evolution to occur by the process of blind variation and selective retention, three conditions must be met. The first is variation or mutation; one cannot speak of evolution without change. The second is the existence of selection criteria. This is provided by the *relative* stability of the selecting environment. If the environment is patternless and chaotic, there is nothing to select which forms will survive and which forms will not.[55] The third consists of mechanisms for the preservation and propagation of the favoured forms. The first of these conditions, namely variation, is readily observed: no culture remains static, and modern cultures change rapidly. The identification of selective criteria is more problematic.

The main difficulty is that of separating what is being selected from the environment which is making the selection. In biological evolution, the selecting environments such as air, water, forest and desert are more easily differentiated from the species which they select. Although the physical world plays an important part in their selection, a major part of the selective environment of cultural products is culture itself. An individual's behaviour is powerfully influenced by the behaviour of others. As Campbell points out, each person's habits are a part of the environment of the others.[56] Moreover, well entrenched cultural parameters such as taboos, superstitions, religious beliefs and perhaps most importantly in the present age, political and bureaucratic systems may supply powerful selection pressures which to one degree or another may insulate cultural products from exposure to the wider environment in the short term. This situation contradicts the popular perception of evolution as something which occurs solely in consequence of pressures exerted by the outside environment.

A little reflection shows that this is not a real hindrance to the application of the natural selection paradigm. For a start, this situation is not without its analogies in biological evolution. The environment which selects species includes other species. Likewise, the environment which selects cultural products include other cultural products. Again, there are parallels between the vicarious internal selection devices of organisms and certain socio-cultural institutions of human communities. Sense organs

---

55   In a state of absolute chaos, there will be no life forms at all.

56   D T Campbell, 'Variation and Selective Retention in Socio-Cultural Evolution' in *Social Change in Developing Areas: A Reinterpretation of Evolutionary Theory* (eds H R Barringer, G I Blanksten and R W Mack), Schenkman Publishing Co, Cambridge, Massachusetts, 1965, p 33.

such as the eye and taste buds represent features of the environment. We heed what these organs tell us about the outside world.[57] Likewise, some cultural institutions such as representative legislatures, churches, universities and governments serve as mechanisms through which we inform ourselves of and respond to our cultural environment. If these selectors become corrupt or outdated they may insulate cultural products from external selection pressures in the short term with catastrophic consequences in the long run. At a more basic level, habit meshing in cultural evolution mimics organic growth through chance fitting molecules. Habit meshing, the process by which the habits of individuals aggregate or coincide to form customs, results from the proclivity of punishing encounters to extinguish and rewarding encounters to reinforce behavioural tendencies of interacting parties.[58]

It seems that however much we try, we cannot really escape natural selection. 'The most general principle', notes Peter Munz, 'is that the environment always constrains the changes which can and will take place'.[59] This principle is seen in action whether we look at pre-biotic change, biological change or cultural change. The difference is that the environment which edits culture is partly our own creation. The question may be asked, then, whether we cannot determine the direction of cultural evolution by engineering this environment? A great deal of 'social' legislation enacted by the modern state attempts to do just this: to change the course of social and cultural evolution through the coercive authority of law. The answer to this question is that we can certainly change the course of cultural evolution by deliberately interfering with the environment, but we can never be certain of producing the results which we desire.

Why we cannot redesign complex (self-organising) orders

It seems beyond doubt that the belief that we can legislate the course of cultural evolution owes much to our successes in science and technology. In those fields we have been able to advance hypotheses and test them in relatively controlled conditions. We have achieved through these means feats that our recent ancestors would have found astonishing if not unbelievable. We have built cities, made immense progress in curing the sick, developed extraordinary forms of communications, landed people on the moon, sent spacecraft beyond our solar system and intervened in the biological world to produce the miracles of modern agriculture and genetic engineering. It is easy to overlook the fact that even in this sphere, the selective elimination process is at work. Scientific theories are able to be falsified by the environment. This falsification process is intensified by the culture of criticism and competition within the scientific community itself.

---

57   D T Campbell, 1965, p 33.
58   D T Campbell, 1965, pp 32–3.
59   P Munz, *Our Knowledge of the Growth of Knowledge: Popper or Wittgenstein?*, Routledge & Kegan Paul, London, 1985, p 280.

Unfortunately, in the social sciences the selective elimination model is rarely applied. Instead, the dominant tendency is to treat all cultural institutions, especially the law, as feats of deliberate social engineering. In organic evolution, complexity of life forms is considered as evidence *against* design theory. In relation to culture, complexity is seen as evidence *of* design. This paradox is noted by Hayek who reminds us that 'it is because it was not dependent on organisation but grew up as a spontaneous order that the structure of modern society has attained that degree of complexity which it possesses and which far exceeds any that could have been achieved by deliberate organization'.[60] Hayek, more than any other thinker, has been responsible for exposing the inadequacy of the design concept of culture. In his monumental work, *Law, Legislation and Liberty*, Hayek advances two major arguments against design theories of culture.

Reason is not antecedent to culture

The belief that cultural institutions including customary law were constructed by human minds presupposes the prior existence of reason capable of generating such designs. From the evolutionary perspective, this does not appear to be possible. It is true that the human brain probably reached more or less its present form before the explosive spiral of cultural evolution. However, it also appears that the brain remained in that condition for a very long time before the cultural explosion occurred. Moreover, it is reasonably speculated that some of the later development of the brain resulted from selection pressures exerted by culture. Hemispheric specialisation, for instance, may have developed in response to the 'unique demands made by language and ... tool construction and usage'.[61]

Reason which fundamentally is the ability to classify and discriminate is found to some extent in all animals. In its rudimentary form it is the result of the selection pressures generated by the physical environment. Its development accelerates as culture emerges among groups of social animals, particularly the hominid ancestors of the *homo sapiens*. But, the explosive spiral occurs only with such breakthroughs as the emergence of language. In fact it is quite clear that higher conceptual thought is impossible without language, yet few today would regard language as an invention.[62] It is true that there would be no culture without the products of the mind. Equally, the mind could not have achieved its present state without the selection pressures of culture. Culture created the challenges and niches which enabled the mind to develop at a much faster rate than the organic evolution of the brain permitted. As Hayek emphasises, mind

---

60   F A Hayek , 1982, note 1 above, vol 1, p 50.
61   K R Popper and J C Eccles, *The Self and its Brain*, Springer-Verlag, Berlin, 1977, p 353.
62   Dawkins uses the Pacific islands as a laboratory to demonstrate the evolutionary nature of language. See his discussion in R Dawkins, *The Blind Watchmaker*, Penguin, London, 1991, pp 217–18.

and culture developed concurrently and not successively.[63] To give a poignant illustration, in the middle of the sixth century BC, Pythagoras was probably the only being on the planet who knew the times table and he dreamed of the day when all humans would know it. At the end of the twentieth century AD, his dream remains unrealised. Although millions of persons have learnt the table, many minds are incapable of grasping it. Mind is still catching up with culture.

The synoptic delusion

There are many things which humans design with great success. We design cities, road systems, and incredibly efficient machinery. We design organisations such as armies, football clubs, trading corporations, universities and government departments. Our success in these fields makes us think that we can also design with equal success things such as moral systems, legal systems and economic systems. Hayek calls this attitude of identifying all successful institutions with design as constructivist rationalism.[64] He sees in this association a fundamental error — the failure to appreciate the critical difference between made orders or organisations (*taxeis*) and grown or spontaneous orders (*cosmoi*).

We can design an organisation such as an army or a trading corporation because we know its purpose, we possess much information relevant to the achievement of that purpose and we can control the components of the organisation, including the personnel and technology. There are other systems such as language and the overall society itself, in respect of which we have neither necessary knowledge nor the capacity of control because they are fundamentally different to organisations. Language has no identifiable purpose. One could say that communication is the purpose but it is too broad to be helpful in designing a language. Similarly customary law had no purpose. It may be speculated, for example, that the institution of the promise (contract) resulted from a coincidence of behaviour and became entrenched as individuals realised its utility for the pursuit of countless disparate aims.

Consequently it is quite impossible to determine the exact form and development of a language or a social order by controlling its elements. Many rulers have attempted this but none have succeeded. We know that even in the most totalitarian socialist societies, informal economies and legal systems subsisted beneath the command systems. This is not to say that a spontaneous order cannot be coercively interfered with. In fact spontaneous cultural orders are subject to incessant interference by governments, individuals and groups. The point though is that despite these interferences the order will retain its spontaneous character. The intrusions may affect the development of the order, but we cannot actually determine its course and secure the results we desire. To appreciate this argument it is necessary to have some idea of the phenomenon of self-organising (or as Hayek calls them, spontaneous ordering) systems.

---

63   F A Hayek , 1982, note 1 above, vol 3, p 156.
64   F A Hayek, 1982, note 1 above, vol 3, pp 8–9.

No serious thinker today doubts the existence of self-organising systems. They occur at certain levels of complexity. To consider an example from nature, given certain conditions of complexity, a self-maintaining rain forest ecosystem may be established. Thanks to environmentalists, it is acknowledged today that interference in such an ecosystem can damage its viability. But, not many people (including environmentalists) seem to recognise that society itself is a self-ordering system in whose operations we can intervene only in a limited way without undermining its efficacy. The reason is that the elements which make up the social order are far too many and their interactions far too complex to let us control the order by regulating its elements. As Hayek explains:

> The reason why such isolated commands requiring specific actions by members of the spontaneous order can never improve but must disrupt that order is that they will refer to a part of a system of interdependent actions determined by information and guided by purposes known only to the several acting persons but not to the directing authority. The spontaneous order arises from each element balancing all the various factors operating on it and by adjusting all its various actions to each other, a balance which will be destroyed if some of the actions are determined by another agency on the basis of different knowledge and in the service of different ends.[65]

Our understanding of complex orders has been augmented from an unexpected quarter, namely, the work of multi-skilled researchers investigating questions concerning the origin of life and the possibility of artificial life. It became quickly evident to these scientists that complex biological systems cannot be understood by mapping out their detailed circuitry. As Stuart Kauffman, philosopher of mind and microbiologist, put it, '... it's very hard to figure out what five things hooked to one another will do. And nobody knows how to think about the behaviour of systems with 100,000 variables acting on each other'.[66] Kauffman hypothesised that these systems were not dependent on micro-designed circuit plans but on self-organising principles which produce order out of chaotic permutations. He used a Boolean network[67] generated out of a Fortran program to test this hypothesis and produced a form of self-organisation (a looping cycle or periodic attractor) after just 14 permutations of the network![68] It became evident that complex systems were produced by 'a bottom-up process'. 'No central plan existed to clear up the confusion, but the accumulation of local actions forced the entire

---

65 F A Hayek, 1982, note 1 above, vol 3, p 51.
66 Kauffman is quoted in S Levy, *Artificial Life: the Quest for a New Creation*, Penguin, London, 1993, p 126. Kauffman's comment was made in relation to the phenomenon of gene switching involved in the process of cell differentiation in animals.
67 A network employing the logical system devised by nineteenth century philosopher George Boole whom Kauffman read at Dartmouth. Levy, 1993, p 125.
68 Levy, 1993, p 130.

system into an emergent behaviour that was not at all predictable from the initial conditions'.[69]

The lesson of this experiment was precisely that which Hayek propounded in his critique of constructivist rationalism, namely, that we cannot improve a self-organising or spontaneous order by specific commands directed at its elements but only by discovering and where necessary 'revising the general rules on which it rests'.[70] With respect to social order, these general rules are the rules of just conduct whose spontaneous emergence brought about the state of orderliness which we call society. We can improve this law while retaining its abstract character but not by changing it to achieve particular results.[71]

Law as a knowledge process

From the evolutionary perspective, we have no reason to despair of our inability to redesign the social order by interfering with its laws. We cannot redesign society because we cannot map out its circuitry. There are just too many elements which react in unpredictable ways. As Hayek points out, 'each member of society can have only a small fraction of the knowledge possessed by all ... and each is therefore ignorant of most of the facts on which the working of society rests'.[72] However, it is this ignorance which caused many social institutions to take the form they actually have.[73] Just as Kauffman found out with his Boolean network, local actions among human actors pursuing their disparate ends produce regularities or patterns of behaviour. Not all of these patterns survive the selection pressures exerted by the physical and cultural environment but those that do form the laws which generate and sustain the social order. They represent adaptations of the social order to its environment and embody knowledge of the environment which no one mind can possess.

Thus, by recognising the social order as a spontaneous system and by observing its selectively retained laws, human beings extend their knowledge far beyond their individual capacities. This is the foundation of culture. To borrow once more Hayek's felicitous language, 'it is the utilization of much more knowledge than anyone can possess, and therefore the fact that each moves within a coherent structure most of whose determinants are unknown to him, that constitutes the distinctive feature of all advanced civilizations'.[74]

69   Levy, 1993, p 127.
70   F A Hayek, 1982, note 1 above, vol 3, p 51.
71   F A Hayek, 1982, note 1 above, vol 3, pp 88, 89.
72   F A Hayek, 1982, note 1 above, vol 3, p 14.
73   F A Hayek, 1982, note 1 above, vol 3, p 13.
74   F A Hayek, 1982, note 1 above, vol 3, p 14.

The role of legislation in the growth of knowledge

The reader could not have failed to notice that in this discussion, the word 'law' has been used in the broadest possible sense. It has been used to refer to rules upon which social order depends, whether or not they have been recognised as law by the competent authorities. These are rules which have performed their social function before they are applied by authorities and rules which continue to perform this function even if they are never officially recognised. Extreme positivism denies the name 'law' to rules in this wider sense. I say 'extreme' because positivists like H L A Hart would have to be excluded. Hart argues that primary rules of obligation may exist even where there are no rules of recognition which enable them to be authoritatively declared, created, modified or repealed.[75] Admittedly, it is of utmost importance in a legal system to be able to identify formal criteria of validity which helps us predict whether a court would accord legal force to a given rule. In other words, we must be able to tell the lawyer's law from the philosopher's and the sociologist's law. However, the epistemological significance of law cannot be fully appreciated by looking only at lawyer's law which represents only a fraction of the rules which guide actions and hence determine the abstract features of the social order.

The grown law is often, to one extent or another, codified or judicially formalised. However, the changing natural and cultural environment cause adjustments leading to new regularities of behaviour upon which members base their expectations. Some of these changes are caused by legislation which rescind or otherwise interfere with the grown law. The new regularities and the altered expectations they generate often invite more legislative interventions. Thus, even in the age of legislation, laws in the broader sense continue to grow. In 'civil law' systems, the absorption of social rules into the formal legal order takes place primarily through the legislative process with the judges playing a secondary role. In the common law countries, the courts continue to perform their traditional function of articulating the law as it emerges endogenously.

It is evident, therefore, that legislation or deliberately made law is very much a part of the cultural environment which selects the social rules that constitute law in the primary sense. We shall also notice presently that a certain type of legislation, namely, that which consists of general rules of conduct, constitute a direct source of law in the primary sense. From the point of view of evolutionary epistemology, these rules represent hypothetical knowledge about our world. These hypotheses are not static but continue to be edited by the ever changing environment.

The fact that the social order is a dynamic self-ordering system does not mean that societies have no need for deliberate law–making. In fact, if we reject recourse to legislation, we deprive ourselves of one of the great advantages of being *homo sapiens*. The need for legislation may be explained by focusing on two facts about evolution which are very easily forgotten.

---

75   H L A Hart, *The Concept of Law*, Clarendon Press, Oxford, 1961, pp 44–7, 89, 208.

Present entities represent adaptations to past environment

It is often overlooked that evolutionary adaptations are always adaptations to past environments.[76] The present environment provides the selection pressures and the niches which determine which of the present entities will survive into the future. The present entities themselves are survivors of the past environment. Vestigial organs of animals are biological reminders of this fact. Decaying social institutions such as the caste system and feudal land tenure provide sociological illustrations. While the present environment remains substantially similar to the past, no great problems are encountered. However, sudden and substantial changes can be catastrophic for animals who cannot change their ways quickly. Here the *homo sapiens* have a distinct advantage. Whereas other species can only change behaviour through random variation and selective retention over many generations, humankind can bring about immediate behavioural changes, by the articulation and dissemination of new rules. In the common law paradigm, rules emerge in the course of time when doubts about new (adaptive) practices arise in the form of disputes. However, where there is a need to enact a rule immediately, the legislative option is available.

Surviving biological and cultural entities as imperfect sources of environmental information

In biological evolution, the environment eliminates organisms which are incompatible with it. It does not follow that every species that survives is perfectly or even well adapted to its environment. This is because a given environment may tolerate a variety of life forms and allow a large margin for error. It is often forgotten that the process of evolutionary change is essentially random. It throws up many changes, some of which may be beneficial and some immediately catastrophic. Others may be dysfunctional but not fatally so. Besides, there may be a substantial time lag before the environment takes its toll on the maladapted species. Hence, as Munz points out, 'each organism only encodes a sketchy description of its own environment'.[77]

In cultural evolution, the knowledge represented by cultural products can be even more deceptive. The emergence of mind and language makes fiction possible. Lower forms of animals cannot lie though some can engage in forms of deception particularly when hunting, courting or avoiding predators. However, humans with their mental and verbal skills can create entire systems of artificial knowledge and insulate them from criticism. Societies ruled by superstition, witchcraft, magic and the like are the paradigmatic examples. These primitive cosmologies may have

---

76   D T Campbell, 'Downward causation in hierarchically organised biological systems' in *Studies in the Philosophy of Biology: Reduction and Related Problems* (eds F J Ayala and T Dobzhansky), Macmillan, London, 1974, p 185.

77   P Munz, 1985, note 59 above, p 281.

had survival value, for example, by improving the cohesion of small bands struggling for survival against great odds. However, as they lose this value they become vestigial and hindrances to progress.

In the case of the lower animals false theories embodied in habits may constitute maladaptations to environment which are eliminated only by the process of life and death winnowing. In the case of the intelligent human beings, practices built on false theories can be criticised, refuted and replaced by new rules of conduct. Animal species are often extinguished because they cannot adjust their genetically dictated customs to ecological changes. Human communities can and do abandon or modify custom before they perish with them. Legislation is the means by which such changes can be effected. The incremental modification of custom by common law adjudication for the most part recognises evolutionary changes that have already occurred in the community, hence represents an integral part of the process by which the spontaneous social order grows.[78] The courts do not have the general legislative authority to reverse, radically change or rescind grown law, although they appear to do just that from time to time.[79] Thus, when the evolutionary legal process is seen to be taking us in undesirable directions, legislation is the only practical solution.

Limits of legislation

The incorrigible self-organising character of the social order places its own limitations on what we can usefully achieve by legislation. These limitations are also implied by the concept of law as a knowledge process.

The basic limitation, entailed by the principle of self-organisation and the theory of knowledge growth espoused in this chapter, is represented by the requirement of generality. As Hayek so brilliantly demonstrated, laws directed at the achievement of particular ends (*thesei*), though appropriate to organisations whose purposes are known, have no place in a spontaneous order. It is easy to illustrate this point. If the legislature in a common law country decides to abrogate the requirement of consideration for the validity of contracts (as many legislatures have done), members of that community will have no difficulty in reordering their affairs to suit the new rule, for they will have a rule which would guide their action — the new rule which displaced the old. If on the other hand the legislature grants a court or other authority the power to vitiate contracts at its unfettered discretion, or even according to subjective notions of justice, equity or good conscience, the citizens' ability to predict the manner in which the relevant officials will treat their contracts is drastically weakened. In this situation, the resulting order of actions in

---

78 See S Ratnapala, 'The *Trident Case* and the Evolutionary Theory of F A Hayek', (1993) 13(2) *Oxford Journal of Legal Studies* 201 at 213.

79 See with respect to the High Court of Australia, G A Moens, 'Mabo and political policy-making by the High Court' in *Mabo: A Judicial Revolution* (eds M A Stephenson and S Ratnapala), University of Queensland Press, St Lucia, 1993, pp 48–62.

the community will be uncertain as it will depend on what social practices, *if any*, emerge as individuals seek to cope with the capriciousness of official decisions. It must be mentioned that courts usually respond admirably to the grant of arbitrary power by quickly developing principles which would govern the exercise of their discretions. The Chancery Court's development of the principles of equity from the exercise of what was essentially an open-ended discretion is, perhaps, the classic example. However, when such discretions are given to non-judicial functionaries there is little prospect of any rules emerging from their decisions.

The generality principle promotes the growth of knowledge in two ways. Firstly, a general rule serves as a theory of the environment which can be examined, criticised and refuted. On the contrary, patternless interventions in the affairs of individuals (which legislation often authorises) do not generate testable theories. Secondly, general rules, being less intrusive and more predictable than *ad hoc* projections of authority promote the free play of elements of the spontaneous order which contributes to adaptive efficiency. On the contrary, legislation which increases the arbitrariness of administration unsettles expectations and impedes the free play of elements. Democracy and hard won basic freedoms give us a unique opportunity to combat those forces which impede the free play of the spontaneous order. The abolition of slavery, the grant of universal adult franchise and the elimination of many forms of discrimination including those based on race, religion and sex have made crucial contributions towards this end. More recently, legislatures have resorted to social engineering of a different type which, by undermining the generality of law and increasing the arbitrariness of government, tend to restrain this free play of the elements.

There is much that we may do to improve the social order through the enactment of general laws. However, there are further limits to what we can achieve. The first problem of social reform is the difficulty of applying experimental methodology to the world of human action. Since an experimental laboratory cannot be established to test theories of human action, every experiment must have actual impact on actual people. If our theories are wrong, some persons *must* suffer. One may disregard this problem on the ground that the alternative of inaction is unacceptable. Then we encounter the next problem, that of testing the correctness of the theory.

Whether one takes a confirmationist approach or adopts the falsificationist method, one has to formulate a testable hypothesis, determine the initial conditions and minimise the perturbations which can affect the outcome. Without achieving these, we cannot identify a confirming or falsifying instance. In relation to human action, the initial conditions are too numerous to identify. Some of them (such as the state of information and tastes and preferences of individuals which are highly relevant in economic theories) cannot be independently verified and they change continually. As von Mises put it, 'in the sphere of human action there are no constant relations between any factors'.[80] Hence, complex structures of human interaction cannot be explained by nomothetic or simple causal theories.[81] This does not mean that some problems of the social order cannot be identified and addressed; it means, however, that we are severely limited in our capacity to engineer social change in the sense of producing specific outcomes according to a design.

Conclusion

Postmodern critical theory has made an important contribution to jurisprudence by reviving in legal context the ancient debate concerning the possibility of objective knowledge. However, in their attempts to demonstrate that all knowledge is subjective and has no source but convention or authority, postmodernists show a profound innocence of much that has occurred in the philosophy of science.

In the final analysis, postmodernists share with the many rationalists they criticise a preoccupation with the search for the foundation of knowledge. Failing to find an origin of knowledge, they conclude that all knowledge is subjective.[82] The evolutionary alternative also proceeds on the understanding that the quest for a foundation is futile. It maintains that all knowledge is dependent on theory, and provisional. However, evolutionary epistemology does not treat knowledge as arbitrary preference, but as theories which are liable to falsification by the environment either naturally or through the deliberate endeavours of human beings to refute them. Such knowledge is considered both normal and useful. Evolutionary epistemologists do not deny that knowledge is often conventional and culturally mediated. However, unlike postmodernists, they examine the cognitive significance of culture and convention and find them to be dynamic processes critical to the growth of knowledge.

In evolutionary epistemological terms, laws in the sense of rules of conduct constitute theories about our environment. These theories are often proposed by legislators in the form of deliberate enactments. However, the self-ordering nature of large societies severely limits the scope for successful social engineering. Yet the understanding of the dynamics of self-ordering structures enables us to extend our knowledge by reliance on the spontaneously grown rules of such orders which, as previously shown, represent adaptations to an environment of countless local actions.[83]

One of the principal objections to the evolutionary approach is that it has no normative content. Evolutionary theory does not assert that what survives is always good, only that what survives fits, or at least is not incompatible with, its ecology. However, the suggestion that the

---

80   L von Mises, 1962, note 26 above, p 62.
81   F A Hayek, *The Fatal Conceit*, University of Chicago Press, Chicago, 1989, p 148.
82   Compare P Munz, 'Philosophy and the mirror of Rorty' in G Radnitzky and W W Bartley III (eds), 1987, note 41 above, pp 370–1.
83   See pp 103–4 of this text.

evolutionary process need not be respected owing to its amoral nature is flawed in at least two respects. First, if evolutionary theory is correct, then the moral standards which we seek to uphold are themselves evolutionary products. If we accept evolutionary theory, we may speculate that social species were naturally selected and that communities which learned to cooperate, to respect basic rights and to engage in charity were selected over those that did not. Hence the argument involves begging the question.

Second, if evolutionary theory is correct, the evolutionary process is inexorable though the outcomes it produces are not predetermined. Since the outcomes are not predetermined, we may influence them. By understanding the process of evolution and the limitations which it places upon us, we may be able to promote more successfully the survival of the things that matter to us, including our moral values.

CHAPTER 6

Law as a Voluntary Enterprise
Francesco Parisi*

Ronald H Coase's celebrated theorem asserts that, with respect to the allocation or distribution of limited resources, individuals can be expected to bargain from any initial endowment of legal entitlements towards a position of optimal equilibrium.[1] Hence, in such a situation, the applicable legal rule would not matter. This expectation will, however, only be fulfilled if information and negotiation costs do not exceed the benefits that individuals hope to obtain from their involvement in potential exchanges. If, however, the costs of information and negotiation are greater than the benefits of the potential exchanges, the Coase theorem implies instead that the choice of legal rules is capable of affecting the final economic outcome, ie depending on the rule, there will or will not be an improvement in economic efficiency. Hence, the choice of legal rules becomes critical to the achievement of efficiency.

Coase's theorem contains an obvious stochastic component in as much as it is possible to introduce an element of statistical relativity into its analysis. Even where transaction costs are high, re-allocations that pursue benefits in excess of such costs will still be carried on. If there is a distribution of transaction costs for each category of situations, the Coase theorem can be restated in stochastic terms. It would then assert that, for any initial assignment of rights, only that part of the population that faces costs higher than the potential benefit of the transaction will be deterred from entering into a mutually beneficial exchange of entitlements.

---

*   Associate Professor of Law, George Mason University. The support of the Sarah Scaife Foundation and of the John M Olin Foundation is gratefully acknowledged, as are the helpful comments of Frank H Buckley, Jonathan C Harris, Ronald A Heiner, Charles K Rowley, Maxwell L Stearns, and Viktor J Vanberg. William D Loeffler provided valuable editorial and research assistance.
1   R H Coase, 'The Problem of Social Cost', (1960) 3 *Journal of Law & Economics* 1.

In light of this restatement, this chapter develops a corollary to Coase's theorem assessing its normative significance in the adjudication of social norms. The normative Coase theorem maintains that, in the presence of positive transaction costs, the efficiency of the final allocation is dependent on the choice of the legal rule, and that the desirable initial assignment of rights is that which minimises the effects of such transaction costs. It is the law-makers' task to select those legal rules which will give this result.[2] The literature on the issue, however, fails to point out that, in pursuing this formidable task, courts and legislators can benefit from observing those situations falling below the threshold of transaction-impeding costs. The point calls for a greater appreciation of spontaneous social arrangements, and for a rediscovery of customary norms as primary sources of law.[3]

The first section of this chapter discusses the formal role played by customary rules as spontaneous sources of legal order. I will discuss both the formative elements of customary rules and their legal effects, with reference to modern domestic and international legal systems. The second section analyses the dynamic structure of customary rules. Different categories of typical social interaction will be examined and with the aid of game-theoretic and evolutionary models, I will define a structural paradigm that could assist courts in the appraisal and enforcement of spontaneous social norms.[4] At that point, I shall revisit the normative foundations of customary law with the aid of evolutionary and game-theoretic tools, with the intent to shed new light on this often neglected source of legal order. It is argued that, in recognising customary rules, courts should pay particular attention to the incentive structure of the originating social environment.

---

2 See eg, A M Polinsky, *An Introduction to Law and Economics*, 2nd ed, Little, Brown and Co, Boston, 1989, p 14.

3 In a similar context, R C Ellickson, *Order Without Law: How Neighbors Settle Disputes*, Harvard University Press, Cambridge, Massachusetts, 1991, p 286, has observed that 'lawmakers who are unappreciative of the social conditions that foster informal cooperation are likely to create a world in which there is both more law and less order'.

4 Game theory is a theory of rational choice which uses hypothetical game scenarios to identify each player's optimal actions in the face of similar actions by other players. The theory aims thereby to understand the common inner structure of all games. Game theory thus provides a rigorous framework for the analysis of problems of strategic behaviour where one individual's actions depend on what other individuals may do. Early in the 1930s the possibility of strategic interaction among individual actors raised difficult and seemingly insoluble problems for economic analysis. The appearance of J von Neuman and O Morgenstern's *The Theory of Games and Economic Behaviour*, Wiley, New York, 1944, provided a point of departure for a number of studies that attempted to confront classical economic problems with the more plausible assumptions of strategic interaction. By the 1970s game theory reached high levels of sophistication, adding mathematical complexity to the more intuitive theorems of the early literature.

Customary rules as a source of law

Nineteenth and twentieth century jurisprudence has attributed residual importance to customary law, often dismissing it as an archaic source of law. In the positivist approach to the issue, the underlying conviction was that spontaneous social forces were institutionally insufficient to create rational rules. The original pre-eminence of customary law therefore had to give way to centralised law-making as the modern state evolved.[5]

In a related development, modern legal realism has largely discredited the older declaratory theory that judges are simply 'law-finders'. The modern view is that courts make law in light of public policy. Accordingly, attention has recently shifted to the incentive structure of common law adjudication.[6]

In an attempt to demonstrate the efficiency of common law, recent studies have focused on litigation models and judges' incentives. Although successful in a number of aspects, these analyses generally overlooked the critical interaction between enacted law and spontaneous social norms.[7] In this chapter, I aim to remedy some of these omissions by considering

---

5   J W Salmond, *Jurisprudence*, 12th ed, Sweet & Maxwell, London, 1966, pp 189–212; M A Eisenberg, *The Nature of the Common Law*, Harvard University Press, Cambridge, Massachusetts, 1980, pp 29–42. For a similar claim regarding international law, see K Wolfke, *Custom In Present International Law*, 2nd ed, Kluwer Academic Publishers, Netherlands, 1993, p xiii. In this respect, it should be noted that, despite the increase in treaty formation during the past century, much treaty interpretation and implementation unavoidably relies on norms of spontaneous compliance based on the practices of the nations.

6   See eg R A Posner, *Economic Analysis of Law*, 4th ed, Little, Brown and Co, Boston, 1992, pp 519–48; P Rubin, 'Why is the Common Law Efficient?', (1977) 6 *Journal of Legal Studies* 51; G L Priest, 'The Common Law Process and the Selection of Efficient Rules', (1977) 6 *Journal of Legal Studies* 65; J Hirshleifer, 'Evolutionary Models in Economics and Law', (1982) 4 *Research in Law and Economics* 167; I Ehrlich and R A Posner, 'An Economic Analysis of Legal Rulemaking', (1974) 3 *Journal of Legal Studies* 257; W M Landes and R A Posner, 'Legal Precedent: A Theoretical and Empirical Analysis', (1976) 19 *Journal of Law and Economics* 249; and B H Kobayashi and J R Lott Jr, *Judicial Reputation and the Efficiency of the Common Law*, manuscript, 1993.

7   This shortcoming has already been criticised by R D Cooter, 'Structural Adjudication and the New Law Merchant: A Model of Decentralized Law', (1994) 14 *International Review of Law & Economics* 215. Much work has been done, however, in the analysis of the evolution of commercial law. See eg B L Benson, 'Legal Evolution in Primitive Societies', (1988) 144 *Journal of Institutional and Theoretical Economics* 772–88; B L Benson, 'The Spontaneous Evolution of Commercial Law', (1989) 55 *Southern Economic Journal* 644–61; B L Benson, *The Enterprise of Law: Justice Without the State,* Pacific Research Institute, San Francisco, 1990; B L Benson, 'Why Did Lawyers Demand Passage of Arbitration Statutes?', in *Florida State University Working Paper* No 91–03–8; H J Berman and F J Dasser, 'The New Law Merchant and the Old: Sources, Content, and Legitimacy', in *Lex Mercatoria and Arbitration: A Discussion of the New Law Merchant* (ed T E Carbonneau), Transnational Juris Publications, Dobbs Ferry, New York, 1990; and L E Trakman, *The Law Merchant: The Evolution of Commercial Law*, Fred B. Rotham & Co, Littleton, Colorado, 1983.

the economic and normative foundations of customary law. This task calls for a rediscovery of the original understanding of the common law as 'the rule acknowledged by all parties as applicable'.[8]

The forgotten idea of common law as common wisdom

The intellectual foundations of private ordering systems of law are built on the idea that any social arrangement voluntarily entered into by rationally self-interested parties is in the beneficial interest of society at large.[9] This belief in the harmony of individual interests has long been challenged by welfare economists. Similarly, positivist jurisprudence has argued that private social arrangements often have harmful effects on third parties, and that legal intervention is, therefore, consistent with economic theory. As a result, the idea of law as a voluntary process is regarded sceptically and much modern legislation purposefully interferes with spontaneous social arrangements. The following analysis discusses the economic basis of this debate, articulating the necessary conditions for the emergence of optimal customary rules.

Voluntary exchanges tend to maximise the welfare of individuals. Attention should therefore be paid to all decentralised social forces that contribute to the general equilibrium. Further, whenever the conditions for the emergence of optimal spontaneous law are met, centralised law-making processes should give way to decentralised and spontaneous law.[10]

Without intending to endorse all existing customary norms, this approach challenges the positivist and Hobbesian beliefs that no order can emerge without deliberately created law. Even where market failure and high transaction costs seem to justify the work of interventionist legislators, spontaneous social arrangements still survive and may indeed reclaim some territory from formal legislation.

The concept of spontaneous order is certainly at odds with the whole theoretical framework of central planning, thus, by its very existence, challenging the positivist belief that rules must come from some higher legislative or judicial body in order to constitute 'proper law'.[11] This point

---

8   F Pollock, *First Book of Jurisprudence*, 6th ed, Macmillan, London, 1929, p 254.

9   G Tullock, *Private Wants Public Means — An Economic Analysis of the Desirable Scope of Government*, University Press of America, Lanham, Maryland, 1987, observes that, if we see 'someone doing something, we believe that it is something that he wants to do and will improve his well-being'. This form of normative individualism further assumes that if several people freely agree to do something or to make exchanges among themselves, society should assume that they all benefit from the transaction.

10   R D Cooter, 1994, note 7 above, noted that as technology and society advances, the ability to manage or regulate becomes more difficult.

11   L L Fuller, *The Morality of Law*, Yale University Press, New Haven, Connecticut, 1969, p 233, argued that government should 'respect the justified expectations created by its treatment of situations not controlled by explicitly announced rules'. Fuller examines the problems inherent in the vertical relationship between state and citizens and contemplates alternative sources of law (ie custom, contracts, and the like) based on the direct relationship of citizens among themselves.

is not new to legal and economic literature. Public choice theory has developed sophisticated tools for the analysis of political decision-making. Research in this field has contributed to the understanding of the political process and of the role played by interest groups in the making of the law. The resulting suspicion of legal centralism has recently revived interest in other sources of social order seen to be free from the shortcomings of the political process.[12] Just as economic theory asserts that the efficiency of the market is determined by its competitive structure, so legal theory should more clearly assert that the efficiency of the legal system should be judged according to the incentive structure of the law-making process.[13] The public choice perspective underscores a unique feature of customary law: unlike statutory law, customary rules are not under anyone's control, and thus their formative process cannot be affected by the pressures of interest groups.

Formative elements of customary law

Customary rules emerge outside of the state legal system as norms that individuals and organisations spontaneously follow in the course of their interactions,[14] and which they consider necessary for the achievement of a more desirable social order.[15]

Customary law is made up of two formative elements that together result in the formation of an enforceable custom:

(a) a quantitative element given by the existence of a norm as a general social practice; and

(b) a qualitative element given by a social conviction that the practice amounts to necessary social behaviour.

---

12   See eg, R C Ellickson, 1991, note 3 above, p 138; and a review of this book by R D Cooter, 'Against Legal Centrism', (1992) 81 *California Law Review* 427. Oliver Williamson refers to a similar concept in terms of 'legal centralism'. O E Williamson, *The Economic Institutions of Capitalism*, Free Press, New York, 1985, p 20.

13   The idea, originally put forward by R D Cooter, departs from the traditional law and economics approach, in that it uses a structural approach to infer the efficiency of a norm, rather than attempting to measure it directly through a cost-benefit analysis. See R D Cooter, 1994, note 7 above, pp 218–27, where the author argues that game theory predicts the incentive structures that produce efficient norms.

14   The school of economists known as the Austrian School, which includes Karl Menger and Friedrich A Hayek has been most active in pursuing this line of thought, as an explanation for the development of currency and various social practices. See generally F A Hayek, *The Fatal Conceit*, University of Chicago Press, Chicago, 1989; and F A Hayek, *The Constitution of Liberty*, University of Chicago Press, Chicago, 1960.

15   With some philosophical overtones, customary law has been viewed as the social expression and endorsement of natural law. Different intellectual perspectives on the idea of customary law are illustrated by R David, *International Encyclopedia of Comparative Law*, Oceana, New York, 1984, 2:3, pp 172–203.

General practice

The first quantitative element consists in the existence of a spontaneous practice among the members of society.[16] Generally, no minimum time period is necessary for the formation of a customary rule,[17] nor is any universality of practice required as a condition for its validity.[18]

These features are consistent with a dynamic and evolutionary approach to customary law formation. Given the different pace of the transformation of social norms, no general time requirement can be established as a condition for their validity,[19] and because of the stochastic origin of social norms, some deviance of individual observations should be expected. Further, the requirement of generality — as opposed to universality — of the practice is consistent with the goal of minimising the effect of positive transaction costs.[20] Accordingly, some cases have restated the requirement of generality in terms of 'increasing and widespread acceptance',[21] allowing for special consideration of emerging clusters of spontaneous practices that are expected to become evolutionarily stable over time.

---

16   In the public international law arena, the participants would be the individual nations.

17   The minimum duration seems to range from a single occurrence to an immemorial practice, according to the nature of the case. Consider, however, the 40 years traditionally required by the French jurisprudence for the emergence of an international custom, and the 30 years generally required by the German doctrine. Further analysis can be found in G I Tunkin, 'Remarks on the Juridical Nature of Customary Norms in International Law', (1961) 49 *California Law Review* 419 at 420; and N M Mateesco, *La Coutume dans les Cycles Juridiques Internationaux*, A Padone Publisher, Paris, 1947, p 212. Obviously, the longer the time required for the formation of a valid practice, the less likely it is for custom effectively to anticipate the intervention of formal legislation.

18   International legal theory is ambivalent on the issue of universality of the practice. See A D'Amato, *The Concept of Custom in International Law*, Cornell University Press, Ithaca, New York, 1971; and J I Charney, 'The Persistent Objector Rule and the Development of Customary International Law', (1986) 56 *British Yearbook of International Law* 1–24. While Charney's thesis suggests that the system of international relations is analogous to a world of individuals in the state of nature, the author rejects the idea that unanimous consent by all participants is a necessary requirement for the formation of a binding customary law. The notions of 'consistency' and 'generality', rather than 'universality', are generally used for defining this requirement. If the fluctuations are so big as to make it impossible to identify a general practice, then the requirement of consistency would not be met. See the *Asylum* case, ICJ Reports (1950) at 276–7; and, already under the jurisdiction of the Permanent Court of International Justice, see the *Wimbledon* case, in PCIJ Reports (1923), Series A, No 1.

19   The flexibility of the time requirement becomes particularly necessary in situations of rapid flux, where the payoff structure of the transaction is likely to be affected by exogenous changes.

20   This is especially true if transaction costs are uniformly distributed.

21   See the *Fisheries Jurisdiction* case, in ICJ Reports (1974) at 23–6; and the *North Sea Continental Shelf* cases, in ICJ Reports (1969) at 42.

Opinio iuris ac necessitatis

Opinio iuris ac necessitatis is the Latin phrase used to describe the second formative element of a customary rule. It refers to the social conviction that general practice amounts to an essential norm of social conduct.

Modern legal thinkers define this element in terms of necessary and obligatory convention.[22] This requirement narrows the range of enforceable customs; only those practices recognised as socially desirable or necessary are raised to the level of enforceable customary law. Not every observable equilibrium, then, amounts to a custom to which legal character is attributed. Those equilibria that are regarded by society as either undesirable (eg, a 'prisoner's dilemma' type of uncooperative outcome)[23] or unnecessary (eg, a common practice of cordially greeting neighbours) will not contain the subjective and qualitative element of legal obligation and so will not generate enforceable legal rules.

The *opinio iuris* introduces, then, a distinction between mere *behavioural regularities* and *internalised obligations*. It is a distinction that, although not reflected by the game-theoretic framework, becomes crucially important in the normative setting. As a result, it is possible to distinguish two categories of social rules:

   (a) those that reflect mere behavioural patterns which are not essential to the legal order; and

   (b) those that reflect an internalised belief in the necessity or the social desirability of the rules.[24]

---

22   For an authoritative example, see H Kelsen, *General Theory of Law and the State*, Harvard University Press, Cambridge, Massachusetts, 1945, p 114; H Kelsen, *Principles of International Law*, Rinehart, New York, 1952, p 307; H Kelsen, 'Theorie du Droit International Coutumier', (1939) 1 *Revue International de la Theorie du Droit* (New Series) 263. See also A D'Amato, *The Concept of Custom in International Law*, Cornell University Press, Ithaca, New York, 1971; and R M Walden, 'The Subjective Element in the Formation of Customary International Law', (1977) 12 *Israel Law Review* 344.

23   Reference here is to A W Tucker, 'A Two-Person Dilemma' in P Straffin, 'The Prisoner's Dilemma', (1980) 1 *UMAP Journal* 101–3. Further discussion of this model of strategic interaction, in which individual actors pursue their self-interest adopting uncooperative strategies that lead to undesirable collective outcomes, can be found in A Rapoport and A M Chammah, *Prisoner's Dilemma*, University of Michigan Press, Ann Arbor, 1965; R Gibbons, *Game Theory for Applied Economists*, Princeton University Press, Princeton, New Jersey, 1992; and E Rasmussen, *Games and Information: An Introduction to Game Theory*, Blackwell, Cambridge, 1989. The prisoner's dilemma paradox provides a rigorous argument in support of Kant's categorical imperative: 'act in the way you wish others to act'. In its generalisation, the 'Tragedy of the Commons' rationale, it has been extensively discussed by G Hardin, 'The Tragedy of the Commons', (1968) 162 *Science* 1243; and A Rapoport, 'Prisoner's Dilemma', in *The New Palgrave: A Dictionary of Economics*, Norton, New York, 1987.

24   On this point, see H L A Hart, *The Concept of Law*, Clarendon Press, Oxford, 1961, pp 50–60.

The existence of a mere behavioural regularity not fostered by the qualitative element of *opinio iuris* does not generate any civil obligation. In legal terms, these norms are identified as mere usages. Those practices that are perceived as necessary for the social wellbeing, however, qualify as proper legal customs, and enter the legal arena as primary sources of law.[25]

The legal force of customary rules

Some legal systems grant direct legal force to customary rules.[26] In those systems, custom is regarded as a primary — although not exclusive — source of law. Courts enforce customary rules as if they had been enacted by the proper legislative authority. In the 'social contract' framework, customary rules can be regarded as an implied — and often non-verbalised — exercise of direct legislation from the members of society. Judicial recognition of such norms amounts to a declaratory as opposed to constitutive act that treats custom as a legal fact.[27] The downside of customary law is found in its insufficiency as an exclusive source of social order, with most modern legal systems having to supplement customary law with extensive legislation.

Two of the commonly made criticisms of customary law concern the problems of accessibility and inelegant fragmentation. Customary law is less accessible than legislation owing to the absence of tangible objective sources which disclose the content of customary rules. It tends to be fragmented because of the need to refer to several potentially heterogeneous factual contingencies in order to establish the existence and content of customary rules. Besides these problems, I intend to show in this chapter that some institutional settings remain outside the reach of

---

25 See, however, the different terminology used in sociological literature. M Weber, *Economy and Society,* vol 1, University of California Press, Berkeley, 1978, pp 319–20. What is a mere usage in legal terms appears defined as custom (*Sitte*) in the sense of typically uniform activities not considered as socially necessary. The legal notion of custom, instead, remains foreign to the sociological classifications. The closest notion is that of convention, which amounts to conduct that is sought to be induced by expressions of approval or disapproval from the other members of the group, but which lacks the element of legal enforceability which characterises a legal custom.

26 The notable illustration is the system of international law, where, in the absence of a central legislative authority, custom stands next to treaties as a primary source of law. See Article 38 of the Statute of the International Court of Justice. A number of other legal traditions, most notably the German, grant recognition to custom as a primary source of law. Although, as a general rule, the effectiveness of custom is excluded in cases of direct conflict with legislation (ie, custom contra legem) the issue remains, in some instances, open whenever the custom supervenes prior legislation (ie, abrogative custom). See also the approach of the US Uniform Commercial Code, Article 2 on general trade practices.

27 This implies that, even after its judicial recognition, a custom remains the actual source of law. In this setting, the judicial decisions that recognised a custom only offer persuasive evidence of its existence.

spontaneous cooperation or 'common wisdom', so that other sources of law become necessary.

Whenever customary rules are granted legitimate status in the legal system, they have the same effect as other typical primary sources of law. Although often placed in a subordinate position to formal legislation, customary rules derive their force from the two formative elements of concurrence of general practice and social conviction without having to be formally incorporated in any written body of law. For this reason, they are usually classified as 'immaterial' sources of law.[28]

Modern legal systems generally grant recognition to customary rules that have emerged either within the confines of positive legislation (*consuetudo secundum legem*) or in areas that are not disciplined by positive law (*consuetudo praeter legem*).[29] Recognition is, however, generally denied to those practices that conflict with the precepts of positive law (*consuetudo contra legem*). However arguments have been made in public international law and in some municipal systems (in Germany, for example) for recognising as law, those emerging practices that come into conflict with obsolete provisions of treaties or statutes (*desuetudo*, or abrogative practice). Some attention shall be given later to the different theoretical and practical significance of these forms of spontaneous social order that compete with law in influencing human choice.

The dynamic structure of customary rules

The study of customary law provides fertile ground for testing the predictions made by game-theoretic and evolutionary models about the emergence of cooperation among self-seeking actors in the absence of a centralised law-making authority.[30] Historically, prior to the formation of a binding legal custom, individuals begin to abide by certain behavioural patterns, in the absence of external legal pressure, binding commitments or enforceable threats.

---

28   For the general classification of sources of law, see among others I Brownlie, *Principles of Public International Law*, 4th ed, Clarendon Press, Oxford, 1990, pp 1–31.

29   One restriction concerning the relevance of customary rules generally imposed by modern legal systems concerns criminal liability. Only formal legislation can restrict individual freedoms by imposing criminal sanctions. The eighteenth century principle *nullum crimen et nulla poena sine lege* calling for accessible criminal legislation is, thus, the generally accepted rule in this area of the law. An interesting unresolved issue (which lies beyond the scope of this chapter) concerns the legal efficacy of practices that evolve in disregard of obsolete criminal law (*desuetudo*, or abrogative practice). These practices would, in fact, eliminate — rather than create — criminal restrictions to individual freedom, avoiding any apparent conflict with the constitutional principle discussed above.

30   The process of formation of customary rules provides a scenario that is, indeed, very similar to the one used in game-theoretical and evolutionary analyses.

Customary law provides a field of study where legal and economic sciences can contribute to each other's advancement. This is possible in two different ways. First, the well-documented evolution of international and domestic customary rules offers the possibility of retrospectively verifying predictions of the game-theoretic model regarding the emergence of spontaneous cooperation.[31] Second, the game-theoretic apparatus offers precise tools for identifying the social settings that are more likely to generate spontaneous welfare-maximising rules. Having first considered the legal approach to the formation of customary law and its acceptance as a series of social norms, it is now possible to revisit the legal categories within an economic and game-theoretic framework. The remainder of this chapter will apply these analytical methods to issues of customary law formation.

The emergence of customary norms

An economic analysis of customary law shows that two conditions are necessary for the emergence of efficient customary rules. First, the practice should emerge from the spontaneous and non-coerced behaviour of the various members of a group, acting in rational response to self-motivated incentives. Economically speaking, this condition amounts to a rather standard assumption of rational choice. The second condition refers to the qualitative element of *opinio iuris*. I claim that a valid *opinio iuris* is established when the emerging rule maximises the aggregate wellbeing of the group. Whenever a given behavioural pattern contributes to the maximisation of the collective welfare of the group, a social norm will emerge underscoring the importance of that conduct for the public good.[32] This belief in social desirability is exactly what lawyers should look for in their appraisal of the qualitative condition of legal necessity and desirability.

Opinio iuris amounts to the realisation and articulation of a collective belief that the norm is necessary for the group's welfare. A norm which is endorsed by an *opinio iuris* is one which nobody should have reason to contest publicly. The emerging consensus, however, does not exclude the possibility that individual members of the group might endorse a rule that they do not plan to follow. Hence instances of strategic deviance from the voluntarily chosen rule should not be regarded as undermining the qualitative element of the custom.[33] The general acceptance of or

---

31   Compilations are available on present and past customary rules. An example can be found in the *Restatement of the Law 3rd, The Foreign Relations Law of the United States*, A L I Publishers, St Paul, Minnesota, 1987.

32   As an illustration, consider the two classical strategies of cooperation and defection, in response to the usual prisoner's dilemma payoff structure.

33   M L Stearns, 'The Misguided Renaissance of Social Choice', (1994) 103 *Yale Law Journal* 1219 at 1243–4 correctly points out that, if the parties were unable to devise rules to govern future interactions, and unanticipated circumstances put them in a position of forced market relationship requiring post-contractual negotiations, courts and legislators may be found to have a

acquiescence to a norm is almost exclusively related to the aggregate effect of the norm on the collective wellbeing of the group. Assuming symmetry of payoffs, the rules that will evolve into norms are those that maximise the expected aggregate welfare of the group. Whenever a general consensus emerges that members of the group ought to conform to a given rule of conduct, and as soon as enough individuals internalise that obligation by disapproving and sanctioning other individuals' deviations from the rule, a legal custom can be said to have emerged. Thus, a legal custom will successfully evolve in a community when the *ex ante* individual incentives are aligned with the collective public interest.[34]

Many social interactions, however, generate inefficient equilibria. Inefficiencies occur when there is a divergence between private incentives of individuals and the collective good. In game-theoretic terms, these conflicts generate Nash equilibria that are non-optimal. Nash equilibria are defined as conditionally best responses to the other players' equilibrium strategies.[35] In such cases, the benefit pursued by each individual actor is insufficient to compensate for the harm suffered by the other players. Members of a group will not openly endorse rules that are expected to harm the aggregate wellbeing of the community. Accordingly, undesirable stabilities in the social evolutionary process will not be bolstered by the requisite belief in the social necessity of the rules.[36] A group ethic which denies recognition to such rules facilitates the process of social evolution, by discouraging strategic behaviour between the parties. Unavoidably, communities that have been able to develop a stronger form of group ethic will enjoy a comparative advantage over the others.

Customary rules for coordination problems

The spontaneous solution of coordination problems is generally not troublesome. Coordination problems are, almost by definition, character-ised by the relative absence of conflicts of interest since every participant gains by having such problems solved. This convergence of individual and collective interests fosters an optimal outcome on the basis of a mere coordination of the self-interested strategies of the individuals involved.

---

comparative advantage over the market participants themselves in devising facilitating rules. Unlike the market participants, courts and legislators would choose among alternative solutions as if the underlying events had not yet occurred, without attempting strategically to maximise the advantage brought about by the random circumstances of the case. More generally on the point, see also M Shubik, *Game Theory in the Social Sciences: Concepts and Solutions*, 4th ed, M I T Press, Cambridge, Massachusetts, 1987, pp 179–216.

34   Robert D Cooter has called this proposition the 'alignment theorem'. See R D Cooter, 1994, note 7 above, p 224.

35   Reference is to J Nash, 'Equilibrium Points in n-Person Games', (1950) 36 *Proceedings of the National Academy of Sciences* (USA) 48–9; and J Nash, 'Non-Cooperative Games', (1951) 54 *Annals of Mathematics* 286–95. See also R Gibbons, 1992, note 23 above, pp 8-9; and E Rasmussen, 1989, note 23 above, pp 32–4.

36   The legal relevance of strategic behaviour between the parties is excluded by a screening based on the subjective or qualitative element of *opinio iuris*.

The solution to a coordination problem, however, may be delayed if it relies exclusively on decentralised processes of spontaneous legal and social order. For example, if everyone in a country needs to coordinate a basic set of traffic conventions, such as driving on the same side of the road, the emergence of spontaneous — but heterogeneous — clusters of traffic customs would consolidate local equilibria that do not possess the features of universality needed in a modern society.[37] Thus coordination problems with no dominant strategy are characterised by the presence of multiple Nash equilibria which create difficulties for decentralised solutions.[38]

Customary rules for cooperation problems

Decision-making can be decentralised to the extent that individuals are expected to generate a desirable cooperative outcome without the intervention of a central law-maker. Cooperation problems, however, may present some difficulties whenever some or all participants are tempted to defect, being attracted by higher payoffs from non-cooperative strategies.

Recent studies have considered the issue of spontaneous emergence of cooperation. Traditional game-theoretic models have been modified by the introduction of evolutionary models of analysis.[39] The assumptions used by these evolutionary models more realistically reflect the normal conditions of social interaction, and so prove particularly useful for the evaluation of spontaneous social norms.

The 'prisoner's dilemma' model predicts that in certain circumstances, rationally self-interested parties will not naturally move towards the optimal

---

37 Ironically, however, the most universal traffic rules are those for water navigation which emerged as a result of spontaneous rule-making processes. For an interesting historical background, see J H Wigmore, 3 *A Panorama of the World's Legal Systems*, vol 3, Wm W Grant, Holmes Beach, Florida, 1928, Chapter XIII.

38 See E Ullmann-Margalit, *The Emergence of Norms*, Clarendon Press, Oxford, 1977, pp 79–133. As discussed above, a Nash equilibrium is defined as a combination of strategies, where no player has incentive to deviate from his or her strategy, given that the other players do not deviate. Nash equilibria are strategically stable best responses to the equilibrium strategies of others, whereas dominant strategies are unconditionally best responses to any strategy the other players may pick. Further analysis can be found in R Gibbons, 1992, note 23 above, pp 8–9; and E Rasmussen, 1989, note 23 above, pp 32–4.

39 Most notably, R M Axelrod, *The Evolution of Cooperation*, Basic Books, New York, 1984. See also V J Vanberg and R D Congleton, 'Rationality, Morality, and Exit', (1992) 86 *American Political Science Review* 418. Intuitive notions of morality and rationality can be shown to be mutually compatible if two assumptions are made: (1) that morality is specified as a general behavioural disposition or program whose rationality is to be determined in comparison to alternative behavioural attitudes; and (2) that the recurrent game is specified as a prisoner's dilemma game with an exit option. See also E Ullmann-Margalit, 1977, pp 18–73; and D M Kreps, P Milgrom, J Roberts and R Wilson, 'Rational Cooperation in a Finite Repeated Prisoners' Dilemma', (1982) 27 *Journal of Economic Theory* 245–52.

equilibrium, for they remain trapped by the tempting strategy of individual payoff maximisation. The 'prisoner's dilemma' is a scenario which illustrates the so-called paradoxes of rationality. By examining the incentives of two prisoners to confess (or not to confess) to a crime, it shows that individually rational behaviour, rather than producing the expected maximum benefit, can produce sub-optimal aggregate outcomes. However, evolutionary models show that, under certain conditions, cooperation develops if such cooperative strategy is conducive to the maximisation of the long-term aggregate welfare of the conflicting parties. The idea behind this model is that members of a close-knit group are more likely, over time, to develop and maintain norms that maximise their aggregate wellbeing. These models attempt to answer with mathematical precision, the often evaded question regarding the proportion of cooperators to game participants that is necessary for the emergence of evolutionarily stable behaviours that lead to welfare-maximising norms.[40] A discussion of the implications of evolutionary models on the emergence of customary norms follows.

The evolution of customary law

Evolutionary theories of cooperation have successfully explained the ability of self-interested individuals to cooperate for the sake of mutual gain. Evolutionarily stable cooperative strategies serve efficiency goals and are recognised as socially obligatory. After emerging, these customary rules generate expectations of other members of society, and those expectations, in time, demand judicial enforcement. The legal system can thus be seen as evolving towards efficiency by giving legal recognition and enforcement to welfare-maximising social norms.[41] In a world of imperfect decision-makers, evolutionary paradigms provide an explanation of the emergence and development of utility-maximising social constraints.

This analysis suggests that there are a number of principles of justice that can emerge spontaneously through voluntary interactions and exchanges between individual group members. Customary law formation relies on a voluntary process through which members of a community develop, by means of voluntary adherence to emerging behavioural rules,

---

40   The mathematical model was developed by Axelrod in an earlier paper. See R M Axelrod, 'The Emergence of Cooperation Among Egoists', (1981) 75 *American Political Science Review* 306–18. The use of terms such as 'small group' or 'close-knittedness' found in much game-theoretic literature acquires a precise content through the use of Axelrod's model.

41   R D Cooter, 1994, note 7 above, pp 217–18. The author argues that legal recognition and enforcement should consequently be denied in the case of non-cooperative practices, with a test that amounts to a structural analysis of the social incentives that generated the norm. Cooter further argues that in the process of common law adjudication, a distinction must necessarily be made between cooperative norms and non-cooperative practices. Courts lack specialisation in the adjudication of most norms. Courts must, therefore, resort to a structural approach, by inquiring first into the incentives underlying the social structure that generated such norms, rather than attempting to weigh costs and benefits directly.

principles that govern their social interactions.[42] The process of defining these common principles relies on the two formative elements discussed above: the quantitative or objective element of practice, and the qualitative or subjective element of *opinio iuris*.

The subjective element of custom-formation may be appraised within a private ordering contractual model. Let us consider a society of rationally self-interested individuals bargaining toward a mutually acceptable social contract. Assume that the various actors play a non-zero-sum cooperative game[43] and that the bargaining occurs behind a Rawlsian veil of ignorance, so that there is uncertainty as to which role, status or condition each member will hold in society.[44] The use of a Rawlsian model of imaginary social interaction is useful for understanding some of

42   J C Harsanyi, 'Cardinal Welfare Individualistic Ethics, and Interpersonal Comparisons of Utility', (1955) 63 *Journal of Political Economy* 315. According to Harsanyi, optimal social norms are those that would emerge through the interaction of individual actors, in a social setting that satisfies the requirement of impersonality of preferences. The requirement of impersonality in individual preferences is satisfied if the decision-makers have equal chance of finding themselves in any one of the initial social positions, and they rationally choose a set of rules attempting to maximise their expected welfare. Further analysis of Harsanyi's insight can be found in A K Sen, 'Rational Fools: A Critique of the Behavioural Foundations of Economic Theory' in *Philosophy and Economic Theory* (eds F Hahn and M Hollis), Clarendon Press, Oxford, 1979, pp 102–3. John Rawls utilises Harsanyi's model of stochastic ignorance in his theory of justice. The Rawlsian 'veil of ignorance', however, introduces an element of risk-aversion in the choice between alternative states of the world, altering the outcome achievable under Harsanyi's original model. See J Rawls, *A Theory of Justice*, Harvard University Press, Cambridge, Massachusetts, 1971, p 12.

43   A zero-sum game occurs where the interests of the players are always opposed, ie for every pair of outcomes, if one player prefers the first, the other must prefer the second.

44   This unrealistic model of social interaction is used, just as Harsanyi had originally conceived it, for the sole purpose of defining what an individual may recognise as good from the social point of view, and distinguishing it from what he would regard as desirable for his own personal interest. See C Harsanyi, 1955, p 12, and A K Sen, 1979, p 103. The Rawlsian assumption of extreme risk-aversion by the contracting parties can be dispensed with for the purposes of the present analysis. Once all parties have agreed on a set of rules that will govern their relationships, there will be full voluntary compliance in all interactions, in spite of possible temptations to violate the agreed-upon rule, arising from occasional higher payoffs. On this point, see the more extensive commentary of R P Wolff, *Understanding Rawls*, Princeton University Press, Princeton, New Jersey, 1977, p 17. If a Pareto-literal test is used to evaluate the voluntary formation of customary rules, a custom cannot emerge if some individual or state consistently objects to the emerging rule. In this setting, it is interesting to note that the persistent objector rule allows any individual or state to opt out of a custom during its formative process. See M W Janis, *An Introduction to International Law*, Little, Brown and Co, New York, 1993, p 151; and J I Charney, 'The Persistent Objector Rule and the Development of Customary International Law', (1986) 56 *British Yearbook of International Law* 1 at 1–24.

the underlying conditions of a valid *opinio iuris* in real situations of spontaneous law. First, it is worth noting that Rawls' social contract does not give opportunity for strategic preference revelation, because parties ignore their respective place, position, class or social status in society, and the odds of being advantaged or disadvantaged are equally distributed for each member of the group. Each individual has incentives to agree on a set of rules that maximises the aggregate welfare of the group, consequently maximising his or her expected share of wealth.

The stochastic harmony of Rawls' imaginary world, however, calls for a rarely obtainable symmetry of payoffs when it is applied to real life situations.[45] In the process of customary law formation, individuals make choices according to their perception of the costs and benefits of alternative rules of conduct. Individual preferences for alternative customary rules are based on a comparative economic evaluation of alternative solutions. This implies that in the presence of asymmetric individual incentives, non-optimal Nash equilibria may possibly obtain in the final outcome. Reciprocity supplies individuals with an optimal set of incentives for choosing optimising strategies. An account of the role played by the concept of reciprocity in the formation of customary law follows.

The robustness of reciprocity in customary law

A game-theoretic restatement of the legal concept of reciprocity gives us one additional insight about the originating conditions of efficient social norms. Symmetry among individual incentives is more likely to be found if the horizons of individual maximisation are extended to include the payoffs from future interactions and the concern for the wellbeing of members within the group. I will contrast two related settings to exemplify this point.

First, let us imagine that a large number of university students live in a small college town, making up almost one-half of the entire residential population. Imagine that the town is also home to a number of senior citizens, who represent an equally large proportion of the resident population. In the process of forming local customary rules, we are likely to notice a conflict between the social norms endorsed by each group. Junior and senior residents will articulate different standards of acceptable conduct, according to their relative preferences. The students, aware that they will not remain in the town after their graduation from college, will tend to articulate rules of social conduct that maximise the enjoyment of their current college lifestyle. Likewise, senior residents will try to impose a rule of conduct that is more advantageous to them than to the students. In this scenario, the likelihood of both groups submitting voluntarily to a common set of norms is rather remote.

---

45 True preferences, thus, will be revealed in situations of stochastic symmetry, whereas strategic choices are more likely to characterise real life situations with asymmetric individual incentives.

Now consider a different scenario, in which the more integrated social structure of the group broadens the horizons of individual maximisation. Imagine a similar generational conflict between junior and senior citizens, this time taking place in a community characterised by increased opportunities for long-term interaction among the various members, and by the existence of familial bonds between the two groups. In this case, the utility curves of each member of the community capture more of the expected benefits derived from a long-term cooperative relationship with the others. The family bond that unites junior and senior residents expands the scope of each individual's utility maximisation, so that the welfare of the members of one group has some direct effect on the members of the other. Because of the more integrated structure of their community, members of close-knitted social groups are more likely to endorse and follow rules that maximise the aggregate utility of all members. This structural reciprocity of incentives allows for a far more optimistic prediction of beneficial spontaneous order. In this example, the young members of the community are more likely to consider that one day they will be old themselves, and that they will be subject to the rules that they are now in the process of articulating. This intuition is consistent with the prediction of evolutionary models of social interaction, where the incentive of future payoffs and the close-knittedness of the group are found to be positively correlated with the emergence of optimal social norms.[46]

Identical conclusions must be reached wherever social relationships are characterised by role reversibility, such as those between traders who sometimes sell and at other times buy.[47] Game situations involving repeated role reversals facilitate the emergence and recognition of customary law:[48] individuals who frequently exchange roles in their social interactions would have incentives to constrain their behaviour to socially optimal norms of conduct, in consideration of reciprocal constraints undertaken by the other members of the community. Thus, in situations characterised by symmetry of payoffs and reciprocity of rights and duties, optimal norms emerge from the non-idealistic and self-interested behaviour of human actors.[49]

---

46 R M Axelrod, 1984, note 39 above; and R M Axelrod, 'The Emergence of Co-operation Among Egoists', (1981) 75 *American Political Science Review* 306–18.

47 L L Fuller, 1969, note 11 above, p 24, observes that the existence of frequent changes of roles in the course of economic interactions facilitates the emergence of mutually recognised and accepted duties. He points out: 'By definition the members of such a society [of economic traders] enter direct and voluntary relationships of exchange ... Finally economic traders frequently exchange roles, now selling now buying. The duties that arise out of their exchanges are therefore reversible, not only in theory but in practice.'

48 B L Benson, 'Customary Law as a Social Contract: International Commercial Law', (1992) 3 *Constitutional Political Economy* 1 at 5–7 considers the role of reputation in situations of repeated market interaction of various players.

49 For an insightful anticipation of this point, see J M Buchanan, *The Limits of Liberty: Between Anarchy and Leviathan*, Chicago University Press, Chicago, 1975, p 54.

Conclusion

According to the theory that classifies customary rules as primary norms of obligation, all welfare-maximising norms that have spontaneously emerged in society are already equipped with the community's authority and should, therefore, enjoy direct legal application. According to paradigms of efficient law-making, this decentralised process has a comparative advantage over more institutional processes. Individuals and social groups have direct, self-interested perceptions of their costs and benefits, and can express their preferences among alternative legal rules by concurring in the formation of enforceable social norms. Unlike individuals, courts and legislators rely on costly, incomplete, and often biased sources of information in their decision-making processes.[50] Whenever possible, then, courts must rely upon the organic capillary process of norm-formation through which society creates rules for itself.[51]

The dynamics of customary law guarantee a purely inductive accounting of objective aggregate values. In the hypotheses discussed above, each participant in the formation of a customary rule contributes through his or her own subjective preferences toward the making of the law. The emerging rule will be the result of aggregate individual choices. This inductive law-making process guarantees an optimal weighing of individual values in public choices, avoiding shifting the burden on third party decision-makers[52] and the need to undertake rather arduous assessments of social welfare values.[53] The growing interest in customary

---

50 G K Hadfield, 'Bias in the Evolution of Legal Rules', (1992) 80 *Georgetown Law Journal* 583.

51 Hayek's work emphasised that individuals must often follow rules due to the inherent limits of reason, and that individuals are unable to articulate and control the complex knowledge that through time and experience led to the formation of customary practices. See, generally, F A Hayek, *The Constitution of Liberty*, Routledge & Kegan Paul, London, 1960; K I Vaughn, George Mason University Working Paper, *Can Democratic Society Reform Itself: The Limits of Constructive Change*, 1982, p 2: 'These rules evolve gradually. They are never fully articulated by any one, nor are they in principle articulatable, yet they are understood and obeyed implicitly. Further, they serve purposes that are often unknown but important for the survival of the community.' See also V J Vanberg, 'Rational Choice, Rule-Following and Institutions: An Evolutionary Perspective' in *Rationality, Institutions and Economic Methodology* (eds B Gustafson, C Knudsen and U Maki), Routledge & Kegan Paul, London, 1993, pp 171–200; and R D Cooter, 1994, note 7 above, pp 225–7.

52 R D Cooter, 1992, note 12 above, p 425, observes: 'In contrast to the anthropological analysis, an economic analysis of solidarity would stress social mechanisms that extend the scope of long-run relationships, thereby increasing the range of decentralised norms without imposing burdensome governance costs'.

53 Many economists emphatically deny that there is any such thing as a social welfare function. See eg J M Buchanan, *The Economics and the Ethics of Constitutional Order*, University of Michigan Press, Ann Arbor, 1991, p 225: 'From a subjectivist perspective, a utility function, as such, does not exist which, even conceptually, could be observed and recognised independently

law represents a long overdue rediscovery of the forgotten wisdom according to which '... every individual, it is evident, can, in his local situation judge much better than any statesman or lawgiver can do for him'.[54]

To the extent that customary practices have spontaneously emerged in social environments which encourage cooperative strategies to maximise aggregate payoffs, we can derive some trustworthy conclusions regarding individual and collective values. Just as we know that prices reveal individual preferences over tradeable goods and services, we should expect that this customary form of social exchange would reveal true collective preferences for alternative social outcomes. And consequently, if we can infer objective market values from the observation of market exchanges, we should give equal inferential weight to spontaneous customary rules. It is in this sense that custom may reclaim full dignity as a primary source of law. The evolutionary and game-theoretic appraisal of the law-making process sheds new light on the normative foundations of spontaneous law, requiring, however, an appropriate analysis of the incentive structure of the originating social environment.

---

of an individual's choice behaviour.' See also J Wiseman, *Cost, Choice, and Political Economy*, Edward Elgar, London, 1989, p 221: 'There is no objective entity called output, no way of measuring aggregate welfare, eg by adding up observed prices (which are disequilibrium prices anyway).' See also J M Buchanan, *What Should Economists Do?*, Liberty Press, Indianapolis, 1979, pp 81–2: 'The principle that exposure to economics should convey is that of spontaneous coordination which the market achieves. The central principle of economics is not the economizing process; it is not the maximisation of objective functions subject to constraints.'

54 A Smith in *An Inquiry into the Nature and Causes of the Wealth of Nations* (eds R H Campbell and A S Skinner), first pub 1776, at IV.ii.10, Liberty Press, Indianapolis, 1981, p 456.

CHAPTER 7

Liberty Misconceived: Hayek's Incomplete Theory of the Relationship Between Natural and Customary Law

Douglas W Kmiec*

Hayek's theory

In contemplating a jurisprudence of liberty, F A Hayek cautions us to separate carefully two conceptions of order: that which is planned or imposed deliberately by man from without and that which arises spontaneously from within. An appreciation of spontaneous order drives Hayek's defence of liberty. The deliberately manufactured order is often heavy-handed, incapable of the complexity of spontaneous order. Deliberately constructed order is rigid, whereas spontaneous order, consisting largely of abstract or general principles, is more pliable or adaptable to new circumstances. Finally, an order imposed by human deliberation has a necessary purpose, where a spontaneous order 'can have no purpose, although its existence may be very serviceable to the individuals which move within such order'.[1]

Hayek favours, in most circumstances, customary or common law over positive enactment because the customary law arises out of the evolution of the spontaneous order. Positive law will often contend with the spontaneous order. In so doing, Hayek posits, that coercion displaces

---

* Professor of Law, University of Notre Dame; Straus Distinguished Professor of Law 1995–1996, Pepperdine University.
1   F A Hayek, *Law Legislation and Liberty*, vol 1, Routledge & Kegan Paul, London, 1973, p 39.

freedom and injects elements of instability and uncertainty which disrupt market as well as personal arrangements. For Hayek, then, positive law has at most a supporting role to play, namely that of corrective legislation. Hayek points to customary laws that have grown in error because 'the development of the law has lain in the hands of members of a particular class whose traditional views made them regard as just what could not meet the more general requirements of justice'.[2] In this, however, Hayek is quick to warn against the use of positive law to seek equality of result, rather than equality of treatment.[3] Eliminating bias that has evolved into customary law does not entail the creation of new bias. Hayek sharply and properly condemns employing the positive law 'to direct private activity towards particular ends and to the benefit of particular groups'.[4] Once this is undertaken, government assumes control of life, liberty and property. And once these are 'administered' to the ends selected by government, there is a disregard of the spontaneous order and personal freedom.

Hayek, God and being

Hayek's conception of spontaneous order and the importance of common or customary law is congenial, though not identical, with the natural law tradition. In this, Hayek is so preoccupied with preserving liberty against the state that there is no acknowledgment that the spontaneous order is itself ordered by the one Supreme Being. Moreover, there is insufficient recognition of each person's role in community, in so far as immunities that apply against governments are too easily allowed to place people atomistically outside their natural contexts. For example, a person may well have a guaranteed 'right', say to free speech, and such right is important as a limit on government or state power. In other words, the right confers an immunity against government restraint (censorship) with regard to certain personal decisions. However, it is important to realise that such rights or immunities from state interference do not leave a person in a posture of unfettered freedom. If the social or spontaneous order is to be tolerable, individual action will often need to be tempered by moral duties that a person may have by reason of being part of a community such as a family. Unlike the state, parents may impose content limitations upon the reading or television viewing habits of children. So too churches may obligate a tithe or redistribution of wealth as a matter of justice towards others. The world cannot be understood in the simplistic 'state v individual' terms. The individual is located within social groups such as family, church, school, and the workplace community. Cultural order depends greatly upon each person being situated in the midst of such intermediary associations,[5] and in so far as these associations are far from spontaneous, Hayek appears to understate their importance.

---

2   F A Hayek, 1973, p 89.
3   F A Hayek, 1973, p 141.
4   F A Hayek, 1973, p 142.
5   See generally, D Kmiec, *Cease-Fire on the Family and the End of Culture War*, Crisis Books, Notre Dame, Indiana, 1995.

Natural law also is more than a spontaneous order or an accumulation of experience over time. Cicero, for example, states that '[l]aw is the primal and ultimate mind of God, whose reason directs all things'.[6] As God has created man in His own image, it is impertinent of any man to call the result of that creation 'spontaneous'. According to Aquinas, natural law is premised upon propositions that are self-evident from our very 'being'. Thus, 'the first indemonstrable principle is that the same thing cannot be affirmed and denied at the same time'.[7] This important precept of non-contradiction secures objective truth against modern claims of moral relativism or scepticism. That something cannot both *be* and *not be* is perhaps implicit in Hayek's praise of the spontaneous order, but it deserves more forthright recognition if the human race is not to become prey for statist claims driven by particular interests.

The purposeless nature of Hayek's conception of spontaneous order also understates man's ultimate purpose according to the Judaeo-Christian precept; namely, to seek that which is good and compatible with his nature, and to avoid that which is incompatible, evil or destructive of that nature. Thus, for natural lawyers the focus is not Hayek's thinner (albeit important) proposition that freedom will prosper where custom and spontaneous order are allowed to flourish, but whether the customs that are undertaken in law coincide with a person's nature or war against it. Again, to quote Aquinas, 'man is directed to an end of eternal happiness which exceeds man's natural abilities ... It is necessary that man should be directed to his end by a law given by God'.[8]

God has given man a purpose. While these purposes become more evident out of the common law traditions that Hayek extols, they pre-exist even his spontaneous order in ways that he ignores or denies. These natural purposes or inclinations include all that 'makes for the preservation of human life, and all that is opposed to its dissolution'.[9] Like other animals, a human being has an inclination to 'sexual relationship, the rearing of offspring, and the like'.[10] Finally, we are intended 'to live in society' and from this is derived all related inclinations, such as the need for knowledge.[11]

Liberty and society

Natural law and Hayek's view coincide on the importance of living in a free society. Thus, Hayek's conception of spontaneous order distinct from that which is deliberately fashioned by persons with administrative or political power is an echo of the important natural law distinction

---

6   Cicero Marcus Tullius, *De Re Publica, De Legibus*, (trans C W Keyes), Harvard University Press, Cambridge, Massachusetts, 1928, pp 379–81.

7   T Aquinas, *Treatise on Law (Summa Theologica Questions 90–97)*, Question 94, Art 2, (1265–1269), reprinted University of Chicago, Chicago, Illinois, 1990.

8   T Aquinas, Question 91.

9   T Aquinas, Question 94, Art 2.

10   T Aquinas, Question 91, Art 2.

11   T Aquinas, Question 91, Art 2.

between living in society and being a mere subject of the state. What is more, Hayek's powerful insights concerning the propensity of the state to be concerned with itself suggest strongly that Aristotle's claim that 'the city or state has priority over the household and over any individual among us [as] the whole must be prior to the parts'[12] cannot be taken at face value. While Aristotle conceived of the human social inclination as an ever expanding structure of self-sufficiency — from individual to family to village to community to communities united as a state — Hayek's work reminds us that there are social as well as economic scale economies. Put more bluntly, as the state grows in size and scope, it tends to lose sight of the purposes that not only are better accomplished, but perhaps only accomplished, in the complex orders of a smaller sovereign, such as the family.

James Wilson, a signatory to both the United States *Declaration of Independence* and its original Constitution was also the United States' most erudite natural law scholar at the time of its founding. Wilson clearly recognises that the state or government exists for individual and family, and not the other way around. Wilson writes:

> Government was instituted for the happiness of society: how often has the happiness of society been offered as a victim to the idol of government![13]

Hayek's distinction between government and society mirrors that of Wilson. Hayek's spontaneous order may be compared with Wilson's comment:

> [C]ivil society must have existed ... before civil government could be regularly formed and established. Nay, 'tis for the security and improvement of such a [condition], that the adventitious one of civil government has been instituted.

However, Hayek's understanding of liberty is misconceived in so far as it is built on an incomplete relationship between natural and customary law. To complete the relationship, individual liberty and the corresponding immunity from state directive must be reconciled with the social inclination of human nature to live in society. From living in society arises the natural obligations between parent and child, husband and wife, neighbour and neighbour and even employer and employee. As Professor David Forte has thoughtfully written:

> [I]f we have too weak a theory of rights, the individuality of the person could be swallowed up in an enforced obligation to assist others and society. If we have too strong a theory of rights, we divide and separate humans from one another, break essential connections between them, and indeed, make weaker, not stronger, the individual human identity.[14]

---

12 Aristotle, *Politics*, Book 1, Chapter 2 (trans T A Sinclair), Penguin, Harmondsworth, Middlesex, 1972, p 29.

13 J Wilson, *The Works of James Wilson*, vol 1, (ed R G McCloskey), Belknap Press of Harvard University Press, Cambridge, Massachusetts, 1967, p 239.

14 D F Forte, 'Nurture and Natural Law', (1993) 26 *U C Davis L Rev* 691 at 703–4.

To make this concrete, Forte, like Hayek, praises the law when it maximises freedom. But with more vigour than Hayek, Forte draws upon the natural law tradition to find in this freedom its essential purpose: namely, multiplying the number of opportunities for individual nurturing of others, and thus ourselves as well.

Social legislation

How active a role can a state take in creating opportunities for individuals to undertake such nurturing activities? Hayek speculated that some appropriate social legislation may be enacted for the provision of 'certain services which are of special importance to some unfortunate minorities, the weak or those unable to provide for themselves'.[15] Admitting that this would increase taxation, Hayek thought this tolerable so long as the funds were raised uniformly and did not make 'the private citizen in any way the object of administration'.[16]

The natural law tradition is similar, but arguably more generous, than Hayek's grudging concession. Aquinas writes: 'in a case of extreme need ... that which [a man] takes for support of his life becomes his own property by reason of that need'.[17] In this, Aquinas is not supporting a right based merely upon need, a proposition that would greatly expand the modern welfare state and coincide with the headiest dreams of those heads of government determined to redistribute wealth. Rather, the right that Aquinas describes is premised upon what is good, objectively defined in terms of human nature. Property is thus understood as an important instrumental device to the security of happiness and the natural end of human beings, and not an end in itself. Further, property ought not be used to defeat a person's right under natural law. It is doubtful whether Hayek would agree.

As a matter of practical politics, what does this authorise the state to do? Let us take the example of health-care reform, an issue in the United States at the time of writing. On the one hand, the current President, Mr Clinton, and his wife, Mrs Clinton, have advocated that every employer in the country should provide basic health-care coverage for their individual employees. In contrast, various amalgams of small and large businesses argue that the way to contain health costs is to place more directly the responsibility for health expenditures upon the individual. Clearly, Hayek would be appalled by the employer mandate. It would destabilise long established business relationships and expectations and curtail economic and personal freedom in the most egregious manner. Yet, for different reasons, it is important to realise that the natural law would also acknowledge Hayek's concern, especially as the mandate would be interfering with individual opportunities (and obligations) to provide nurture. But in saying this, the natural law would

---

15   F A Hayek, 1973, note 1 above, pp 141–2.
16   F A Hayek, 1973, p 142.
17   T Aquinas, note 6 above, Question 66, Art 7.

not take the position that the state could not arrange for incentives for these individually-directed nurturing opportunities to occur. Thus, while it may be best to leave the individual responsible for his or her health care, tax deductions or credits might facilitate a son or daughter providing for the health care costs of an elderly parent.

Along similar lines, Professor Forte comments that the early welfare practice in the United States 'required a personal relationship between the giver and receiver, the distribution of assistance for special needs, and the requirement that the recipient "do something" if at all possible in exchange for help'.[18] How different this is from the present-day statist programs of food and housing assistance that are anonymously administered in accordance with census and financial data. These programs not only encourage a culture of poverty on the part of the recipient,[19] they impoverish the taxpayer donor by separating the donor and donee and thereby break the bonds of the natural law community.

The function of the state and its relationship to natural law

In misconceiving liberty, Hayek fails to realise, or chooses to ignore, that the spontaneous order can be either one of pursuit of virtue and the good or the pursuit of greed (or lust or fame) and evil.

It is natural law that answers this omission by both preserving liberty and recognising the purpose of liberty as the pursuit of the good. Building in prudence and notions of limited enforceability, natural law — like Hayek — cautions against the enforced virtue of the state. Persons are to be brought to virtue, not suddenly, but gradually. Natural law, unlike Hayek, explicitly recognises that it is virtue that is being pursued. Yet, virtue is not — as Hayek sometimes seems to imply — a naked choice between coercion and freedom. Virtuous habits are usually learned within families with a good deal of parental coercion. So, too, the state must play this role to protect life itself from attack, for example by making criminal the murder of human beings.

But the state is more than a fail-safe device against extreme evil. From a natural law perspective, the state — at least in its limited form — is part of our search for the good. The state performs a coordinating function, and at its best, it permits those with outstanding talents to create conditions for the individual pursuit of the good. In this, the state is not merely the result of people's fallen or sinful nature or some deliberately planned order originating solely in our nature, it is part of the society known to, and prefigured by, God. We have only one end: our reunification with God. It is to that end that individual and state action ought to be directed. As Father Copleston comments:

---

18   D F Forte, 1993, note 13 above, p 724.
19   See generally, M N Olasky, *The Tragedy of American Compassion*, Crossway Books, Wheaton, Illinois, 1992.

St Thomas does not say that man has, as it were, two final ends, a temporal end which is catered for by the State and a supernatural, eternal end which is catered for by the Church: he says that man has one final end, a supernatural end, and that the business of the monarch, in his direction of earthly affairs, is to facilitate the attainment of that end.[20]

If the state is to carry out this proper function, it must respect the freedom of the spontaneous order, but only as that is understood in terms of natural law. In this, the Catholic principle of 'subsidiarity' is instructive:

[A] community of higher order should not interfere in the internal life of a community of a lower order, depriving the latter of its functions, but rather should support it in case of need and help to coordinate its activity with the activities of the rest of society, always with a view to the common good.[21]

The principle of subsidiarity is an important, if judicially disregarded,[22] portion of the United States Constitution's Tenth Amendment which reserves to the state, or to the people, 'powers not delegated to the United States by the Constitution'.[23] The principle of subsidiarity looms large on the international scene as well, with individual European nations referencing this principle as a source of restraint in the face of the strengthening of the European Union.

Hayek makes a substantial contribution to the understanding of law by reminding his reader that '[a]s late as the seventeenth century, it could still be questioned whether parliament could make law inconsistent with the common law. The chief concern of what we call legislatures has always been the control and regulation of government'.[24] In the modern age, where the substance of a person is the substance of legislative rights — eg welfare entitlements, minimum wages, housing assistance, pension mandates, hiring (affirmative action) preferences — it is important to be reminded of how recently legislatures have usurped the power to displace what Hayek calls the 'rules of just conduct', or more precisely the natural law. It is useful to examine Hayek's contribution from both an institutional and individual standpoint. Institutionally, of course, Hayek's observation goes to the relationship between the legislature and the court. Individually, it concerns what standards or methodology governs an individual judge.

20 S J F Copleston, *A History of Philosophy*, vol II, Burns, Oates & Washbourne, London, 1954, p 416.

21 Pope John Paul II, *Centesimus Annus*, Art 48, para 4, Daughters of St Paul, Boston, Massachussetts, 1991.

22 *Garcia v San Antonio Metropolitan Transit Authority*, (1985) 469 US 528 holding that the Constitution, including the Tenth Amendment, does not substantively affirm state sovereignty as a limit on federal commerce authority; rather, states must fend for themselves in the political process.

23 US Constitution, Amendment X.

24 F A Hayek, 1973, note 1 above, p 124.

Natural law and common law

Separation of powers

At the institutional or structural level, Hayek as before does not fully appreciate the natural law significance of democratic checks and balances and the separation of powers. His main task is again to defend the common law and the spontaneous order from an overbearing positive law state. With that task in mind, he is most concerned with shrinking the conception of enacted or positive law. He writes: '[w]hat is important for our purposes is that ... to conceive of legislation as a distinct activity presupposes an independent definition of what was meant by law'.[25] The proper historical account, Hayek argues, is that, except for Benthamites who demanded an 'omnicompetent legislature', the accepted British view was that the scope of positive enactment was necessarily constrained not only by the requirement that statutory law be general in form and application, but also that it not upset the common law. Of course, modern legislatures do not fully observe such limitations on their substantive law-making power, and it is here that the utility of the separation of powers is made apparent. It is also here where the separation of powers should be clearly linked with the natural law.

Pre-existence of natural law

Again, part of Hayek's shortcoming is his unwillingness to see the common law, not as merely spontaneous, but as the necessary outgrowth of a divine law-giver. Without due acknowledgment of the Almighty, Hayek is left to defend the common law as a matter of tradition or expectation. Important matters to be sure — at least, that is, for those who are predisposed to conserve or maintain the established order. It is no answer, however, to those who wish to subvert it. On a structural level, it leaves Hayek to maintain that written constitutions are 'essentially a superstructure erected over a pre-existing system of law to organize the enforcement of that law'.[26] Again, Hayek's purpose is to exalt the common law, even as against modern positivist claims that the common law must give way to the primary or supreme constitutional charter. But if all that supports the common law is that it pre-exists, and not that it is also consistent with the pursuit of goodness or human nature as designed by God, the defence of the common law is weak. Only when the common law is seen in the natural law tradition do structural limitations on law-making such as the separation of powers become embodiments of principle, not merely useful props for the status quo.

25   F A Hayek, 1973, p 128.
26   F A Hayek, 1973, p 134.

Coke

The best illustration of the structural, natural law importance of the separation of powers can be located in the history of the founding of the United States. Roscoe Pound, who lectured widely on the natural law at the University of Notre Dame and at Harvard, commented that just as English common law lawyers utilised the principles underlying the Magna Carta to contest with the Stuart monarchs, so too, colonial American lawyers used Coke to justify the separation of the United States from England.[27] But Coke, unlike Hayek, was not bashful about locating the significance of common law in the hand of God. Coke writes:

> The Law of nature was before any judicial or municipal law [and] is immutable. The law of nature is that which God at the time of creation of the nature of man infused into his heart for his preservation and direction; and this is the eternal law, the moral law, called also the law of nature. And by this law, written with the finger of God in the heart of man, were the people of God a long time governed ... before any laws written and before any judicial or municipal laws.[28]

Coke's writings are restated in Blackstone. The 1765 publication of Blackstone's commentaries, and a subsequent 1771 edition printed especially for the American colonies, reiterated the relationship between the common law and the will of the Creator. To Blackstone:

> [God] has so intimately connected, so inseparably interwoven the laws of eternal justice with the happiness of each individual that [happiness] cannot be attained but by observing the former; and if the former be punctually obeyed it cannot but induce [happiness].[29]

And as Dean Manion in this century correctly concludes, Blackstone not only interweaves the natural law with the pursuit of happiness, but also finds the natural law to be 'the inspiration of the common law of England'.[30] It is because this is so that the common law is respected. It is not, as Hayek puts it, merely that the common law is a better reflection of useful social arrangements that have evolved through time to be accepted as rules of just conduct. It is also that the common law derives its validity from the natural law dictated by God himself.

Liberty

A spontaneous order without God is not liberty, but licence. Such order can be as much driven by lust as by the pursuit of the good. The only true liberty is that which is necessarily constrained by the natural law. Animals

---

27   R Pound, 'The Development of Constitutional Guarantees of Liberty', (1945) 20 *Notre Dame Lawyer* 347 at 348.

28   *Calvin's Case* (1608) 7 Coke Rep 12(a); 77 Eng Rep 392.

29   W Blackstone, *Commentaries*, vol 1, 14th ed, Cadell & W Davies, London, 1803, p 40.

30   C Manion, 'The Natural Law Philosophy of Founding Fathers', *1947 Natural Law Institute Proceedings* (ed A Scanlon), University of Notre Dame, Notre Dame, Indiana, 1947, p 11.

without the power of reason have no choice in this; '[their] existence depends on obedience', says Blackstone. Endowed with reason, humans have a choice, and in this, a natural liberty. But it is a natural liberty that can only be meaningfully exercised if it is understood as necessarily dependent upon the will of God. Again, Blackstone instructed the American colonists and all of us who follow:

> The absolute rights of man considered as a free agent endowed with discernment to know good from evil, and with power of choosing those measures which appear to him to be most desirable, are usually summed up in one general appellation and denominated the natural liberty of mankind. This natural liberty consists properly in a power of acting as one thinks fit without any restraint or control unless by the law of nature ...[31]

In comparison, Hayek's conception of the common law and its judicial discernment is incomplete. Hayek sees the judge not in pursuit of right reason, but in the maintenance and improvement of:

> [A] going order which nobody has designed, an order that has formed itself without the knowledge and often against the will of authority, that extends beyond the range of deliberate organisation on the part of anybody, and that is not based on the individuals doing anybody's will, but on the expectations becoming mutually adjusted.[32]

If this is all that anchors the common law, it is not surprising that modern scepticism can dispense with it for sport. An order that no one designed is subject to redesign at will. An order where no principle of right conduct, other than that which is 'mutually adjusted', is an order that ultimately sees no relationship between conduct and character. In short, it is modern life where the subscript is 'anything goes'. And tragically for Hayek and his libertarian followers, it is an order subject to repeal not only by positive enactment, but also — in some partisan administrations in the USA at least — by unilateral executive order.

The rise of legislative supremary

The seeds of Hayek's hollowness unfortunately were planted long ago. Blackstone himself would compromise the common law to positive enactment, writing:

> [I]f there arise out of [acts of Parliament] collaterally any absurd consequences, manifestly contradictory to common reason, they are, with regard to those collateral consequences, void. I lay down the rule with these restrictions; I know it is generally laid down more largely, that acts of Parliament contrary to reason are void. But if Parliament will positively enact a thing to be done which is unreasonable, I know of no power in the ordinary forms of the Constitution that is vested with authority to control it.[33]

With this, Blackstone separated himself from Coke. Pound in his Notre Dame lectures speculated that Blackstone accepted legislative supremacy

---

31   W Blackstone, 1803, note 28 above, p 125.
32   F A Hayek, 1973, note 1 above, p 119.
33   W Blackstone, 1803, note 28 above, p 79.

because of the English Revolution of 1688, but that this acceptance was not transferred to the colonial United States. Pound writes unequivocally of the United States' rejection of an 'omnicompetent' legislature: 'The Seventeenth Century polity as set forth in Coke's doctrine, was the one we accepted at our Revolution and put into our Constitution'.[34]

Pound is right that the United States Constitution was fashioned to be subservient to the natural law, but we also know that this keen insight is at present greatly disputed. And the dispute comes not only from the totalitarian troops feared by Hayek, but also Hayek's philosophic, and nominally conservative, successors, who view the positive enactment of the Constitution as supreme. Curiously, however, Hayek speculates that judicial decisions 'have shocked public opinion' most when judges have 'had to stick to the letter of the written law'.[35] This is, of course, directly contrary to the litany of 'judicial restraint' espoused by Robert Bork and his fellow conservative originalists.[36] Something is obviously amiss in these contradictory reasonings.

To untangle this confusion, Hayek gives us a semi-useful postulate that he knows is not observed, namely, that a constitution is better understood as a rule of organisation, rather than a rule of just conduct. Hayek labours for this postulate because it leaves room for the spontaneous order of the common law. This is all well and good, but just as predicted, those dissatisfied with the status quo have not hesitated to utilise every positive law source, including the Constitution, to overturn it. Without any meaningful claim that his spontaneous order is premised upon the objective good to which we are inclined by the Creator, Hayek's order and preference for the common law thus becomes a matter of historical curiosity. Recognising Hayek's dilemma, modern advocates of judicial restraint have sought to avoid the displacement, or at least the distortions, of the common law by making a small concession that Hayek would resist; specifically, that democratic majorities under the Constitution do have substantive power to displace the common law so long as it is all written down. Reminiscent of Blackstone, although not Coke, this version of judicial restraint and blind acceptance of majoritarianism is hardly in the historical tradition of the founding of the United States. What's more, this 'small' concession, of course, is the tip of the iceberg. Indeed, given what this concession allows to be enacted into positive law, from preferences for conditions such as homosexuality to oppressive laws that take private property by regulation, it seems fair to say that this concession has taken over natural law.

Like Hayek's misconception of liberty, Bork's version of originalism overlooks the fact that certain constitutional provisions are themselves a product of the natural law. As Dean Manion observed:

---

34 R Pound, 1945, note 26 above, p 367.
35 F A Hayek, 1973, note 1 above, p 117.
36 See D W Kmiec, *The Attorney General's Lawyer*, Praeger, New York, 1992, pp 35–8. Judge Bork's argument is contained in R Bork, *The Tempting of America*, Free Press, New York, 1990.

> Just as firmly as [the founders] believed in natural law and natural rights, therefore, they believe in practical as well as theoretical checks upon the possibility of governmental violation of those rights. It was not enough ... to belabor sovereignty with sound philosophy. Sovereignty had to be split and checked and degraded to the point where it was obviously a servant of the people's God-given rights.[37]

In this, the specifications of the United States Constitution were not ends, but means to the intended natural law purpose. Thus, the separation of powers not only secures liberty from overbearing positive law, it is also reflective of man's fallen condition, and his inability to fully grasp objective truth. A recent commentary on the natural law of St Augustine puts it nicely:

> The Augustinian attitude thus has doubts not about the existence of an ultimate, supralegal moral goodness but about the possibilities of its embodiment in human law... [This attitude] supplies a compelling justification for an American constitutional system that fragments both the power to define the good and the power to do it.[38]

Court-watchers in the United States well know that Hayek is wrong in saying that judicial opinions have shocked the majority of the public most when they have stuck to the written law. The mention of the United States Supreme Court's decisions transforming the crime of abortion into a constitutional liberty is sufficient to make the point. But Bork's prescription for curing this judicial misbehaviour, an example of textualism uninformed by natural law, is as unsatisfactory as Hayek's embrace of the common law without God. As noted above, natural law is embodied in the very structure of the United States Constitution. It exists in substantive provisions as well. For example, the Ninth Amendment recites that '[t]he enumeration in the Constitution, of certain rights, shall not be construed to deny or disparage others retained by the people'.[39] Here is the positive law directly adverting to the 'pre-existing system of law', to use Hayek's terminology. But it is a pre-existing system that is transcendent in nature, not merely spontaneous as Hayek would have it. In this regard, legal historian Edward Corwin found natural law to be the essential purpose of the Ninth Amendment. The only difference Corwin noted is phraseology, since 'the principles of transcendental justice have been [there] translated into terms of personal and private rights'.[40] Corwin is clear that the founders' intent was not to confer legitimacy on these personal rights by their incorporation into the Constitution, but to confer legitimacy on the Constitution by not assuming the pretence that natural rights can be legislatively limited. Corwin thus writes that these transcendental rights 'owe nothing to their recognition in the Constitution — such recognition was necessary if the Constitution was to be regarded as complete'.[41]

---

37   C Manion, 1947, note 29 above, p 22.
38   G Walker, *Moral Foundations of Constitutional Thought*, Princeton University Press, Princeton, 1990, p 150.
39   US Constitution, Amendment IX.
40   E Corwin, 'The "Higher Law" Background of American Constitutional Law', (1928) 42 *Harv L Rev* 149 at 152–3.
41   E Corwin, 1928, p 153.

Rights conferred by natural law

The rights derived from natural law have been stated differently over time, but chiefly they are:

> The 'rights' revealed by nature, 'animate and inanimate', includ[ing] a right to be, and therefore includ[ing] a right to continue to be (from which [is] derive[d] the right of self-defence and a duty of protecting from wanton destruction human, animal and vegetable life); [and] these imply 'a right to the conditions of existence', from which [is] implie[d] the right to the exclusive ownership and possession of property.[42]

These same sentiments are captured by the shorthand employed by the United States founders' concern for 'life, liberty and property or the pursuit of happiness'[43] known to every American schoolchild. Fundamentally, then, the natural law of the United States Constitution prescribes the right of self-preservation of life as well as the right to live and develop in the community.[44]

As thus stated, natural law cannot be relied upon to either create 'new' social rights or entitlements of concern to Hayek or to result in the general subversion of democratic choices that troubles Bork. With respect to the containment of the modern fabrication of rights, natural law as a source of authority has an obvious and immutable limitation: the fixed character of human nature that exists as a matter of divine, not human, specification. As for Bork's majoritarian preference, 'natural law ... is not a hunting licence empowering judges to impose their own morality to invalidate legislative decisions in genuinely debatable cases'.[45] Economic regulation that does not threaten personal existence or disregard private property, subject of course to the explicit textual constraints of other provisions of the Constitution like the 'taking clause',[46] would not be

---

42 E Patterson, *Jurisprudence: Men and Ideas of Law*, Foundation Press, Brooklyn, 1953, p 368.

43 Professor Antieau asserts that from this the framers of the Constitution derived the following natural rights: (1) freedom of conscience, (2) freedom of communication, (3) the right to be free from arbitrary laws, (4) the rights of assembly and petition, (5) the property right, (6) the right of self government: C Antieau, 'Natural Rights and the Founding Fathers — the Virginians', (1960) 17 *Wash and Lee L Rev* 43 at 45.

44 C Rice, 'Some Reasons for a Restoration of Natural Law Jurisprudence', (1989) 24 *Wake Forest L J* 539 at 562. In summarising the work of Thomas Aquinas, another commentator describes the basic inclinations of man as follows: (1) to seek the good, which is ultimately his highest good which is eternal happiness; (2) to preserve himself in existence; (3) to preserve the species, that is, to unite sexually; (4) to live in community with other men; and (5) to use his intellect and will, that is, to know the truth and to make his own decisions: T Davitt, 'St Thomas Aquinas and the Natural Law', in *Origins of the Natural Law Tradition* (ed A L Harding) Southern Methodist University Press, Dallas, 1954, pp 26, 30–1.

45 C Rice, 1989, p 568.

46 The Fifth Amendment of the US Constitution provides: '[N]or shall private property be taken for public use, without just compensation'.

subject to challenge on natural law grounds. Thus, the state could take one's property for public use upon the payment of just compensation and the state could also regulate that property ownership without compensation so long as it performed its task in even-handed and proportionate ways directed at the prevention of harm. What the state cannot do, because the natural law against theft would preclude it, is redefine property ownership in ways that would render the taking clause and the due process clause meaningless. Property, being in part a natural law concept, cannot be wholly subject to state redefinition.

Natural law thus does far more than Hayek's mere perpetuation of an order that nobody has designed and that has just grown. Natural law has the intellectual power to reject not only spurious social entitlement claims, but also claims for 'new' rights that are destructive of human nature itself. Obviously, a judicial decision striking down state laws protective of human life can have no natural law foundation. Indeed, a decision like *Roe v Wade*,[47] which manufactured the right to kill the unborn, is perhaps the best example of where the natural law context of the American Constitution has been most seriously offended.[48] So too, a claim that the Constitution guarantees individuals the 'right' of homosexual practice would have no natural law foundation. In so far as homosexual behaviour undermines the societal interest in procreation, the stable transmission of cultural values within families, and is one of the primary ways in which the deadly HIV or AIDS virus is transmitted, a law limiting that behaviour promotes natural law by safeguarding existence and promoting health. The US Supreme Court's conclusion in *Bowers v Hardwick* that 'to claim that a right to engage in [homosexual] conduct is "deeply rooted in this Nation's history and tradition" or "implicit in the concept of ordered liberty" is, at best, facetious',[49] is an echo of this natural law understanding.

The relationship between natural and positive law

Properly understood, natural law accords respect for positive law, and thus recognises that government — even legislative government — kept within natural law bounds is a necessary part of man's pursuit of the good or happiness. This is missing from Hayek, yet it is apparent, for example, in Aquinas.[50] Of course, respecting the legislative process to an extent greater than Hayek's characterisation of it as one of the gravest inventions

---

47   *Roe v Wade* 410 US 113 (1973).

48   Professor Rice comments: 'Only rarely would a judge be entitled or obliged to rely on supra-constitutional principles to refuse to uphold or enforce an enacted law. As the German courts indicated after World War II, judges should take this step only when the conflict between the law or precedent and justice is "intolerable" or "unendurable". Such a conflict could occur in the context of *Roe v Wade*, since that ruling authorizes the execution of a certainly innocent human being': Rice, 1989, note 43 above, p 569.

49   *Bowers v Hardwick* 478 US 186 at 194 (1986).

50   T Aquinas, 1990, note 6 above, Question 95, Art 1, reply objection 2.

of man 'more far-reaching in its effects even than fire and gun-powder',[51] does not require approval of all its manifestations.

This proper relationship between natural and positive law was outlined long ago by Aristotle, and it has been restated more recently by the respected American philosopher, Dr Mortimer Adler. Adler, like Aristotle, observed that:

> Of political justice part is natural, part legal — natural, that which everywhere has the same force and does not exist by people's thinking this or that; legal, that which is originally indifferent, but when it has been laid down is not indifferent.[52]

Thus, there are distinct, immutable principles of natural law, such as to seek the good, and precepts, such as not killing, stealing, or committing adultery, but 'many things [are left] undetermined which must be determined by the conventions of political or civil law'.[53]

To fully understand how natural law gives a wide, but not unlimited, berth to the operations of positive law, it is necessary to comprehend the fundamental differences between natural and positive law.[54] If one wanted to learn the law of a particular state, Adler commented, one would not ask someone to teach us this law by demonstrating rational conclusions from sound premises: 'the law of [a state] can only be taught by statement and it can only be learned by memory. This is due to its arbitrary character as positive law'.[55] In contrast, natural law is discovered by the individual through rational inquiry and it can be taught by others through rational instruction. Adler highlighted other differences, too. Positive law compels obedience through force and fear; there is no such temporal, external force with natural law. Positive law involves a free choice among several options, indifferent possibilities as the philosophers would say; whereas, with natural law, as with an accurate mathematical answer, there is no choice. Positive law is binding only within the limited sphere of temporal political authority; natural law is binding on everyone.

The differences Adler highlighted between natural law and its positive counterpart should not be taken to mean that they are irrelevant to each other. Quite the contrary, as Adler instructed: '[p]ositive law without a foundation in natural law is purely arbitrary. It needs the natural law to make it rational. But natural law without positive law is ineffective for the purposes of enforcing justice and keeping the peace'.[56]

---

51   F A Hayek, 1973, note 1 above, p 72.

52   M J Adler, 'The Doctrine of Natural Law Philosophy', in *1947 Natural Law Institute Proceedings* (ed A Scanlon), University of Notre Dame, Notre Dame, Indiana, 1947, p 69.

53   M J Adler, 1947, p 70.

54   Adler relies for this distinction on the definition of law supplied by St Thomas Aquinas: law is an 'ordinance of reason, for the common good, promulgated by him who has charge of the community'. M J Adler, 1947, p 76.

55   M J Adler, 1947, p 79.

56   M J Adler, 1947, p 83.

Over time, lawyers have sought to further elaborate the natural law/positive law difference by drawing a distinction between principles or precepts and rules. Principles and precepts — like the injunction to seek the good or the proscription against killing or theft are not capable:

> [B]y themselves of governing action, — for different reasons ... in the case of principles, because they specify only one end, and action depends on specification of means; in the case of precepts, because they specify the means only generally and without reference to the contingent circumstances which are always involved in action.[57]

It is the contingent circumstances that make rules, the usual stuff of positive law, far different from principle and precept. Two consequences flow from the introduction of contingent circumstances, or facts:

> The first is that since facts are infinite in number, they cannot all be comprehended by human reason. Therefore any rule which is based upon them must be based upon the generality of experience and will be defective to the extent that it fails to provide for the unknown or the unusual case. The second is that facts change, and therefore laws must change, to preserve a reasonable relation to facts.[58]

In short, natural law principles and precepts are immutable, whereas rules are 'relative, contingent and changeable'.[59]

The role of judges

Hayek views the legislative process as a latter-day invention that poses grave danger to individual liberty. He would confine the process to 'definite limited tasks required to bring about the formation of a spontaneous order'.[60] The bulk of the work is to be performed by judges articulating abstract rules of conduct or principles that do not disappoint expectations. Thus, the small corrective role that Hayek assigns to positive law does not provide any significant guidance to judges who occupy positions where legislatures are not largely inert — that is, in most places. These judges face real conflicts that are largely unresolved by Hayek's yearning for modern nation-states where judge-made law predominates. Confronted with prolix federal statutes that not only weaken individual liberty, but more importantly, displace the sovereign authority of smaller natural law communities, such as families and churches, one can readily agree with Hayek's utopian desires. But what is a judicial officer, not resident in utopia, to do in the face of these positive enactments? It is not enough to say that it would be better if legislatures would defer to the common law or adopt its methodology.

One further significant consequence, therefore, of a proper recognition of natural law is that it does not leave real life judges instructionally

---

57 H McKinnon, *1947 Natural Law Intitute Proceedings* (ed A Scanlon), University of Notre Dame, Notre Dame, Indiana, 1947, p 97.

58 McKinnon, 1947, p 98.

59 McKinnon, 1947, p 98.

60 F A Hayek, *Law Legislation and Liberty*, vol 3, Routlege Kegan Paul, London, 1979, p 6.

adrift. In particular, natural law judges are not usually or generally directed to second-guess the legislative process, but contrary to Blackstone and Bork, that power is reserved. When the legislative process yields a true conflict between the explicit text of the Constitution or a natural law principle or precept, a judge is duty bound to act to set a statute aside. Thus, natural law is capable of harmonising a judge's duty to follow the law as written with the judge's duty to do justice; to ensure that the positive law is not itself an injustice. Natural law, unlike the positivism of Bork or the weaker spontaneous order of Hayek, does not shrug off Nazi atrocity with the response 'well, the law is the law'. Hayek feebly claims that his spontaneous order-based conception of law surmounts the positivist's dilemma with respect to atrocity,[61] but his claim ultimately drowns in abstraction and the lack of content of what he ascribes to the order itself. What morality is reflected in the law of the spontaneous order is merely a function of 'rules to which the recognized procedure of enforcement by appointed authority ought to apply'.[62] This is either a weaker, more inchoate form of positivism, or it begs the question.

Conclusion

At bottom, the jurisprudence of liberty that Hayek prescribes fails to deal with the world as we know it. But more profoundly, Hayek's philosophic search flounders because he asserts that 'there can be no justification for representing the rules of just conduct as natural in the sense that they are part of an external and eternal order of things, or permanently implanted in an unalterable nature of man'.[63] Why not? Where is his positive proof of the denial of God? Hayek is correct to warn us against the perils of modern day legislation with its mistaken burdens, mandates and impositions. He is right that the common law process would give greater liberty. Yet, because of Hayek's incomplete appreciation for the natural law basis of customary law, the greater liberty he extols would still be subject to ill-purpose, abuse and misdirection. Thus, in his warning to us, Hayek gives us no adequate defence against powerful attacks on social order. Ultimately, Hayek seeks to recast as 'objective truth', not man's God-created nature, but 'the views and opinions which shape the order of society, as well as the resulting order of that society'.[64] 'Views and opinions' antagonistic to God's plan, whether fashioned in legislative enactment or 'spontaneously' over an extended period of time in judicial decree, are hardly immutable first principles and they have led, and continue to lead, to the defeat of our happiness.

61   F A Hayek, *Law Legislation and Liberty*, vol 2, Routlege Kegan Paul, London, 1976, p 56.
62   F A Hayek, 1976, p 58.
63   F A Hayek, 1976, p 59–60.
64   F A Hayek, 1976, p 6.

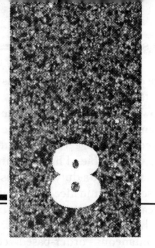

CHAPTER 8

The German Borderguard Cases: Natural Law and the Duty to Disobey Immoral Laws

Gabriël A Moens*

A jurisprudential problem

The circumstances giving rise to an individual's obligation to disobey laws that are incompatible with higher moral principles have been the subject of an enduring jurisprudential debate since the end of the Second World War. The Nuremberg trials attributed individual criminal responsibility for acts against humanity performed in obedience to superior orders, or done pursuant to the laws of the regime holding power at the time at which they were committed. The trials imposed upon individuals a duty to disobey laws which are clearly recognisable as violating higher moral principles. This has become known as the 'Nuremberg Principle'.

The Nuremberg trials contributed to a revival of natural law thinking in post-war Germany. In its widest form natural law theory holds that certain rights exist independently of the legal system and are incapable of abolition by legislative act. Any law purporting to violate these rights ceases to be law and cannot command the obedience of citizens. In contrast, legal positivists support the separation of law and morals. They recognise constitutionally valid laws as legally binding upon citizens even if these laws infringe upon human rights.

In the recent borderguard cases, German courts were asked to consider the applicability of the 'Nuremberg Principle'. These cases are a direct consequence of German reunification which occurred on 3 October 1990. Following reunification, there were incessant demands by the German public to initiate legal action against East German borderguards who, before

---

* Professor of Law, T C Beirne School of Law, University of Queensland, and Director, The Australian Institute of Foreign and Comparative Law.

reunification, killed East Germans trying to escape to the West. Most borderguards accused of these shootings sought to rely on justifications found in the law of the former East Germany. In particular, they relied upon a defence of obedience to superior orders. This defence caused the German courts to assess the applicability of the 'Nuremberg Principle'.

In this chapter, I propose to discuss two of these borderguard cases. The first case resulted in a judgment of the *Bundesgerichtshof* (BGH) on 3 November 1992.[1] The second case was resolved by a decision of the District Court of Berlin on 20 January 1992.[2] Relying at least in part on the 'minimum content' theory of natural law, these judgments held that borderguards responsible for killing fleeing civilians may be prosecuted by the courts of a reunified Germany. It is not the purpose of this chapter to offer a fully developed account of the 'minimum content' theory of natural law. Instead, this chapter aims to describe the use made by the two German courts of this theory and to make some tentative comments regarding the appropriateness of such use. In addition, it will be argued that these judgments were unsatisfactory as they were based on West German judicial and philosophical concepts alien to East Germans.

Relevant German laws

Section 315 EGStGB

Article 8 of the Reunification Treaty (*Einigungvertrag*) provides for the application of West German law to former East German territory from the date of reunification (3 October 1990). However the borderguard cases deal with acts committed *prior* to reunification. These cases required a determination, by the courts of a reunified Germany, of the continuing applicability of East German law to fatal shootings which occurred on East German soil prior to reunification.

The Reunification Treaty introduced s 315 EGStGB[3] which provides for a modified application of West German law to crimes committed in East Germany *prior* to reunification. Section 315(1)-(3) EGStGB implements the Criminal Code of West Germany (StGB) which provides in its s 2(3) that when a crime is committed and there is a subsequent change in the law the milder of the laws is to be applied.[4] Reunification involved a change in the law because West German law took the place of East German law. In the usual situation s 315 EGStGB and s 2 StGB immunise from punishment acts committed on East German soil prior to reunification if these acts were not punishable under East German law. This avoids the imposition of a penalty which did not exist at the time the act was committed.

1   BGH Urt 3.11.1992, *Neue Juristische Wochenschrift*, 1993, No 2, p 141.
2   LG Berlin Urt 20.1.1992, *Neue Justiz*, 1992, p 269–73.
3   BGBl II 1990, p 955.
4   Section 315(2) and (3) implements this rule for fines and other punishments.

Relationship between s 315 EGStGB and s 7 StGB

By virtue of s 315(4), the immunity from punishment in s 315(1)-(3) does not apply where West German law was already the applicable law at the time an act was committed. Of particular importance is s 7 StGB, under which prosecutions of those responsible for fatal border shootings in East Germany could proceed in West Germany prior to reunification.[5] This section applies West German law to acts committed on foreign soil when:

(a) the acts are committed against Germans (s 7(1)); or
(b) the person who committed the act becomes a resident of West Germany or comes to its territory (s 7(2)).

Professor Erich Samson argues that since upon reunification East Germany became part of West German territory, s 7(2) StGB applies to all former East German citizens since they have become 'West German residents'.[6]

A similar argument could be made under s 7(1): that the East Germans against whom the acts were committed were Germans. Before reunification, West German law was applied to foreigners who committed crimes against East German citizens. Under West German constitutional law, East German citizens were deemed to have West German citizenship. They were thus 'Germans' for the purposes of s 7(1).

While technically sound, this interpretation is strained because in all other contexts East Germans were regarded as foreigners under West German law. Furthermore, application of s 7 StGB to the borderguard cases would allow the unqualified application of West German law to all acts committed against East German citizens before reunification. This would effectively exclude the protection given by the provision requiring application of the milder law (s 315(1)) since s 315(4) would mandate the application of the West German law which existed when the act was committed. For this reason, the BGH rejected the applicability of s 7 StGB to the borderguard cases. Therefore, s 315 operates so that the milder law will be applied to actions committed prior to reunification provided that West German law was not already applicable at the time the act occurred. Under the territoriality principle of ss 3 and 9 of the West German Criminal Code (StGB), an act committed in East Germany was subject to West German law if the consequences of the act occurred on West German territory. West German law also applied to acts occurring in East Germany when:

---

5   See J Bohnert, 'Die Amnestien der DDR und das Strafrecht nach dem Beitritt', (1993) *DtZ* No 3 at 167-73; G Küpper and H Wilms, 'Die Verfolgung von Straftaten des SED-Regimes', (1992) *ZRP* No 3 at pp 91-6; J Renzikowski, 'Zur Strafbarkeit des Schusswaffengebrauchs an der innerdeutschen Grenze', *Neue Justiz*, 1992, pp 152–5; H J Scholzen and M A Gladbeck, 'Zur Bedeutung von s 7 StGB für die Verfolgung von Straftaten des SED-Regimes', *ZRP*, 1992, No 12, pp 476–80.

6   E Samson, 'Die strafrechtliche Behandlung von DDR-Alttaten nach der Einigung Deutschlands', (1991) *Neue Juristische Wochenschrift*, No 6 at 335–40.

(a) the act was committed against a German whose permanent residence was in West Germany (s 7(1)), hence, not applicable in the borderguard cases;

(b) when an act was carried out by a West German (s 7(2)), hence, again not applicable to the borderguard cases; or

(c) when the perpetrator of a crime moved to the former West Germany before reunification which occurred on 3 October 1990: s 7(2)(ii).

The 'milder' law

Murder was a criminal act in both West Germany and East Germany. Under the West German Criminal Code (StGB-BRD) murder was punishable with imprisonment for not less than five years (s 212). In less serious cases the sentence could be reduced to a period of between six months and five years (s 213). In contrast, under the East German Criminal Code (StGB-DDR) murder was punishable with imprisonment from six months to ten years (s 112). When the possible reduction of punishment under West German law is taken into account, West German law was the milder law.

On the other hand, if East German law provided justifications for the killings, East German law would be the 'milder' of the two competing laws. In cases where East German law provided a total justification for fatal shootings at the border, East German borderguards could be exempt from punishment.

The issue thus arose as to whether justifications available under East German law could be relied upon by borderguards. In its judgment of 3 November 1992, the BGH considered two possible justifications under East German law. The first involved s 27(1) of East Germany's border law (*Grenzgesetz*). It provided that the use of firearms was justified to prevent the imminent completion of a 'crime' at the border. A definition of 'crime' was found in s 3(1) StGB-DDR. This section not only classified certain acts as 'crimes' but also provided that acts which were not listed could retrospectively become 'crimes' by the imposition by courts of a sentence of imprisonment for more than two years. Section 213 StGB-DDR provided for the imposition of terms of imprisonment of between one year and nine years in cases of 'serious crime'. A crime was a 'serious crime' if carried out with 'dangerous means' (s 213(2) StGB-DDR). East German courts invariably characterised ladders and other climbing devices used in escape attempts as 'dangerous means'. Thus, if a court imposed a penalty of more than two years' imprisonment for an unsuccessful attempt to climb the Berlin Wall with such 'dangerous' devices, then the use of firearms at the scene of the crime was retrospectively justified. As interpreted by the East German authorities, s 27 (*Grenzgesetz*) obliged guards to prevent attempted escapes by killing if necessary.

The second justification under East German law was found in s 258 StGB-DDR. It provided that a soldier (or borderguard) following orders was not criminally responsible for carrying out the order unless the order constituted a blatant violation of international or criminal law or it was obvious that it was contrary to higher morals.

The majority of the BGH decided that the borderguards could not avail themselves of these justifications under East German law. Borderguards would not be able to evade criminal liability altogether because the 'milder' West German law would be applied in cases where East German justifications are rejected. It is appropriate to provide a more detailed examination of the facts of the borderguard cases and of the reasons of the court in the next section of this chapter.

The judgment of 3 November 1992

The facts of the case

In late 1984 Michael S decided to escape over the border from East Berlin to West Berlin. He used his ladder to climb over a signal fence. He was observed from a watchtower by defendant W, who ordered his co-defendant H to prevent the escape. W called out to Michael S to 'stay put'. Michael S did not heed W's order, and ran to the Berlin Wall with the ladder. W fired a series of shots at him. As Michael S prepared to climb the ladder, co-defendant H realised that his escape could be prevented only by shooting. From a distance of 110 metres H shot at least 25 bullets at the calves of Michael S. From a distance of 150 metres defendant W also shot 27 bullets aimed at Michael S's legs.

A shot from W's rifle hit Michael S in the knee, and he fell to the ground. He was left without medical assistance for two and a half hours despite repeated requests to be taken to a hospital. When Michael S was finally taken to hospital he died within a short time. Had he received medical assistance sooner his death could have been avoided. Both defendants carried out the 'shoot to kill' order which they received in training and considered to be binding.

Following reunification, both defendants were found guilty of murder by the youth court of the Berlin District Court. W was sentenced to one and a half years' imprisonment. H received a jail term of one year and nine months. Both sentences were subject to probation. W appealed to Germany's highest court, the BGH.

Act of State doctrine

W argued, among other things, that the Berlin District Court had failed to consider the 'Act of State Doctrine'.[7] Under this doctrine, a defendant acting in the course of duty under the auspices, and in the interests, of another state, enjoys immunity from legal action and, therefore, cannot be called to account for his actions. The Act of State doctrine is based on the

---

7   The Court's judgment is discussed in Amelung K, 'Strafbarkeit von 'Mauerschützen' – BGH Neue Juristische Wochenschrift, 141', *JuS*, 1993, no 8, pp 637–643, and Schroeder F C, 'Die Rechtswidrigkeit der Flüchtlingeerschiessungen zwischen Transzendenz und Immanenz', *Juristische Rundschan,* 1993, no 2, pp 45–51, and 'Rechtfertigung von Todesschüssen an der Mauer', *NStZ*, 1992, no 10, pp 492–495.

notion that all nations are equally sovereign. The doctrine was described by Fuller CJ of the United States Supreme Court in *Underhill v Hernandez*[8] where he said that '[e]very sovereign state is bound to respect the independence of every other sovereign state, and the courts of one country will not sit in judgment on the acts of the government of another done within its own territory'.

The BGH held that this doctrine did not command universal respect, being essentially limited to the Anglo-Saxon world. It pointed out that in Germany, as elsewhere in continental Europe, there is no binding rule that foreign acts, adopted by authorities of a sovereign state, are exempt from consideration by the courts. Moreover, the Reunification Treaty did not stipulate that actions attributable to the East German authorities are exempt from consideration in post-reunification German courts. In fact, the opposite is quite true since the Treaty provided in Articles 18 and 19 that decisions of the courts or of the bureaucracy of East Germany remain valid but can be disregarded if they are found to be incompatible with fundamental principles of the rule of law. In any event, the BGH decided that even if the 'Act of State Doctrine' did apply, it could not be used by defendant W since he cannot be treated as a representative of a foreign state that no longer exists.

Section 27 Grenzgesetz-DDR

The BGH indicated that s 27 could be interpreted in three ways. First, it could be seen as a total justification for border shootings resulting in the death of escapees. Secondly, it could be interpreted in the light of other East German legal and constitutional provisions, leading to the conclusion that the excessive and disproportionate use of firearms at the border was not justified. Thirdly, s 27 could be challenged as contrary to natural law or internationally acknowledged human rights. The BGH mainly concentrated on this third interpretation which involved a consideration of the 'minimum content' of natural law.

The minimum content of natural law

The BGH considered the compatibility with higher law of the interpretation of s 27 by the East German authorities. If the shootings offended the 'minimum content' of natural law[9] the order to shoot could not be recognised as valid 'law'.

Before the Second World War, the noted legal philosopher Gustav Radbruch was one of Germany's chief representatives of the school of jurisprudence known as 'relativism'.[10] This school accepted that a legal character can be attributed to a 'law' if it has been adopted in accordance

---

8   168 US 250 at 252 (1897).

9   Known in Germany as the heart of the law (*Kernbereich des Rechts*).

10   G Radbruch, 'Legal Philosophy' in *The Legal Philosophies of Lask, Radbruch, and Dabin* (trans K Wilk), Harvard University Press, Cambridge, Massachusetts, 1950, p 57.

with the state's procedural requirements; the content of the law itself was irrelevant, thereby separating law and morals.[11] Radbruch also suggested that effective, yet pernicious, laws may be valuable since they promote legal certainty.[12] However, following the Second World War, Radbruch recognised that there are fundamental principles of morality which are part of the very concept of *Recht*. He argued that no law could be valid if it contravened basic principles of morality, even if it conformed with the formal criteria of validity of the legal system. A law which completely denied human rights could not possess the quality of 'law'. A duty of obedience to the law can never be grounded on the mere factual existence of a formally valid command, irrespective of the contents of the relevant legal rule. Thus in extreme cases of conflict between law and justice, statute law must yield to superior requirements of justice. These requirements could not be obviated by a return to an outmoded and immoral positivist system.

If the 'minimum content' of natural law had been breached by the 'shoot to kill' order, East German legal justifications could not prevail and would in effect be irrelevant. The BGH was reluctant to apply the Radbruch formula to the borderguard cases since the killing of escapees at an internal border cannot be equated to the genocide practised during the National Socialist era. Nonetheless, the principles applied in respect of Nazi atrocities could have been considered in determining whether East Germany had violated the requirements of natural law, and whether it had overstepped the limits which are generally accepted in civilised countries. The BGH did not decide whether the former East Germany had exceeded those limits. The BGH found that only in extreme circumstances should a justification existing at the time of the commission of the crime not be considered. Only in such circumstances would it be appropriate to rely on Radbruch's formula.

The BGH's reluctance to rely upon natural law reasoning can probably be explained by the obvious difficulties associated with any attempt to define the 'minimum content' of natural law. However, it is significant that the BGH admitted, in principle, that laws could be disregarded if they violate basic principles of justice and human rights.

International human rights

Instead of invoking natural law, the BGH based its decision on more positivistic grounds: East Germany's breach of international human rights law. The court especially considered the International Covenant on Civil and Political Rights.[13] On 2 November 1973, East Germany became a signatory to the Covenant. However, the Covenant remained unimplemented in domestic law. State practice did not correspond to the formal written laws which superficially appeared to comply with

---

11 G Radbruch, 1950, p 113.
12 G Radbruch, 1950, p 118.
13 999 UNTS 171.

international human rights instruments. The BGH opined that the Covenant could not be interpreted, by ratifying states, so as to make it conform to their ideological or political systems. Indeed, the Covenant sets a minimum level of protection of civil and political rights to which all parties must adhere.

Article 12(2) of the Covenant deals with the freedom to leave one's country. The court decided that East Germany's passport law of 28 June 1979 breached Article 12(2) of the Covenant since restrictions on a person's right to leave his or her country should be limited to clearly specified circumstances.

According to Article 6 of the Covenant, a person cannot be arbitrarily deprived of his or her life. The border practices of East Germany contravened this Article. The BGH interpreted the prohibition upon arbitrary deprivation of life as importing a 'proportionality principle',[14] requiring a rational relationship between a 'crime' and its 'punishment'. The East German interpretation of s 27 violated this principle since it condoned the killing of a person simply for attempting to cross the national border. Shootings at the border could only be justified in situations of absolute necessity.

The BGH discussed a fatal border shooting by a *West* German customs official. The official fired a machine gun at two people on a motorbike from a distance of around 100 metres. The BGH found the shooting justified since it appeared that the two people were smuggling hard drugs, leading to a real likelihood of a life threatening situation. This finding left the BGH open to accusations of applying a double standard: one for West German customs officials and one for East German borderguards. It also shows that in the view of the BGH, a fatal border shooting does not of itself constitute a breach of the Covenant. A violation only occurs if the fatal use of firearms is unnecessary for the purposes of enabling the state to achieve its objective. The BGH distinguished East German practice on the ground that there was unquestionable evidence that borderguards were encouraged to kill fleeing people in order to prevent them from reaching the West. The requirement that the means used be proportionate to the objective to prevent escapes was conveniently overlooked. On 3 May 1974, Communist Party Leader Erich Honecker decreed that ruthless use of firearms was to be resorted to and that if escape was prevented the shooter would be rewarded. Up until 1987 guards were instructed to capture or exterminate escapees.

The BGH concluded that the disproportionate use of firearms at the border violated the Covenant. The shootings were not absolutely necessary for the security of the border because the execution of a fleeing person with machine guns and mines was grossly disproportionate to the aim of preventing border crossings. The BGH noted that the East German practice of keeping fatal shootings secret deprived the state of its excuse for the shootings: the deterrence of future border crossings.

---

14   See *Tennesee v Garner* 471 US 1 (1985) with regards to the proportionality principle in an American context.

The defence of following orders: s 258 StGB-DDR

It will be recalled that s 258 StGB-DDR provided that a soldier (or borderguard) following orders was not criminally responsible for carrying out the order unless the order constituted a blatant violation of international or criminal law, or it was obvious that it was contrary to higher morals. Thus, if a soldier was subjectively aware that his conduct was illegal he would not be exempt from criminal prosecution. Also, a soldier could not avail himself of the defence if, on an objective test, it was obvious that his conduct was incompatible with higher moral norms.

A similar provision is found in s 5 of the West German Military Code (*Wehrgesetzbuch*). In 1921, in the celebrated *Llandovery Castle* case, the German Supreme Court convicted two lieutenants of murder for killing the defenceless passengers of a lifeboat, even though they had followed the commands of a superior officer.[15]

The BGH held that borderguards could not rely upon this defence because they could not have been unaware of the inherent immorality of the order they were given. Despite the indoctrination, rearing and education in East Germany, the fatal shooting of fleeing people offends ethical norms to such a degree that the defendants could not have been unaware of the immorality of the order to 'shoot to kill'. For example, on state holidays, when international guests were in the country, guards were given strict orders only to use firearms in emergencies. Such orders would have alerted borderguards to the possibility that the fatal use of firearms was immoral. Surely, borderguards should have reflected on why the use of firearms was condoned and even required on some days but restricted on other days. And while it was the practice that after a border killing a guard would be decorated, most guards did not wear their medals for fear of abuse from members of the public.

Furthermore, all reports of shootings at the border were suppressed. Because of the secrecy surrounding border killings, people were not always aware about what would happen when they attempted to flee. The point is, to the extent that the East German government kept its ruthless prevention of border crossings from the knowledge of its own people, they may have been responsible for an increase in the number of attempted escapes and associated deaths. In this way, the leaders of the former East Germany may be liable for inciting people to harm themselves.

The BGH examined whether border killings came within the category of 'crimes against humanity'. Article 6 of the Charter of the International Military Tribunal[16] defined 'crimes against humanity' as:

> [M]urder, extermination, enslavement, deportation, and other inhumane acts committed against any civilian population, before

---

15   Lord Russell of Liverpool, *The Knights of Bushido*, Corgi Books, London, 1972, pp 244–8. On the status of the defence of following orders in common law jurisdictions, see P Gillies, *Criminal Law*, 3rd ed, The Law Book Co Ltd, Sydney, 1993, p 212.

16   82 UNTS 284.

or during the war, or persecutions on political, racial or religious grounds in execution of or in connection with any crime within the jurisdiction of the Tribunal, whether or not in violation of the domestic law of the country where perpetrated.

The killings at the German border were not deemed to fall within the category of 'crimes against humanity'. This approach certainly enabled the court to give the impression that its decision was based on East German law existing at the time of the fatal border shooting, for s 258 StGB-DDR placed an obligation on soldiers to disregard orders that were clearly incompatible with higher moral principles.

Judgment of 20 January 1992

Facts of the case

This widely publicised case in the Berlin District Court involved the border killing of Christian Gueffroy and the wounding of his friend Christian Gaudian on 6 February 1989.[17] Four former borderguards were tried for murder. Defendant Ingo Heinrich was sentenced to three and a half years' imprisonment. Andreas Kühnpast was given a two year suspended sentence for attempted murder. His sentence was suspended because he showed genuine remorse. A not-guilty verdict was returned in the case of Mike Schmidt because he had not shot at any of the escapees. A not-guilty verdict was given in the case of Peter Schmett because it had been proven that he had targeted the feet of the escapees or the ground. The court reasoned that both Schmidt's and Schmett's actions were proportionate to the problem with which they were faced on 6 February 1989 and that therefore, they had acted in accordance with the letter of the East German law.

Different treatment of the defendants

The defence wanted a not-guilty verdict, because the deadly shots fired were in accordance with East German law. But the prosecution demanded suspended sentences for the four accused because they should have known that the relevant East German law was unjust. The prosecution argued that an unequal (and less severe) sentence could only be justified in the case of Schmidt, who gave the order to shoot but did not shoot himself.

So in effect both the defence and the prosecution urged the court to treat the four accused equally: they should all be declared not guilty or the same suspended sentence should be imposed upon all of them. However, the court declined to follow this course, rejecting the claim that the

---

17 See about this case J Hruschka, 'Die Todesschüsse an der Berliner Mauer vor Gericht', (1992) 13 *JZ* 667–70; K A Adams, 'What is Just? The Rule of Law and Natural Law in the Trials of Former East German Border Guards' (1993) 29 *Stanford Journal of International Law* 271 at 295–301.

accused be treated equally in matters of guilt and sentence. What these four accused did on the 6 February 1989 was not seen by the court as a *common* act against the two escapees. The court differentiated the states of guilt of the accused. According to the court, no law was broken by two of the soldiers. In targeting the feet of the escapees, Schmett acted in accordance with East German law. No law was breached by Schmidt's order to shoot. East German law was violated in the cases of Kuehnpast and Heinrich. Kuehnpast fired at the escapees from a great distance, thereby endangering the lives of Gueffroy and Gaudian, though he did not seriously injure them. There was incontrovertible evidence that the deadly shots were fired by Heinrich.

The court's judgment was based on untenable distinctions. If the shooting resulted in death, the shooter was guilty whereas the soldier who sought to inflict bodily injury may escape punishment. The court's judgment sought to identify a *main* culprit, ie a defendant who was more guilty than the other defendants. It could be argued that Heinrich was not the main actor in these events, but was only a tool in the hands of his criminal employer.

Minimum content of natural law

In a feeble attempt to come to terms with Radbruch's 'minimum content' of natural law, the court affirmed that such a concept limits the power of the state. Not every statute is law.[18] There is a right to life which no statute (*Gesetz*) may violate. The order to shoot did not deserve to be obeyed.

The court should have answered some of the most difficult, yet perennial, issues of jurisprudence. These include the following questions. Under what circumstances is it impossible to attribute a 'legal' character to the orders of the authorities? When should people disobey laws which have been validly adopted by the legislature? Can the acts of the defendants be justified on the ground that they were following orders? The court did not adequately consider any of these questions.

Importance of the borderguard judgments

While the Berlin District Court relied more on natural law principles, the BGH chose to base its decision on international human rights codifications. Either way, in both judgments, the courts of reunified Germany have insisted that its people should have had a more acute moral vision.

Both judgments will undoubtedly influence the many other borderguard cases which are pending in German courts. These judgments are authority for the proposition that, under present legal developments in Germany, it is possible to prosecute the executors of 'immoral' orders given by higher authorities. As a result of the BGH finding that the East

---

18 'Statute' is translated into German as *Gesetz*; 'law' is translated as *Recht*. The Judge said (literally translated) that 'what is *Gesetz* (statute) is not always *Recht*'. Thus, *Recht* and *Gesetz* do not always overlap.

German implementation of the laws (rather than the letter of laws) breached international human rights standards, former members of the East German legislature who passed these laws will not be prosecuted.[19]

The fact that the BGH did not equate fatal border shootings with crimes committed in the National Socialist era will not detract from the criminal liability of judges and prosecutors who were involved in the legal justice system. They include the judges who imposed harsh sentences on those who were unsuccessful in their attempts to cross the border; these judges themselves were involved in breaching their own East German laws.

The duty to disobey an immoral law

The attribution of criminal responsibility to borderguards who conducted themselves according to rules which were regarded as 'law' when the actions were committed is a highly controversial step because it may be argued, with some plausibility, that it violates the principle that no person should be punished except for the breach of the law (*nulla poena sine lege*). The invalidation of a 'law' is based on the ground that its provisions are too inhumane to be characterised as law. In both judgments, discussed above, the courts assumed that the 'shoot to kill' policy violated the 'minimum content' of natural law, but failed to examine this issue in detail. In particular, the courts did not establish any guidelines which could be used as benchmarks against which the morality or immorality of the borderguards' conduct could be tested. The reasoning of the courts rested on the assumption that people possess a critical moral and legal vision which enables them to readily recognise the 'immoral laws' that higher law requires them to disobey.

Natural law versus legal positivism

The question whether there is a duty to disobey immoral laws was debated by two influential legal philosophers, H L A Hart and Lon L Fuller, in the *Harvard Law Review* in 1958. The debate was triggered by the changed views, after the Second World War, of Radbruch, and the treatment, by German courts, of grudge informers. Professor Hart took the view that what is law and what ought to be law are two separate issues.[20] Professor Fuller, a proponent of natural law theory, argued forcefully that law must contain a minimum moral content for it to be characterised as law. A rule, which did not satisfy this minimum content, could not legitimately command the obedience of citizens. For Fuller law

---

19   Prominent members of the former East German regime and security service have also been prosecuted. Some of these prosecutions have been successful. However, Erich Honecker succeeded in avoiding prosecution on the grounds of old age and ill-health. See M J Lasky, 'The Trial of Erich Honecker — Before and After', (Winter 1993) *Australia and World Affairs* 11.

20   H L A Hart, 'Positivism and the Separation of Law and Morals', (1958) 71 *Harvard Law Review* 593.

is 'an object of human striving'[21] and a formal description of a human institution which does not include a description of its purposes must be inadequate. He revealed his preference for natural law theory when, in his assessment of Nazi atrocities, he stated that:

> We have ... to inquire how much of a legal system survived the general debasement and perversion of all forms of social order that occurred under the Nazi rule, and what moral implications this mutilated system had for the conscientious citizen forced to live under it.[22]

In his book *The Morality of Law*,[23] Professor Fuller makes a distinction between the external and the internal morality of law. Whereas his concept of external morality relates to the extent to which laws deserve to be respected and obeyed, internal morality deals with the minimum conditions which every mature legal system must satisfy in order to achieve its purpose. These conditions, which are inherent in the concept of 'law', include the requirements that rules must be prospective, must not be constantly changing, and their implementation by officials must not be perverted. It could be argued that the relevant East German laws failed to meet these conditions since, in accordance with s 3(1) StGB-DDR, certain acts could retrospectively become 'crimes' and there was a discrepancy between the rules and the way in which they were implemented. Although Fuller's conditions do not, in themselves, guarantee that legal rules will be just — a point made by Hart — their satisfaction will usually promote respect for the rule of law. Therefore, these conditions possess moral value which is worthy of preservation.

Difficulties in the application of the natural law theory

However, arguments which are based on the 'minimum content' of the law suffer from serious intellectual infirmities. The notion of a 'minimum content' of natural law must somehow be given an objective existence. That is, there must be shown to exist some objectively valid body of ethical rules with which laws must be compatible. Natural law proponents argue that these rules derive from the 'nature of humans' or come from God, as revealed in the scriptures. The problem with this line of argument is that it involves the attribution of the property of 'goodness' or 'badness' to state-imposed acts. However, ethical concepts such as 'goodness' and 'badness' cannot be treated as properties. If I were to say that this page is green then it can easily be ascertained that it is green because 'green-ness' is a property. In contrast, ethical rules codify values that are subject to disagreement. It is not the purpose of this chapter to consider this issue in detail. It suffices for my present purposes to point out that there are obvious complications involved in any attempt to identify those ethical

---

21 L L Fuller, 'Positivism and Fidelity to Law — A Reply to Professor Hart', (1958) 71 *Harvard Law Review* 630 at 646.

22 L L Fuller, 1958, p 646.

23 L L Fuller, *The Morality of Law*, rev ed, Yale University Press, New Haven, Connecticut, 1969.

rules which are part of the 'minimum content' of natural law. It may plausibly be claimed that this 'minimum content' consists of nothing else but standards set by individuals for themselves, according to their own experiences. Hans Kelsen encapsulated this view in his book *What is Justice?* He argued that the question of whether one value is superior to another cannot be resolved in the same way as the question whether iron is heavier than water or water heavier than wood. He continued:

> This latter question can be resolved by experience in a rational scientific way, but the question as to the highest value in the subjective sense of the term can be decided only emotionally, by the feelings or the wishes of the deciding subject. One subject may be led by his emotions to prefer personal freedom; another, social security; one, the welfare of the single individual; the other, the welfare of the whole nation. By no rational consideration can it be proved that the one is right or the other wrong.[24]

If Kelsen is right, incompatible values can claim equal validity, even though they cannot coexist in the same value systems. Both the objective and subjective (or relativist) approaches to the 'minimum content' of natural law are, however, inflexible in that they are implacably opposed to compromises.

To question natural law arguments is not to reject the *pursuit* of high ideals, only to question that such ideals have any inherent legal character. The pursuit of such ideals undoubtedly contributes to the betterment of society. Indeed, Eugene Kamenka, to whom this book is dedicated, recently reminded us that:

> A crude concept of 'value-free' social science as implying moral, cultural and even epistemological relativism, together with a levelling version of democracy, does indeed end in the desire to excise the concept of judgment from social and moral life and in giving the word 'culture' many meanings and thus no meaning at all.[25]

The German tradition versus the critical tradition

Reliance upon natural law theory by German courts also overlooks the fact that, historically and traditionally, the *German tradition* of obedience to the law placed a heavy onus of justification on people who wanted to disobey 'unjust' laws. This tradition certainly lasted in West Germany until after the Second World War when it was superseded gradually by what could be called a *critical tradition* which made it feasible for West German citizens to contemplate disobeying a law which is recognised by them as 'immoral' or obviously offends supra-positive norms. In contrast, the German tradition of obedience to the law largely persisted in East Germany until reunification. Subject to the validity of this point, it can reasonably be argued that the judgments of the courts, discussed above,

---

24   H Kelsen, *What is Justice?*, University of California Press, Berkeley and Los Angeles, 1957, p 141.

25   E Kamenka, 'Australia Made Me...But Which Australia is Mine?', the John Curtin Memorial Lecture, Australian National University, Canberra, 1993, p 16.

involve the imposition of the post-war West German critical tradition on East German borderguards who, regardless of the morality of the relevant orders or laws, were undoubtedly imbued with the German tradition of unqualified obedience to the law.

The German tradition to obey the state's laws was a derivative of the individual's obligation to obey God. Georg G Iggers, in tracing the origins of German historicism, discussed the role which Lutheran theology played in the development of this tradition:

> In the place of a concept of a rational law of Nature, Luther substituted an irrational law of Nature. Luther argued in accordance with St Paul's admonition that 'there is no power but of God: the powers that be are ordained of God.' Every state represented the will of God, and thus required the complete obedience of the Christian in all matters temporal. Reason therefore expressed itself not in abstract moral commandments, but in historical institutions. The positive authorities were the concrete manifestations of natural law.[26]

As the state was ordained by God to govern the secular sphere, it followed that obedience to God demanded obedience to the state. Where the morality of the individual came into conflict with the morality of the state, the morality of the state prevailed. Lutheran theology, however, recognised the existence of the doctrine of resistance to the state. But it only condoned disobedience to the state in cases where the state stepped outside the secular sphere and trespassed into the spiritual sphere.

The idea that the state is the secular expression of God's will is, of course, not novel. St Thomas Aquinas argued in his great treatise *Summa Theologica* that the state is part of a divine order which is controlled by God. Consequently, humans are bound to obey human laws to the extent that they are compatible with natural law, which is discoverable through reason, or divine law. But for Aquinas, the duty to disobey human rules which violate natural law or divine law is, however, not absolute. For him, the subjects of rulers may, in exceptional circumstances, be obliged to obey even immoral laws when necessary to avoid 'scandal or some particular danger'.[27] This latter point indicates that Aquinas was of the view that the consequences of disobeying immoral laws must be considered by people. If the dangers resulting from disobedience substantially outweigh its benefits, people should choose obedience.

In Germany, the religious tradition of obedience to authority was reinforced by Herder's thesis of the benevolence of history. Herder contended that history was the secular expression of a higher order.[28] The German nation, being the product of its own historical experience, was considered to be the product of a higher order of history and the secular expression of the will of God. By implication, the nation's spirit was an historical force and was, therefore, the product of a higher order.

---

26 G G Iggers, *The German Conception of History*, Wesleyan University Press, Middletown, Connecticut, 1968, pp 33–4.

27 T Aquinas, *Summa Theologica*, 1a 2ae, Question 91, Arts 1 and 2.

28 G G Iggers, 1968, note 26, pp 34–7.

Hegel translated this tradition of obedience into political terms. Hegelian theory rejected the existence of a universal standard of value. This precluded the construction of an ethical norm against which the moral standards of the state could be compared. In the absence of an universal norm the morality of the state was defined by the state itself. The Hegelian state 'is not an institution for the realization of ethics but is this realization itself.'[29] Thus the morality of the individual came to be subordinated to the morality of the state: where the individual acted under the dictates of the state, the individual was subject to the moral standards of the state.

This German tradition of obedience to the law influenced the positivist theory of law which arguably dominated German legal thinking until after the Second World War.[30] Although a number of competing criteria could be used to clarify the possible meanings of 'positivism', in the main, its proponents argued that the validity of law depended on the satisfaction of minimum procedural requirements and did not involve an examination of its content.[31] Legal validity implied an obligation to obey the law. Such obligation was usually religiously observed by judges. Loewenstein observed that, traditionally, a German judge 'is unaffected by intellectual doubts as to the intrinsic justice of the legal rule he has to apply, provided it is enacted by the authority of the State, and he does not question whether the authority is legitimate or not'.[32] The formulation of the judges' obligation to obey the law was as important to German law as the formulation of due process of law was to the law of the United States.[33] This understanding of the law was also formulated by Léon Duguit when he said that if 'the State is by nature a sovereign will, that is to say, a will which commands individuals and is not subordinated to any other will, how can it be in subjection to a rule binding upon it, since by definition there is no other will capable of imposing a rule upon it?'[34] In 1883, the German Imperial Court asserted that 'the constitutional provision that well-acquired rights must not be injured, is to be understood only as a rule for the legislative power itself to interpret, and does not signify that a command given by the legislative power should be left disregarded by the judge because it injures well-acquired rights'.[35] Positive law, by definition, is the product of the higher order and, therefore, commands unswerving loyalty.

---

29   C J Friedrich, *The Philosophy of Law in Historical Perspective*, the University of Chicago Press, Chicago, 1963, p 131.

30   K Loewenstein, 'Reconstruction of the Administration of Justice in American-Occupied Germany', (1948) 61 *Harvard Law Review* 419.

31   H Rottleuthner, 'Legal Positivism and National Socialism: A Contribution to a Theory of Legal Development' in *Critical Legal Thought: An American-German Debate* (eds C Joerges and D M Trubek), Nomos Verlagsgesellschaft, Baden-Baden, 1989, pp 88–9.

32   K Loewenstein, 1948, note 30 above, p 432.

33   H Nagel, 'Judicial Review in Germany', (1954) 3 *The American Journal of Comparative Law* 236.

34   L Duguit, 'The Law and the State', (1917) 31 *Harvard Law Review* 1 at 7.

35   Decision of 17 February, 1883, RGZ 9 (1882), 235. See D P Kommers, *Judicial Politics in West Germany. A Study of the Federal Constitutional Court*, Sage Publications, Beverly Hills and London, 1976, p 36.

The critical tradition: judicial review of legislation

As the German tradition combined morality and power in the state, it denied the need to restrict the state's legislative power. In West Germany, this was reflected in the absence until 1949 of a system of judicial review of legislation involving the testing of laws in the light of a higher human law, for example, the Constitution, or higher moral principles. The German tradition had the effect of subordinating the power to review the actions of the state to the obligation to obey the state and its laws. Judicial review of legislation was seen by proponents of legal positivism as an impediment to the legislature. The obligation to obey the law was contained in Article 102 of the Weimar Constitution according to which the judges, whilst independent, were subject only to the (positive) law. This obligation is also contained in virtually the same form in Article 97(1) of the Basic Law of 1949 according to which '[t]he judges shall be independent and subject only to the law'.

However, some standards of a higher moral order which had been part of the German Civil Code, for example, good faith and good morals, were rehabilitated after the Second World War by courts.[36] More importantly, the Basic Law of 1949, in providing for judicial review of legislation, overcame the restriction on the power to review the content of the law. Indeed, in its Article 1(3) it provided that the 'basic rights shall bind the legislature, the executive and the judiciary as directly enforceable law'. Article 20(3) stipulates that '[l]egislation shall be subject to the constitutional order; the executive and the judiciary shall be bound by law and justice'. It could be argued that these constitutional provisions jointly recognise the right of the individual to resist an immoral law (*gesetzliches Unrecht*) that violates the basic rights of people. Thus, under present constitutional arrangements, judges have an implied power to review the content of the ordinary law in the light of the Basic Law. Since 1949, West German citizens can challenge laws which are opposed to the fundamental moral values of the community or of the individual. German jurisprudence since the Second World War interpreted the rights enshrined in the Basic Law not as granted by the Constitution, but as existing before it and independently of it.[37]

The absence of the critical tradition in East Germany

However, the critical tradition adopted by the West Germans after the Second World War, as exemplified in the Basic Law, could not be extended to East Germany because any review of legislation would have involved a challenge to the ruling communist elite. As seen in earlier parts of this chapter, in East Germany, the German tradition of unquestioned obedience to the law remained a controlling influence. In their training

---

36 See, eg *Luth's Case* 7 *BVerfGE* 198 (1958).
37 See cases discussed in D P Kommers, *The Constitutional Jurisprudence of the Federal Republic of Germany*, Duke University Press, Durham and London, 1989.

and education, borderguards were imbued with the German tradition of unqualified obedience to the law. The West German critical tradition, which allows West German citizens to disobey laws offending higher moral principles, was alien to East German law. While West Germany repudiated the German tradition after the Second World War, East German law elevated it as an ideal. It is thus necessary to take into account that East German social thought and practice were inimical to the development of a critical tradition. In advocating non-critical obedience to the state, the German tradition which continued to exert an inordinate influence in East Germany precluded the development of a critical tradition which would have facilitated a decision by East German citizens to disobey an 'immoral' law. If this understanding of the borderguard cases is right, then the willingness of East German borderguards to follow orders is not an historic aberration of the German tradition.

A consideration of the actions of borderguards accused of fatal shootings should ideally take into account the strong influence that the duty to obey laws has had in German history. When this tradition is overlooked as it was in the two German judgments, ideas foreign to the borderguards were imposed upon them. The difficulties involved in the identification of the 'minimum' content of natural law by people who have not sufficiently been exposed to the critical tradition are apparent. Such imposition may result in 'unjust' decisions because it involves the application of West Germany's critical tradition to East German conditions.

The injustice lies in the fact that the apparently 'just' convictions of East German borderguards do not appropriately consider the German tradition of obedience to law. This injustice relates also, among other things, to the difficulties involved in the identification of the 'minimum content' of natural law by people who have never been exposed to the critical tradition. Why should the conduct of citizens who lived in a communist dictatorship, where freedom of action was severely circumscribed, be judged in accordance with standards which apply in a liberal democracy, where freedom of action is broad? Why should an obligation to disobey an immoral law be imposed on ordinary soldiers who may not have the means to discover the extent of the alleged immorality? How is it possible for people, in general, to distinguish actions that are compatible with the 'minimum content' of natural law and actions that are not? *But what of r.v.?*

The failure of the courts of the reunified Germany to find justifications in East German law for the fatal shootings, under the guise of adherence to natural law, erodes the certainty of the law and the legitimate expectations of the borderguards. It is worthwhile to speculate whether the erosion of these expectations leads to the unintentional development of a mobocratic society, since the 'minimum content' of natural law is not defined by any unanimously recognised set of values. It is useful, in this context, to be mindful of Kamenka's prophetic reminder that '[v]irtues pressed beyond a certain point become vices, and particular virtues need to be balanced by others that make inconsistent, even contradictory, demands'.[38] As seen before, Aquinas also alerts us to the need to balance the 'higher' moral principles which the German courts indicated should have been followed by the borderguards, against other principles which require obedience to laws which have been validly enacted. Kamenka's and Aquinas' message is not unimportant. It points to the societal cost which is inevitably associated with irrational and indiscriminate disregard for the legal system. As Fuller reminds us, compliance with his internal conditions satisfies the rule of law, which, itself, is a moral value worthy of protection. If this admonition is disregarded, the duty to disobey an immoral law might erode and adversely affect respect for law and result in instability within a legal system since the validity of legal rules would constantly be in doubt.

Conclusion

Since the Second World War, there has always been much speculation as to whether the development of an anti-positivist attitude would be ephemeral in character or whether it would result in a lasting reorientation of legal philosophical thinking in Germany. The application by the post-war German courts of the 'minimum content' of natural law to borderguards indicates that natural law thinking reasserts itself whenever there is a need to react against the evils committed by a totalitarian regime.

The judgments discussed in this chapter suggest that the prosecution and conviction of the borderguards result in injustices masquerading as justice. Although the borderguard cases appear, on the surface, to have delivered substantive justice, the legal system of the reunified Germany failed to achieve a satisfactory resolution to the perennial problem of whether there is a duty on citizens to disobey immoral laws.

---

38 E Kamenka, 1993, note 25 above, pp 13–14.

CHAPTER 9

Liberty, Law and Economics

R Ian McEwin*

Introduction

Law and economics has become, at least in the United States, a major school of jurisprudence in the last twenty years. However combining economics and law is not a new endeavour. Beccario and Bentham adopted economic approaches to criminal law in the nineteenth century.[1] In the late nineteenth century in the United States, a law and economics movement arose as a reaction to the rise of neoclassicism. This movement was dubious about the benefits of markets and tended to be concerned with the relationship between law and wealth redistribution.[2]

The new 'law and economics' began in the 1960s with sophisticated economic analyses of nuisance by Coase[3] and of tort law by Calabresi.[4] Since then economic tools have been utilised not only to examine the legal system in market settings but also to examine non-market phenomena such as rioting, church attendance, divorce and so on.[5]

Mainstream economic analysis of law examines legal doctrine in terms of economic cost-benefit analysis using the *hypothetical Pareto improvement* concept of economic efficiency to draw conclusions about the impact and

---

*   Reader and Director, Centre for Law and Economics, Faculty of Law, Australian National University.

1   See R A Posner, *Economic Analysis of Law*, Little, Brown and Co, Boston, 1992, p 22, footnote 2.

2   H Hovenkamp, 'The First Great Law and Economics Movement', (1990) 42 *Stanford Law Review* 992.

3   R H Coase, 'The Problem of Social Cost', (1960) 3 *Journal of Law and Economics* 1.

4   G Calabresi, 'Some thoughts on Risk Distribution and the Law of Torts', (1961) 70 *Yale Law Journal* 499.

5   See T Burrows and C G Veljanovski, 'Introduction: The Economic Approach to Law' in *The Economic Approach to Law* (eds P Burrows and C G Veljanovski), Butterworths, London, 1981, pp 2–3.

social value of particular legal arrangements. Economic analysis has been used to look at the likely impact on behaviour of changes in criminal sanctions or changes in liability for accidents. Mainstream economic analysis also uses the tools of neoclassical analysis to describe the economic content of legal rules.

Much of the mainstream economic analysis of law has been based on work undertaken by Richard Posner, now a Federal Court judge in the United States but formerly a law professor at the University of Chicago. Posner makes a descriptive claim that judge-made common law rules generally maximise wealth. Not only does Posner argue that existing rules are best explained by this wealth maximisation hypothesis but he also makes a normative claim — judges should maximise society's overall wealth. Posner's approach has come in for a great deal of criticism from scholars with varying philosophical backgrounds including libertarian and classical liberal scholars.

This chapter provides an introductory overview of the relationship between liberty and modern law and economics analysis. It begins by outlining the approach and basic methodology of modern mainstream economics. Some knowledge of economics is a *sine qua non* for understanding the debate about the relevance of liberty to law and economics. Next, the concept of economic efficiency is described followed by a discussion of a variant of it called 'wealth maximisation', which is propounded by the most prolific writer on law and economics, Richard Posner. The relationship between liberty and wealth maximisation is then considered followed by a brief discussion of the question whether concerns with liberty can be incorporated into mainstream law and economics analysis.

Modern economic approaches to law

There are as many economic approaches to the law as there are political philosophies (eg conservative, liberal, libertarian, Marxist, classical liberal).[6] This chapter focuses on mainstream economic analysis of law. Until recently, neoclassical economics provided the main methodological basis for law and economics. Now transaction cost economics provides a different analytical base, although there are many methodological features in common.

Neoclassical economics mainly focuses on markets and the determination of price and output. Buyers' preferences are aggregated and generalisations made about the cost conditions facing firms to develop abstract market models. In order to make the study of markets tractable, simplifying assumptions are made about the economic actors in markets and the institutions in which they operate. In general, background laws and values are 'givens' outside the bounds of the analysis.

───────────────────────

6   For references to these different approaches, see R P Malloy, 'Is Law and Economics Moral?' in *Adam Smith and the Philosophy of Law and Economics* (eds R P Malloy and J Evensky), Kluwer, Dordrecht, 1994, p 154.

Neoclassical economics

Five basic concepts underlie the neoclassical approach. They are:

    (a) maximising behaviour (utility maximisation);
    (b) stability of preferences (economic rationality);
    (c) marginal analysis;
    (d) opportunity cost; and
    (e) a focus on the future rather than the past.

The neoclassical economic approach takes the market as the basis of analysis. Within the market, self-interested buyers (who maximise their utility) interact with sellers (who maximise profit). While economists model self-interested behaviour in terms of maximising utility, neoclassical economics is not based on utilitarianism nor any interpersonal comparisons of utility. Instead, utility is used in an entirely subjective sense to mean that people will try to satisfy their preferences in a consistent way. Thus, faced with a choice, individuals will pick the option that gives them the most satisfaction given their own individual preferences.

Unlike psychology, economics does not attempt to explain why individuals prefer certain outcomes or certain goods over others. Instead, individuals are assumed to be the best judges of their own welfare. The assumption of stable preferences means that individuals make consistent choices. Without consistent choices over time, there cannot be prediction.

Neoclassical economists do not argue that all individuals are rational (have stable preferences) and maximise their own utility. Instead, they assume that, at the margin, some rational, self-interested individuals will respond to changed incentives. Economists develop models that show how a rational economic individual would react to changes in the relative prices of alternative outcomes. Changes in laws are seen as affecting the relative costs and benefits of engaging in activities to which rational people respond. These assumptions about behaviour are used, essentially, as *working hypotheses* that have proved to be very useful in predicting the overall behaviour of groups. For example, an increase in the size of fines for careless driving may make only some people drive more carefully. However, in aggregate, there may be a perceived decrease in accidents because some take extra care.

Transaction cost economics

Following the work of Commons, transaction cost economics focuses on the transaction as the unit of analysis.[7] The costs of market exchange include the costs of searching for people with whom to exchange, including information costs; the costs of meeting and negotiation; contract costs; and the costs of enforcing any contract. Due to the less aggregate nature of the inquiry, some of the simplifying assumptions of the neoclassical school are done away with as the inquiry is more concerned with the

---

7   J R Commons, *Institutional Economics*, Macmillan, New York, 1934.

determinants and impediments to market exchange. Individuals are assumed to be 'boundedly rational' and to behave opportunistically. In the context of market exchange, laws are seen as providing 'default' rules that govern the exchange. Default rules reduce the transaction costs of exchange so that a greater number of exchanges occur.

Transaction cost economics focuses on individual transactions to explain why, for example, economic production is organised within firms rather than in markets. The costs of market transactions and the costs of internal organisation are contrasted to predict the circumstances under which markets or organisations are likely to occur. Transaction cost analysis does not require a high degree of abstract reasoning because its prime focus is on individual relations. The highly simplifying assumptions needed for the study of a large number of economic actors are not necessary. As well, because laws and institutions are directly relevant to individual decisions, they cannot be assumed away. As a result transaction cost economics is more likely to appeal to lawyers and the types of problems with which law and economics is concerned.

Methodological underpinnings of modern law and economics analysis

Before the tensions between modern law, economics and liberty can be understood it is first necessary to have a basic understanding of modern economic methodology, what it is trying to achieve, and its limitations.

Opportunity cost

The concept of opportunity cost is basic to modern economics. Opportunity cost is based on the idea that, given limited resources and competing ends, if one goal is pursued then it must be at the expense of another goal. Thus, if a farm decides to produce apples it is at the expense of producing pears or if a consumer buys a chocolate bar it is at the expense of another purchase. More formally, opportunity cost is the value of the best foregone alternative use of a resource. The concept of opportunity costs is fundamental both to market and non-market choices. Thus we can talk about more justice being achieved through a greater concern with procedural fairness but this may come at the expense, given limited resources, of better substantive rules. Economists' focus on costs, which is in terms of alternative opportunities foregone, often alienates lawyers concerned with rights, liberty, morality and so forth. Who can put a price on liberty, it is argued? Economists reply that real resources are used to protect liberty and rights and to promote justice. These resources could be used for other ends such as reducing poverty and so there is a 'cost' in pursuing values which should be taken explicitly into account.

Ex ante versus ex post

Economic analysis of law also looks to the future in that it uses an ex ante approach to focus on the incentives that laws give to people. Thus the response of a rational, self-interested individual can be used as the basis for predicting aggregate responses to changes in the law. The ex ante approach of economics can be contrasted with traditional legal analysis that looks back at the past and past cases. This different methodological approach can be a source of confusion between economists and lawyers.

Positive and normative analysis

Economists distinguish between normative and positive analysis. As Katz puts it:

> [F]oremost among the cultural differences between law and economics is economists' commitment to positivism — the idea that it makes sense to distinguish between things as they are and things as they should be, between fact and value, is and ought. While this tradition has a long tradition in Western thought, it has come under substantial attack in the twentieth century and is today regarded as controversial if not problematic in the field of philosophy in which it originated, and in most social sciences other than economics. Economists, however, adhere strongly to the idea of positivism within their own professional culture, and tend to believe as an article of faith that fact and value can be distinguished and that one can talk about the former without talking about the latter.[8]

Normative economics (usually called welfare economics) is concerned with the goals of private and social resource allocation. The aim is to develop a model of the economy or a market that is efficient and then to examine real life situations to see whether or not the actual outcomes differ. If they do, economists prescribe the best way of moving towards that more efficient allocation. How efficiency is defined is, of course, crucial.

The standard starting point for much normative analysis is the model of perfectly competitive markets. It can be shown that perfectly competitive markets result in social efficiency or an optimal allocation of resources (where efficiency is defined as Pareto efficiency in a world without exchange costs — see the next section). It is important to note that economists do not say that actual markets are perfectly competitive or should be perfectly competitive. The efficiency of perfectly competitive markets depends on a set of highly restrictive assumptions that include:

(a) no firm has any market power;
(b) products in each market are homogenous;
(c) there is a full mobility of all resources;
(d) there are no entry and exit barriers; and
(e) all economic participants are well informed and do not impose uncompensated costs and benefits on others.

---

8   A Katz, 'Positivism and the Separation of Law and Economics', paper presented to the 1995 Annual Conference of the American Law and Economics Association, Berkeley, p 2.

Under the perfectly competitive assumptions, goods and services are produced at least cost and go to those who value those goods and services the most. Value here depends on individual willingness and ability to pay. Socially efficient outcomes depend on the initial distribution of income and wealth because it is initial wealth that determines willingness to pay. Given different initial wealth entitlements there will be different socially efficient outcomes. For example, the socially efficient outcome where everyone had the same initial wealth will differ from a situation where one person has 99% of the initial wealth. In the latter case the preferences of the person with nearly all the wealth will determine the 'value' of goods and services.

Welfare economics uses the model of perfect competition in a prescriptive sense when market failure is present. Market failures are defined as situations where the assumptions underlying the perfectly competitive market model are not met in practice. In other words, a 'failure' occurs when an ideal world is not attained. Market failures, it is argued, provide a *prima facie* case for government or legal intervention. These 'failures' include monopoly power, imperfect information and, very importantly for legal analysis, external costs or benefits.

An external cost is a loss imposed by an economic agent (an individual or firm) on others. These external losses are not compensated by those causing the external cost. Examples of external costs include pollution, crime and road accidents. Because external costs are not compensated by those creating the harm, there is an excessively high level of activities imposing the costs.

However, in an important paper in the development of law and economics, Coase demonstrated in 1960 that competitive markets could control external costs effectively as long as there are fully enforceable property rights and no exchange costs (called transaction costs, ie zero search, bargaining and contract enforcement costs).[9] Because people can bargain and enforce without cost in this zero transaction cost world, only the cost-justified level of external cost would be imposed, ie external costs would continue as long as the benefit from each additional unit of the activity causing the externality exceeded the additional cost imposed by each unit. Coase demonstrated that, in this costless exchange world the same level of externality would result irrespective of who was liable for the damage, those creating the externality or those affected by it. The only difference between the liability rule would be who paid the compensation (a distributional issue not an efficiency concern). For example, those affected by, say, pollution would have to pay those creating the pollution not to pollute if the polluter had the right to pollute. Those polluting would have to pay those affected if the latter had the right not to be affected. Compensation will only be paid as long as the benefit is greater than the cost imposed (compensation paid). The outcome is efficient whoever is liable for the pollution damage as long as both sides can pay the other either to pollute or not to pollute.

---

9   R H Coase, 1960, note 3 above.

However, the real point Coase made was that, in reality, liability laws do matter because people cannot bargain without cost. Transaction costs had been ignored by economists. The value of Coase's analysis is that it focuses attention on the obstacles to the social efficiency of markets. At the same time social efficiency should be defined with transaction costs explicitly taken into account, not in terms of an ideal world where they do not exist. Coase's analysis stresses that market participants take costs of exchange into account and devise ways of maximising the value of exchange by reducing their impact. Thus people develop strategies to take account of information deficiencies, work out ways of minimising external costs given the practical constraints they face and so on. The ability of market participants to minimise the costs of exchange and so increase the value of exchange means a more limited role for government than envisaged in traditional neoclassical analysis, where social efficiency was defined in terms of a world without exchange costs.

Much of the law and economics literature has been concerned with normative analysis, ie with designing legal rules that maximise economic efficiency.[10] A considerable literature exists which examines the efficiency consequences of liability rules such as strict liability and negligence. This concern with efficiency has not been welcomed by many legal scholars who see other values as being just as important as wealth redistribution or personal liberty. Whether economic efficiency is an appropriate goal will be discussed in more detail below.

Positive economics can be divided into two branches. The first is concerned solely with deriving testable hypotheses or predictions that can be verified by empirical evidence — termed predictive positive analysis. The second uses economic analysis to describe legal processes — termed descriptive positive analysis. Here economics can play a useful role in identifying the costs and benefits of social/legal policies.

Predictive positive economics judges the usefulness of a model (a model is simply a framework for analysis) by the ability of the model to predict the responses to a change in law. The assumptions used in deriving these models are relatively unimportant; it is the predictive ability that is important, rather than the realism of the assumptions. As a result, many predictive models or positive models are derived from highly simplified assumptions.

Lawyers often see positive economic models as being far too simplistic, ignoring many real-world complexities that lawyers regard as important. Economists argue that these models are necessarily abstract, that they are not supposed to be descriptions of reality and that it is only the predictions that are subject to verification, not the assumptions. Thus, predictive models are used to examine the impact of legal changes on behaviour, eg the impact of the death penalty, changes in tort law or rules on accidents.

---

10   See, for example G Calabresi, *The Costs of Accidents: A Legal and Economic Analysis*, Yale University Press, New Haven, Connecticut, 1970.

Economists largely adopt positive methodology for pragmatic reasons.[11] Model assumptions do not matter if used solely for predictive purposes. But sometimes models developed for predictive purposes are used to explain or to set normative goals. Sometimes models developed to predict are used to describe or explain why certain legal rules evolve. Again, this is a legitimate method of analysis. Rules are explained in terms of their economic efficiency in the same way as feminists explain the world in terms of gender or Marxists in terms of class.

The usefulness of a descriptive-positive economic model depends on how closely the assumptions of the economic model resemble reality. A model that assumes that consumers have full information may be useful for predicting the impact of a law that increases seller's liability. The same model cannot be used to explain why buyers respond to 'image' advertising. Thus, unlike the test for a predictive-positive model, descriptive models should be assessed by an empirical verification of their assumptions.

But economists often use models developed for positive purposes as the basis for making normative claims, and in doing so, they implicitly or explicitly claim that efficiency is a goal to be pursued. While most economists see that as self-evident, non-economists may not. It is at this point that jurisprudential problems arise. So what do economists mean by efficiency?

Economic efficiency

When using the term efficiency, economists generally mean Pareto efficiency. A Pareto improvement occurs if someone is made better off without anyone else being made worse off. Mutually beneficial trade is thus a Pareto improvement because both sides gain, ie there is a net increase in utility. Note that this criterion does not involve making interpersonal comparisons of utility. People make their own minds up as to whether the trade will increase their own welfare or utility.

Exchange can continue until Pareto efficiency is reached. At this point no more Pareto improvements (ie mutually beneficial trade) can be made. Thus efficiency, in an economic sense, means that no trades can be made that can improve welfare. Each party to a transaction makes his or her mind up about the transaction. On the assumption that each party knows his or her best interests, net welfare (and utility) must be increased.

Pareto efficiency does not imply utility maximisation. If, for example, a woman decides to sell her last piece of family jewellery for $1 because she is desperate to feed her family, as long as she receives enough money to induce her to part with it then the transaction improves economic efficiency even though the piece may be bought by a millionaire for whom $1 is a mere pittance. Overall utility is increased because each side judges they will be better off. But overall utility could be increased by compulsorily transferring an additional $1 to the woman if the value (or utility) of the $1 was greater in the hands of the woman than in those

---

11   See A Katz, 1995, note 8 above.

of the millionaire. Maximising utility necessarily involves making interpersonal comparisons of utility. Maximising wealth implies that the value of a dollar is the same whoever receives it. Economists eschew making these comparisons and adhere to the Pareto criterion of efficiency, at least in theoretical discussions, to avoid having to make statements about distribution.

Voluntary market exchange between well-informed traders will necessarily mean an improvement in welfare because, by assumption, transactions will only occur if all participants benefit. However, different initial wealth distributions will lead to different allocative outcomes. The initial distribution of property rights determines what exchange can take place. Thus there is no single 'efficient' resource allocation. A large number of efficient resource allocations are possible depending on the initial allocation.

However, the Pareto efficiency standard is impractical because nearly all changes, including rule changes, result in winners as well as losers. As Cooter points out:

> ... it is almost impossible in practice to identify new policies or new laws that make someone better off without making anyone worse off. This fact is even more apparent in litigation than in legislation. In litigation, there is disagreement over how to distribute the stakes in dispute. When the court reaches a decision about how to distribute the stakes, the holding in the case creates incentives for future behaviour. When viewed retrospectively, resolving a legal dispute distributes the stakes, and when viewed prospectively, resolving a legal dispute creates incentives that may be efficient or inefficient.[12]

Because the Pareto efficiency standard is impractical as a guide to policy-making, economists adopt a more pragmatic standard. Economic efficiency is improved if the change in policy or the law results in the beneficiaries gaining more than the losers lose. In theory, if all those losing are properly compensated then this criterion is consistent with the Pareto standard. Some must gain sufficiently from the change to fully compensate those losing.

But if those who gain could compensate those who lose why doesn't market exchange achieve Pareto efficient outcomes through consensual exchange? The answer is that reaching a more efficient outcome is hindered by the costs of using the market. Exchange will not take place if the costs of getting together, negotiating and enforcing contracts are too high.

It matters whether Pareto efficient outcomes are defined in terms of a world with or without transactions costs. If efficiency is defined in terms of a world without transaction costs then there is much more scope for intervention to replicate the zero transaction cost world. Defined to include transaction costs, there is less scope for intervention: the world is accepted as it is and the only intervention that can be justified is action to reduce transaction costs in order to facilitate the gains from exchange.

---

12   R D Cooter, 'Liberty, Efficiency and Law', (1987) 50(4) *Law and Contemporary Problems* 141 at 151.

If a central planner knew everyone's preferences then the planner could determine the resource outcome that would be reached if everyone could bargain without cost. This would be an efficient outcome, reached without incurring exchange costs but incurring planning and regulatory costs. For there to be an improvement, the planning and regulatory costs must be less than the additional net exchange benefits.

Attempting to replicate a zero transaction cost world is pure fantasy. A central planner can never have sufficient information about consumer preferences and production economics to mimic the outcome that would be reached by market participants bargaining without cost. Note the considerable information requirement needed to be sure that there will be an increase in efficiency.

Even on a more limited scale, valuing the losses of those who lose as the result of a relatively simple change in the law (say from negligence to strict liability for workplace accidents) is a difficult exercise, particularly as it is likely that people will exaggerate their true loss in the hope of maximising their compensation claim. As a result, economists become even more pragmatic by further assuming that compensation need not be actually paid. It is enough that those who gain can *hypothetically* compensate those who lose. This efficiency criterion provides the basis for cost-benefit analysis and is termed the *hypothetical Pareto improvement* or the *Kaldor-Hicks* criterion.[13]

Of fundamental importance to the Kaldor-Hicks approach is the calculation of the amount gained and lost. To be consistent with the Pareto approach, individual preferences and willingness to pay should determine market outcomes and not the preferences of the policy decision-maker. Thus the calculation should include individual valuations about losses or gains. Cost-benefit analysis tries to take account of individual preferences by attempting to measure the value people place on changes to them in terms of their willingness to pay for the change or the minimum amount they would accept as full compensation if the change went ahead. However, this is a notoriously difficult exercise. Inevitably, cost-benefit involves judgments by the decision-maker about individual preferences. This calculation may or may not include a valuation of individual liberties. Thus the Kaldor-Hicks criterion overrides the concern with consensus in the Pareto criterion.

In practice, economists use the Kaldor-Hicks or hypothetical Pareto improvement approach in determining whether a change in policy or the law improves efficiency. There is considerable scope for getting it wrong and for decision-makers to impose their own valuations. Worse still, the criterion only assumes that compensation could be paid. It does not have to be paid for a change to be deemed an improvement.

---

13 For a good discussion of the differing concepts of economic efficiency as applied to law see J Coleman, 'Efficiency, Exchange, and Auction: Philosophical Aspects of the Economic Approach To Law', (1980) 68 *California Law Review* 221.

A variant of the hypothetical Pareto improvement criterion is *wealth maximisation* which has been used by many law and economics scholars, in particular Richard Posner and it is to his contribution that we next turn.

Posner's wealth maximisation

Posner adapts the concept of hypothetical Pareto improvement or Kaldor-Hicks efficiency and argues that efficiency denotes 'that allocation of resources in which value is maximised'.[14] An increase in wealth is not the same as a hypothetical Pareto improvement. Economic wealth is measured by market prices but market prices do not necessarily measure individual costs and benefits. For example, the market price of a painting may be well below its owner's valuation. Measuring loss by market prices will underestimate the loss from compulsory acquisition.

It can be shown that, in a perfectly competitive market, prices measure the value that people at the margin place on them as well as the social cost of the resources. For small changes, market prices represent consumer willingness to pay or the value that consumers place on the product (or the amount that consumers would need to be compensated to give up the product). In a perfectly competitive market, maximising wealth (or gross domestic product in the aggregate) also maximises overall net benefits, measured in terms of willingness to pay. This only happens because wealth is measured at prices which represent the proper valuation of costs and benefits.

In the real world case of imperfect markets, prices do not represent the value that people would place on them if there are no market failures. In the case of monopoly, a product's market price is well above the value of resources used in producing it. Economic cost-benefit analysis tries to adjust prices to reflect market failures so that it can be determined whether there is an hypothetical Pareto improvement using proper valuations. Simply maximising wealth does not ensure efficiency in the Pareto sense because current prices usually do not represent opportunity costs, ie the benefits of alternative resource allocations.

When the costs of market exchange are low, governments and courts can improve efficiency by facilitating bargaining (through ensuring property rights are properly defined and bargains enforced). Resources will tend to go towards those who value them the most. But when the costs of market exchange are high, bargaining does not occur. Whoever initially holds the property right will continue to hold it. The initial allocation of property rights is Pareto efficient because no change is possible. If we wish to maximise the value of resources, then we should allocate initial property rights over resources to those who value them the most.

What should we do about high transaction cost situations? Posner's approach is to ask the following question: faced with high transaction costs under what circumstances will involuntary exchange increase efficiency? When exchange costs are too high Posner suggests that the law should *mimic the market*. His approach:

---

14   R A Posner, 1992, note 1 above, p 13.

> [W]hich is in the spirit of Kaldor-Hicks ... is to try to guess whether, if a voluntary transaction had been feasible, it would have occurred ... This approach attempts to reconstruct the likely terms of a market transaction in circumstances where instead a forced exchange took place — to mimic or stimulate the market, in other words. A coerced exchange, with the legal system later trying to guess whether the exchange increased or reduced efficiency, is the less efficient method of allocating resources in a market transaction — where market transactions are feasible. But often they are not, and then the choice is between the necessarily crude system of legally regulated forced exchanges and the even greater inefficiencies of forbidding all forced exchanges, which could mean all exchanges, as all have some third party effects.[15]

As a practical matter mimicking the market requires considerable knowledge of what bargains people would have made in the absence of exchange costs, ie knowledge of personal preferences. More fundamentally, it begs the normative question of whether that goal should be pursued, given that valuations of property rights depend on the existing income distribution. For example, if, in a two person society, one person owns most of the resources and the issue is who should be given the property right to a new resource discovery, the answer using Posner's approach would be to give the new property right to the rich person because that would most likely be the outcome from unrestricted exchange. A different outcome would result if the positions were reversed.

Posner recognises that wealth maximisation implies that those with more wealth have a greater say in the determination of the use of society's resources. As Posner puts it:

> Another implication of the wealth maximisation approach, however, is that people who lack sufficient earning power to support even a minimum standard of living are entitled to no say in the allocation of resources unless they are part of the utility function of someone who has wealth. This conclusion may seem to weight too heavily the individual's particular endowment of capacities. If he happens to be born feeble minded and his net social product is negative, he would have no right to the means of support even though there was nothing blame-worthy in his ability to support himself.[16]

Posner describes himself as a 'pragmatic economic libertarian'.[17] By this he means that he believes in minimum government, that economic theory can define the boundaries of the state (governments should only concern themselves with correcting market failures) and pragmatic in the sense that maximising wealth best promotes common human goals. Posner is scornful of moral philosophy saying that:

---

15 R A Posner, 1992, p 15.
16 R A Posner, *The Economics of Justice*, Harvard University Press, Cambridge, Massachusetts, 1981, p 76.
17 R A Posner, 'Law and Economics is Moral' in *Adam Smith and the Philosophy of Law and Economics* (eds R P Malloy and J Evensky), Kluwer, Dordrecht, 1994, p 169.

I do not derive my economic libertarian views from a foundational moral philosophy such as the philosophy of Kant, or Locke's philosophy of natural rights, or utilitarianism, or anything of that sort. I regard moral philosophy as a weak field, a field in disarray, a field in which consensus is impossible to achieve in our society.[18]

By adopting a limited, pragmatic approach based solely on wealth maximisation, Posner argues that slavery can be consistent with wealth maximisation and that the main objection to slavery is that it is inefficient, not that it is morally wrong.[19]

Posner has been criticised extensively. Dworkin rejects the idea that wealth is a value (ie a value that can justify the use of coercive power).[20] Coleman and Lange question whether economics can operate solely in a positive way, ignoring ideals and values:

Can the distinction between positive and normative economic analysis be sustained? In one view, the point of legal theory is to provide an interpretation of law or of some body of it. An interpretation of law requires seeing it as having a purpose or point which is usually expressed by a principle or goal. Economic efficiency is one such goal; corrective or distributive justice might be another ... Law is coercive. It imposes constraints that are enforceable by the use of political power ... Thus, the principles that bring the law together in a coherent way must also justify the exercise of authority. Those who would claim that economic efficiency provides the best explanation of a body of the law are committed to the view that economic efficiency is an attractive moral ideal, sufficiently attractive to justify the use of political authority in implementing it. Thus, the hard and fast distinction between prediction and prescription, between positive and normative law and economics cannot be sustained. If efficiency provides the best interpretation of the common law, then efficiency must be a desirable moral ideal.[21]

Malloy argues that Posner's work 'reflects a conservative ideological approach to law and economics' because it argues for the preservation of the *status quo* and therefore fits within traditional conservative political ideology.[22] Michelman also argues that wealth maximisation is a principle biased in favour of the wealthy.[23]

---

18 R A Posner, 1994, p 170.
19 R A Posner, 'Wealth Maximisation Revisited', (1985) 2 *Journal of Law, Ethics and Public Policy* 85 at 93–4.
20 R M Dworkin, 'Is Wealth a Value?', (1980) 9 *The Journal of Legal Studies* 191–226.
21 J Coleman and J Lange, *Law and Economics*, vol II, Dartmouth Publishing, Aldershot, Hampshire, 1992, p xxi.
22 R P Malloy, 1994, note 6 above, p 153. Earlier he said: 'Conservatism is fundamentally Platonic, being based on privileged elitism, mysticism, and collective order, whereas liberal libertarianism is fundamentally Aristotelian, being based on reason, objectivity, and individual self sufficiency. While conservatives are concerned with protecting the status quo, patriotism, law and order, and religion, libertarians are concerned with individual self-actualisation in a society that respects and protects individual autonomy and human dignity while greatly restricting the power of the State.' R P Malloy, 'Invisible Hand or Sleight of Hand? Adam Smith, Richard Posner and the

More recently Posner has recognised that efficiency is not the sole social goal:

> Since economics does not answer the question whether the existing distribution of income and wealth is good or bad, just or unjust (although it can tell us a great deal about the costs of altering the existing distribution, as well as about the distributive consequences of various policies), neither does it answer the ultimate question whether an efficient allocation of resources would be socially or ethically desirable. Nor can the economist tell us, assuming the existing distribution of income and wealth is just, whether consumer satisfaction should be the dominant value of society. Thus, the economist's competence in a discussion of the legal system is limited. He can predict the effect of legal rules and arrangements on value and efficiency, in their strict technical senses, and on the existing distribution of income and wealth, but he cannot issue mandatory prescriptions for social change.[24]

Posner and liberty

Libertarians place major emphasis on the individual and tend to view individuals as having certain natural or inalienable rights. Richard Epstein, a prominent proponent of the libertarian perspective in law and economics, says:

> Whatever their differences, at the core all theories of natural rights reject the idea that private property and personal liberty are the sole creations of the state, which itself is only other people given extraordinary powers. Quite the opposite, a natural rights theory asserts that the end of the state is to protect liberty and property, as these conceptions are understood independent of and prior to the formation of states. No rights are justified in a normative way simply because a state chooses to protect them, as a matter of grace. To use a common example of personal liberty: the state should prohibit murder because it is wrong; murder is not wrong because the state prohibits it. The same applies to property: trespass is not wrong because the state prohibits it, it is wrong because individuals own private property.[25]

Classical liberalism's central thesis is liberty under the law. Individuals must be allowed to pursue their own interests, subject only to laws which limit their impact on the liberty of others. Classical liberals see a role for government in protecting individual rights and liberties from powerful groups or individuals. But classical liberals are suspicious of the potential of the state to abuse these powers and so seek to preserve private power via competitive markets. Classical liberals tend to see the market place as a means to an end, that end being individual liberty. Neither the market, nor

Philosophy of Law and Economics', (1988) 36 *The University of Kansas Law Review* 246–47.

23 F T Michelman, 'A Comment on Some Uses and Abuses of Economics and Law', (1979) 46 *University of Chicago Law Review* 307.

24 R A Posner, 1992, note 1 above, p 14.

25 R Epstein, *Takings: Private Property and the Power of Eminent Domain*, Harvard University Press, Cambridge, Massachusetts, 1985, pp 5–6.

efficiency, is seen as an end in itself. Unlike libertarians who seek a minimal state, classical liberals attempt to define a state in terms of counterbalancing private power. Competing power sources and decentralised decision making are important.

Milton Friedman, a long-time exponent of classical liberal philosophy, argues that economic efficiency is of secondary importance compared with concerns about individual freedom and liberty. He states:

> A free society, I believe, is a more productive society than any other; it releases the energies of people, enables resources to be used more effectively and enables people to have a better life. But that is not why I am in favour of a free society. I believe and hope that I would favour a free society even if it were less productive than some alternative, say, a slave society.[26]

Classical liberals like Friedman and Hayek see economics as providing a tool for evaluating law and social policies. As such it provides a framework for examining and evaluating alternatives. But economic models are not seen as a substitute for individual moral judgment.

Posner's *de facto* acceptance of the status quo contrasts starkly with classical liberal and libertarian ideology. As Malloy puts it:

> Posner's theory of wealth maximisation is not only amoral, but is disrespectful of a concept of individual liberty. Freedom and individual liberty cannot be protected by a theory of law that systematically rejects the claims of the poor, that tolerates a taste for discrimination, or that legitimises totalitarian dictatorships as an incidence of a perpetuation of a status quo. Such a theory of law is antagonistic to the libertarian values of Adam Smith. Us believers in free market philosophy and capitalism must reject Posner's approach to law and economics as surely as they must denounce the commissions of crimes against humanity.[27]

Classical liberals support government programs such as minimum income, public education, training for unemployment and public housing. In attempting to achieve these goals, classical liberals use economic analysis to ensure that these programs are provided efficiently and with the minimum of government intervention.

Classical liberals see a role for moral judgments in assessing law and economic policy with primacy given to the protection of individual liberties:

> In pursuing the protection of individual liberty through social co-operation, the classical liberal is willing to restrain certain individual conduct by implementation of general rules through a process which respects the human dignity of each person. Furthermore, the classical liberal envisions affirmative government action when there is a significant social purpose involved, such as the protection of basic human dignity by providing food, shelter, medical care, and education when the private market is unlikely to provide these goods and services without government intervention and when the intended recipients are poor and have no purchasing power with which to command the attention of private suppliers.[28]

---

26   M Friedman, 'Free Market and Free Speech', (1987)10 *Harvard Journal of Law and Public Policy* 1 at 7.
27   R P Malloy, 1994, note 22 above, p 254.
28   R P Malloy, 1994, p 255.

Because classical liberalism places paramount value on freedom and individual liberty (and sees capitalism and the free market as the best way of achieving and maintaining those objectives), classical liberals (unlike conservatives) reject all laws or social policies that seek a justification on the basis of prior or existing political and economic arrangements. Concerns for individual liberty are placed well ahead of economic efficiency.

Liberty and efficiency analysis

In general, economists who regard themselves as 'Chicago' economists tend to be concerned solely with efficiency. Most other economists support efficiency as a goal in conjunction with other goals. Libertarians and classical liberals prefer to define Pareto efficiency as the appropriate efficiency measure. Other economists, for pragmatic reasons, support utility maximisation, Kaldor-Hicks or wealth maximisation.

Although Posner recognises that the wealth maximisation criterion depends on the pre-existing distribution of resources and wealth, he justifies his approach on pragmatic grounds. Many, if not most, economists would agree. Increasing the size of the economic pie is the concern of economists and for most the limit of their expertise. Rights and morals are not part of economic discourse.

But it is one thing to say, at descriptive level, that law promotes efficiency (however defined) but quite another to say that it should, particularly when efficiency is defined in a way that other values such as liberty are overridden, as wealth maximisation does.

While economics can help to describe the costs and benefits of alternative actions and predict the consequences of laws, can a concern with liberty be incorporated more directly into economic efficiency analysis? Can concerns for liberty be incorporated into what is for economists an essentially positive endeavour? The answer to this question depends on whether one believes that normative issues can be separated, properly, from positive analysis, ie can 'ought' questions be kept separate from 'is'? Cooter sees values such as liberty as being 'normative resources' determined prior to analysing efficiency:

> An initial distribution of resources is needed to supply the prices that are used to reduce different goods to a single metric for purposes of comparing their value. Once prices are given, it is possible to ask whether a particular policy increases or decreases value. When this framework is applied to law, the initial distribution of resources corresponds to the fundamental rights and duties that law assigns to people. These rights and duties may be characterised as normative resources. The efficiency analysis of law, as the present author understands it, takes as its objective maximising the value of these normative resources as measured by the preferences of the people to whom they are initially allocated.[29]

Cooter goes on to say that:

---

29   R D Cooter, 1987, note 12 above, pp 141–2.

The initial distribution may be described by an historian, explained by a social scientist, or evaluated by a philosopher. Theories that describe, explain, or evaluate an initial distribution of normative resources are logically prior to an efficiency analysis. This can be called the *foundational argument* for the priority of fundamental legal values over efficiency.[30]

Can we define a liberty property right that can be incorporated into our 'normative resources' as Cooter suggests? How should this be done? Liberty has a number of meanings. Liberty may mean the right to do any thing regardless of the consequences. Or it may mean the right to be free from interference by others. Or it may mean the right to do anything subject to either an absolute prohibition on interfering with others or a limited prohibition on interference with others. How should those limits be determined? Should people be able to trade liberty? If so, economic efficiency analysis can help.

Once initial rights or entitlements (the right to do things and the right to be protected from others) and their limits have been determined and assigned how should they be protected? Entitlements (including liberty) can be protected by property rules, liability rules and inalienability rules.[31] Property rules prevent others from affecting entitlements unless the holder agrees to sell the right for a mutually acceptable price. Liability rules allow others to infringe entitlements but require that they pay compensation after the event — the amount being determined independently and not being, necessarily, what the holder would have accepted for the infringement if bargaining had taken place beforehand. If the compensation is less than what the affected party would have accepted for, say an infringement of liberty, then it is not a Pareto improvement. Rights protected by an inalienability rule cannot be transferred. For example, individuals cannot sell their liberty to a would-be slave-owner, irrespective of whether both fully consent and agree on a price. Protecting liberty by an inalienable rule means foregoing efficiency because mutually beneficial exchange is prohibited. But apart from moral objections, prohibition on such transfers can be justified on economic grounds — people who would willingly sell themselves as slaves either lack full information or are irrational.

This chapter has provided a brief overview of modern law and economics and its concern with liberty. Economists' concern to establish a 'value-free' science by relying solely on consensual exchange is useful for providing a descriptive analysis of the consequences of certain actions. Used descriptively efficiency means no more than being better off through mutually advantageous exchange. But exchange depends on the pre-existing set of property rights, trading rules and moral values. Economics takes this as a given for positive analysis.

---

30   R D Cooter, 1987, p 15.
31   G Calabresi and D Melamed, 'Property Rules, Liability Rules and Inalienability: One View of the Cathedral', (1972) 85 *Harvard Law Review* 1089.

When arguing that efficiency should be pursued economists cannot ignore values such as liberty by arguing that they are determined prior to the economic analysis. For example, in assessing the efficiency of legal rules, economic efficiency is defined in a way that assumes preferences and tries to replicate the outcome that people with those preferences would try to reach if they did not have any bargaining impediments. In doing so economists are describing an ideal or utopian world where values such as liberty are protected by assumption.

Liberty is not explicitly taken into account in economic analysis except in the sense that economic efficiency is derived, in principle, from individual valuations and that society's welfare is the sum of individual welfare. Liberty is also taken into account through a recognition of the importance of private property rights and a realisation by economists that markets will better improve economic welfare because planners do not have sufficient information about the workings of the economy.

In practice, moving from an existing situation to another involves winners and losers. The Kaldor-Hicks criterion says that economic efficiency is improved if the winners could compensate the losers. Individual valuations are not determined before policy recommendations are given. Instead a policy is recommended as being efficient if, in the theoretical world of zero transaction costs, winners in that world could pay compensation and be better off. In general, no one asks the actual losers in the economic analysis of law. Wealth maximisation also overrides values and rights. Until economic efficiency can be defined in such a way as to incorporate values such as liberty more explicitly in the efficiency analysis, economic analysis should only play a limited, descriptive role in dealing with legal issues. Normatively, economics has little to say about the desirability of alternate legal rules and institutions.

CHAPTER 10

Dworkin, Hayek and the Declaratory Counter-Revolution

Professor Alan Fogg*

Geoffrey Robertson QC is well known in Australia as creator and moderator of the ABC *Hypotheticals* programs. He is also a human rights lawyer domiciled in London. He prefers continental restaurants to those in Britain, and has a similar preference for law contained in the European Convention of Human Rights. '[I]t's stimulating for a lawyer trained in Anglo-Australian common law (which argues from a rag-bag of old cases and precedents) to argue instead from first principles enshrined in human rights treaties.'[1]

What Robertson contemptuously dismisses as a rag-bag is for F A Hayek the core of our liberty, and common law judges are liberty's gatekeepers. Hayek gives a descriptive theory of classical common law adjudication which translates by osmosis into a normative theory of justice. He parallels Ronald Dworkin in condemning the prevailing climate of legal realism, in which the discovery process is linked with formalism, as defects justifying the emancipation of courts to perform a creative modern role. This dimension of Hayek is surprisingly neglected in legal theory; he rarely rates a mention in jurisprudence texts, although philosophers, economists and political scientists have for some time been interested in other aspects of his ideas. Yet his descriptive theory of judicial adjudication is grounded in classical common law, and is supported by fully-fledged theories of knowledge and society that lead naturally to it. By contrast, the pyrotechnical development of a superficially similar theory by Ronald Dworkin has been lavishly exposed to the extent that one commentator has lamented that it sometimes seems if an author is

---

* Professor of Law, T C Beirne School of Law, University of Queensland.
1 *The Australian Magazine*, 22–3 October 1988, p 70.

not prepared to focus primarily on Dworkin's work he or she is not 'doing jurisprudence'.[2]

It is piquant to compare the results of Hayek's self-confessed 'muddler's mind'[3] with Dworkin's elaborately constructed alternative.[4] Both are pre-Benthamite in saying that judges find the law, both have a descriptive theory that is a predicate for a normative theory that denies law-making, both identify similar opponents in realism and positivism and anchor their propositions in citizens' rights. Yet their tests for judicial authenticity differ considerably, and the outcomes of those tests on hard cases are so radically opposed as to make any superficial identity of description a minor item for cataloguing. Descriptive theories are usually advanced in the service of normative theories, and analysis of what judges are alleged to do unsurprisingly becomes a normative thesis of what they ought to do; if judicial behaviour fails the description, then normative theory fills the gap.[5] Beyond that, theories reflect the ways in which their authors believe society ought to operate. In that contest of ideas it will be argued Hayek's priority of liberty is superior to Dworkin's juggling act of reconciling liberty with equality.

Legal realism often appears to be the dominant theory of the judicial function and seems to constitute the official doctrine of the High Court of

---

2   G C Christie, 'Dworkin's "Empire"', (1987) *Duke L J* 157 at 157–8.

3   F A Hayek, 'Two Types of Mind', *New Studies in Philosophy, Politics, Economics and the History of Ideas*, Routledge & Kegan Paul, London, 1978, Chapter 4. He prefers 'puzzlers' to 'muddlers', but did not object to the latter as a self-description. His point (pp 53–4) is that 'muddleheadedness' is a condition precedent to independent thought, while compartmentalised minds that master areas of knowledge are particularly susceptible to intellectual fashions that are temporarily dominant. Some law students may sympathise with Hayek's confession (p 52) that he took no lectures notes and had to swot information for exams, thereafter promptly forgetting it. They may also be encouraged that such a student was subsequently awarded a Nobel Prize in Economics in 1974.

4   Stephen Guest is Dworkin's main supportive interpreter, and reveals that when studying law at Harvard Law School, Dworkin did not take jurisprudence as one of his subjects: S Guest, *Ronald Dworkin (Jurists: Profiles in Legal Theory)*, Edinburgh University Press, Edinburgh, 1992, p 5. Dworkin currently holds the Chair of Jurisprudence at the University of Oxford, to which he was appointed in 1969.

5   F A Hayek's theory of judicial adjudication is descriptive of classical common law only, and the gap between description and modern examples of aberrant judging thereby revealed constitutes his normative dimension. By contrast, Dworkin's descriptive theory has always contained his controversial equality principle that many would count normative. John Finnis goes so far as to assert that the theory is fundamentally normative in offering guidance to the judge in his or her judicial duty, although with many illuminating moments of description. J Finnis, *Natural Law and Natural Rights*, Clarendon Press, Oxford, 1980, p 21. Finnis made his comment in 1980, and in later writings Dworkin has so submerged the descriptive element that the comment is even more obviously true today.

Australia.[6] A plain presentation of modern attitudes is necessary to provide a contrasting departure point for the descriptive and normative counter-revolution led by the new declaratory theorists. This point will be illustrated in this chapter by case studies and two familiar examples will be given to show how even the hardest of hard cases surrender more persuasively to critical analysis from the counter-revolution based on rights than to the cynicism and pragmatism of modern realism. The lesson from Hayek in particular is that liberty is protected by classical technique, allied to a sense of judicial function immanent in common law, far better than by adherence to liberty as a constructed objective.[7] The dangers of manufacturing purposes for law explains the preliminary contrast between constructivist and evolutionary or critical rationalism which provides yardsticks for evaluation that permeate subsequent commentary.

The errors of constructivist rationalism

The difference between constructivist and evolutionary or critical rationalism is one of Hayek's important antinomies which goes to the heart of sorting the sheep from the goats in terms of liberty. As a separating rod it is not only fundamental to Hayek's ideas, but a valuable useful tool of analysis for the ideas of others.

The pith of constructivist rationalism in relation to law is exemplified by Voltaire's brutal assertion that if you want good laws, burn those you have and make new ones.[8] This eighteenth century arrogance continues today both in overt modulations and restatements and in the hidden premises which underlie practical propositions. Twin philosophical engines for constructivist rationalism are the rationalistic epistemology of Descartes and the positivism and utilitarianism of Bentham, both of which have continuing, and according to Hayek, damaging effects on civilisation. Cartesian rationalism came to mean only such action as was determined entirely by a known and demonstrable truth and from this it was an easy step to the idea that only what is true can lead to successful action. This puts reasoning as the exclusive basis for human achievements.[9] And the link between the French rationalists and Bentham is no mere historical

---

6   A Mason, 'The Role of the Courts at the Turn of the Century' (1993), 3 *Journal of Judicial Administration* 156–67 at 164. 'In Australia we have moved away from the declaratory theory and the doctrine of legalism to a species of legal realism.'

7   By F A Hayek's criteria Dworkin's theory has constructed objectives since the fundamental equality principle is not merely formal but substantive and colours his entire theoretical enterprise by requiring particular results. Dworkin also identifies preferred liberties, while F A Hayek declines to atomise liberty in this way.

8   F M A Voltaire, *Dictionnaire Philosophique*, sub verbo 'Loi', in *Oeuvres complètes de Voltaire*, Book xviii, Hachette, Paris, 1977, p 432.

9   F A Hayek, *Law, Legislation and Liberty*, Routledge & Kegan Paul, London, vols 1–3, 1982, vol 1, p 10. This book coalesces three previous publications: vol 1 (*Rules and Order*, 1973), vol 2 (*The Mirage of Social Justice*, 1976), and vol 3 (*The Political Order of a Free People*, 1979).

coincidence; Bentham wrote to Voltaire in 1776 expressing his admiration and saying he had taken counsel of him much more frequently than of Coke, Hale and Blackstone.[10] Coke and Hale constitute important props for the maintenance of the alternative Hayekian view based on evolutionary rationalism,[11] while Blackstone's approach is entirely consistent if his formal obeisance to natural law is excluded.

It is important to identify the principal stigmata of constructivist rationalism from this alternative standpoint, because they have application as critical tools in the dissection of the authentic function of common law judges. They comprise a collection of propositions that are counted false and dangerous in terms of Hayek's theory:

(a) all knowledge concerning human actions can be possessed by a single mind;

(b) all human institutions and practices (including law) are purposive and were created for a purpose;

(c) there can be no law without a deliberate act that invents the law, so that everything that counts as law is either written or announced;

(d) the inclusion of common law rules and legislation as components of the same definition of law; and

(e) democracy necessarily means the unlimited power of the majority exercised through a periodically elected legislature.

This is a catalogue of points at varying levels of generality and not all the ascribed convictions have a direct and obvious relation to judicial adjudication, but they provide a context for identifying a view of society that may, consciously or unconsciously, affect the duty of judging. More than 300 years ago, Lord Chancellor Nottingham identified the judicial responsibility of segregating 'natural and internal conscience' from 'civil and political conscience', and basing judicial decisions only on the second of those consciences.[12] In short, a judge is not licensed to impose personal preferences. It is doubtful that this crucial division is always maintained today; indeed, the contaminations of realism and positivism have gone so far as to convert breaches of Lord Nottingham's test into dominant philosophies of judicial behaviour.

Hayek's alternative can be concisely stated: constructivist rationalism has two major defects. First, it wrongly assumes that all relevant knowledge is available to a decision-maker so that consequences can be calculated in advance. Constructivists act as if they controlled the appropriate knowledge. They believe that 'since man has himself created the institutions of society and civilisation, he must also be able to alter them at will so as to satisfy his desires or wishes'.[13] This dimension to the

---

10   F A Hayek, 1982, vol 2, p 155, note 15, referring to C W Everett, *The Education of Jeremy Bentham*, Columbia University Press, New York, 1931, pp 110 ff.

11   F A Hayek, 1982, vol 1, pp 73–4, where contrasting lists of evolutionary and constructivist rationalists are supplied. Blackstone does not there figure on the side of the angels but can undeniably be recruited.

12   *Cook v Fountain* (1676) 3 *Swanst* 585 at 600.

13   F A Hayek, 1978, note 3 above, p 1.

impugned rationalism has special appeal to the educated ignorant, those self-appointed intellectual elites who know what is best for other people, or as Michael Oakeshott puts it, 'men in a hurry to appear educated but incapable of appreciating the concrete detail of their total inheritance'.[14]

But there is more to criticise in constructivist rationalism than an intellectual distemper. Hayek's second charge concerns the damage done to society by restriction of the means by which mankind can succeed. Success frequently lies in the observance of social practices and rules, the origin and content of which is unknown to the actor. There is a tradition of behaving available to us that cannot be encompassed by a single mind, but the constructivist fallacy leads to the belief that everything is deliberately designed and that knowledge is limited to words. This contradicts the fact that we are governed by rules which have evolved in society by a process of selection and which are the product of the experience of generations.[15]

Modern realist theories of judicial adjudication

Modern theories of judicial function contradict Blackstone's statement that judicial decisions are the best evidence of the existence of customary law.[16] The declaratory theory of judicial adjudication is consigned to the rubbish tip of history; it is out of temper with the requirements of the age, being at best a conservative deceit and at worst an impediment to the achievement of social justice. Chief Justice Mason of the High Court of Australia has recently joined Lord Reid[17] in deriding Blackstone's approach as a fairy tale, and sees Blackstone's approach to judging as an 'Open Sesame' one, where bad decisions only occur when a judge muddles the password.[18]

The dominance of modern realism as a theory of judging has its explanatory basis in Herbert Hart's treatment of hard cases in his influential book *The Concept of Law*.[19] When contested curial issues cannot be brought under a clear rule laid down by some institution in advance, then the judge has a strong or semi-legislative discretion to decide the case either way. His judgment is written in language which seems to assume that one or the other party has a pre-existing right to win, but this is a fiction. In truth, he has legislated new legal rights and applied them retrospectively

---

14 M Oakeshott, *Rationalism in Politics and Other Essays*, Liberty Press, Indianapolis, 1971, p 23.
15 F A Hayek, 1982, note 9 above, vol 1, p 11.
16 *The Sovereignty of Law: Selections from Blackstone's Commentaries on the Laws of England* (ed G Jones), Macmillan, London, 1973, p 50. A similar modern opinion is given by Sir Owen Dixon, former Chief Justice of the High Court of Australia: O Dixon, *Jesting Pilate and Other Papers and Addresses*, The Law Book Co Ltd, Melbourne, 1965, p 154: 'Ours is a system of law which makes the utterance of judges the best evidence of the state of the law'.
17 Lord Reid, 'The Judge as Law Maker', (1972) *JSPTL* (NS) 22 at 22.
18 A Mason, 1993, note 6 above, pp 22–3.
19 H L A Hart, *The Concept of Law*, Clarendon Press, Oxford, 1986, pp 128–32.

to the case in hand.[20] Hart has subsequently maintained this analysis against Dworkin's argument for the preponderance of legal principles:

> For though the search for and use of principles underlying the law defers the moment, it cannot eliminate the need for judicial law-making, since in any hard case different principles supporting competing analogies may present themselves and the judge will have to choose between them, relying like a conscientious legislator on his sense of what is best and not on any established order of priorities among principles already prescribed for him by law.[21]

This is the rule-book idea which acknowledges as law only what is laid down, and the raw judicial power it releases on citizens differs from an untrammelled parliamentary power to legislate only in constraints inherent in the judicial process. Those limitations circumscribe opportunities for social engineering, but do not extinguish them.

What would Jeremy Bentham say if his mummy in University College, London, could be cross-questioned? A lifelong and vituperative opponent of Blackstone, he would have celebrated modern theories for showing the demolition of a shibboleth. But his joy would probably be comparatively modest for two reasons. First, the number of common law judges in superior courts has multiplied by several algebraic factors since Bentham's era. Second, a number of present day judges, probably constituting a majority, give support to modern theories concerning their proper function. The first circumstance is likely to produce a wrathful response in Bentham, since he regarded common law as sham law or quasi-law leading to the exercise of 'power everywhere arbitrary'.[22] Because the common law cannot be written or announced with precise accuracy it cannot be said to exist,[23] yet its judicial high priests have multiplied and common law systems have colonised extensive parts of the planet. The modern rejection of classical declaratory theory would probably be sneered at as a cunning defensive ploy by the judges, calculated to preserve their indefensible privileges and functions.

But Bentham might also celebrate the winning of a battle that promises a successful conclusion to his trench warfare against Blackstone. It was always his hope that an increase in legislation based on the utility principle would gain community advantages that either cannot be delivered by judicial decisions or will be delivered at snail's pace, and complementing this social purpose is the political purpose of reducing the power of an unelected and undemocratic group he scornfully called 'Judge

---

20 This compressed account is translated into Dworkin's language for convenience. Hart talks of the open texture of rules and cases on the margin of rules and precedents; he also compares the rule-producing function of courts with that of administrative bodies.

21 H L A Hart, *Essays in Jurisprudence and Philosophy*, Clarendon Press, Oxford, 1983, p 7.

22 J Bentham, *The Works of Jeremy Bentham*, vol IV, William Tate, Edinburgh, 1843, p 460.

23 J Bentham, *A Comment on the Commentaries* (eds J H Burns and H L A Hart), Althone Press, University of London, London, 1977, p 119. ('As a system of general rules, the common law is a thing merely imaginary.')

& Co'.[24] Although Bentham's principal objective of codification is as far away as it was 200 years ago, abandonment by the judges of their impartial historical role entrenches the dominance of legislatures and reduces judges to the status of minor functionaries. Law made on a utilitarian basis by parliaments is now seconded by the courts who become interstitial legislators,[25] although the judges emphasise that they are engaged in interpretation rather than overt law-making, and that there is a qualitative difference in the exercise of the judicial function.

Before the two dominant modern models are given detailed examination some preliminary points must be made. Analysis and commentary in this area are bedevilled by descriptive issues of whether judges do or do not legislate, rely on principles or policies, and find or make law. And should they continue whatever they characteristically do, or do something else? Since these antitheses are commonly used they will appear as minor premises in subsequent discussion, but they are in truth only semantic distinctions. Arguing about the properties of words is a fruitless bagatelle similar to identifying how many angels can dance on the head of a pin, because the essence of issues is delivered by a different process of inquiry which accounts for institutional history rather than word-play. Second, explanations of adjudication come from two main sources: legal theory and the accounts the judges themselves give. It is rare for judges to acknowledge a theoretical explanation of their role, so that the majority of judicial pronouncements are self-originated and based on what they see as practical understandings of function. A comparatively rare exception to this atheoretical preference is Chief Justice Mason's recent acknowledgment that the High Court of Australia currently pursues 'a species of legal realism'.[26]

The labels given to the two prevalent theories are deliberately theoretical. Geoffrey Walker accurately penetrates controversies between positivists and realists to identify the underlying truth: that they are factional disputes, since realism is a form of positivism.[27] Positivism is a command-based or rule-based theory, depending on whether Austinian or modern versions are believed in; it is an established branch of European inquiry, and dominant in the British legal system.[28] Realism in its factional sense is best understood as exemplifying the American judicial context where the emphasis is on beneficent results rather than identification of the historical origins of common law or acknowledgment of restraints

---

24 Michael Lobban incorporates Bentham's comment in relation to procedure: M Lobban, *The Common Law and English Jurisprudence 1760–1850*, Clarendon Press, Oxford, 1991, p 129 ('From first to last, Bentham saw the common law of procedure as being the gravy-train of Judge & Co alone').

25 *Southern Pacific Co v Jensen* 224 US 205 (1917) at 221 per Holmes J.

26 A Mason, 1993, note 6 above.

27 G de Q Walker, *The Rule of Law: Foundation of Constitutional Democracy*, Melbourne University Press, Melbourne, 1988, p 173.

28 The essence of modern British positivism is usually taken to be represented by H L A Hart in his book *The Concept of Law*, 1986, note 19 above. For a detailed positivist approach to judicial decision-making, see N MacCormick, *Legal Reasoning and Legal Theory*, Clarendon Press, Oxford, 1978.

inherent in spontaneous social systems.[29] Positivism has utilitarianism as its usual companion theory, while realism has slid from description to prescription of judicial functions.[30] But they come from the same stable, and share the common assumption that law has an identifiable author and is an act of will.[31]

Strong realism

The American realists provide a number of colourful apothegms, such as that law is simply a prophecy of what courts will do[32] and what officials do about disputes is the law itself.[33] It is a judge-centred approach that is sceptical of the existence of legal principles, emphasising instead the uncertainty of the law and the importance of contemporary judicial attitudes. Central to realism is the proposition that law is a means to social ends and must be evaluated in terms of its effects; the focus is on litigation, empiricism and the influences which affect judges. This last can range from the words in statutes and cases to the state of the judicial digestion.[34] At the level of modern judging, realism is epitomised by a famous passage from the judgment of Justice Holmes in *Southern Pacific Co v Jensen*.[35] '[J]udges do and must legislate, but they can do so only interstitially, they are confined from molar to molecular motions.'[36] Those who take the strong realist view have a disdain for the declaratory theory, and forswear as antiquated the process of analogical reasoning from settled rules of law. In common law cases policy considerations are taken into account, although with the careful caveat that legal principles are extracted from them.[37]

---

29   These are Hayek's perspectives. Dworkin joins him in recognising history though as a guide only.

30   G de Q Walker criticises the slide into the normative, stating : 'it was something else entirely to encourage judges to make their own theories and prejudices, their own predisposition to one party or another, unrestrained by any pre-existing principle, the basis for their decisions'. Walker, 1988, note 27 above, p 174. Legal realists who are judges do, of course, stoutly deny that such preferences and predispositions are translated into their judicial decisions.

31   Location of the author tends to vary between the Supreme Court in the USA and the Westminster parliament in the UK. The differences are clearly ascribable to the function of judicial review with respect to the US Constitution.

32   O W Holmes, *Collected Legal Papers*, Peter Smith, New York, 1952, p 173.

33   K Llewellyn, *The Bramble Bush*, Oceania, New York, 1960, p 3.

34   The extravagances tend to come from academics, so that the state of judicial digestion, for example, is no part of what modern judges say they do, whether in court or out. The careful identification of proper functional constraints is part of the camouflage of judicial realism, and may indeed occasionally be believed in.

35   224 US 205 (1917).

36   224 US 205 (1917) at 221.

37   These patterns are marked in recent papers given by Sir Anthony Mason, the recently retired Chief Justice of the High Court of Australia. See for example, A Mason, 'Future Directions in Australian Law', (1987) *Monash ULR* 149 and A Mason, 1993, note 6 above.

Partnership with the legislature is emphasised. In Chief Justice Mason's words: 'The very scale and pace of social and economic change has meant that the legislative process could not cope with what has been and will be required.'[38] Dworkin has roundly condemned theories of function that put judging in the shadow of legislation, and identifies two levels of unacceptable subordination. The first is that, in developing the law, judges should act as deputies to the legislature by producing law they think the legislature would have enacted if it had attended to the problem. A deeper subordination is where judges act as deputy legislators, and develop law in response to utilitarian arguments that parliaments usually employ.[39] An English example of judges acting in both impugned capacities is *Herrington v British Railways Board*.[40] A child accessed an electrified railway line from common land through a broken fence, and was electrocuted by the live rail; the Board was aware that children intermittently crossed the track, but had not repaired the fence for some time before the accident. The child was a trespasser, and under pre-existing tort law an occupier owed no duty of care to a trespasser, save when the harm was caused recklessly or deliberately.[41] In overturning the old law, a number of the Law Lords made clear the realist basis for their decision. The failure of parliament to reform English law concerning trespassers in the Occupiers' Liability Act 1957 was contrasted with the Scottish position achieved by the Occupiers' Liability (Scotland) Act 1960, where the pre-existing rule was replaced with a duty stemming from reasonableness. Lords Morris and Wilberforce concluded that a new court-created rule would not be contrary to legislative policy, nor so daring a development of the law as to be wrong for the House of Lords to introduce;[42] Lord Reid, a Scottish judge, believed that the legislative silence so far as England was concerned accrued from indecision rather than principle.[43]

There are four realist points to be drawn from *Herrington*.[44] First, the House of Lords had no doubts that it was making new law. Second, it did so in the shadow of legislative policy, taking the form of second-guessing parliament in terms of the absence of a rule in the 1957 statute. Third, the judges partly relied on analogy with the legislative principle of reasonableness in the Scottish statute to justify a new common law rule. Fourth, it is clear that the court regarded its function as striking a balance between the interests of occupiers and a perceived community need to extend categories of protection against injury. This dimension was satisfied by a judicial juggling act that maintained a distinction between trespassers and those permitted by an occupier to enter by identifying the

---

38 A Mason, 1993, note 6 above, p 26.
39 R Dworkin, *Taking Rights Seriously*, 3rd impression, Duckworth, London, 1981, pp 82–4.
40 [1972] AC 877.
41 *Addie & Sons (Collieries) Ltd v Dumbreck* [1929] AC 358.
42 [1972] AC 877 at 904 and 921.
43 [1972] AC 877 at 897.
44 For a commentary on the *Herrington* decision, see J Bell, *Policy Arguments in Judicial Decisions*, Clarendon Press, Oxford, 1983, pp 60–3.

occupiers' duty as a citizen, measured against inherent dangers on the property and the likelihood of trespassing.[45]

Sometimes, realist judges use analogy with statute more forcefully than the *Herrington* court. Justice Michael Kirby is President of the New South Wales Court of Appeal and an avowed realist, and in his book *The Judges* has urged judges to be sociologists in the cause of law reform.[46] In court, Justice Kirby has employed analogy with modern legislation designed to reconstruct our attitudes and behaviour in order to justify extension of the common law in a related area. In *Ralevski v Dimovski*,[47] the NSW Court of Appeal set aside a damages award to a young man scarred in a motor accident on the basis that the trial judge had wrongly considered the injury would have been more serious if suffered by a woman. The NSW anti-discrimination legislation had no direct effect on personal injury damages, but was employed by Justice Kirby as a moral basis for extending the common law. He thought the statute contained the wholesome principle that sex-stereotyping was wrong and moved the common law in step with statutory example. There was no existing common law basis for the extension; indeed, Justice Mahoney dissented in *Ralevski*, pointing out what is highly probably the community attitude, namely that females are more likely to feel strongly than males about facial scarring.[48] If that dissent is right, then Justice Kirby undertook a self-appointed role as judicial enforcer of state policy by ramrodding an extension about which there was no community agreement. On this issue, Dworkin and Hayek divide. For Hayek the *Ralevski* decision would be double damned: once for ignoring genuine community opinion as the moral basis for common law and twice for allowing impermissible statutory sources to influence the separate spontaneous order represented by rules of common law. Under Dworkin's theory reaction is more ponderable but he expressly requires a judge to construct an overall political theory that integrates statutes with common law, and when allied to his fundamental principle of treating citizens with equal concern and respect, the combination is likely to justify *Ralevski*.

Realists characteristically take a statist attitude with respect to statutory interpretation. They apply the test of legislative intention rather than citizens' rights, and condemn the literal rule of statutory interpretation

---

45 J Bell, 1983, p 62. Balancing of interests is a familiar realist technique. It is inconsistent with the duty to find the uniquely correct answer required by Dworkin and Hayek. For conclusions concerning Hayek's theory see Robin O'Hair, *The Bankruptcy of Judicial Restraint and Judicial Activism*, PhD thesis, University of Queensland, St Lucia, 1986, pp 260–1. O'Hair describes balancing of interests as arbitrary and intellectually bankrupt and as an attempt to legislate a principle of positive justice. Hayek himself is firm about the inappropriateness of balancing since it is concerned deliberately to bring about a just state of affairs. F A Hayek, 1982, note 9 above, vol 2, p 39.

46 M Kirby, *Boyer Lectures 1983: The Judges*, Australian Broadcasting Corporation, Sydney, 1983, pp 40 and 59.

47 (1987) 7 NSWLR 487 at 491–4.

48 (1987) 7 NSWLR 487 at 502.

as part of the antiquated intellectual furniture of formalism.[49] None of this means that courts produce law, either in non-statutory or statutory cases, that necessarily accords with the transient preferences of governments commanding temporary parliamentary majorities. That would be too crude, and a deliberate surrender of judicial independence. Consequently, when realists exercise judicial power in partnership with parliament, they are careful to emphasise differences between judicial and legislative decision-making. Chief Justice Mason has catalogued some of the distinctions.[50] A judge decides a particular dispute between parties, and does so primarily by reference to the arguments which they present. It is a constraint recognised by Lord Scarman:

> The judge, however wise, creative, and imaginative he may be, is 'cabin'd, cribb'd, confin'd, bound in' not, as was Macbeth, to his 'saucy doubts and fears' but by the evidence and arguments of the litigants. It is this limitation, inherent in the forensic process, which sets bounds to the scope of judicial law reform.[51]

The legislator is in a different case, because the preoccupation of parliaments is said to be with the prescription of a rule of general application, and in achieving that rule a legislator is untrammelled by limitations of institutional role or any particular methodology. To expand Justice Holmes's colourful example, a legislator could create a rule that banished the requirement of consideration as an element in the making of a valid contract, but a judge could not say, 'I think the doctrine of consideration a bit of historical nonsense and shall not enforce it in my court'.[52] This is the antithesis of Hayek's view, which allocates generality to the rules of just conduct that comprise common law and regards statutes as the particular commands of an organiser, the legislature.[53]

The doctrine of precedent is presented as a further constraint acknowledged by realist judges,[54] but the solemnities taught to first year law students are torpedoed by an explanation relayed by Lord Justice Asquith. 'The rule is quite simple: if you agree with the other bloke, you say it's part of the *ratio*; if you don't, you say it's *obiter dictum* with the implication that he is a congenital idiot.'[55] This is realism at its most brutal, but the anecdote has the implied support of American realists like Justice Holmes and Karl Llewellyn who argue that precedents are

---

49 A Mason, 1987, note 37 above, p 158. ('Likewise, the emphasis is on purposive interpretation ... literal interpretation being a hallmark of formalism.')

50 A Mason, 1993, note 6 above, pp 26–8.

51 *Lim v Camden Health Authority* [1979] 2 All ER 910 at 914.

52 *Southern Pacific Co v Jensen* 244 US 205 (1917) at 221.

53 F A Hayek, 1982, note 9 above, vol 1, pp 48–52. Dworkin makes no such distinction.

54 A Mason, 1987, note 37 above, pp 159–60; A Mason, 1993, note 6 above, p 27: 'Respect for precedent severely restricts judicial freedom of action'.

55 Lord Justice Asquith, 'Some Aspects of the Work of the Court of Appeal' (1950) 1 *JSPTL* 350 at 359. The anecdote emanated from one of our greatest legal luminaries and was at least half in jest. Legal realists do not regard such propositions as humorous. See R Cross, *Precedent in English Law*, 3rd ed, Clarendon Press, Oxford, 1977, pp 50–3.

incapable of covering all situations, so they can be manipulated to cover a number of possible outcomes. This is especially true when the court is the final court of appeal and is not bound by its previous decisions. Added force is then given to techniques of distinguishing and overruling, a flexibility that seems peculiarly to the appetite of realist courts which seem tempted to avoid previous decisions and substitute a different rule.[56] A startling modern example is *Mabo v Queensland (No 2)*,[57] where the High Court of Australia recognised native title retrospectively to European settlement, and in so doing overruled or declined to follow a series of previous decisions that had been thought to settle what two of the judges called 'the basis of the real property law of this country for more than a hundred and fifty years'.[58] The inherent danger of realist manipulation of precedents contradicts the priority accorded *stare decisis* in Hayek's theory, where it is seen as uniquely assisting judges to articulate organic principles of common law without pretending to know everything about the nature of the order they affect or about any societal interests the decision may serve.[59] Dworkin's reaction is less trenchant, and appears limited to criticism that the sceptical realist view means that judges merely pretend that citizens have existing rights.[60] But he accepts legal realism as a strong competitor to his idea of law as integrity.[61]

Another hedging qualification lies in the relationship of policies to principles. Realist theory accommodates policy considerations, but only in a radical and iconoclastic version are policy matters applied directly to facts and law to produce judicial conclusions. Lord Denning is an iconoclast, and in *Spartan Steel & Alloys Ltd v Martin & Co*[62] distributed liability for economic loss on the basis of whether a decision in favour of the plaintiff was a sensible policy. According to Lord Denning, when courts limit the boundaries of duty with respect to economic loss they do it as a matter of policy to limit the responsibility of the defendant; when they limit the damages recoverable they do it as a matter of policy to limit the liability of the defendant.[63] That heresy was firmly rejected by the High Court of Australia in *Caltex Oil (Australia) Pty Ltd v The Dredge 'Willemstad'*, where Justice Stephen acknowledged the relevance of policy only as a source of legal principle; direct application of generalised policy

---

56 This is not so obvious a temptation in the ordinary run of appellate decisions. Richard Epstein has aptly commented that ideology often asserts itself in precisely those bedrock cases that mark a departure from established principle. R Epstein, 'The Static Conception of the Common Law', (1980) IX *Journal of Legal Studies* 253 at 273.

57 (1992) 107 ALR 1.

58 (1992) 107 ALR 1 at 82 per Deane and Gaudron JJ.

59 F A Hayek, 1982, note 9 above, vol 1, p 119.

60 In the non-academic version, naked judicial power is decently clothed by mention of the standard constraints already canvassed. R Dworkin, *Law's Empire*, Fontana, London, 1986, pp 154–5. For a summary of Dworkin's views of realism (he calls it pragmatism), see S Guest, 1992, note 4 above, pp 207–11.

61 R Dworkin, 1986, Chapter 5.

62 [1973] 1 QB 27.

63 [1973] 1 QB 27 at 36.

considerations would invite uncertainty and judicial diversity.[64] Justice Stephen's view represents a standard convention of the realist view,[65] but again is illicit in Hayek's theory, in which common law and statute represent two different types of law where statutes are prohibited from influencing constructivist development of the common law, and policy is for the legislature alone.[66]

The final realist constraint concerns the consequences of decisions, whether economic or social. The court must 'have an eye to the utilitarian object in a broad sense',[67] but not in the same ways that are open to the legislature. Consequences are wider than economics, but economics can no doubt form an important ingredient in them. Chief Justice Mason has emphasised that the focus of the judicial process is both wider and more constrained than economics. 'Doing justice between a plaintiff and a defendant, between one class of persons and another class, may require a court to bring down a decision or formulate and apply a principle which proceeds along lines which are at variance with [economic objects]'.[68] In his earlier and clearer writings, Dworkin rejects utilitarian objects as elements in judicial adjudication, since judges should be solely concerned with legal principles that respect or secure an individual or group right. The collective goals of a community are the province of the legislature alone.[69] Hayek would similarly exclude consequences in the utilitarian sense so far as common law is concerned.[70] The function of the judge in a hard case is to articulate a rule of just conduct that is genuinely authorised by community morality, and the only relevant consequences are that conflicts giving rise to litigation should in future be prevented by a system of mutually compatible rules.[71]

Other relevant considerations identified by legal realists include morality, culpability, justice and fairness, all of which are expressly not subordinated to economic goals.[72] So simply stated, the list is something of a 'rag-bag'. But it is appropriate to identify realist justice as result-oriented justice. The native title recently given to Australia by *Mabo v Queensland (No 2)*[73] is justice concerning results that go towards curing what the majority saw as historical unfairness to indigenous Australians. This is constructivist rationalism for Hayek, who accepts only the formal justice of equality before the law, contrasting with Dworkin whose underlying principle of equality drives judicial conclusions that would accord with the *Mabo* decision, which can accommodate within his

---

64 (1976) 11 ALR 227 at 254–5.

65 See A Mason, 1993, note 6 above, p 24.

66 F A Hayek, 1982, note 9 above, vol 1, Chapter 6, especially pp 139–40.

67 A Mason, 'Law and Economics', (1991) 17(1) *Monash ULR* 167 at 173.

68 A Mason, 1991, pp 173–4.

69 R Dworkin, 1981, note 39 above, p 82.

70 For an illuminating analysis, see C Kukathas, *Hayek and Modern Liberalism*, Clarendon Press, Oxford, 1990, pp 191–201. Kukathas rejects the idea that Hayek is either a direct or indirect utilitarian.

71 F A Hayek, 1982, note 9 above, vol 1, p 101.

72 A Mason, 1991, note 67 above, p 174.

73 (1992) 107 ALR 1.

idea that discrimination in favour of a disadvantaged minority is a judicial duty.[74]

Weak realism

Weak realism is closet realism. It reflects the disfavour into which Blackstone's declaratory theory has fallen among judges who cannot always bring themselves to say so in court. No longer is classical theory standardly recruited as a genuine alternative to legal realism; instead, as John Bell puts it, judges who take the declaratory approach 'frequently combine an apparent adherence to this latter model in judicial utterances with extra-judicial statements admitting a certain degree of creativity'.[75] Bell then parks such judges in what he calls a consensus model. A more fruitful tack is taken by Patrick Atiyah[76] who identifies declaratory theory as never having fully recovered from Bentham's onslaughts, and as being currently in serious disrepute among legal commentators and some English judges. Declaratory theory may be invoked on the bench as a protective facade, but the true picture is of actual adherence to realist theory in contradiction of those public acknowledgments.[77]

The motive for the compromise is that to be too openly realist would shake public confidence in the impartiality of the judiciary.[78] There are five arguments for retaining the declaratory facade.[79] First, it is useful for a judge to be able to disassociate himself from the law, in the sense that the law decides issues rather than the judge and thereby, in Lord Devlin's phrase, 'leaves no sense of personal injustice'.[80] Second, it is undemocratic for unelected judges to make law. There are two separate issues bound up in this bald statement: whether it is democratically undesirable for judges to legislate, and if they do legislate, whether it is undesirable to admit the fact. An adherence to the classical doctrine of separation of powers would resolve the first issue in the negative, but dominant modern attitudes place that idea on the backburner. Nonetheless, the doctrine has sufficient lingering influence to persuade some judges that their creativity should be decently masked from public view to avoid legislative intervention in matters such as the judicial appointment process, tenure and salaries.[81]

---

74   This conclusion can be persuasively drawn by Dworkin's approval of claims by racial and ethnic minorities to reverse discrimination in the obtaining of admission to tertiary demand disciplines. See, for example, R Dworkin, 1981, note 39 above, Chapter 9.

75   J Bell, 1983, note 44 above, p 10.

76   P S Atiyah, 'Judges and Policy', (1980) 15(3) *Israel LR* 346.

77   P S Atiyah, 1980, p 369.

78   P S Atiyah, 1980, p 360.

79   P S Atiyah, 1980, pp 362–9.

80   P Devlin, *The Judge*, Oxford University Press, Oxford, 1979, p 4.

81   Such dangers are genuine. Realist Australian judges now feel obliged to conduct campaigns through published papers and articles on precisely these issues. A Mason, 'Judicial Independence and the Separation of Powers — Some Problems Old and New', (1990) 13(2) *UNSWLJ* 173; M Kirby, 'Judicial Independence in Australia Reaches a Moment of Truth', (1990) 13(2) *UNSWLJ* 187. There seems little understanding that legal realism in the courtroom has been a large factor in producing the pressures they resist.

This leads to the third point that discretion is the better part of valour when parliament can cut down judicial power. Not all 'creative' decisions by judges are welcomed by legislatures, and allegedly malign effects of individual decisions have been statutorily reversed; moreover, political majorities in parliament can fluctuate from election to election. Lord Scarman made this fear explicit in *Duport Steels Ltd v Sirs*:[82]

> Great judges are in their different ways judicial activists. But the Constitution's separation of powers, or more accurately, functions, must be observed if judicial independence is not to be put at risk. For, if people and Parliament come to think that the judicial power is to be confined by nothing other than the judge's sense of what is right (or, as Selden put it, by the length of the Chancellor's foot) confidence in the judicial system will be replaced by fear of it becoming uncertain and arbitrary in its application. Society will then be ready for Parliament to cut the power of the judges. Their power to do justice will become more restricted by law than it need be, or is today.

The passage occurs in a controversial case concerning trade union immunity from suit that raised partisan political passions, and in which the judges felt it necessary to make careful distinctions between applying existing law and creating new law in order to emphasise that the judiciary should not be embroiled in controversial social issues.

A fourth point concerns the source of judicial principles of justice and fairness. Is it the judge's inherent notions or is it community convictions? The traditional answer to the conundrum lies in Lord Nottingham's distinction between the two types of judicial conscience, but modern judges tend to translate the dichotomy into an alternative between strict adherence to the law's letter, and ad hoc discretionary justice of the 'palm tree' variety.[83] Given the simplistic modern antithesis it is unsurprising that some judges cling to the declaratory theory, at least in formal public statements, like a mountaineer anchoring to a piton on a slippery glacier. A final argument made by Lord Devlin is that a community consensus is necessary for judicial activism, otherwise a judge's impartiality may be prejudiced since he or she will be thought to have taken sides when 'judgments should be immune from the sort of comment that is appropriate to the hustings'.[84] This connects with Sir Henry Maine's comment many years ago of an apparent contradiction in the claim that, although the courts do not legislate, the law is kept contemporary by the judges adapting principle to new circumstances thereby avoiding legislative intervention.[85] The declaratory approach accommodates the Devlin view better than realist theory, but by speaking of judicial activism in terms of it being unlikely that the common law will 'invent a completely new [principle]', Lord Devlin appears to acknowledge that invention is theoretically available but tactically unwise.[86]

---

82   [1980] 1 All ER 529 at 551.
83   P S Atiyah, 1980, note 76 above, p 367.
84   P Devlin, *Samples of Lawmaking*, Oxford University Press, London, 1962, p 23.
85   H Maine, *Ancient Law*, University Press, London, 1931, p 27.
86   P Devlin, 1979, note 80 above, p 5.

Atiyah condemns weak realist theory for intellectual dishonesty, for an elitism that will not work, and for practical disadvantages concerning loss of reputation for impartiality and diminution of effectiveness in adjudication.[87] No doubt for these reasons, senior Australian judges show an increasing tendency expressly to abandon declaratory theory, although Bell is able to say that weak realist theory is the most popular with the English judiciary.[88]

The counter-revolution: two modern declaratory theories

The rise of modern realism has parallels with post-classical Roman law. After the death of the emperor Alexander Severus in 235 AD, Roman law gradually moved into an era of 'vulgar' or degenerate law marked by Visigothic codes and a general decline in the intellectual level of law.[89] Important trends of the post-classical era resonate with contemporary developments. Legal principle gave way to the intellectual short cut of a generalised equity represented by woolly tags such as *benigne tamen dicendum est* (nevertheless one must speak gently). Atiyah has criticised modern law for a similar declension from principle to the pragmatism of an increased use of judicial discretion to decide particular cases, a development which matches erosion of the hortatory function of law as a complex of incentives and disincentives. Rules governing future behaviour are increasingly replaced by remedies to cure wrongdoing after the event.[90] A second trend of 'vulgar' law protected the weak against the strong at the expense of general security and credit, and in *Mabo v Queensland (No 2)*[91] a self-confessed realist court was prepared to destabilise a long-settled real property regime in order to cure what it identified as historical injustice to indigenous Australians. The final

---

87   P S Atiyah, 1980, note 76 above, pp 369–71.

88   J Bell, 1983, note 44 above, p 10.

89   H F Jolowicz, *Historical Introduction to the Study of Roman Law*, 2nd ed, Cambridge University Press, Cambridge, 1954, Chapter XXIX. The comparison with what were then legal developments has been made by G W Paton, *A Text-Book of Jurisprudence*, 3rd ed (ed D P Derham), Clarendon Press, Oxford, 1964, pp 59–60. Paton comments at p 60: 'It is easy to sneer at the desire for legal elegance, but if a system loses its underlying unity it becomes hard to teach and difficult to apply [and] may cease to be a system and become a collection of *ad hoc* rules'.

90   P S Atiyah, *From Principle to Pragmatism: Changes in the Function of the Judicial Process and the Law*, Clarendon Press, Oxford, 1978. This is an inaugural lecture delivered before the University of Oxford on 17 February 1978, and reproduced in (1980) 65 *Iowa LR* 1249. For a realist counterattack see J Stone, *Precedent and Law*, Butterworths, Sydney, 1985, Chapter 13. Atiyah's account is dismissed as 'nostalgic error-ridden traditionalism': see p 247.

91   (1992) 107 ALR 1 at 27, 28 per Brennan J; and at 79, 82 per Deane and Gaudron JJ. Mason CJ and McHugh J agreed, with an exception here irrelevant, with Brennan J's judgment.

characteristic of post-classical Roman law, emphasis on intent rather than form and an impatience with technicalities, also permeates modern case law.[92]

Post-classical Roman law met a considerable revival of classical learning before Justinian, and Justinian's compilers were concerned to preserve and restore the greatness of Roman law.[93] The modern counter-revolution against realism is led by Dworkin and Hayek, and the renaissance of declaratory theory lies at the centre of what Hayek says and what Dworkin once asserted. Dworkin's ideas are malleable to the extent that in 1980 one commentator identified two versions, Dworkin Marks I and II.[94] The publication of *Law's Empire* in 1986 constitutes what could be seen as Dworkin Mark III, while subsequent development of his theory has produced other variations. By contrast, the main strands of Hayek's thought are contained, without variation, in his three-volume *Law, Legislation and Liberty*.

Early Dworkin writings are the clearest, when his sharp-edged analysis sliced through the basic propositions of positivism and produced a third theory of law that sketched a via media between positivism and natural law in which law was reconnected with morality.[95] Subsequent writings such as *Law's Empire* are often dense and complicated,[96] and successive amendments have sometimes undermined the clarity and power of earlier ideas.[97] *Law's Empire* is substantially concerned with the interrelationships

---

92   For example, in contract. Atiyah refers to the modern device of refusing to enforce a promise on the ground that the promisor did not 'intend' to create legal relations. This is a disguisement for refusing to enforce a promise the courts think is unjust or impolitic to enforce. A century ago courts would have dealt with such problems in terms of consideration. Compare *Shadwell v Shadwell* (1860) 9 CBNS 159 and *Jones v Padavatton* [1969] 1 WLR 388. P S Atiyah, *Essays in Contract*, Clarendon Press, Oxford, 1988, pp 184–5.

93   H F Jolowicz and B Nicholas, *Historical Introduction to Roman Law*, 3rd ed, Cambridge University Press, Cambridge, 1972, p 477.

94   P S Atiyah, 1980, note 76 above, pp 350–5. Atiyah identifies Dworkin Mark I as concerning the rejection of the positivists' distinction between law and morals and the inclusion of principles and policies as the raw material for judicial decisions represented now by Chapter 1 of *Taking Rights Seriously*, 1981, note 39 above. He finds Dworkin Mark II in the insistence that judges should decide only on principle (not policy) and the 'single right answer' thesis. These dimensions of Dworkin are now in *Taking Rights Seriously*, Chapter 4 and 'No Right Answer?' in *Law, Morality and Society* (eds P M S Hacker and J Raz), Clarendon Press, Oxford, 1977, p 58. Fourteen years on, the division is more obviously between propositions in *Taking Rights Seriously* and those in *Law's Empire*.

95   Notably the essays and articles collected in *Taking Rights Seriously*, especially Chapters 2, 3 and 4. In *Law's Empire* Dworkin calls positivism 'conventionalism' and produces a diluted set of arguments in criticism. For clarity's sake, the earlier criticism is set out here.

96   Dworkin's friendly interpreter Guest acknowledges that his writing is not easy to many and that it is sometimes hard to dig out the different strands of thought. S Guest, 1992, note 4 above, p 1.

97   See, for example, criticisms by T R S Allan, 'Justice and Fairness in Law's Empire', (1993) 52(1) *Cambridge Law Journal* 64.

of three highly abstract ideas. 'Fairness' concerns the adoption of procedures, which distribute political power correctly, and in practice necessitates institutions and arrangements which allocate each citizen an equal influence on official decisions. 'Justice' takes over from fairness once appropriate institutions are in place, and concerns the distributive decisions that legislators and other officials ought to make in order to achieve a morally defensible outcome. The link between the two is 'law as integrity' which is Dworkin's vehicle for his theory of law; it is a morally persuasive interpretation of existing legal practice where there is lack of agreement on the correct principles of justice and fairness. There is a further notion of 'political integrity' which requires governments to embrace a consistent set of principles of justice and fairness, with which is linked Dworkin's adjudicative principle of integrity by which judges should identify legal rights and duties in service of a coherent conception of political morality. Judges should adjust principles of justice, fairness and procedural due process to produce 'the best constructive interpretation of the community's legal practice'.[98]

These lofty ideas from *Laws Empire* are perhaps too elevated for useful synthesis. It becomes sensible to concentrate on Dworkin Marks I and II for his analysis of judicial function, because the essays in *Taking Rights Seriously* contain his most effective attacks on positivism as well as presenting the clearest picture of his constructive alternative. However, *Law's Empire* contains valuable illustrative examples that are absent from earlier work. Subsequent writings expand his political theory by identifying the different weights and functions to be attached to equality and liberty. In brief, Dworkin's theory of law is that the nature of legal argument lies in the best moral interpretation of existing social practices. His theory of justice is that all citizens should be treated with equal concern and respect irrespective of where they are born on the ladder of life.[99] Those theories are based on intuitive assumptions about democratic societies that are foreign to Hayek's arguments.

The case against positivism and realism

Hayek and Dworkin agree that positivism and realism are flawed. Dworkin chooses Hart's model of rules as his main target. In hard cases he asserts that judges have recourse to standards other than rules, including principles and policies. His distinctions between principles and policies are stipulative and technical, but form a foundation for the theory he erects upon them. A policy establishes a community goal in terms of an improvement in some economic, political, or social feature of the community; a proposition that seat belts should be compulsory to reduce death on the roads is a policy. A principle is a standard to be observed because it is a requirement of justice or fairness or some other dimension

---

98   R Dworkin, 1986, note 60 above, p 225.
99   This summary mimics S Guest, 1992, note 4 above, p 1.

of morality.[100] Legal maxims are a fruitful source of principles; for example, 'no man may profit by his own wrong'. Principles are propositions that describe rights; policies are propositions that describe goals. These distinctions are vital for Dworkin because they identify the appropriate functions of judges in the doctrine of separation of powers.[101] The difference between rules and non-rule standards like principles and policies concerns function not substance. Rules have an 'all or nothing' quality; they are either valid or invalid, binding or not binding on a judge. Non-rule standards are different; they have the dimension of 'weight'. A judge may find a principle is relevant but not dispositive of the issue before him, but if it is not applied this does not mean it is invalidated and removed from potential future effect.[102]

Hart's rule book idea is thus incomplete. Dworkin further assails the core belief of positivism, the distinction between fact and value, and argues that acknowledgment of non-rule standards collapses the dependent schism between the issue of what the law is and what it ought to be. Legal principles derive from a society's morality, and can only be identified by a moral test for which the rights thesis supplies the correct judicial technique. By contrast, policies are inappropriate sources for courts and belong to governments. Judges should rely only on arguments of legal principle which 'justify a political decision by showing that the decision respects or secures some individual or group right'.[103] Rights have three characteristics that segregate them from goals. They are accorded individuals in terms of an opportunity, resource or liberty, so that whether a plaintiff has a right to succeed is a matter of principle that should not be decided by arguments based on the collective welfare of a society.[104] They have 'threshold' weight against the goals contained in community welfare arguments, and fundamental or 'strong' rights trump the collective goals that represent community advantage.[105] Finally, rights must be distributed consistently throughout society, while goals can be achieved by an unequal distribution of burdens and benefits. Dworkin's example is of a subsidy to an aircraft factory in one city, but not another. There are other definitions and distinctions in Dworkin's theory that are important with respect to judicial adjudication. Institutional rights provide

---

100 R Dworkin, 1981, note 39 above, pp 22, 90 and 91. These definitions are adopted wholesale in *Law's Empire*. See Dworkin, 1986, note 60 above, p 438, note 2.

101 S Guest, 1992, note 4 above, p 60.

102 R Dworkin, 1981, note 39 above, pp 24–8.

103 R Dworkin, 1981, p 82.

104 R Dworkin, 1981, p 84. Dworkin criticises Lord Denning's decision in *Spartan Steel and Alloys Ltd v Martin and Co* [1973] 1 QB 27 for saying that a decision on economic loss should be based on whether it was economically wise to distribute liability as the plaintiff suggested rather than ask whether there was a right to recovery.

105 The idea of rights as anti-utilitarian is now diluted and rights are now measured against 'background' justifications for community goals that include utilitarian theories. See S Guest, 1992, note 4 above, p 65, and R Dworkin, *A Matter of Principle*, Clarendon Press, Oxford, 1986, p 359.

justification for a decision by some particular and specified institution; they have current force as law and are contrasted with moral and political background rights which exist without the express support of written law. The latter powerfully influence what concrete rights citizens actually have, because they are part of the fabric of an 'overall political theory' which a judge must deploy in identifying rights. Sources-based positivism is, according to Dworkin, incompatible with the rights thesis because it trivialises rights by making them the plaything of retroactive law-making in hard cases.[106]

Hayek has a simpler pattern of attack, targeting the earlier version of positivism of Austin and Bentham for the constructivist rationalism of locating the source of all laws in sovereign commands.[107] The idea that all laws are willed by an originator is false by Hayek's custom-based theory, and has demonstrably malign effects. It debauches rules of just conduct that express the customs of the spontaneous order, are end-independent, and the outcome of social practices of individual citizens comprising society. Not only is judicial law subordinated to statute, but the doctrine of parliamentary supremacy readily metamorphoses into the conviction that all laws are deliberately designed for a purpose. This leads to the myth that a government runs the country in the same way that an incorporated company runs a factory, and results in legislative interferences with the spontaneous order of private actions. Positivism supplies the mainspring for parliament's ultimate authority, while utilitarianism gives justification for the substance of its meddlesome programs of legislation. But it is positivism that puts a platform under such programs by identifying all law as being of the same character, with its content determined by the will of the legislature. This collapses the distinction between rules of just conduct and rules of an organisation, effectively between private law and public law, that Hayek counts as so important to liberty. He marries this mistake to positivist rejection of an objective test for justice, for this second error leads to the proposition that 'if nobody can ascertain what is just, somebody must determine what shall be legal'.[108] The two related fallacies cooperate to produce the conviction that law controls the content of justice rather than the reverse, which moves comfortably to the conclusion that distributive justice supplants the corrective justice inherent in ideas of just conduct.

Realism is targeted by both theorists. For Hayek this is an implicitly necessary extension to more general arguments. He identifies a gap in positivism where authority is confused with substance; the ultimate authority of parliaments as law-givers does not necessarily mean that they automatically determine the content of law, or indeed are aware of that

---

106 R Dworkin, 1981, note 39 above, pp 81–6, 93, 279–90.
107 F A Hayek, 1982, note 9 above, vol 2, Chapter 7. He also (see pp 48–56) criticises Kelsen's pure theory for treating all norms as 'created' and blurring the distinction between law and legislation. Hart's rule-based positivism escapes real attack by Hayek, apparently partly because it is possible to agree that many legal rules have no relation to moral rules. F A Hayek, 1982, vol 2, p 56.
108 F A Hayek, 1982, note 9 above, vol 2, p 47, quoting Gustav Radbruch.

content outside statutes that are passed. It is open to parliaments to instruct courts to enforce customary rules and maintain the common law, so that positivist argument is illicitly extended by its assumption that the existence of ultimate power necessarily leads to wholesale exercises in determining the content of law. Realism fills this gap and is separately condemned for dangerous myopia and empiricism.

> The spurious 'realism' which deceives itself in believing that it can dispense with any guiding conception of the nature of the overall order, and confines itself to an examination of particular 'techniques' for achieving particular results, is in reality highly unrealistic.[109]

Hayek's comment was made in relation to science, but is readily transferable to law.

O'Hair has taken Hayek's criticisms and brilliantly charted the value of them in relation to adjudicative issues raised by the doctrines of judicial restraint and judicial activism, antinomies he identifies as the progeny of legal realism.[110] *Soi-disant* judicial restraint is a realist misnomer, since concepts such as mootness, locus standi, exhaustion of remedies and the like are integral to the notion of jurisdiction and separate execution from adjudication.[111] Failure to abide by the inherent jurisdictional limitations represented by these issues opens the door to judicial usurpation of the executive and the legislature.[112] Judicial activism is equally misconceived and means judicial imperialism.[113] It is part of Bentham's attack on the common law to postulate the alternative of an all-powerful magistrate ruling directly with the theoretical consent of the people, bypassing such constitutional protections as parliaments and juries and with no constraint save his own understanding of the people's will.[114] This is destructive of individual liberty since it entails judicial management and control of society.[115] O'Hair highlights the dangers of realism to a free society. 'It causes the courts to move from "principles to pragmatism" and destroys the legitimacy of judicial review in a democracy, quite apart from the de-stabilising character of unprincipled decisions emerging from the judiciary, so far as the spontaneous order and government are concerned'.[116]

These strictures connect naturally to those of Dworkin, who counts realism as a sceptical conception of the law because it denies that past decisions create rights, thereby liberating judges to abandon settled rights in favour of their view of what is best for the future.[117] In a more subtle version of realism, judges will act in most cases 'as if' citizens have rights;

---

109 F A Hayek, 1982, vol 1, p 64.
110 R O'Hair, 1986, note 45 above, p 973.
111 R O'Hair, 1986, pp 929–31.
112 G de Q Walker, 1988, note 27 above, p 165.
113 R O'Hair, 1986, note 45 above, pp 938–41.
114 See R Nisbet, *The Twilight of Authority*, Heinemann, London, 1976, pp 175–6, extracted in R O'Hair, 1986, pp 938–9.
115 R O'Hair, 1986, p 940.
116 R O'Hair, 1986, p 973.
117 See S Guest, 1992, note 4 above, pp 207–10. In *Law's Empire*, Dworkin calls realism by the tag 'pragmatism'.

they retain the facade but behind it are free to reconstruct.[118] This demeans rights by denying them an independent existence: '[t]he right exists only in so far as its recognition is in accordance with a decision that is the best practical one for the community'.[119] Realism is an approach that fails to take Dworkinian rights seriously; it rejects genuine non-strategic rights in favour of what judges believe to be the best community for the future. In the subtle version, judges deceive citizens into thinking they have rights, whether based on precedents or not; in fact rights can be ignored by legal realists if they prefer their view of the community interest. The unsubtle version has at least the merit of candour in that primacy is openly given to the community interest and the rights argument made into a sham. But citizens are not likely to find abundant incentives in going to court when the issue is always whether a new rule should be created, not the enforcement of existing rights. In *Law's Empire*, Dworkin ultimately rejects legal realism because it is false to his notion of law's integrity, an idea that requires genuine sense to be made of a group's history as well as its future.[120]

The role of the judge

The modern counter-revolution depends crucially on an authentic explanation of the judicial function that reinstates nuanced versions of declaratory theory. Legal realists commonly caricature the declaratory approach applied by earlier judges, whose processes for changing the law are stigmatised as mechanistic.[121] For example, Chief Justice Mason has condemned the outcomes of Australian declaratory theory for being exclusively limited to inductive and analogical reasoning from precedents in the evolution of legal principles.[122] No such stultifying proposition is found in either Dworkin or Hayek. In different ways their theories require an organic link between law and morality that controls a judicial function in which strictly logical processes have a subordinate place.[123] Each supplies an explanation of the judicial function that resolves perceived tension between declaratory theory and the obvious fact that the content of laws changes over time, and in so doing falsify the realist idea of judicial activity as akin to the highwire act of a circus tightrope-walker

---

118 R Dworkin, 1986, note 60 above, pp 152–3.

119 S Guest, 1992, note 4 above, p 209.

120 R Dworkin, 1986, note 60 above, pp 220–1, 225–6, 244. Dworkin joins with O'Hair in identifying the judicial activism of realists with judicial imperialism. He denies that judges are 'independent architects of the best future' free from a duty to 'act consistently in principle with one another'. R Dworkin, 1986, p 410.

121 N Barry, *The Crisis in Law*, Centre for Independent Studies, Sydney, 1989, p 8, has felicitously identified this characteristic. 'The realist movement made all its intellectual profit from its alertness to the simple truth that a mechanical jurisprudence is impossible.'

122 A Mason, 1993, note 6 above, p 23.

123 See, for example, F A Hayek, 1982, note 9 above, vol 1, pp 105–6. Dworkin powers Justice Hercules by political morality and principles, not logic.

where it is crucial to balance the different constitutional responsibilities of legislatures and courts. Legal realists remit themselves to a masterless decision about where such balance should be struck, since vague statements of the relevance of community consensus and an underlying philosophy lack a legal profile when unmoored from a moral inheritance they seem unable to understand.[124]

A comparison of Hayek and Dworkin discloses superficial similarities in descriptive approach to judicial adjudication. They have rights at the centre of what they say, anchor their theories in community morality, deny the relevance of governmental policies to the exercise, and require decisions to have an institutional fit with existing law. But if the shade of Blackstone could be invoked as a modern critic, there is no doubt what his response would be. Dworkin's theory has moved from the freshness of its original contentions to highly abstract propositions such as integrity, fairness and justice. In particular, his current theory is interpretive, which appears to have the effect of subsuming questions of institutional fit under controversial equality propositions, foreign to Blackstone's ideas. By contrast, Hayek's theory is eighteenth century Blackstone updated; the fact that Blackstone is commonly regarded as a crusted Tory and Hayek counts himself an Old Whig becomes a minor difference compared with the gulf that separates Dworkin from classical theory of two centuries ago. That separation arises from the normative spin that Dworkin puts on his descriptive approach, for it is increasingly difficult to segregate the two categories in what he writes.[125]

Both Dworkin and Hayek concentrate on a judge's function in common law cases. There are greater difficulties with their separate approaches to statutory interpretation. Dworkin only fully explains this component of his theory in *Law's Empire*, while Hayek gives limited attention to how statutes should be construed. The gap is understandable because Hayek's main purpose is to condemn statutory intrusions into the spontaneous order as part of his distinction between law and legislation. The advice offered to judges on how to deal with the modern phenomenon of encroachment on customary rules of common law is sparse, but is dealt with by O'Hair in a lawyerly application of Hayek's larger ideas.

Common law cases

Justice Hercules is the superhuman judge Dworkin postulates in order to deal with hard cases. He is the ideal judicial performer modern judges should attempt to emulate. Description of his duties used to be plain: he must construct a political and moral theory that best explains and justifies existing legal materials in constitutions, statutes and cases, and the theory arrived at will be the best guide to the rights he should apply to reach the

124 R O'Hair, 1986, note 45 above, p 974.
125 Even before *Law's Empire*, Finnis considered that Dworkin's theory was fundamentally normative. J Finnis, 1980, note 5 above, p 21.

uniquely correct answer that is discoverable in the hardest of hard cases. He will always decide on principle rather than policy in his pursuit of vindicating the rights people already have. In this way he avoids criticism that he is legislating or that he is unfairly applying law at the time of his decision that was absent when the facts of the case occurred.

Dworkin argues that his third theory of law avoids the traps of Hart's rule book approach that gives judges a strong discretion to make new law on policy grounds. Justice Hercules has no real discretion in the sense commonly understood. His decisions run on principled rails to a conclusion that is uniquely right, so that in *McLoughlin v O'Brien*[126] it was not properly open to the court to decide whether the plaintiff was entitled to damages for emotional injury suffered away from the scene of the accident on the basis of whether awarding damages in such cases would be economically efficient in terms of increasing the community's wealth. The true competition lay between an abstract principle of 'private apportioning', whereby negligent defendants should pay for the consequences of their fault, and a 'collective sympathy' principle at the same level that excuses defendants otherwise required to pay large sums for a momentary negligence. If the unvarnished 'private apportioning' principle applies, then the plaintiff succeeds on the basis of foreseeability of injury; if the qualified 'collective sympathy' principle prevails, the defendant wins because the emotional injury was so remote as to create an unfair burden. In the result Dworkin has Justice Hercules decide on the 'community sympathy' principle, at least where liability insurance for motor accidents is available privately on sensible terms.[127]

The right answer to issues of litigants' entitlements is controlled by two types of general test: 'fit' with settled law, and 'substance' which concerns matters of political morality. There is ambiguity about how conflict between the tests should be resolved, but the likely solution in favour of substance reinforces Dworkin's status as a constructivist rationalist.[128] On fit, he compares judges with chain novelists to illustrate the permitted circumference of legal arguments on which they can properly rely. If a number of authors are each allocated the writing of a chapter in the same novel there are obviously constraints of fit, since they are at minimum limited by the names of characters, the plot, and the language in which the novel is written. A framework controls literary interpretation in much the same way that existing legal materials control judicial decisions; the use of precedent within this framework is expressed by an early point Dworkin makes about previous decisions exercising gravitational force based on fairness, provided they are decided on legal

---

126 [1983] 1 AC 410. See analysis in R Dworkin, 1986, note 60 above, pp 238–50 and S Guest, 1992, note 4 above, pp 69–71.
127 R Dworkin, 1986, pp 270–1.
128 T R S Allan, 1993, note 97 above, pp 85–6, finds Dworkin's dichotomy between fit and substance confusing, and says they are properly understood as references to fairness (or consistency) and justice. For a summary of Dworkin's account, see S Guest, 1992, note 4 above, pp 49–57.

principle rather than policy.[129] This is an account of the *ratio decidendi* of a decision which limits construction of it in subsequent cases to those elements that are justified by fairness. It is here that Dworkin is accused of total faith in analogical arguments.[130] But unlike positivists who themselves accept analogy as a proper and useful judicial tool, Dworkin insists on sharpening a moral point with respect to fairness arguments of this kind before precedents can be used by Justice Hercules.[131] In vetting alternative interpretations of precedents in *McLoughlin*, Justice Hercules will reject success for the plaintiff either limited to physical injury or only where injury is the direct consequence of the accident. Neither interpretation fits the pre-existing case law. He will also rule out a distinction between emotional injury suffered at the accident scene and similar injury suffered away from it. Although no previous decision prior to *McLoughlin* covered injury away from the scene, to draw a line is morally arbitrary. Arbitrariness is apparently a double error; it does not fit common law decisions and is also a matter of substance like treating people differently because of their skin colour.[132] A parallel double mistake knocks down an interpretation in *McLoughlin* that adopts economic efficiency as the naked policy basis; it does not accurately translate the integrity of the precedents and travels beyond fit to substance by brutalising the plaintiff's right to be treated as an equal.

The substance test requires as the ultimate principle of political morality that others should be treated with equal concern and respect. Here Dworkin collapses the two tests, because the moral point of the second invades the first and overwhelms it. In distancing himself from positivists' attempts to colonise him, he has denied that he wishes to replace the idea of law as a system of rules with a theory of rules plus principles:

> There is no such thing as 'the law' as a collection of discrete propositions, each with its own canonical form. People have legal rights, and principles of political morality figure in deciding what legal rights they have.[133]

Integrity of decision-making based on existing materials is always linked to ideas of justice and fairness, behind which lurks the ultimate equality principle: 'Legal argument must proceed on the basis that the best way to

---

129 The early point is made in *Taking Rights Seriously*, Chapter 4, but S Guest, 1992, note 4 above, pp 58–9, considers that Dworkin modifies the idea of 'gravitational force' in *Law's Empire*. Fairness is a matter of right structure for a legal system, and the doctrine of *stare decisis* is assimilated to procedural due process. See R Dworkin, 1986, note 60 above, p 405.

130 See J Raz, *The Authority of Law*, Clarendon Press, Oxford, 1979, p 205, note 19. 'Dworkin's theory of adjudication is the most extreme case of total faith in analogical arguments.'

131 S Guest, 1992, note 4 above, p 58.

132 S Guest, 1992, p 70.

133 R Dworkin, 1981, note 39 above, p 344. Dworkin is here rejecting the idea that Hart's rule of recognition can be modified to capture an indirect relationship of legal principles to rules. See N MacCormick, 1978, note 28 above, p 244, for the colonising proposition.

make sense of the law must be to read it so that it represents the state's striving to treat people as equals'.[134] This propels Justice Hercules to cast aside decisions like *Saif Ali v Sydney Mitchell & Co*[135] that preserves an exemption from liability for negligence in favour of barristers and thereby offends against foundational principle. A device that encourages such firmness of purpose is the distinction between 'bare' and 'strategic' consistency. Bare consistency means treating all past decisions as if they could not be mistakes, while strategic consistency leads back to the controlling equality test.

Very little of this comports with Hayek's theory concerning judicial function, and it is increasingly difficult to maintain that Dworkin offers a genuine declaratory theory. Those early descriptive elements that caused Dworkin to be called Blackstone in modern dress[136] are swamped by the ultimate normative imperative of treating people equally. There are no similar problems with Hayek, who is unselfconscious in his fidelity to classical common law and its processes. It is a declaratory theory that depends on correct judicial articulation of customary rules of just conduct belonging only to non-statutory common law, and which is sharply distinguished from the law of legislation. His objective is to show that liberty is vulnerable if the two types of law are not kept separate, because only rules of just conduct should rightly be enforced against citizens. A rule of just conduct must be:

   (a) abstract, in the sense of being end-independent and applicable to an unknown number of future instances;[137]

   (b) negative, in the sense of preventing 'actions towards others' that interfere with a citizen's autonomy and protecting the domain within which he or she can make feasible plans;[138]

   (c) capable of being universalised so that it fits with existing rules of common law;[139] and

   (d) applied over the long run so that it becomes a settled and tested rule.[140]

There is no imposed will, such as that of parliament in relation to legislation. This is evolved customary law, and rules which are judicially articulated are only part of the corpus of rules that citizens observe,

---

134 R Dworkin, 1986, note 60 above, p 263.

135 [1980] AC 198. See discussion of the case in R Dworkin, 1986, note 60 above, pp 219–20. Although the House of Lords limited the exemption in *Saif Ali*, this is not enough for Dworkin. 'Integrity will not be satisfied, however, until the exemption is entirely erased.'

136 H L A Hart, 'Law in the Perspective of Philosophy', (1976) 51 *New York ULR* at 538, 548.

137 F A Hayek, 1982, note 9 above, vol 1, pp 1, 19; vol 3, p 100.

138 F A Hayek, 1982, vol 2, pp 36–7 (negative character); vol 1, p 86 (private feasible plans).

139 F A Hayek, 1982, vol 2, pp 27–9.

140 F A Hayek, 1982, vol 2, pp 29–30. Hayek is not here dealing with technical validity. A bad decision may be valid, but in a meaningful sense contrary to law. See vol 2, pp 50–1.

including unwritten rules within a common sense of justice and fair play.[141] Such rules are as much a part of the law as those declared or articulated by judges, and our ignorance of them and our incapacity to verbalise them with precision is immaterial since we can know how to act without thinking about it.[142] They illustrate Hayek's central proposition that it is possible to have order without design; it can be a spontaneous order growing out of a web of culturally inherited rules which have adjusted to each other by processes of time and experience. Legislation has a part to play and may provide a regularised context within which rules of just conduct operate, as where company law provides a platform for the operation of trading corporations, but the transactions of corporations are governed by rules of just conduct.[143]

The judge's task with respect to common law is restoration of the spontaneous order when it has broken down, and not the imposing of an order by resort to result-orientated criteria.[144] He will follow customary principles and apply the rule that should have been followed by the parties; such a rule is one which would have been consistent with the spontaneous order.[145] A judge's especial talent is for articulation, even in hard cases. Hayek's theory acknowledges that hard cases like *Donoghue v Stevenson*[146] alter the nature of articulated common law and extend its scope, but the exercise remains articulation and not judicial legislation, since legitimate expectations within a community are capable of being divined by the professional talents of the judge. This is Hayek's answer to the characteristically perceived difficulty of reconciling declaratory theory with the obvious fact that judge-made law changes. Judging is not an act of will, and positivists and realists are wrong to think that when articulated rules run out the only answer is a strong judicial discretion to change the law by reference to external standards. The sole permissible authentication of the decision in a hard case is genuine social custom in the community,[147] so that the decision will integrate with other rules of just conduct in the spontaneous order. In easy cases where existing rules

---

141 F A Hayek, 1982, vol 1, pp 74–6. Hart calls these social rules, but excludes them from legality under his rule of recognition.

142 F A Hayek's view chimes with that of Sir Owen Dixon, who recognised that inarticulate rules exist, including rules concerning the legal profession. Dixon, 1965, note 16 above, p 129.

143 Legislation may also be necessary in common law if a series of judges entrench undesirable rules. This is a rescue function that cannot usually be performed by courts alone. But the touchstone for rescue is the restoration of genuine rules of just conduct, not the imposition of social objectives. See F A Hayek, 1982, note 9 above, vol 1, pp 88–9.

144 F A Hayek's most systematic account of the judicial function is in *Law Legislation and Liberty*, 1982, note 9 above, vol 1, pp 94–102 and 115–22.

145 For a compatible judicial opinion, see *Robinson v Mollett* (1875) LR 7 HL 802 at 816–17 per Brett J; R O'Hair, 1986, note 45 above, pp 231–2.

146 [1932] AC 562.

147 Customary opinion arises from community morals. There can, of course, be morals supporting customary opinion that do not qualify as rules of just conduct because they lack the dimension of 'action towards others' required by Hayek. See R O'Hair, 1986, note 45 above, Chapter 5.

supply the answer, a judge must identify the facts from the evidence of the parties and then decide on the remedy most appropriate to restore the party injured by the infraction to the position he or she would have occupied apart from the breach.

Identification of relevant customary rules commences with resort to judicial precedent as their contemporary expression. Here Hayek is prepared to acknowledge that a decision can be logically deduced from existing rules, but this is not the controlling technique since its exercise must produce a result that is factually consistent with the body of existing rules. A new rule must lead to an order of compatible actions, and although it may logically seem to be wholly consistent with recognised rules it 'may yet prove to be in conflict with them if in some sets of circumstances it allows actions which will clash with others permitted by the existing norms'.[148] Facts prevail over logic where they lead to different conclusions. This priority answers realist criticisms that declaratory theory necessitates a narrow, mechanistic logic. Moreover, the source of new legal principles is different from sources that both Dworkin and legal realists find acceptable, since they are prepared to find persuasive analogies assisting development of common law in statutes as well as judicial decisions. Statutory analogy is unacceptable to Hayek, since judges will be drawing from the potentially poisoned well of an order that reflects the imposed will of its organiser. Adventures of this kind carry the danger that an influential statutory rule will not meet the abstract, end-independent requirements for a rule of just conduct.[149] Common law and legislation are different types of law and should not be commingled.

The primacy of the legitimate expectations of the parties in a hard case also separates Hayek from Dworkin's constructive rationalism contained in a manufactured equality principle. O'Hair has pointed out that hard cases are concerned with what those expectations *ought* to have been in the context of the spontaneous order as a whole, and brilliantly summarises the pith of Hayek's argument by adding:[150]

> This, in itself, may be sufficient to yield the right answer. It is certainly a serious limitation on the attempt to make law out of 'whole cloth'. A law that comports with conceptions must turn on features of the situation that are capable of repetition. It must comport with the whole law. It must concentrate on features of the situation, that according to the structure of local custom, could be relevant. The rule cannot be one that leaves the bulk of the community doubtful as to its justice. It must not create classifications the support for which depends upon which classification one falls into, prior to any dispute arising. This is tied to the conception of justice which is relevant to the dispute ... The rule articulated must be one confirmed by acceptance and likely to produce the response, 'Of course'.

---

148 F A Hayek, 1982, note 9 above, vol 1, pp 105–6.

149 See criticisms of modern judicial use of statutory analogy in G de Q Walker, 1988, note 27 above, pp 187-8. Modern legislation tends to be aimed at reconstruction of society, and an unbridled use of statutory analogy turns courts into a legislature in their own right.

150 R O'Hair, 1986, note 45 above, p 146.

Freedom of speech, for example, is compatible in abstract terms with both the presence or absence of the idea of private or severally held property. But freedom of speech in a spontaneous order compellingly implies acceptance of several property in practice.[151]

Hayekian hard cases arise where there is genuine doubt about what is required by established custom, and a real gap exists in recognised law.[152] A judge still finds the law, which is recognised as being appropriate after it is stated; if it is not so accepted, then it is wrong. The possibility of judicial error is expressly accommodated:

> The judge may err, he may not succeed in discovering what is required by the rationale of the existing order, or he may be misled by his preference for a particular outcome of the case in hand; but all this does not alter the fact that he has a problem to solve for which in most instances there will be only one right solution and that this is a task in which his 'will' or emotional response has no place.[153]

In the selection of hypotheses to test, primacy is given to judicial intuition which is beyond whim, being the legal expression of a judge's lawyerly acculturation to a proper sense of function that excludes a deliberate balancing of interests or preference for a particular result.[154] The doctrine of precedent largely cocoons the judge from such errors, and is a far more orthodox constraint than in Dworkin's theory where it is converted to gravitational force subordinated to an equality principle. A Hayekian judge adds to his intuitive sense of justice by the experience accumulated from 'the constant necessity of articulating rules in order to distinguish between the relevant and the accidental in the precedents which guide him',[155] and thereby obtains a capacity for discovering principles unavailable to a judge operating under a Benthamite codification. The spontaneous order is dynamic not static, and the distillation of legal principles from the *rationes decidendi* of previous decisions is the vehicle for its development while simultaneously constraining judicial imperialism. Hayek's legal principles are inchoate rules and inherently open to conversion to rules *stricto sensu*;[156] they do not suffer the barren, logical demarcation that Dworkin imposes on categories of rules and principles. That linkage defeats criticism of Hayek as a rigid conservative and is an important prop to an evolutionary rationalism justifying development of common law rules.

Similarities between Hayek and Dworkin can be teased out of their respective theories. They agree that common law cases are based on discovering the uniquely correct answer to a litigated dispute, even in a hard case. They join in identifying crucial differences between the judicial and legislative minds, and condemn a legislative attitude with respect to the common law. An authentic judicial approach dissolves the idea of a

---

151 R O'Hair, 1986, pp 235–6.
152 F A Hayek, 1982, note 9 above, vol 1, p 100.
153 F A Hayek, 1982, vol 1, pp 119–20.
154 What may appear just as an outcome should sometimes be rejected since it will disappoint legitimate expectations in society. F A Hayek, 1982, vol 1, p 115.
155 F A Hayek, 1982, vol 1, p 87.
156 F A Hayek, 1982, vol 1, p 119.

strong discretion that is semi-legislative and based on policy choice. But these are agreements on formalities, and differences of substance are crucial to whatever persuasion the theories may individually exert.

Statutory interpretation

A theory of adjudication must persuasively accommodate statutory as well as non-statutory cases. Hayek does not offer a detailed theory in this area, and deductions must be made from general propositions concerning appropriate legislative function. His distinction between *cosmos* and *taxis*, and between the different types of law that properly emanate each of the two areas, is directed towards an ideal state of affairs, whereas in practice courts must interpret numerous examples of social legislation that affect private conduct within the *cosmos* or spontaneous order.

Thesei are the rules of the *taxis* and are defined as rules which are applicable only to particular people or in the service of ends of rulers; they are necessary to operate an organisation and are commands representing an act of will by the organiser which requires to be executed.[157] The most important example is the legislature and statutes created by it. It is possible for legislation to be modelled on rules of just conduct in the sense of being a codification of such rules, and examples can be found in Sale of Goods and Bills of Exchange legislation. These are perfectly acceptable to Hayek, who also acknowledges that case law may find itself in a cul-de-sac and require legislative rescue.[158] Reasons for rescue are various, but Hayek specifically refers to bodies of law that have historically been unfairly weighted in favour of a dominant class: master over servant, creditor over debtor, and organised business over customer.[159] The corrective of legislation is then justified, since it is beyond the capacity of courts to alter the law by decisions in particular cases in the light of existing precedents.

Rules of organisation are part of an imposed order and require execution, whether by public or private persons. A model of interpretation of such rules by courts rests initially on the doctrine of separation of powers, a doctrine relatively recent as is shown by *Bagg's* case nearly 400 years ago when Chief Justice Coke denied any sharp schism between judicial and legislative power.[160] Legislatures are omnicompetent within a constitutional framework today because courts accept that they are; but courts reserve the right to assess the validity and application of statutes while simultaneously acknowledging parliamentary supremacy. There are two main approaches that can be adopted in the exercise of this judicial function: the protection of citizens' rights or the comprehensive integrity of legislative intention. Hayek's propositions point to the first alternative:

---

157 Comparison of *taxis* with *cosmos*, and the different rules which emanate permeate Hayek's writings. See F A Hayek, 1982, vol 1, pp 35–54; vol 2, pp 46–8.
158 F A Hayek, 1982, vol 1, p 88, and see note 143 above and accompanying text.
159 F A Hayek, 1982, vol 1, p 89.
160 (1615) 11 Co Rep 93 at 98.

> The role of the courts in statutory cases should not then be the superintendence of government. It should be the protection of private rights from government. This latter role is somewhat analogous to the role of the courts in the spontaneous order.[161]

There are virtues in not expecting all statutes to be systematically enforced, because otherwise courts will assume an executive role spurred by ideological litigants and lose their crucial reputation for impartiality.[162] Powers will no longer be separate and the doctrine that supports separation will be dead. The alternative of protecting citizens' rights assimilates statutory construction to the role of the judge in the spontaneous order by identifying and applying valid statutes at the suit of an aggrieved party.[163]

A major purpose of the normative dimension of Hayek's theory is to protest the illegitimacy of transforming private law into public law by social legislation. The term 'social', which Hayek calls a weasel word,[164] may refer to removal of discrimination as between landlord and tenant, provision of government services to disadvantaged minorities, or direction of private activity to particular ends and to the benefit of groups who thereby obtain privileges.[165] The English Trade Disputes Act 1906 falls into the third category, and attracts Hayek's criticism for conferring unique privileges on trade unions and destroying the main characteristic of rules of just conduct, the equality of all under the same rules.[166] Although he laments the socialisation of private law, a prescription for the proper judicial approach to social legislation of the third type is absent; the remedy is in the different direction of radical constitutional reform of the composition and powers of parliaments.[167] Until that millennium is achieved, the best safeguard consistent with Hayek's other propositions is for statutory interpretation to be firmly based on protection of citizens' rights. The High Court of Australia has recently adopted this approach to constitutional issues,[168] and one member has suggested extra-judicially that the court might articulate the contents of the limits on parliamentary power arising from common law liberties.[169]

---

161 R O'Hair, 1986, note 45 above, p 390.

162 R O'Hair, 1986, p 385.

163 R O'Hair, 1986, p 400.

164 Hayek points to 160 nouns qualified by the adjective 'social'. F A Hayek, *The Fatal Conceit*, University of Chicago Press, Chicago, 1988, pp 115–16. See also pp 116–17: 'a weasel word is used to draw teeth from a concept one is obliged to employ, but from which one wishes to eliminate all implications that challenge one's ideological premises'.

165 F A Hayek, 1982, note 9 above, vol 1, pp 141–3.

166 F A Hayek, 1982, vol 1, p 142.

167 F A Hayek's proposals for reform are found in *Law Legislation and Liberty*, 1982, note 9 above, vol 3, Chapter 17.

168 *ACTV Ltd v Commonwealth* (1992) 177 CLR 577, where the court invalidated legislation banning media comment prior to elections on the basis that an implied guarantee of free speech with respect to political discussion was inherent in Australian constitutional democracy.

169 Justice Toohey. See the *Australian Financial Review*, 6 October 1992.

By contrast, Justice Hercules freely acknowledges the majority's right to legislate invasively and adopts this as the rationale for his approach to statutory interpretation; the legislature has a right to have its legislation made effective by the courts.[170] But Dworkin's first real attempt to integrate statutory interpretation into his theory in *Law's Empire* has been criticised for undermining the clarity and power of his earlier analysis.[171] Legal principles then applied equally to statutes as to common law. Probably his best-known early illustration of legal principle is in *Riggs v Palmer*,[172] where the court disqualified a murderer from inheriting under the will of his victim despite the plain language of an inheritance statute. The principle that 'no man may profit from his own wrong' was applied as a justification for making an exception to the otherwise literal effect of the legislation. There was no doubt in the early Dworkin that a judge should construe a statute in the light of legislative policy, but would be controlled by the assumption that the legislature was adding to or subtracting citizens' rights with legal principles providing the propellant for rights-based conclusions. The subsequent and extended treatment of the same issues in *Law's Empire* has drawn criticism that Justice Hercules is now infected in his judgments by a crude form of popular morality rather than the rights of the parties stemming from background moral rights that are independent of populism or majority opinion.[173]

Justice Hercules will apply many of his common law techniques to the interpretation of statutes. The example in *Law's Empire* is *Tennesee Valley Authority v Hill*[174] where the United States Supreme Court halted the construction of a dam costing more than one hundred million US dollars because otherwise the habitat of a small fish called the snail darter would be destroyed. The court applied the clear words of the Endangered Species Act 1973, even though it thought the consequences silly. Justice Hercules judges the case *ex post facto*. He joins the dissidents on the Supreme Court by bowing to the popular view in the country that the dam should be completed, because death for a fish is not the same as unjustly favouring some humans at the expense of others.[175] The will of the people at large prevails over their will as expressed in statute if this factor is absent, since there is no equality principle for fish and thus no conflict between Dworkin's abstract ideas of justice and fairness. But if a statute produces justice issues, reverse discrimination or abortion for example, then both public and parliamentary opinion is excluded as irrelevant since the fairness of lawfully created statutory policy cannot stand against the justice contained in the equality principle. It also appears that Justice Hercules will adopt the form, if not always the substance, of strict construction. Common law rights will yield to

---

170 S Guest, 1992, note 4 above, p 59.
171 T R S Allan, 1993, note 97 above, p 64.
172 115 NY 506 (1889). R Dworkin, 1981, note 39 above, p 23; R Dworkin, 1986, note 60 above, pp 18–20.
173 T R S Allan, 1993, note 97 above, pp 66–7.
174 437 US 153 (1978).
175 R Dworkin, 1986, note 60 above, p 341.

statutory policy only to the extent that the best interpretation requires them to be overruled; such an approach is consistent with the idea of law as integrity, which envisages trade-offs between justice and fairness.[176]

There is no judicial resort to popular morality in Dworkin's early writings unless it is distilled in rules, and its later intrusion has been condemned for displacing the critical morality of the judge. The importance Justice Hercules must place on fairness is more accurately limited to correct procedures for decision-making. 'It neither requires nor permits resort to popular morality — in so far as it differs from justice — beyond the morality enacted into the statute, interpreted correctly in accordance with justice.'[177] But public opinion is apparently different from popular morality, and is accepted both by critics and Dworkin himself as an appropriate determinant of the snail darter case.[178] Unlike the majority of the Supreme Court, he is not prepared to accept a silly interpretation of a statute simply because the statutory words are clear and supported by legislative history showing that Congress intended to give a high level of protection to endangered species. The relevance of public opinion to a single project affecting a single species of fish is an odd and potentially perverse idea, particularly since there is no suggestion that this is Hayekian common opinion that has evolved over the long run; moreover, the calculation of the spread and intensity of popular opinion with respect to momentary issues must be speculative.

Dworkin also permits reference to more orthodox parliamentary materials, including committee reports and speeches by elected representatives, as evidence of legislative purpose, but treats them as part of the state's commitment to a background scheme of political morality.[179] In the snail darter issue the legislature had attempted to make clear in several decisions after the statute was passed that the dam was not to be prevented from being completed, and Justice Hercules will allow himself to take this into account as the Supreme Court majority did not. 'He has no reason of textual integrity arguing against that reading, nor any reason of fairness, because nothing suggests the public will be outraged or offended by that decision.'[180] The flexibility of this approach pivots on Dworkin's rejection of 'speaker's meaning' whereby the construction of legislative language is fixed in the meaning it has for legislators who passed the statute, because Justice Hercules is given the power to alter the interpretation of statutory words. If public opinion veers from the zealous environmentalism present when the Endangered Species Act was passed

---

176 R Dworkin, 1986, p 341. Common law rights are clearly extremely vulnerable to the equality principle here.

177 See T R S Allan, 1993, note 97 above, p 78.

178 See R Dworkin, 1986, note 60 above, Chapter 9 and T R S Allan, 1993, note 97 above, pp 79–80. Allan is concerned to sanitise Dworkin's *Law's Empire* account to exclude the corrupting influence of popular morality by making a hairline distinction between it and public opinion as relevant criteria in statutory interpretation. The distinction seems semantic and unpersuasive.

179 R Dworkin, 1986, note 60 above, pp 343, 346.

180 R Dworkin, 1986, p 347.

to firm support for completion of expensive public utilities, then he may decide differently on fairness grounds at the two different points in time; in particular he will note the failure of the legislature to repeal or amend the statute consistently with changed opinion.[181] Arguments from textual integrity may also shift because of subsequent political decisions or changing ecological circumstances, as may legislative history since official statements can alter. So Justice Hercules is not pinned to original intention nor consequently to judicial precedent concerning the construction of particular words, but has an empowering freedom to adapt judgment to changed circumstances.[182]

The question of the weights to be given to different tests in particular circumstances is left substantially open by Dworkin, but Justice Hercules must meet the sceptical view that the web of possibilities contained in the combination of tests leave him free to exercise a personal choice. Of those tests, community opinion appears to have strong force in the absence of the equality principle, and opinion in the sense acknowledged by Dworkin appears a moveable feast. But if the question under the statute concerns rights citizens may have against others or the community then the equality principle is called upon, since the issue is whether some citizens are unjustly favoured at the expense of others. In either condition he has considerable discretion as to sources and conclusions. Even rejection by legal realists of the literal or 'plain meaning' rule of construction does not result in so wide an ambit claim for the judicial function, although they share with Dworkin the belief that the common law can be developed by statutory analogy. In the Hayekian canon this latter constitutes an illicit commingling of two different types of law. Hayek would undoubtedly also disapprove of *Furniss v Dawson*[183] in which the House of Lords abandoned the literal rule of construction of tax legislation that protects private plans to avoid the incidence of tax. As O'Hair shows, the decision jettisons long-established constitutional principles that include a presumption against wide grants of revenue power to the Crown and contradicts bicameralism; moreover, it allows arguments of state necessity to pre-empt bargains between interest groups. More generally, it contradicts the fundamental principle of liberty: that what is not clearly prohibited is lawful, and is thus an invasion of the spontaneous order.[184]

The great eighteenth century constitutional case of *Entick v Carrington* can serve as an example of the way disputes under statutes should be assimilated to disputes between citizens within the spontaneous order. Lord Chief Justice Camden is clear about the approach to statutory

---

181 R Dworkin, 1986, p 350.
182 The chain novelist idea is taken from common law and applied to statutes. See R Dworkin, 1986, p 313.
183 [1984] AC 474.
184 R O'Hair, 1986, note 45 above, p 440.

interpretation that is most likely to preserve liberty: 'The best way to construe modern statutes is to follow the words thereof.'[185]

The priority of liberty?

Liberty and equality are commonly thought of as polar opposites in justifications for society and its laws, but this is a superficial dichotomy. Dworkin and Hayek each have a normative extension of descriptive theory, although Dworkin blurs the distinction by including his controversial equality principle in the description of the functions of Justice Hercules by contrast with the duplication of rules of just conduct which is Hayek's simple translation. Dworkin is also more complex in theoretical substance, attempting an uneasy marriage of equality and liberty that is labyrinthine when compared with the simple propositions of Hayek's negative liberty which is based on formal equality; and the interferences in the spontaneous order that Dworkin's normative theory compels, identify it as an example of constructivist rationalism by Hayek's standards.[186] The two normative theories go beyond judicial function to give accounts of what human societies should be, and may thus be identified as theories of justice, although both retain intimate links with adjudication. The rules of just conduct wholly constitute Hayek's theory of justice and judges are their authentic articulators, while Dworkin sees hard cases as pivotal for testing fundamental issues of justice.[187]

Hayek's intentions are to demonstrate that socialism is wrong and that a truly civilised society is governed by liberal institutions sustaining a market economy and the rule of law. Central to the idea of maintaining the spontaneous order that underpins liberty is a rejection of distributive or social justice and the adoption of corrective or commutative justice. The touchstone is due to a citizen under a general rule, so that when negligence, breach of contract or stealing disturb the general customary rule the balance of the spontaneous order is restored by legal remedies. It is a backward-looking concept of justice and claims are assessed in terms of pre-existing rights rather than future claims based on reformist ideas. Result-orientated justice of the latter kind must be an invention in which arbitrary choices are made between contending interests, and for which no genuine principle of decision-making can be found.[188] In the customary rules of the spontaneous order the idea of social justice has no profile because no one controls the system as a whole or the income it

---

185 (1765) 2 Wils KB 275 at 290. This reflects the classical common law approach identified by R Pound in a celebrated article 'Common Law and Legislation', (1907) 21 *Harvard LR* 383. According to Pound, courts will not only refuse to analogise legislative innovations to the common law, but will also give statutes a strict and narrow interpretation.

186 Dworkin's most recent writings on the subject are not in standard sources. An excellent synthesis of both old and new ideas is in S Guest, 1992, note 4 above, Chapters 9, 10 and 11.

187 S Guest, 1992, note 4 above, p 211.

188 F A Hayek, 1982, note 9 above, vol 2, Chapter 9.

generates;[189] it follows that social justice is destructive of the end-independent rules of the *cosmos* if judicial decision-making is patterned on a constructed justice. Implementation of social justice by common law judges diminishes the liberty of citizens to pursue private plans consistently with rules of just conduct, which Hayek identifies as true liberty. There is no positive test for justice, only the negative tests of the rules of just conduct, otherwise society is altered by result-orientated rules of organisation into a *taxis* that contains the seeds of totalitarianism. This coheres with Sir Owen Dixon's conviction that judges who pursue a reformist justice put the common law at risk, and with his prediction that courts would then come to exercise 'an unregulated authority over the fate of men and their affairs which would leave our system indistinguishable from the systems we least admire'.[190]

The only equality for Hayek is formal equality before the law, what he calls the principle of treating all under the same rules where the rules concern individual conduct. This is to guarantee that each citizen has the best chance of realising private plans, since the main advantage of spontaneous orders is that citizens can achieve more by cooperation than by acting alone, even when their goals differ.[191] Justice is the property of individual conduct premised upon those rules, and permits the common law judge to develop customary law as an evolutionary rather than a constructivist rationalist. The philosophical engine room for propositions is Hayek's reconciliation of Kant and Hume, wherein the twinned bases of Kant-based universalisation and Hume's inflexible general rules of stability of possession, its transference by consent and the performance of promises, underpin justice as a common law process. That reconciliation has been criticised in philosophical terms as an unstable alliance,[192] and as producing a negative idea of justice contained in the result of unintended individual action that gives the unlucky no more than the right to sleep under bridges.[193] The universalisation test is, however, not merely formal for Hayek but moral in the sense that any provisional new rule must be measured against another rule that it may be preferable to preserve, so that community opinion is subjected to the test of fit with the order as a whole.[194] An order which contains conflicting rules has its own dimension of injustice because legitimate expectations are compromised. Hayek's approach is similar to that of Popper concerning scientific discovery as a series of failure tests rather than success tests, where truth is achieved through falsification of hypotheses rather than their verification.[195] Justice

---

189 R O'Hair, 1986, note 45 above, p 247.
190 O Dixon, 1965, note 16 above, p 165.
191 R O'Hair, 1986, note 45 above, p 229.
192 C Kukathas, 1990, note 70 above, p viii. Hume's propositions are extracted in F A Hayek, 1982, note 9 above, vol 1, pp 167–8 note 34.
193 N MacCormick, *Legal Right and Social Democracy*, Clarendon Press, Oxford, 1982, p 10.
194 F A Hayek, 1982, note 9 above, vol 2, pp 28–9. See also R O'Hair, 1986, note 45 above, p 248.
195 F A Hayek, 1982, note 9 above, vol 2, p 43.

becomes a sorting principle for provisional rules that places hurdles in the path of constructivist inventions, and serves to protect the common law and its courts compatibly with Sir Owen Dixon's view of them as the foundation and steel framework of the community, but 'unable to do more than support a structure with stability and at rest'.[196]

Hayek's descriptive theory of adjudication is transferred wholesale to his normative theory of a justice that is focused on Humean property rights and incapable of disaggregation. Dworkin has never accepted this view of liberty as a priority, and in early writings rejects the notion that it is a seamless web.[197] Liberties to use property and to enter into contracts are less important than liberties such as freedom to speak, so that any general right to liberty is misconceived and incoherent. Undifferentiated liberty does not agree with Dworkin's jealously guarded idea of rights as trumps of utilitarian arguments, because if everyone has the right then everyone holds the trumps in his hand; if all cards are trumps, then none are. Dworkin also focuses on liberties rather than liberty because he wishes to discriminate between fundamental and less important liberties to explain his organising equality principle which depends on such argued distinctions.

This theme is subsequently developed in an attempt to reconcile liberty with equality which is more puzzling than illuminating because of the dominance accorded the abstract principle of equality; he assumes that we should treat people as equals in his special sense of those words, and then deals with the problem as one of distribution.[198] A crucial ingredient in Dworkin's idea of equality is its derived conception of resource egalitarianism in which a citizen is distinguished from his environmental or physical circumstances.[199] Citizens without recognisable talents or who are handicapped physically or mentally count just as much as humans as those who are not, and must be treated as equals by being given an equality of resources. Reverse discrimination in separate university quotas for disadvantaged groups is justified in terms of redressing the equality imbalance of resources. But a sharp distinction must be drawn between compensable lack of talent and physical incapacity and non-compensable tastes and ambitions, and liberty is to this extent disaggregated.[200] Hayek will have none of these fine distinctions, for circumstances of birth or status or physical and mental capacity are not compensable under rules of just conduct, and the base line of personal qualities and wealth is purely a matter of luck. We cannot say who is

---

196 Inaugural address as Chief Justice of the High Court, (1952) 85 CLR xi at xv. See also O'Hair, 1986, note 45 above, p 256.

197 R Dworkin, 'We Do Not Have a Right to Liberty' in *Liberty and the Rule of Law* (ed R L Cunningham), Texas A & M University Press, College Station, 1979, p 169. F A Hayek does not disaggregate liberty as Dworkin does, but counts economic liberties as important as others. On this, see R O'Hair, 1986, note 45 above, pp 954–8.

198 S Guest, 1992, note 4 above, p 298.

199 Guest considers that Dworkin fails to make the derivations he seeks to show. S Guest, 1992, p 263.

200 S Guest, 1992, pp 271–2.

unjust in these circumstances since there is no person called society and no one controls, or should control, processes within the spontaneous order; moreover, any disturbance of formal equal justice similarly disturbs the end-independent nature of rules of just conduct. There can be no unequal starting line that is properly remediable through law.[201]

Dworkin is determined to locate liberty within his special idea of equal respect and concern, and the bright line he attempts to draw places deficits due to prejudice and victimisation in the remediable category. The arguments are complex, but the lower average intellectual achievement of black candidates for standard quotas for tertiary disciplines in demand justifies special quotas for such disadvantaged candidates which do not infringe the rights of majority candidates who would otherwise obtain a university place.[202] Minority candidates otherwise suffer a resource deficit. On the other hand, a citizen who is deprived of liberty for the sake of improving equality may be unfairly victimised. How does this square with the equality principle? In *Buckley v Valeo*[203] the United States Supreme Court invalidated congressional legislation which restricted the amount a citizen could pay to assist in the election of a political candidate as contrary to the First Amendment freedom of speech. Dworkin thinks the court was wrong. In an ideal society there are equal resources and the legislation would be unfair, but the rich benefit from lack of financial restriction more than the poor and Dworkin approves the statute because the restrictions on liberty do not in practice count as victimisation. The question is whether the reduced liberties would in practical terms be less than under an ideal distribution.

Similarly, in *Lochner v New York*[204] the same court declared legislation unconstitutional that limited hours and conditions of work in the bakery industry. The surface answer is that the decision is right because the statute restricts freedom of contract and victimises employees, but Dworkin disagrees on grounds that the decision ignores inequality of bargaining power and insufficiently canvasses health and safety issues. More importantly, the *Lochner* case transgresses the idea of integrity central to *Law's Empire*, namely that the court should have assumed that the legislature was acting in pursuit of a policy to treat all its citizens with

---

201 A good focus for F A Hayek's ideas is inheritance, which is often the target of social policy through taxation. For a short summary, E Butler, *Hayek: His Contribution to the Political and Economic Thought of Our Time*, Temple Smith, London, 1983, pp 101–2.

202 This has long been Dworkin's determined view, and is perhaps one of the main reasons why many see his theory as intuitive and subjective. Probably his best known and most accessible argument for reverse discrimination is in *Taking Rights Seriously*, 1951, note 39 above, Chapter 9, where he rejects the plaintiff's claim in *DeFunis v Odegaard* 416 US 312 (1974). The wealth of passionate writing by Dworkin in this area is listed by S Guest, 1992, note 4 above, p 251, note 33 and p 252, note 42. F A Hayek's concept of formal justice, the treating of all under the same rules, most nearly approaches the idea of a right to equal treatment rejected by Dworkin in his analysis of *DeFunis*.

203 424 US 1 (1976). See S Guest, 1992, p 280.

204 198 US 45 (1905). See S Guest, 1992, pp 281–2.

equal concern and respect, so that it should have assumed that employees who were dismissed because of the decision would be compensated by the state for loss of income and status. By ignoring this dimension, the *Lochner* court usurped the legislative function.

There is no doubt that Hayek would regard all this as an agile trapeze act deserving of applause for its skill, but ultimately false to the liberty principle. It constitutes constructivist rationalism in its interference with the spontaneous order and pursues a moral and political agenda which combines rules of organisation with rules of just conduct and exactly typifies the dangers to the latter type of rule.

Conclusion

Although technically part of the counter-revolution, Dworkin is closer to the realist camp since by significant tokens he qualifies as a constructivist rationalist. His initial descriptive declaratory approach was always skewed by inclusion of the fundamental imperative that judges treat citizens with equal concern and respect rather than the rejected idea of equal treatment, and subsequent theorising so submerged Blackstonian propositions as to drown them. The early theory that Finnis identified as fundamentally normative becomes in *Law's Empire* totally so.[205] Dworkin's complex drive for law as integrity is essentially intuitive and dependent on a moral and political agenda that is inherently controversial. Common law rules and legislation are yoked as sources of law based on the equality idea, and not separated as Hayek insists. Dworkin's atomising of liberty stems from Hobbes' definition of liberty as licence, and his concern to entrench only preferred liberties as strong claims of right amounts to an attempt to exempt those chosen from social feedback, and a concomitant silent assent to the priority of government power outside those strong claims. The exclusion of liberty-based property rights is unjustified; citizens have those rights not property itself, and property has priority in Hayek's theory for good Humean reasons.[206] The later sophistication into resource and liberty deficits does not alter the basic thrust of Dworkin's agenda.

Hayek's theory stands alone without serious support from Dworkin, and shows Hayek rather than Dworkin is Blackstone in modern dress. It is astonishing that a theory supplied by a non-common lawyer with a muddler's mind should so accurately capture the essence of classical common law adjudication. Hayek's theory accords with the temper of the High Court of Australia at the time when Sir Owen Dixon was Chief Justice, which recognised that judges had only riparian rights in the common law.[207] The court rejected constructivist rationalism in arguments made to it, and declined to invent new rules to meet ideological claims of

---

205 J Finnis, 1980, note 5 above, p 21.

206 For a libertarian critique of Dworkin on these lines, see S Macedo, 'The Public Morality of the Rule of Law: a critique of Ronald Dworkin', (1985) 8 *Harvard Journal of Law and Public Policy* 79.

207 *Rootes v Shelton* (1967) 116 CLR 383 at 387 per Kitto J.

changing social needs.[208] The pendulum has swung, however, and the modern High Court is a realist court which condemns past justifications as formalism.

There are two final observations. First, condemnations of formalism are still made, and in some detail, to highlight the comparative advantages of realist adjudication.[209] Only a strong opponent justifies such systematic treatment, so that what is called formalism at the practical level of judging clearly still exerts a powerful hold on lawyers' ideas of what is right. Hayek can help here. His theory explodes the realist myth that sterile logic necessarily controls development of the common law under old ideas, and thus can be the vehicle for a successful counter-revolution based on genuine community opinion rather than the constructivist ideas of an intellectual elite. The second point is short. Realism in judging means that judges will be perceived as unelected politicians with an agenda, especially in those landmark cases which do not reflect genuine community opinion. Departure from the idea of what realists call a priestly caste administering a mystery means that judicial independence will be threatened. There are signs that this is already occurring.[210]

For much of his life, Hayek was ridiculed for his views. But he constantly preached the power of ideas over politics and intellectual fashion. It is not necessary to agree with his particular proposals for constitutional reform to celebrate in that.

---

208 See, for example, *Rootes v Shelton* (1967) 116 CLR 383 at 386–7 per Kitto J. ('[I]t is a mistake to suppose that the case is concerned with "changing social needs" ... or that it is to be decided by "designing" a rule'.)

209 See A Mason, 1993, note 6 above, and A Mason, 1987, note 37 above.

210 Contemporary examples of Australian realist judges resisting political intrusions into their independence are collected at note 81 above.

CHAPTER 11

Contemporary Radicalism and Legal Theory

Alice Erh-Soon Tay and Eugene Kamenka*

Disintegration of the Marxist system

When Marx died in London in March 1883 just 11 people attended his funeral. Yet, in the late twentieth century, more than one-third of the world's population was led or governed in his name. Politically, Marxism, or at least Marxism-Leninism, has achieved some remarkable successes. The two major twentieth century revolutions, the Russian Revolution and the Chinese Revolution, ended with Marxist-Leninists in control and Marxism the ruling ideology of an all-powerful state and party. A worldwide communist movement has preached revolution in most countries. With Soviet or Chinese help, the movement took power in several countries, often doing so by brutally destroying any challengers. For a period, the anti-colonialist and anti-imperialist sentiments that have come to dominate modern international relations and the politics of developing countries were heavily tinged with, or even inspired by, the language, assumptions, and prognostications of Marxism-Leninism. To some extent, they still are.

In modern post-industrial societies, the working class and the parties that have the main electoral allegiance of that class have neither made nor advocated revolution. They have either not adopted, or have departed from, the tenets, tactics, and fundamental concepts that Marx preached. Yet in some countries, the Marxist and neo-Marxist left has strong, often disproportionate, influence. As Marx predicted, capitalism has been

---

*   Alice Erh-Soon Tay is the Challis Professor of Jurisprudence, Department of Jurisprudence, Faculty of Law, University of Sydney. The late Eugene Kamenka was at the time of writing this essay, the Professor of the History of Ideas, Research Institute of Social Sciences, Institute of Advanced Studies, Australian National University, Canberra.

significantly socialised from within. Private property and control as the reification of individual will and individual rights, as an area in which the citizen or the bourgeois is free from outside interference, stand in glaring theoretical 'contradiction' to the increasingly corporate, non-individual nature of ownership and its ever-growing dependence on the state for economic support. The public perception of the social ramifications, social power, and social dependence of large-scale private enterprise is widespread. Increasingly, such enterprise in welfare states is not distinguished in the public's mind or the worker's mind from state-owned enterprise. Many countries subject large-scale private enterprise to strong political and 'public interest' controls. The ideology of *laissez-faire* capitalism and the political and legal beliefs of liberal individualism have come under increasing attack and become more eroded in the new societies of mass production, mass services, and mass consumption. A new 'knowledge class' composed of (some) educators, media and social workers, actors, public servants, and technical experts has replaced the 'militant' proletariat as the bearers of hostility to capitalism. This 'knowledge class' is most receptive to aspects of the Marxist message which elevate the public sector against the private sector, compassion against competition, and culture against money.

The revival of Marx-based radicalism and the astounding shift in its clientele were dramatised by student upheavals in 1968, primarily in the prosperous democracies of western Europe and North America. The largely temporary alliance of students and young workers that emerged in some countries failed to mask the fact that the new radicals and their New Left coalitions saw the universities as the powerhouse of revolution in modern capitalist societies. The New Left thought that the students, not the proletariat, would expose the 'repressive tolerance' of late capitalist societies and throw off their cultural hegemony, their military-industrial complexes and their alienated and alienating economic, political, legal, and cultural institutions. Once these institutions fell, the capitalist economic system could not survive.

The actual 'happenings' of 1968, significantly set in motion by the progress of the Vietnam war, China's Great Proletarian Cultural Revolution, and the enormous expansion in the number of tertiary education students was shortlived. Student strikes do not bring the wheels of industry to a halt. Nevertheless, the sudden revival of radicalism and of Marxist or neo-Marxist sentiment in the heart of western post-war democracy was both striking and significant. It has had some lasting impact. The movement was hostile to capitalism and the established order, and at the same time, was sharply critical of the dogmatism and repression that characterised the Soviet Union and those communist parties that followed its instructions. The radicals of 1968 elevated anti-authoritarianism, egalitarianism, and sexual and cultural freedom against the determinism of classical Marxism and its concentration on economic grievances and economic classes. These ideas were popularised earlier in the Free Speech movement at Berkeley and the 'youth protests' in America as part of a sexual 'liberation'. The radicals rejected nationalism, racism, male chauvinism, and any authority relations. Within the Marxist tradition the radicals looked back to the unsuccessful revolutions: the Paris Commune of 1871 and the 1918–1919

Workers' Councils Movements in Germany, Austria, and Italy. Their heroes were typical 'oppositionists': Luxemburg, Trotsky, Pannekoek, and Bakunin, or anti-Soviet anti-determinist 'Marxists' like the later Mao. Participation was the catchword for the future; alienation the concept that brought out the evils, both of capitalism and the communist-dominated 'state capitalisms' or 'new class' bureaucracies of the Soviet bloc. The New Left was a loose coalition of left radicals, neither pervasively Marxist nor wedded to any common theoretical positions. The New Left emphasised certain aspects of Marxism, the work of Kirsch, Lukacs, Gramsci and the members of the Frankfurt School of Critical Theory, or the anti-authoritarian quasi-Marxist socialism of Erich Fromm and Herbert Marcuse.

The economic recessions of the 1970s somewhat dampened the New Left's concentration on the cultural and ideological features of capitalist society which the New Left regarded as evils which offset the ever-increasing affluence of the people in advanced economies. The fall in growth rates and the renewed plight of the poor, blacks, immigrants and other disadvantaged groups in advanced western economies produced a revival of the economic work of Marx from his mature period. Many Marxists returned to exposures of the contradictions of the capitalist economy in place of the 1960s critiques of the alienation and reification that they saw in capitalist (and Soviet) culture. 'Traditional' Marxist analysis of capitalism with its critique of private ownership of the means of production, distribution, and exchange still have much to say to us. The intellectual feeling that traditional Marxism is relevant has been strengthened and revived in the last 15 years by the growth of a new conservatism, by the increasing rejection by governments of Keynesianism, by the expansion of the welfare state and by the increasing concentration and internationalisation of capital.

Nevertheless, even 'traditional' Marxists now emphasise the role of multi-national corporations in the world economy, the 'imperialist' and anti-communist role of the United States 'ruling classes' (implicitly treated as power elites), and the limits that these world protagonists and the unplanned world economy place on the capacity for action by social democratic or socialist national governments anywhere in the world. Most Marxists recognise that neither the industrial proletariat nor the factory owner is the main actor in economic struggles, problems, and decision-making today. Marxists believe that one characteristic of late capitalism is the consummated transfer of 'control' from the mill-owner to finance capital, to great international corporations, international banks, and holding companies working in partnership or collusion with state and military bureaucracies. Another characteristic is that the 'subjective' class structure and the economic reality in advanced economies resemble a diamond shape rather than the traditional class pyramid. Wage earners who see themselves as actual or aspiring members of the middle classes, rather than the proletariat, form an ever-increasing part of the population in capitalist countries. The wage earners do own or aspire to own houses, cars, and other consumer goods.

By the 1970s in Great Britain and in the United States the term 'bourgeoisie' had virtually disappeared from the vocabulary of political writers and politicians. 'Bourgeoisie' was replaced by 'middle class,' and people who worked for wages used the term 'working class' less frequently as a self-description. Deviation from the traditional Marxist two-class model was apparent in the nineteenth century. The Marxist R S Neale in his *Class and Ideology in the Nineteenth Century* argued that a five-class model was the minimum necessary for recognising the important differences that the terms 'proletariat' and 'bourgeoisie' glossed over. An expanded model was necessary to capture the realities recognised in the twentieth century by the ever-growing use of the term 'middle classes'. The hostility of the hardcore poor to the system is easily understood. They are as much the product of cultural, social, religious, and personal disadvantages as of any direct economic 'exploitation'. The vast majority of working poor are not receptive to the revolutionary message. Many Marxists, therefore, view them as in thrall to capitalist culture, ideology, and political illusions rather than as victims of direct physical or economic repression.

The greater appeal of the Marxist message to underdeveloped countries has kept alive and even revitalised the 'capitalism is to be destroyed through its weakest link' theory elaborated by Lenin. Primarily agrarian populations today suffer from 'feudal' (ie, landowner) repression, military dictatorship, and 'neocolonial' exploitation. Recent Marxist re-examinations of Marx's political writings tend to stress that these interpretations do not conform to interpretations of Marx that have him predicting revolution in advanced industrial economies as coming first. Much of Marx's political sympathy, like that of revolutionary socialists generally in the nineteenth century, focused on Ireland as Britain's economically most backward and politically most troublesome possession, and focused also on Poland as a symbol of the ideology of national liberation. The practical political policies of Marxist movements today have largely kept to these realities, seeing South America as the weakest link of United States imperialism and Asia, Africa, and now the Pacific, as the sites where European 'colonialism' and 'neocolonialism' might be humbled. Some Marxist writing has emphasised an independent dimension of political enthusiasm and social dislocation in the making of revolutions. Some Marxists argue that this produces revolutionary situations in the early development of capitalism or in its initial unsettling intrusions into pre-capitalist economies more readily than in an established capitalist economic system.

As a result of all this, contemporary Marxism in the western world has become an infinitely more complex movement in doctrine and ideology than it was in the days of monolithic communism. During that period the term 'Marxist' was increasingly abandoned to those who called themselves Marxist-Leninists or communists and who claimed to find in capitalism the simple struggle of bourgeois and proletarian. Marxist thought now displays neither a common set of beliefs nor a common methodology. Different types of Marxist thought are less sharply distinguishable from one another than Marxism once was distinguishable from radical and revolutionary movements and individuals who did not see themselves as 'orthodoxly' or 'properly' Marxist. Marxist thought varies considerably in the critique of capitalism — some concentrating on one set of evils and some on another.

Few Marxists now believe that all these evils can be simply and directly reduced to a single determining factor, such as private property or commodity-production. Few Marxists now argue that the evils of capitalism can be removed simply and with logical inevitability by abolishing both. Behind this is an implicit, unacknowledged but increasingly important recognition of the fact that there is a difference between traditional capitalist (*laissez-faire*) economic assumptions and the present 'capitalist' social order, its politics, its ideologies, and its culture. In the nineteenth century, it may have looked as though the economic 'base' of capitalist society inevitably created a powerful and superficially coherent version of the 'superstructure'. Economics, politics, and culture appeared to exemplify the same dominant assumptions, values, and ideology as capitalism. Today, in private enterprise societies, the economic order, the political order and the cultural order have parted company. As Daniel Bell argues, the economic order emphasises efficiency, political equality and cultural 'self-expression'. This parting is due to many factors. It is partly the result of a disillusionment with economic progress and the growing importance of planning and 'rationalisation' of production, partly the product of political democracy, trade union power, and the increasing subjection of private property and private interest to various forms of state and public control, and partly the consequence of a striking alienation of a new 'knowledge class'.

In advanced post-industrial societies, this conflict is at least as important and often more evident than any bitter conflict of class interest and class ideology within the economic system. This, too, helps to explain the extent to which Marxists no longer simply reduce the political and the ideological to the economic even though many would reject our analysis or at least be uncomfortable with it, insisting that the political and the ideological are at best only 'relatively autonomous'. In the end, the traditional Marxist argument runs, they all still serve capitalism or express the intrusion of working class demands.

Marxism as a social science and Marxism as the philosophy of human emancipation have taken some very hard knocks. Increasingly, they now are viewed by intelligent Marxists as intellectual and political programs requiring careful rethinking and re-examination in the light of twentieth century history and of deeper historical knowledge and social understanding. Politically, Leninism, the Marx-based strategy for gaining and keeping power in agrarian societies undergoing the dislocations and rising expectations that follow the impact of the industrial and post-industrial world, did well. In the most difficult conditions, by abandoning democracy, communist parties and governments for a time were remarkably successful in maintaining internal 'order' and external security. They climbed into the well-worn seats of power and made their states stronger than ever at whatever cost to their peoples. They imposed major social and economic transformations, destroyed traditions, and reshaped cultures. They found non-Marxist and quasi-Marxist imitators from Uganda to Burma. However, the social and the economic costs of these programs were great. The capacity of communist countries to maintain economic efficiency in terms of their own goals became increasingly questionable. But state and law (in a certain sense) flourished in these Leninist societies.

There was nothing utopian or legally 'nihilist' about these countries' conceptions or methods of state and legal control. Their own practice, and to a significant extent their theory, constituted a daily rejection of the belief that state, politics, and ideology express or reflect existing economic realities. For communists, the state exists to create them.

Post-industrial western societies have their own, rather different, problems, which is why Marxist or pseudo-Marxist 'critiques' of law and even legal nihilism in western societies have not become totally unfashionable, especially among younger law teachers. Such radicals are happiest ignoring, or knowing as little as possible about, social ideology, law and legal theory in the communist countries. Their outlook is firmly provincial, selecting the parts of the world that suit them best. These Marxists especially rely on those cultures closest to home or most favourable to their concerns. They have little admiration for Soviet-type states, although they may still prefer these societies to 'United States imperialism' and 'liberal bourgeois individualism'. They are likely to treat communist societies as not 'truly' Marxist; as having been created in adverse conditions and consequently departing from the proper path. Implicitly, though, many carriers of this sort of Marxism and Marxist critique of law in English-speaking societies abandon Marxism as an unproblematic science, as a body of general laws and attested conclusions organised and organisable into a plan of history and historical development. They are concerned, rather, to choose sides against the power of capital and the profit motive and to support the cause of peace, community, and 'rational' social relations. They draw from Marx a committed attitude and a radical research program. They emphasise economic and class interest, social conflict, the insensitivity and prejudice of ruling groups and elites, 'the structure of domination', the longings, interests, culture, the fate of the poor and exploited, and the view of law from below. This approach provides such younger Marxists with themes, rather than with laws. Some find in selected aspects of Marx's thought all that they need; others adhere to his categories and pronouncements very loosely.

Increasingly, these newer radicals see themselves as post-Marxist, 'radical,' or 'critical' theorists. For some, 'patriarchal' oppression and 'exploitation' of women throughout history is now more important and more pervasive than the exploitation of serfs and workers. For others, blacks or 'coloured' races and indigenous peoples, or even the 'poor' (not a Marxist category), are the most important categories. These people are the truly exploited on a world scale. Many thinkers may have started with classical Marxism, but much of their radicalism has turned to a loose coalition of this with reasons for dissatisfaction with 'bourgeois' society and ideology or 'European' domination.

These viewpoints span the radical continuum, from women to the nuclear disarmament and gay liberation, from indigenous peoples who have lost their land and culture, to the poor nations taking part in what is alleged to be the international class struggle between south and north, or between allegedly noncapitalist, nonindividualist ideologies such as Islam and the individualist decadent west. Even former members of the Old Left, as historians, find more inspiration in studying rural bandits than in looking at the proletariat today. The leading 'revisionist' Marxist, Roger Garaudy, expelled in the 1960s from the French Communist Party for substituting 'salariat' for 'proletariat,' has been converted to Islam and attended the UNESCO-sponsored commemoration of the centenary of Marx's death as an observer from the World Muslim Federation.

In recent years, 'exploitation' again has begun to replace 'alienation' as the key word expressing and mobilising hostility toward capitalism and capitalist firms among many classical Marxists. This is especially true for an intelligent new sector of 'analytical' Marxists. But for all the economic overtones or undertones of that word, the fragmentations sketched above have undermined further the political centrality and effectiveness of economics and the notion of economic determinism in Marx. The new radicals increasingly emphasise cultural and ideological factors over economic factors, although they intermingle them with economic factors. Above all, the socialist and Marxist belief in the superior rationality and efficiency of public ownership and the planned economy of the socialist mode of production is almost completely eroded. Planned, state-run economies have their own problems promoting innovation, flexibility, productivity, and capacity to deliver goods that consumers want. Such economies can be and are just as dehumanising and production-oriented as capitalist economies, except that in capitalist economies, workers are 'undisciplined' and may opt out of the system. Nor have these state-run economies continued to deliver economic growth. Most Third World countries ceased admiring the Soviet Union or China as economic models or as economic patrons (though they often liked the Soviet legal model for its simplicity and its elevation of state power). Increasingly, western Marxists and radicals no longer criticise capitalism for failing to deliver the goods that a socialist economy can or could produce. They criticise capitalism for producing too much, for creating excessive consumption and hopes of consumption, for creating *international* inequality, for ravaging the environment and not only exploiting people, but elevating an internalised but still enslaving work ethic.

New radical legal groups and concerns

Since the remarkable revitalisation of Marxism and radical thought in the western world accompanying and following the events of 1968, in which the official communist parties played no important role and in which universities and university intellectuals were central, discussions in western Marxism have been increasingly independent, pluralist, and multifaceted. These discussions are no longer subject to any consistent or coherent attempt at centralised communist party direction or to dogmatic orthodoxies, but Marxists remain an internally quarrelsome lot, constantly accusing each other of departing from Marx or Marxism. The decline of allegiance to a dogmatic Marxism as a coherent and universal science has been so great that interest has shifted, especially among the growing number of academically trained Marxists, to the task of exploring Marxist lines in particular fields, thus seeking to throw fresh illumination both on Marxism and on the field in question. More and more would-be Marxist intellectuals earn their living as tutors, assistants, younger lecturers, or radical new-wave professors in universities, technical colleges and teacher training colleges. They do not seek to elaborate a Marxist theory for the proletariat, but rather a Marxist approach and program for their own discipline, to radicalise the understanding of their subject, to transform 'bourgeois' university courses into radical university courses and thus undermine capitalist culture. We now have schools, or at least discussion groups and conferences that explore Marxism and philosophy, Marxism and literature, Marxism and sociology, Marxism and anthropology, Marxism and history, or rather Marxism and particular histories, and Marxism and law. In some areas, such as sociology and 'revisionist' history, Marxists have become both organisationally and intellectually very prominent, but by adopting, to some extent, the wider jargon and concerns of their trade. In other areas, including classical and seventeenth century English history, they have been able to latch on to and build upon the widely recognised achievements of a somewhat older generation of politically committed but intellectually independent Marxists and neo-Marxists. These older Marxists have brought out the fruitfulness of the Marxist approach and shown a sense of its limitations.

Like leftist groups generally, such like-minded groups — 'conferences' and 'collectives' — have tended initially to be organised by and around a 'hardcore' group of committed people, often not more than one or two. These usually have been more conscious and wide-ranging in their 'Marxism' than the rest, both at the level of theory and of involvement in practical action, at least within the academy. Nor do such groups display striking permanence or stability: in continental Europe, where there has been a richer tradition of past Marxist philosophical and other academic endeavour to draw on, their membership and their interests shift as new social problems, new radical causes and new intellectual trends or disagreements come to the fore. Thus, the very non-Marxist work of Professor Bodenheimer reflects the philosophical seriousness and sophistication of continental Europe and the capacity of non-Marxists to deal with Marxism. European Marxists are somewhat less academically amateurish than Marxists in English-speaking countries, where the general background education of professional academics, especially lawyers, in the wider subjects of philosophy, history, and modern European thought often has been deficient. In all countries, Marxist groups, seeing universities as politically and academically conservative institutions, have pursued organisational and intellectual influence. They have de-emphasised and devalued ability without political commitment, and have sought to promote, in any way that will succeed, the appointment of like-minded teachers and the framing of 'Marxist' courses.

However, the removal of dogmatic constraints by a number of western European Communist Parties, including the British, has led to some important and basic discussions of Marxist methodology and Marxist conceptions of the relation between theory and history, and economics and culture. In continental Europe much of the Marxist discussion concerned the relationship between Marx and Hegel and the correct understanding of the philosophy of Marxism. There were also important discussions of the rise, character and internal dynamic or lack of dynamic of social formations, eg feudalism, the Asiatic mode of production, and how to classify African history. In Britain, a series of works by the late Raymond Williams — *Culture and Society* (1958); *The Long Revolution,* (1961); *Marxism and Literature,* (1977)[1] — attracted widespread popular and radical attention. These works led to a major debate between Williams and the editors of the *New Left Review* on Marxist methodology and the relation of culture to the economic base.[2] Williams, emphasising popular culture against the abstract reification and categorisation imposed upon social thinking by historical elites, nevertheless insisted on the relative autonomy of popular culture and literature. He specifically rejected the past Marxist tendency to overemphasise the economic and political and to treat culture as superstructural. In *Marxism and Literature,* Williams argued for the 'materiality' of culture as a form of production. Human beings create language, meanings, and values, just as they create products. They do so out of the 'living experience' of ordinary people and not just that of artists and writers. Language is thus a form of practical consciousness and not merely a reflection of practical activity:

> The social and political order which maintains a capitalist market, like the social and political struggles which created it, is necessarily material production. From castles and palaces and churches to prisons and workhouses and schools; from weapons of war to a controlled press: any ruling class, in variable ways though always materially, produces a social and political order. These are never superstructural activities.[3]

For the Marxists of the *New Left Review*, this was more than they could take. They complained justly, but without sharpening the issue or facing deeper confusions involved in the term 'material,' that Williams had lapsed into 'a new circularity in which all elements of the social order are equal because they are all material'.[4] In truth, the *New Left Review* Marxists said, 'some forms of matter are more materially effective than others'[5] (shades of Mr Pickwick!). More intelligently, Terry Eagleton in *Criticism and Ideology* commented that 'Williams often manoeuvred himself into the contradictory position of opposing a crippling hegemony whose power he had simultaneously to deny because not to do so would have suggested that ordinary people were not after all the true creators of meanings and values'.[6]

More solid and significant was the attack launched by the Marxist historian E P Thompson, author of *The Making of the English Working Class*

---

1   R Williams, *Culture and Society, 1780–1950*, Chatto & Windus, London, 1958; R Williams, *The Long Revolution,* Chatto & Windus, London, 1961; R Williams, *Marxism and Literature,* Chatto & Windus, London, 1977.

2   R Williams, *Politics and letters*, NLB, London, distributed in the United States and Canada by Schocken Books, New York, 1979, pp 350–1.

3   R Williams, 1979, p 351.

4   R Williams, 1979, p 351.

5   R Williams, 1979, p 351.

6   T Eagleton, *Criticism and Ideology*, Verso, London, 1978, p 28.

(1968) and *Whigs and Hunters: The Origin of the Black Act* (1975).[7] Thompson dismissed Althusserian and economic-technological determinism on behalf of an empirically based and historically based Marxist writing of history. In *The Making of the English Working Class* Thompson set out to show that class was not the product simply of economic developments, steam power, and cotton mills. The formation of the English working class was a fact of political and cultural history as much as of economic history. The former was not reducible to the latter. The foundation texts of the English working class movement were Bunyan's *Pilgrim's Progress* and Paine's *The Rights of Man*. The movement drew on an older and wider tradition of protest on behalf of liberty of conscience, trial by jury, communitarianism, a ('slumbering') sense of democracy, and the notion of a free-born Englishman. These were formed in the struggle against arbitrary arrest, absolutism, rising food prices, the disruption of paternalism, and the moral economy, which was represented by the concept of the 'just price' through the pre-industrial eighteenth century growth of *laissez faire*, the free market, and the cash nexus. Field labourers, artisans, and weavers were among the most radical in popular protest. Thompson argued in his *Patrician Society, Plebeian Culture* that cultural hegemony was only secondarily an expression of economic or physical (military) power.[8] Cultural hegemony rests on 'images of power and authority' with which the rulers — described for eighteenth century England variously as the 'patricians,' 'the ruling class', 'the great', and 'the gentry' — exercise cultural hegemony and social control, and also rests on the 'popular mentalities of subordination' that make this possible. In the eighteenth century, the regular and practical exercise of patrician paternal authority and responsibility declined. Authority was increasingly expressed in symbolic gestures and occasional dramatic interventions which masked the fact that the patricians were becoming distant from the village and from plebeian cultures. Patricial cultural hegemony required more and more the 'theatre' of the law and politics to establish an image of social order and social control. The people, given more space to develop a plebeian culture by the withdrawal of the patricians, developed their forms of popular action — anonymous letters, arson, houghing of cattle, opening of fishpond sluices — and the counter-theatre of the poor, threatening 'sedition' by burning effigies, hanging a boot from the gallows, illuminating windows, and punishing plebeian offenders against popular norms by charivari.

Thompson, in rejecting the base and superstructure model, wanted to reject the direct determining role of economic structures and relations as well. In an article called 'Folklore, Anthropology, and History',[9] he quoted with approval a passage in the *Grundrisse* in which Marx speaks of a specific

---

7   E P Thompson, The Making of the English Working Class, Penguin Books, Harmondsworth, 1968; E P Thompson, *Whigs and Hunters: The Origin of the Black Act*, Penguin, London, 1975.

8   E P Thompson, 'Patrician Society, Plebian Culture', (1974) 7 *J Soc Hist* 382 at 405.

9   E P Thompson, 'Folklore, Anthropology, and History', (1977) 3 *Indian Hist Rev* 247 at 261.

or determinate production and its relations as a 'general illumination in which all other colours are plunged which modifies their specific tonalities' — a view that is neither causally nor structurally determinist.

Thompson's specific attack on Althusserianism, published as *The Poverty of Theory* in 1978, saw structuralism as promoting elitism and vanguardism and as deliberately obscuring or denying the role of ordinary people as active historical agents. Structuralism is a dangerous reversion to Stalinism, just as Marxism is liberating itself by seeing facts and caring about people. For the structuralist, Thompson writes:

> [W]e are *structured* by social relations, *spoken* by pre-given linguistic structures, *thought* by ideologies, *dreamed* by myths, *gendered* by patriarchal sexual norms, *bonded* by affective obligations, *cultured* by *mentalities,* and *acted* by history's script.[10]

Against this, as a historian as well as a Marxist, Thompson insisted that:

> [T]here is a real and significant sense in which the facts are 'there' and . . . determining, even though the questions which may be proposed are various, and will elucidate various replies . . . the facts will disclose nothing of their own accord, the historian must work hard to enable them to find 'their own voices'. Not the historian's voice, please observe; *their own voices,* even if what they are able to 'say' and some part of their vocabulary is determined by the questions which the historian proposes.[11]

An essential part of the historian's task is 'getting it right' and no theory can do that alone or without recognising an objective, independent 'it' for historians to explore and interrogate. There was no shortage of Marxists to tell Thompson that he had failed to understand that historical facts are 'valid' only if they are arrived at through theory and are consistent with theory. This will surprise no one acquainted with Marxism or with the extent to which the word 'valid' has become fashionable as a substitute for recognising the objectivities of truth and of true assertions. The scope of Thompson's empirical and humanist revolt against Marxist abstraction, Marxist dogma, and Marxist elevation of theoretical categories can be gauged by the fact that Thompson distinguishes the younger Marx from the older Marx. He sides with the humanist Marx of the 1840s against the abstract economist Marx of the 1850s and later. Political economy, for Thompson, had sucked the later Marx into a 'theoretical whirlpool' in which such abstractions as value, capital, labour, and money reappear again and again, are interrogated, categorised, re-interrogated, and recategorised.

The debates that have surrounded these pronouncements and others like them range from re-examinations and re-interpretations of Marxist theory to disputes over the relations between history and theory and over the facts themselves. These discussions are reflected in Perry Anderson's *Considerations on Western Marxism* (1976), in his *Arguments within the English Marxism* (1980), in the pages of the *New Left Review,* the *Socialist Review, Marxism Today,* the annual *Socialist Register, Telos, Contemporary Crises,* and other Marxist and radical journals. Some argument is sharp,

---

10   E P Thompson, *The Poverty of Theory and Other Essays,* Merlin Press, London, 1978, p 345 (emphasis in original).

11   E P Thompson, 1978, pp 222–3 (emphasis in original).

knowledgeable, and important, some obtuse and scholastic. The basic difficulty in resolving the disputes lies in the imprecision and open-endedness, sometimes even the systematic ambiguity, of such key Marxist terms as 'material', 'economic', 'productive forces', 'relations of production' , 'determines', 'in the last instance', 'structure', and 'mode of production'. To the non-Marxist, it seems clear that Marxists become more interesting, and their Marxism becomes less dogmatic and theory-laden, as they work with more knowledge and in greater detail on any history or social situation. Increasingly, for the most intelligent, Marxism suggests themes to explore, hypotheses to test for possible falsification, approaches that may be fresh, and areas that may have been under-investigated. By and large, the results of honest investigation have complicated Marxist theory at best and in many respects undermined it, though often demonstrating its initial fruitfulness as an approach to be revised or modified in the light of what actually happened. Marx's reflections on the significance of the Silesian weavers' revolt, after all, were derived principally from a poem on the subject by Heinrich Heine, not from any investigation of working class or artisan unrest. In others, this threat to Marxist dogma and general theory produces a sharp reversion to elevating theory over and against 'the facts' or denying that there is any question of 'fact' independent of theory.

Together with a considerable loosening of Marxist discussion in the western world and a willingness to grapple in more detail with historical and theoretical problems has come a more serious discussion of the relationship between Marxism and the study of law. Some of the discussion reappraises the orthodox Marxist-communist conception of law as the command of a state that expresses and serves the interest of the ruling class. This discussion draws on the more complex view of state, politics, and ideology presented in the work of Gramsci and Althusser, in Nicos Poulantzas' *Nature des choses et droit* (1965) and his *Political Power and Social Classes* (1968, T O'Hagan trans, 1973), in Ralph Miliband's *The State in Capitalist Society* (1969), and in the writings of Perry Anderson. Others have come to their critique of law through criminology — studying either the history of crime or the concept of crime or both. In the United States, a critical legal studies movement has developed out of the initially non-Marxist radicalism of Students for a Democratic Society (SDS), drawing on and developing conflict sociology and social theory, the questioning of legal impartiality and the authority of legal rules by American realism and a host of other contemporary trends. Certainly, the last 15 years have seen no major Marxist legal theory or Marxist legal work comparable to the work of Renner or Pashukanis. However, there has been a rediscovery of both these thinkers and active discussion and publication of Marxist 'critiques' of law. Most of these are 'exposures' of the way in which law abstracts and reifies ideology, conceals repression behind a facade of impartiality, represents or consolidates class interests and the structure of domination, produces 'fetishistic' attitudes and responses in its practitioners and exacerbates the social evils it is meant to cure. But debate also exists over the specifically legal — 'the form or forms of law' — and the bases for cultural hegemony such as the 'mobilisation of consent'.

In France, Germany, and Italy, reappraisals of Marxism and the theory of law began in the late 1950s and early 1960s with the renewed consciousness of Marx's early writings on law and a subtler interest in Marxist approaches to law as a form of alienation and reification. The Gramscian emphasis on the state and cultural hegemony and the Althusserian interest in the nature and relative autonomy of political and ideological levels or substructures had pushed this development further and exercised more direct influence on English-speaking lawyers and sociologists. So had the work of Poulantzas. By the late 1970s, Z Bankowski and G Mungham had published their *Images of Law* (1976); I Taylor, P Walton and J Young had published *The New Criminology* (1973); I D Balbus had produced the widely discussed *The Dialectics of Legal Repression* (1973); and M Cain and A Hunt had issued their selection *Marx and Engels on Law* (1979) and launched the British journal *Law and Society*. A debate on law and ideology had taken off in a major way with three books published in 1979: P Hirst's *On Law and Ideology*, J Larrain's *The Concept of Ideology*, and C Sumner's *Reading Ideologies*. J Holloway and S Picciotto edited *State and Capital: A Marxist Debate* (1978) and B Fine, R Kinsey, J Lea, S Picciotto, and J Young edited, for the National Deviancy Conference, *Capitalism and the Rule of Law: From Deviancy Theory to Marxism* (1979). In the same year, B Edelman's *Ownership of the Image: Elements for a Marxist Theory of Law* was translated from the French. A debate on Pashukanis and his 'commodity-exchange theory of law' also developed in several journals on both sides of the Atlantic.[12] Soon, standard and conventional texts in jurisprudence, such as Lord Lloyd of Hampstead's text, were devoting space to Marxist jurisprudence and considering both communist legal theory and legal systems and the new western Marxist critique of law. The 1979 British Sociological Association Conference began with a plenary session on 'law and the capitalist state'. The opening speaker was Nicos Poulantzas, who tragically committed suicide in September of that year.

In radical discussions of Marxism, philosophy, and legal theory, allegiance to a specific brand of Marxism or radical faction is now neither required nor always evident. Some of those taking part in contemporary 'radical' discussions of law and mentioned as authors above prefer not to describe themselves as Marxists but as radicals, critical theorists, or sympathetic to anarchism. In the United Kingdom increasing discussion within the British Communist Party was accompanied by the founding of the Conference of Socialist Economists held at Cambridge University in 1970. The Conference, which began issuing a Bulletin in 1971, was originally conceived as a nonsectarian discussion group for socialist economists of all persuasions, but between 1972 and 1975, Marxists became dominant and many non-Marxists withdrew. The Conference is

---

12 I D Balbus, 'Commodity Form and Legal Form: An Essay on the "Relative Autonomy" of the Law', (1977) 11 *Law & Soc Rev* 571–88; R Kinsey, 'Marxism and the Law: Preliminary Analyses', (1978) 5 *Brit J Law & Soc* 202-7; R Warrington, 'Pashukanis and the Commodity Form Theory', (1981) 9 *Int J Soc Law* 1–22.

organised into regional and interest groups. Its law and state interest group was centred mainly in Warwick University, the Middlesex Polytechnic, and Edinburgh University. Though small in membership, it was of some importance in introducing and furthering serious Marxist discussion on law and 'the legal form' in the United Kingdom. Younger Oxford dons have now jumped on the bandwagon.

The United Kingdom discussion of law originated largely with Marxist economists, sociologists, and historians who took interest in Marxist analysis of law, radical criminology, and eighteenth century criminal legislation. In America, the principal radical group, the Conference on Critical Legal Studies (CLS), was formed by left liberal, radical, and Marxist lawyers concentrated at Harvard Law School and the Wisconsin Law School. Founded in 1978, CLS described itself as 'a national organisation of lawyers, teachers, students, social scientists and others committed to the development of a critical theoretical perspective on law, legal practice and legal education'.[13]

The group is not officially Marxist and began as a breakaway group from conflict studies, legal realism, and the 'law and development' approach. It was based on the radicalism of the SDS founded at Wisconsin in the 1960s rather than on any native Marxist or communist intellectual heritage, which it discovered later in the work of Sweezey, Genovese, and others. CLS sharply rejected the liberal jurisprudential approaches of Rawls, Posner, and Dworkin. It was strongly influenced by the earlier work of CLS member Roberto Mangabeira Unger at Harvard, and it sees itself as developing and transcending legal realism with the aid of Marxian and other radical insights. In recent years it has done much of its most serious work in the area of legal history, though that, too, has been subjected to sharp criticism which alleges inaccuracy and selectivity.

Marxist critique of law, even in Britain, did not burst fresh upon the world in the 1960s. The communist parties of the 1920s and 1930s contained a number of active lawyers in Germany, France, Italy, Spain, Great Britain, and many other countries, including the colonies. There were even more Marx-influenced leftists and social democrats who, in the Weimar Republic for instance, earnestly set about 'socialising' the law and its concerns by emphasising public interest legislation, industrial law, and social welfare provisions. In Britain, the National Council of Civil Liberties was founded in 1934 by social democratic and leftist lawyers, and the Haldane Society of Socialist Lawyers was established soon after. After the Second World War the Society of Labour Lawyers also campaigned for socialist legal reform rather than against law. Generally, communists completely rejected law as a form of class justice, while social democrats believed law could be reformed and shaped for socialist ends. Depending on

---

13   For details and an indication of the extent to which the group can adopt a childishly undergraduate tone, see the 'Symposium on Critical Legal Studies', (1984) 36 *Stan L Rev* 1–674 and D Kennedy, *Legal Education and the Reproduction of Hierarchy: a Polemic Against the System*, Afar, Cambridge, Massachusetts, 1983.

the wider political situation, Marxist and social democratic lawyers would either cooperate in specific protests and demands, or denounce each other.

Before the Second World War and for a period thereafter, the typical subjects and interests of the radical lawyer were criminal law, industrial and especially trade union law, political trials, and civil liberties. The radical lawyer, such as the communist D N Pritt, put his legal skills — his advocative powers, his expertise in the law as it was, his capacity to convince the judge and persuade the jury — at the service of 'deserving' clients. These clients included trade union leaders and members, poor tenants, political protesters and detainees, student rioters, 'subversives', and agitators in the colonies. For some, as summarised by Taylor, the law became, in practice at least:

> [A] body of rules that can be used to arbitrate between conflicting interests in an essentially neutral fashion. In so far as law has operated otherwise in the twentieth century, and in so far as it has appeared to operate in the interests of property as against labour, it has done this because of the undemocratic and class-bound procedures of recruitment of judges and magistrates and the narrow and unsociological training of professional lawyers. Law has been an instrument through which the hierarchies of class society and the pre-eminence of propertied interest are reproduced, but it is not an essential feature of law that it must operate instrumentally in this direction. The remedy for this bias in law has been seen to be the reform of the class character of recruitment of legal personnel, and in particular, in some writing by social democrats, the introduction of a full-time professional magistracy and the radical reform of the training of the judiciary as a means of wrestling [sic] control of law from aristocratic amateurs.[14]

J G Griffith's *The Politics of the Judiciary* (1977) is principally devoted to this sort of 'American realist' exposure of the alleged class bias of (UK) judges. This approach is always welcome to Marxists but is considered inadequate theoretically if it is accompanied by the belief sketched by Taylor (and sharply repudiated by him) that law in principle, and as a formal system, is neutral. Even D N Pritt, in his four volume *Law, Class and Society* (1972), was affected by the European post-war labour-liberal consensus in favour of social democratic reform of the law. He writes:

> The law is not, therefore, the merely automatic reflection of a particular economic structure, but takes shape, develops and changes in ways determined by actual class interests and class struggles. The ruling class by no means uses its power impartially for the benefit and protection equally of all classes that make up the community. Nor are its servants, including the legislators, judges and lawyers, in any sense neutral. It governs in its own interests, which it professes to believe, and perhaps sometimes does believe, to be identical with the interests of the whole people.[15]

But in modern democratic society, the ruling class cannot govern without the acquiescence or approval of the working class, which is a significant

---

14   I Taylor, *Law and Order: Arguments for Socialism*, Macmillan, London, 1981, p 165.
15   D N Pritt, 'The Apparatus of the Law ', (1972) 2 *Law, Class & Society* 7–8.

constituent of society. Therefore, for Pritt, law is not entirely engineered by the ruling class: the worker and his fellow citizens contribute every day to its formation and development. They do so 'by their resistance to — or their acquiescence in — the proposals of their rulers by their positive demand for reforms, and by their apparently intangible but real and indeed powerful influence on the formation of public opinion'. From this it follows that 'the working class today has much more influence on the development of our law than appears on the surface, and working people have a corresponding responsibility to maintain continuously the greatest possible pressure on public opinion and on the government to secure the most healthy development possible'.[16]

With the collapse of the protest decade of the 1960s and the swing back to conservatism in Britain and other parts of the western world, hostility to law once again increased among Marxists. One area that helped to shape aspects of this new 'legal nihilism' — although it also provided some more complex considerations of law and its social role — was the radical criminology and historical studies of crime and criminal law that came to the fore in the late 1960s.

Law and legal theory

The serious formal discussion of law, legal systems, and legal theory from a Marxist standpoint is a recent and still poorly developed aspect of Marxist endeavour in the English-speaking world. It is a phenomenon principally of the 1970s and early 1980s. It tends, therefore, to endorse modern 'interpretations' and re-interpretations of Marx; it distances itself both from the dogmatism of Stalin and his heirs, and from the 'reformism' and 'revisionism' of the Second International and of contemporary labour parties. It ignores the systems, legal history, and the legal theories (regarding law under socialism) of Marxist-governed countries. Some of this 'Marxist' writing reflects a tone of strident non-responsibility — the non-responsibility of those who do not see themselves as having to participate in the work of society or even to carry out the sustained work of social transformation. There is also a totally un-Marxist resentment of a world that does not instantly and directly satisfy the needs and assuage the insecurities of the young, especially of the not very able young, by making them feel important and central to the work of society. That society, in much of this radical writing, turns out to be the law school and the underlying values, those of a strident rights-oriented post-historical individualism, elevating relevance, emotional security, and 'fulfilment' above all.[17]

---

16   D N Pritt, 1972, p 10.
17   For a remarkable and often embarrassing display of such emotionally centered juvenile self-importance based on the reluctance to recognise that insight and achievement require *sustained* work and *technical* skills, see generally the 'Symposium on Critical Legal Studies', 1984, note 10 above. The issue is devoted to letting the Critical Legal Studies movement speak for itself.

Marxists used to distinguish themselves from anarchists by saying: 'The anarchist wants to know when the revolution will come, Marxists ask, "What must we do in the hour of a revolution?"' Given the rather different cultural climate and social *niveau* in which those developing contemporary analyses and 'critiques' of law now operate, it is not surprising that these writers should increasingly moralise Marxism, turn it into an ideological *praxis,* and see it as having a life independent of historical determinism and great mass movements, at least in their own societies. More and more, some writers avoid calling themselves Marxist and prefer to speak of themselves as 'working in the Marxist tradition'. Others react to this by emphasising that one cannot be in the Marxist tradition without being a Marxist. Nevertheless, there is an increasing tendency to insist — at least some of the time — that Marxism is not a finished or dogmatic set of conclusions, an objective science of society, or a form of economic determinism. Many of the writers are discussing whether Marxism provides a philosophical basis, a theoretical framework, and a set of fundamental concepts for understanding how the social world is organised and how it changes and develops.[18]

Almost all of these new radicals now deny that Marxism is properly interpreted as asserting a one-way economic determinism between base and superstructure. Many deny that the base–superstructure analogy is appropriate at all. They prefer, with Althusser, to focus on social modes of production, on structured totalities and practices, or sub-structures within those totalities. Some attach great, if mysterious, importance to denying that Marx elevates the economic, insisting instead that he elevates the 'material' process of production and reproduction. This claim is mysterious because the substitution of 'material' for 'economic' illuminates nothing and does not in any way alter the discussion of what Marxism means. Courts, police forces, and schools are as 'material' as factories. If Marx is saying that factories and what they imply — the system of ownership, production for a market, etc — are more central, more important than courts, schools, and police forces, he is not doing this by focusing on the materiality of factories or of what they produce, but on their economic functions. If the 'materialists' say that production is production only when it produces material objects, and not when it results in services, administrative organisation, or the promotion of knowledge — all of which have economic functions and uses — they are saying something silly.

The simple and basic point is that Marx's conception of 'material' in the materialist interpretation of history has nothing to do with the 'materialist' doctrine in philosophy incorporated into Soviet 'dialectical materialism'. There, materialism quickly was reduced to the claim that there is an objective, independent reality prior to and distinguishable from the consciousness or conscious being that apprehends it (the implications of which many 'Marxist' philosophies now seek to evade)

---

18 The view taken, for instance, in the radical pamphlet prepared by the Critique of Law Editorial Collective, *Critique of Law: a Marxist Analysis,* UNSW Critique of Law Society, Sydney, 1978, pp 8–15.

and not to the claim that only matter exists (indeed, matter is now seen as convertible to energy). On the social side, in 'historical materialism', the term 'materialism' means the elevation of a process of production as central to the understanding of society. The alleged centrality of such a process of production is better expressed by speaking of the economic activities in a society than by confusing a host of issues in the term 'materialism'. Marx himself, in consonance with the most obvious feature of early industrial production, concentrated on the making of material objects — a path along which Marxist socialist societies followed him with disastrous results.

Clearly, 'economic' is a wider and more apposite term to describe production that satisfies human needs and demands than the term 'material'. These wider terms are needed precisely because an entire mode of production, rather than a technologically determinist conception of productive forces evoking relations of production is the central explanatory tool with which Marxism operates. Contemporary Marxists, we would argue, are mistaken in thinking that they convey this by using the term 'material' instead of 'economic'. In the end, they simply are talking about the *social* and failing to distinguish clearly the economic or the material as a specific structure within it. This is made even more evident by the contemporary Marxist predilection for replacing the term 'economics' with the older term 'political economy'. Suddenly, the new Marxists imply that one cannot understand the economic except as it relates to the political, that is, as a part of the whole society.

Others, while never abandoning the primacy of the economic, put special weight on Marxism as a doctrine of human *praxis* and interpret that to mean a rejection of 'blind' determinism. These writers emphasise the role of human consciousness and activity in history and elevate class and ideological struggle. For them, state and law are essential features of an oppressive social system that now relies on more than physical and economic coercion. They reach this view by elevating the strength and importance of cultural and political institutions — some writers rely on Gramsci's conception of cultural hegemony, others on Althusser's elevation of the relative autonomy of political and ideological 'practices' in society. Gramsci's conception of a pervasive, or at least very strong, cultural ruling class hegemony that goes beyond physical repression and the intrusion of the state into educational systems, political parties, professional groups, art, literature, religion, family, etc, makes the ideological critique of law important and worthwhile. The Althusserian view maintains that there is no 'economic base,' and no determining ruling class interest that forms the 'essence' of state and law or of political and ideological practices in society. To lawyers, Althusser's conception of his own science as a closed and self-validating system is more familiar and less suspect than it is to those whose intellectual endeavours deal more directly with actual, infra-legal human, or natural behaviour.

All of these developments, of course, take account of and reflect important social changes that have occurred since Marx's time. Marxists now recognise that capitalism has passed through several stages: an early mercantile capitalism; the industrial capitalism of individual factory owners and firms; a further stage of finance and monopoly capital, variously described but representing a movement of economic power from factory owners to banks and trusts or corporations (these stages were all described or predicted by Marx); and a 'late' capitalism (not directly predicted by Marx) that saw the rise and development of the welfare state and an economically increasingly interventionist, semi-independent, state apparatus. The function of the latter, most Marxists would still hold, is to save the capitalist system by conceding what can no longer be withheld, but the relative independence and direct significance of the state and law is now widely recognised among Marxists. This becomes even more important as many Marxists implicitly accept what Gramsci argued in his *Prison Notebooks*: that a Leninist *coup,* a communist seizure of power, was not a viable political strategy for western societies. In Russia, Gramsci argued, the state was overwhelmingly powerful while civil society, the entire network of non-state relations and institutions, was weak. Russian society could be transformed from the top. In the west, when the state trembled, a sturdy structure of civil society was at once revealed. That civil society was a network of fortresses and earthworks that remained standing even when the state's outer ditch had fallen. If law and legal ideology are such earthworks, they need to be captured and destroyed by specific, planned assaults based on detailed reconnaissance.

The contemporary critique of law 'in the Marxist tradition', then, represents as many views as there are ambiguities in Marx's thought and as there are subsequent interpretations and emendations of his work. Of course, as Marxists become more 'open', they increasingly fit in with wider developments in the contemporary discussions of law, with the greater emphasis on social and sociological context and function, with the historicisation of legal values and principles, and with the 'demystification' of law. Their intellectual guns, trained at natural law and legal formalism, now simply point the wrong way. Marxists also emphasise, not uniquely but especially sharply, the need to go beyond mere intellectual criticism, to oppose, destroy, transform, and rebuild society, laws, and human relations. The emphases vary as much as, and inversely with, the quality.

For some, for example Zenon Bankowski and Geoff Mungham in their *Images of Law* as well as the young Lukacs, revolutionary practice, including the critique of law, must be inspired by a merciless revolutionary intention and a missionary consciousness. Decisions and resolutions must be the masters and not the slaves of facts. The circle within which Lukacs himself operated in 1918 strove to propagate these aspirations by working out the most radical methods and by completely breaking with every institution and mode of life stemming from the bourgeois world. Lukacs, in such lectures and pamphlets as *Terror as Source of Law, Legal Order and Violence, Tactics and Ethics* and *The Changing Function of Historical Materialism,* sharply emphasised that law was organised violence. As an institution, it was only an institutionalisation of means subordinate to external ends. These concepts of order at most possessed a relative validity; they were based on violence and its acceptance. Therefore, communists should be fearless in the face of the law. 'The risk of breaking the law should not be regarded any differently,' Lukacs wrote in *History and Class Consciousness,* 'than the risk of missing a train connection when on an important journey'. Bankoswski and Mungham say that the message of their book is simple:

> [L]aw in the forms that it is practised and taught means domination, oppression and desolation. Law does not help but rather hinders people in the way to free society. In this book we concentrate upon a particular brand of law and a particular way of teaching law. What we have in mind here are movements to liberalize law; to give it a 'human face'. We claim that this liberalization and the concomitant idea that law can be used to transform society by alleviating its problems cannot work, that there is no difference in form from this sort of law and the traditional 'rich man's' law.
>
> [W]e want society to be transformed and the socio-legal enterprise prevents this. We want to get across what trying to solve the problems of the world with the help of law and men with 'lawyer-like' skills really means. We do not want to create 'radical law' for law is locked in the interstices come together and decide how to run their lives.
>
> [O]ne thing that we know is this: law is an imperial code, it emasculates man by offering the solution of his problems to 'experts'; it reflects the professionalised society. The only way out is for men to seize their lives and transform themselves and the world.[19]

For others, as for Lukacs himself in a subtler mood, and for Bankowski and Mungham in the less conspiracy-mongering parts of their book, law is above all, but necessarily, a system of abstraction, reification, and alienation. Law subordinates human activities and human beings to abstract categories. Laws are treated as having an actual independent existence to which these activities and beings are subordinated. That theme, perhaps the most subtle and most interesting Marxist critique of law, has produced the revival of interest in Pashukanis, the enthusiastic reception of Bernard Edelman's *The Ownership of the Image,* and a debate among Marxists concerning the legal form. Yet a third strand, never totally absent from any Marxist work, sees law as based on economic requirements or economic interests whether these be those of a class or a 'system'. Some Marxists have criticised radicals' over-concentration on criminal law and slowness in looking at the role of law in ordering and regulating the economy.

An Australian Marxist pamphlet, *Critique of Law,* distinguishes 'infrastructural laws which serve to structure and bolster the economic power of the capitalist class over the working class' from:

> [S]uperstructural laws ... essentially concerned with regulating social behaviour and consciousness ... Whereas infrastructural laws are primarily concerned with ensuring that capitalist economic activities are most effectively developed, superstructural laws are primarily concerned with the social and political domination of the working class and repression of those elements of that class who undermine or challenge the reality and ideology of capitalist ownership of the means of production.[20]

---

19   Z Bankowski and G Mungham, *Images of Law,* Routledge & Kegan Paul, London, 1976, pp xii-xiii.

20   Critique of Law Editorial Collective, note 18 above, pp 37, 45 and, more generally, pp 47–123.

The Crimes Act, the Mental Health Act, the Summary Offences Act, the Education Act, the Social Services Act and laws governing mass communication are cited as examples of the latter, but so are criminal law and family law. The law of contract, law of trade practices and labour regulations, and the law of torts on the other hand are examples of infrastructural law. Ultimately, though, all Marxists want to insist that law as oppression, law as alienation, law as the furtherance of class interest, or law as the requirement of an economic system, are all related facets of a system based on private property, the appropriation of surplus value, and the pursuit of power and profit by the capitalist class. Alternatively, they argue that this is a system based on the power and requirements of capital and the contradiction between capital and labour, and the private and the public sectors.

A fundamental difficulty in writing about contemporary Marxist critiques of law remains. Most such critiques adopt or parallel the unresolved lacunae and ambiguities of Marx's position, especially fatal in the case of law, without taking law seriously enough. These theories of law do so even when they initially claim to do the opposite, that is, to develop a Marxist theory of law. Marx's most recent disciples for the most part reject any view of law as an independent force or as a social institution or tradition. However, some of them, as we shall see, are becoming more ready to concede or even emphasise that legal forms — structured laws and regulations and systems of interpretation and appeal within such structures — will not disappear under socialism. A recent sympathetic, but not especially perceptive or tough-minded expositor of their views, Hugh Collins, writes (as though this were sufficient excuse):

> To demand a general theory of law from a Marxist is to ask him to run the risk of falling prey to what can be termed the fetishism of law . . . the belief that legal systems are an essential component of social order and civilization.[21]

In line with this, many Marxists, with support from Collins, launch an attack on what they take to be the centrepiece of 'liberalism' (a term of abuse in Marxist and radical American quarters): the elevation of the rule of law. Marxists do and, according to Collins, should reject the view that 'law is a unique phenomenon which constitutes a discrete focus of study',[22] and they should not endorse the rule of law, which is the doctrine 'that political power should be exercised according to rules announced in advance'.[23] (One needs to live in Oxford, not in Moscow or Beijing, to be as silly as that!) Collins does, however, recognise a fundamental tension between historical materialism as 'class-instrumental' explanation of law and the 'relative autonomy' thesis, which he has some commitment to:

> If [Marxists] stick to a purely instrumental explanation of legal reasoning . . . then the whole enterprise of ensuring coherence and consistency in legal reasoning has to be dismissed as false

---

21 H Collins, *Marxism and the Law*, Clarendon Press, Oxford, 1982.
22 H Collins, 1982, pp 11–12.
23 H Collins, 1982, pp 11–12.

consciousness, perpetrated by lawyers who are concerned to mystify their desire to support the interests of the ruling class. On the other hand, an acceptance of the autonomy thesis poses a threat to the whole theory of historical materialism.[24]

The doctrine of relative autonomy of law, if derived from or constituted by 'the plasticity of the dominant ideology', has the greatest difficulty in relating law to relations of production or the material base alone. Collins, who espouses this view, is promptly attacked by some other Marxists for being insufficiently emancipated from positivism and Herbert Hart. These Marxists argue that Collins remains constrained by the habit of drawing distinctions and does not see the problem of 'legal form' or Marxism subtly enough. Reviewing *Marxism and Law,* Alan Hunt insists that Collins' theory of 'relative autonomy' fails because it cannot or does not provide an explanation of what determines the limits to the degree of relative autonomy. Collins' concept of 'dominant ideology' is not adequately or coherently explained in connection with either the state or social relations of production. For Hunt, ideology is not simply and unproblematically superstructural:

> This solution is in my view inadequate and ultimately contradictory. The proposition that legal rules are 'superstructural in origin' says no more than that they have their origin *in ideology*. If ideology is unproblematically assigned to the sphere of the superstructure, then it follows that legal rules are in some fundamental or primary sense (which Collins seeks to capture by his reference to 'origin') superstructural. As soon as we question the simple assumption that ideology is part of the superstructure, the solution proposed by Collins collapses. For just in the same way as legal relations (for example, as property relations) are part of or constitutive of the relations of production so too is ideology inseparable from an empirical description of the relations of production. Or to put the same point in a different way, ideology is a necessary condition ('condition of existence') of the relations of production. Ideological elements such as language, normative environment, elementary labour discipline are all inescapably part of or constituents of the relations of production.[25]

Here, fundamental and damaging criticisms of Marxism suddenly appear as its proper interpretation. Hunt, indeed, proposes that the problem of law in historical materialism can only be solved by pursuing a different approach which:

> [L]ies in abandoning rationalist and empiricist assumptions in favour of the adoption of a focus on 'Marxism as method' in which a radically different understanding of the relationship between concepts as 'abstractions' and the 'concrete' in which the concepts function not to embrace or incorporate the concrete, but to propose lines or stages of inquiry in a process of successive movements between the realms of abstraction and the concrete. Such an approach abandons any assumptions that concepts such as 'social relations of production' or 'mode of production' correspond to

---

24   H Collins, 1982, p 70.
25   A Hunt, 'Marxist Legal Theory and Legal Positivism', (1983) 46 *Mod L Rev* 236 at 238.

concrete economic practice. The concepts function to specify or give priority to certain sets of relations, for example, the relations of separation and possession (which are of special importance with respect to legal relations) or class relations.[26]

The withering away of law and Pashukanis' conception that law under socialism will be replaced by policy and regulation in the light of socio-technical norms are similarly modified and reinterpreted by Hunt into a question to which there are several possible answers:

> [T]o what extent will the *legal form* or *legal forms* (of rules, procedures and institutions) be the characteristic mechanisms necessary for the resolution of different forms of conflict? Without engaging in a full examination of this re-formulated problematic, certain possible answers may be sketched:
>
> (i)   Increased consensus over primary social rules diminishes need for legal form;
>
> (ii) Increased political democracy will result in decisions of economic and social priorities taking a political form (*eg*, the political resolution supplanting the legislative device);
>
> (iii) The need to secure conditions of democratic participation will require protection against centralist or bureaucratic tendencies; hence the need for a stronger legal form of civil and political liberties;
>
> (iv) The complex interrelation between public institutions and agencies will continue to require legal forms governing interinstitutional relations.
>
> I repeat that this scenario is advanced for illustrative purposes only and that the argument is in no way dependent upon any particular conclusion. Its essential feature is the insistence on the need to abandon a simplistic conception of the consensus-conflict opposition so as to facilitate a more adequate analysis of the *forms of conflict* and their conditions and their relationship to the *forms of law* in order to more adequately address the problem of the role of law under socialism and communism and for that matter under capitalism.[27]

Thus, against Collins' position that the principal aim of Marxist jurisprudence must be a program for demystifying the preponderant bourgeois ideology of the rule of law, Hunt argues that a program for Marxist jurisprudence must put behind it the naive radicalism of conflict theory of the 1960s. Hunt argues that the Marxist program must recognise that Lenin's picture of communism as involving universal participation, abolition of the division between legislation and administration, and the instant recall of delegates, is theoretically coherent only at the level of the city-state and small communities. A legal framework that posits representative institutions and universal participation on a larger scale requires a developed or augmented rule of law — a socialist rule of law based on the development of a socialist theory of rights, of the socialist judicial process, and of socialist justice. On the other hand, Collins, on the last page of his book, presents Marxists and non-Marxists with a dilemma. Marxists

---

26   A Hunt, 1983, pp 239–40.
27   A Hunt, 1983, p 24.

cannot have any wider belief in the intrinsic merit of preserving the legality of government action and defending individual rights without making the mistake of taking at face value the ideology of the Rule of Law, which obscures class domination. But can we believe in the importance of these principles under socialism without supporting some version of the concept of the Rule of Law and of the pretensions of legal systems? Soviet and Chinese communists, whose experience is more relevant than ours, no longer do so.[28]

---

28   This essay was previously published in (1988) 21(3) *U C Davis Law Review* 605–44.

CHAPTER 12

The Role of Ideas in Political Change

Igor Grazin*

Ideas and realities

The Marxism-Leninism ideology denied the role of ideas in the political changes that occurred in the twentieth century. This ideology quietly originated from the comfortable circles of academic philosophy of mid-nineteenth century Germany. Following its introduction in Russia, it split Europe and, later, the whole world for more than seven decades. Neither Marx nor most of his contemporary disciples denied the active role of ideas in the course of history, but nevertheless, this role was never considered to be anything decisive within the realm of the forces that determined the course of history. One of the most sophisticated and academic Russian followers of Marx — who because of these qualities was so hated and ridiculed by an under-educated, pragmatic, cynical Lenin — George Plekhanov, made an effort to find a 'dialectical' solution to the ever-existing contradiction between the realities of (economic, objective, material) actual life, on the one hand, and the ideas (aspirations, values, convictions) of people, on the other.

Plekhanov, when analysing the careers of outstanding Napoleonic generals, wrote:

> In 1789, Davout, Desaix, Marmont and MacDonald were subalterns, Bernadotte was a sergeant-major ... Augerean was a fencing master; Lannes was a dyer, Gouvion Saint-Cyr was an actor; Jourdan was a peddler; Bessières was a barber; Brune was a compositor ... Had the old order continued to exist ... it would never have occurred to any of us that in France at the end of [XVIIIth] century, certain actors,

---

* Professor of Law and Economics, University of Notre Dame, and Member of the National Parliament of Estonia.

compositors, barbers, dyers, lawyers, peddlers and fencing masters had been potential military geniuses.[1]

The circumstances created the personalities. Plekhanov is even more specific: 'The final cause of social relationships lies in the state of the [material] productive forces'[2] that develop somehow by themselves.

In spite of all reservations, it seems to be evident that the ultimate cartesian question — what determines what; whether the matter determines our ideas or whether the spirit designs the actual life — was answered by Marxists and socialists in favour of the first option.

But to put aside all other historical evidence and to simplify the whole issue, I need to point to one crucial question never answered by strictly materialistic (and Marxist) theories of history. Referring back to Frederick Engels' classical Marxist work *The Origins of Family, State and Private Property*, we may explain the origins of the social classes and then of the state and the political society in the following way. In pre-historic times, when humans as a whole and individual societies (tribes, pre-ethnic groups, etc) were economically on the level of passive consumption of natural goods, society remained stagnant. But once people were able to *produce* and to have available more than was needed, the surplus product caused the politicisation of society's basic structure. The reason was that surplus product was capable of being concentrated in the hands of a few who gradually became the ruling and economically dominant elite. Even within the framework of Marxism, some phenomenon, standing outside the mere materialistic circumstances, is needed to explain human progress.

Directly opposing himself to Marx (whose social theory he calls 'absurd'), von Mises argued that 'technology follows from (capitalist) mentality and not vice versa'.[3] Hundreds of books and thousands of pages have been written on the causes of the Bolshevist counter-revolution in Russia of October 1917. I think that in spite of the vast variety of opinions among the scholars of the subject (former official Soviet ones excluded) they all would agree on one point: whatever were the circumstances in Russia in 1917, the seizure of power by Bolsheviks and their establishment of a totalitarian type of state socialism were neither inevitable nor the only possible outcome. What determined the course of history were (besides, of course, historic-materialistic reasons like the economic situation) a set of factors which, to a very large extent, were of an ideological character. To name some of them: unpreparedness and unwillingness of Russian democratic forces to take power and responsibility; the German interest in destroying the military enemy (Russia) from within; the existence of a small, but well organised leftist opposition; and the semi-socialist traditions of Russian peasant ideology. What actually determined the further developments of the Soviet socialist state was again not the material circumstances, but its ideology. To be more precise: not one, but

---

1   G Pelakhanov, *The Role of the Individual in History*, International Publishers, New York, 1940, p 51.
2   G Pelankhanov, 1940, p 44.
3   L von Mises, *Liberalism in the Classical Tradition*, Cobden Press, San Francisco, 1985, pp 86–7.

at least two principal ideologies. The first — the explicit and official one — is the ideology of Marxism that theoretically served the purpose of justifying the whole system of state socialism. The second is the ideology of justification of the elitist, above-the-law status of the leadership and nomenklatura of the Communist Party.[4]

The method by which this contradiction (between Marxism which states that the development of the society is an objective, materialistic process; and the discretionary, irrational and purely ideological character of the decisions of Marxist leaders) was actually solved, reveals something about the relations between socialism, liberty and the legal ideologies that correspond to them.

Legal ideas and legal realities

The very existence of some law in its normative sense has always been a theoretically inconvenient fact to the Marxist. Hans Kelsen in his *The Communist Theory of Law*, published in 1955, has demonstrated that all classical authors on Soviet theory of law always had to interpret the very phenomenon of law in socialist society as something very exceptional, transitional or temporary. E B Pashukanis wrote:

> It must ... be borne in mind that morality, law and state are forms of bourgeois society. The fact that the proletariat may be compelled to use them by no means signifies that they can develop further in the direction of being filled with a socialist content.[5]

In the works of P Stuchka and E B Pashukanis, the law was replaced by a system of economic relationships. As direct and constant economic management was one of the most important functions of the state, the state was not bound by the constraints of law, which was only one among many other means of social regulation. Kelsen pointed out that, according to Marxism, '[t]he state as a meta-legal fact cannot be conceived of as subjected to the law and hence not as a legal subject'.[6] He correctly concluded that in reality Marxism meant the extreme form of sociological relativism in legal theory combined with political pragmatism of communist ideology.[7]

---

4   It needs much more than a book to list all the idiocies of the communist decision-makers from Lenin to Brezhnev. More notable are Kruschev's infamous idea of cultivating corn in northern areas of Russia where it was botanically impossible to accomplish it, and Brezhnev's plans to divert the flow of great Siberian rivers. Many other examples could be given. See P G Roberts and K LaFollette, *Meltdown: Inside the Soviet Economy*, CATO Institute, Washington DC, 1990, Chapter 1.

5   As quoted in H Kelsen, *The Communist Theory of Law*, F A Praeger, New York, 1955, p 106.

6   H Kelsen, 1955, p 95.

7   H Kelsen, 1955, p 195. The awesome reality of this doctrine has been brilliantly described in A Solzhenitsyn, *The Gulag Archipelago*, vol I, Collins and Harvill, London, 1978, Chapters 8–10.

The shift made by the Nineteenth Conference of the CPSU (Summer, 1988) that re-introduced the notion of the law-governed state was of principal significance.[8] As Pashukanis had warned prohetically six decades earlier, the supremacy of law and socialism are incompatible. This statement, although it has been vindicated by events, is not always correct from a formal positivistic point of view because the principle of legality itself can be removed by means of positive law.

That is exactly what happened in the course of Soviet constitutional development. The latest (and the last) Soviet Constitution (of 1977) introduced a special clause (Article 6) that actually abolished not only the rest of its text but that of the rest of the legislation also. That article reads as follows:

> The leading and guiding force of Soviet society and the nucleus of its political system, of all state organizations, is the Communist Party of the Soviet Union. The CPSU exists for the people and serves the people.
>
> The Communist Party, armed with Marxism-Leninism, determines the general perspectives of the development of society and the course of the home and foreign policy of the USSR, directs the great constructive work of the Soviet people, and imparts a planned, systematic and theoretically substantiated character to their struggle for the victory of communism.
>
> . All party organizations shall function within the framework of the Constitution of the USSR.

Under such limitless power the 'framework' that otherwise would be offered by the Constitution is non-existent.[9]

Without any further details and specifications (there were none, and even the textbook interpretations remained brief), the article put political and legal discretion above the rule of law. So technically, even the formal 'legalisation' of the notion of law-governed state did not exclude the subordination of the rest of legality to the superiority of the dominant monopolistic party. The question remained, however, whether Article 6, though formally valid, was really a valid law meeting other extra-positivistic criteria of validity?

Administration versus litigation

The sphere of civil law (as understood in continental European tradition) primarily regulates property-related interests (ownership, contracts, wills, etc). The civil law is based upon the assumption that people are, from a legal point of view, equal under the law and that they enter into legal relationships with a sound mind and free will and, therefore, are

---

8   For more details, see M Susi, *The Meaning, Genesis and Perspectives of the Concept of Law-Governed State (Pravovoe Gosudarstvo) in Recent Soviet Legal Theory* (LLM Thesis), University of Wisconsin, Madison, 1991.

9   We can only speculate as to why the previous Soviet constitutions, including Stalin's of 1936, did not contain such a clause. Most probably, the openly totalitarian regime did not care too much for the image created by it and did not feel any real need to mask its actions by such types of constitutional covers.

responsible for their own acts. It has to be specially proved if that was not the case and if such proof is presented, the court may invalidate the whole transaction.[10] This material assumption is reflected in its procedural counterpart in that the parties in a civil dispute, the plaintiff and respondent, are not subordinated to each other and hold the same rights and have equal procedural standing. Equality in this sense, however, requires that parties are independent and control their own resources, acts and obligations. This independence is the main reason why the civil law and civil procedure were, from the very beginning, in some conflict with the methods and aims of socialist society. The basic feature of the socialist society in its Soviet or Soviet-influenced version requires that 'all means of production, all productive organisations, are state owned [or controlled]'.[11] As 'all' here really means almost all, there are no legal entities, no independent individual owners needed for the applicability of civil law and procedure. This was already clearly understood by Pashukanis who used the term 'law' only to refer to those un-noteworthy remote provinces of socialist society that were still not covered by direct state regulation.[12]

So, from the purely legal point of view, socialism caused the replacement of civil law by something else. When describing the organisation of the Soviet economy, Stalin used the metaphor of a '[h]uge single factory'. Although the excesses of his version of totalitarianism vanished after his death, the metaphor remained sound. Indeed, the factory owned by the state was operated by state-appointed managers who were subordinated to government ministries and departments. The latter were themselves under the orders and directives of the bodies in charge of planning, price setting and distribution.[13] In other words, these were relations in the sphere of direct execution of state power based on subordination, ie, the sphere of regulation by administrative law. As Guy Sorman puts it, '[s]tate enterprise in the socialist world is [not an economic but an] administrative unit subordinated to the logic of administration'.[14] Thus civil law was replaced by administrative law.[15]

---

10   The lack of free will and clear understanding invalidated certain legal actions under Roman law. Justinian's *Institutes* elaborate on this topic specifically when dealing with the validity of wills (Book II, Chapter 10). The invalidation of contracts due to their inequality was based on the proof of mistake, fraud and duress. Ph J Thomas, *Introduction to Roman Law*, Kluwer Law and Taxation Publishers, Amsterdam, 1986, p 83.

11   M Keren, 'On the (Im)Possibility of Market Socialism', in *The Road to Capitalism* (eds D Kennett and M Liebermann), Dryden Press, Fort Worth, 1992, p 45.

12   H Kelsen, 1955, note 5 above, pp 93–4.

13   On the mechanisms of planning and plan-enforcement, see Heinz Köhler's and Larina Popkova-Pijasheva's articles in Kennett and Liebermann, 1992, note 11 above, pp 5–14 and 53–8.

14   G Sorman, *Sortir du socialisme*, Novosty Press, Moscow, 1991, p 176.

15   There were also other replacements. The rejection of civil law also automatically involved the rejection of one of the most important parts of private law: property relations. Initially the core of private law fell under the regulatory means of public law.

It does not mean, of course, that administrative law used generally in the sphere of the economy or specifically in the sphere of industrial production automatically creates lawlessness and discretion. Though principally different from the civil law, administrative law is still law and, although it is subordinated to the Party, it does not involve the absence of rights. Administrative law does not affect the administration of labour law.[16] This is demonstrated by the fact that a minister who wants to fire an incompetent subordinate faces in some cases the risk of being involved in labour litigation with the necessity to prove and defend his or her position under labour law. Even within the province of administrative law itself, certain procedural guarantees were granted to the subordinate. For instance, under the former Soviet administrative legal system, the advisory boards of ministries (usually made up of the department heads of the same ministries) had the right in the case of their disagreement with the minister to appeal to the next level of government, the Council of Ministers.

In any event, the mere fact of subordination to someone higher in the administrative hierarchy does not deprive that person of his or her principal rights; the inequality involved in hierarchical structure is part of the 'rules of the game' known in advance. A person applying for a position in the Department of Agriculture in Washington DC knows in advance that he or she will be expected to obey certain commands and that certain consequences will follow any failure to obey. Subordination was, however, very different in the case of the Soviet-type administration in the sphere of economy. Although theoretically controlled by the state, ruled by its plan-orders and managed by nominated officials, the system failed to operate as designed and left loopholes in the initially designed mechanism. It may be said that the system of control through the plan-orders did not function and in principle could not work.

What really kept the economy moving, albeit inefficiently and at cost, were those parts of it that were not controlled by the plan and plan-fulfillment orientated legislation. Shortcomings in supplies had to be compensated by a strange system of expedients, semi-legal and illegal transfers of goods and equipment through a semi-legal market. John H Litwack puts it very succinctly: 'It is impossible to be a successful manager in a Soviet-type economy without continually breaking the law.'[17] Take the example of a manager who cannot continue production because he has not received adequate supplies of raw materials through official channels of distribution. Faced with this problem, he asks some individual hired for that purpose to get the materials 'directly' (ie not through the chain of

---

16   Labour law, by itself, may be both a branch of administrative law and of civil law. If the labour contract is based on the assumption of legal equality of the partners (ie the contract is for the free sale and purchase of labour) then it is part of civil law in the widest sense of the word. On the contrary, if one party is not free to give up the contract without disciplinary or other coercive consequences, then these elements of labour legislation start to resemble administrative law.

17   Kennett and Libermann, 1992, note 11 above, p 113. The excellent description of managerial acrobatics imposed upon the managers under this system can be found in Roberts and LaFollete, 1990, note 4 above.

state provided supplies) from the producers — in exchange for some other sort of 'favours' (bribery, cash payments, etc). This is what keeps his business going. At the same time such activities were covered by Article 153, s 2 of the Criminal Code which provided that 'commercial mediations' of this kind were punishable by up to five years of imprisonment and confiscation of personal property.

As almost all the managers had to violate the law,[18] including the criminal law, they could not all be punished lest the economy ground to a halt. In reality, only some managers were punished even though most violated the law. The decision to punish managers was a discretionary decision which was not based on law.[19] A decision involved a combination of thousands of individual circumstances that determined whether a successful manager went to jail or was awarded the Order of Lenin. The 'rules of the game' for the Soviet manager included the risk that resulted from abandoning the automatism of rule applications in favour of administrative discretion.

Legal ideology in political change

In spite of the acute legal nihilism and the inability to explain the normative character of the law (so well pointed out by Hans Kelsen), Marx once came quite close to a proper understanding of some crucial elements of the nature of law. In his *Critique of the Gotha Programme* he mentioned that: 'Right by its very nature can only consist in the application of an equal standard [to the otherwise unequal people and circumstances]'.[20] However this comment of Marx's produced quite an unexpected theoretical implication. To avoid the inequality produced by actual life, 'right, instead of being equal, would have to be unequal'.[21] The crucial conflict still remained. Whereas a law-governed state presupposes

---

18   This inevitability is a really crucial point. Mancur Olson makes an ingenious relevant observation on this point:

> Though economists have a relatively well developed theory of why markets work, neither they nor specialists in any other discipline have any satisfactory explanation of why Soviet-type economies worked at all.

One of the elements of the explanation is offered in the following quotation from *The Emergence of Market Economies in Eastern Europe* (eds C Clague and G C Rauser), Basil Blackwell, Oxford, 1992, pp 56 and 63:

> Paradoxically, they performed as well as and survived as long as they did in part because of the many markets, legal and illegal, explicit and implicit, that they contained ... Though not all of the implicit and illicit transactions were socially desirable, many of them were indispensable for correcting the shortcomings in the state plans and for maintaining production in state enterprises.

19   Let us use a more familiar analogy to clarify this point. On the toll road with a speed limit of 80 kilometres per hour, the traffic moves at the speed of 100 kilometres per hour. This situation does not result from a rule-based decision, but from the discretion of a traffic police officer who decides who to stop and fine and who to let go.

20   K Marx, *Critique of the Gotha Programme*, International Publishers, New York, 1938, p 9.

21   K Marx, 1938, p 10.

that the 'game' is played in accordance with predetermined rules, socialist administrative engineering involves the playing of the game by any means available or means made available. As has been stated quite forcefully by Hayek — the greatness of liberal (libertarian) law lies in its impartiality, its 'blindness'. He wrote:

> Although competition and justice may have little else in common, it is as much a commendation of competition as of justice that it is no respecter of persons. That it is impossible to foretell who will be the lucky ones or whom disaster will strike, that rewards and penalties are not shared out according to somebody's views about the merits or demerits of different people but depend on their capacity and their luck.[22]

In this sense the very idea of a state or any political organisation governed by law (ie by impartiality) contradicts the very idea of opportunistic administration based upon principles of socialism. Assuming that the two types of political organisations of society, namely socialism and democracy, correspond to 'administrativism' and the 'supremacy of law', it could be said that once Gorbachev had adopted as his official policy the idea of creating a law-governed state the days of socialism in Russia and eastern Europe were numbered.[23]

We can only speculate now on how clearly this was understood by Gorbachev and Gorbachevists themselves. Dr Mart Susi in his dissertation has demonstrated very clearly that the general idea of a state being governed by law was transformed in the USSR several times during only two or three years.[24] It started with the monstrously illogical concept of a 'socialist law governed state'.[25] However, the idea that everybody including the all-powerful and unshakeable Communist Party, is subordinated to law gave the democratic opposition the most potent political and ideological weapon against Gorbachev and other communists.

In another context — that of the aspirations of Soviet republics to (re)gain their sovereignty — Zbigniew Brzezinski wrote:

> Gorbachev's emphasis on greater legality — so necessary to the revival of the Soviet economy — gave the non-Russians a powerful weapon for contesting Moscow's control over their destiny ... A constitutional framework for the full assertion of national sovereignty has formally existed, almost inviting the increasingly assertive leaders of the non-Russian nationals to take deliberate advantage of it.[26]

---

22 F A Hayek, *The Road to Serfdom*, University of Chicago Press, Chicago, 1958, p 101.

23 The anti-legalistic tendency of socialist ideology was discovered much earlier by Hayek in his analyses of influential left-wing ideologies in England between the World Wars. For criticism of H F Laski's works, see F A Hayek, 1958, pp 61–3.

24 M Susi, 1991, note 8 above.

25 The options here are either: the state is governed by law, or it is not. Political and ideological characteristics (socialist, liberal, conservative, etc) do not have anything to do with this. The issue is also whether all people and corporate subjects are equal under the same rules or whether a privileged position is given to some of them based on political priorities.

26 Z Brzezinski, 'Post-Communist Nationalism', (1989) 68 *Foreign Affairs* 2–8.

This legal-political advantage was exploited by the republics and as a consequence, communism no longer exists in the former USSR and in Europe (at least in its classical Soviet version).

Right and 'right', left and 'left'

Since the French Revolution of the eighteenth century the occidental political tradition has accepted quite a vague division of ideologies and policies into the right and the left. In spite of the serious ambiguity of these classifications, until very recent times their content seemed to be sufficiently clear: *right* wing was traditionally associated with classical democracy, libertarianism, entrepreneurship, 'minimal state' and American conservatism, whereas *left* was related to socialism, social engineering, redistribution and American liberalism. Political changes in 1989 in Europe forced us to rethink our understanding of these ideologies. Conservatism (being on the right wing of the political spectrum) in post-communist society means the adherence to old socialist ideology (ie left ideology) and conversely, the restoration of traditional human and democratic values is carried out by political groups that in this new context compose the left wing. Although these changes contribute to terminological confusion, it is still not so hard to understand the real role of these ideologies if we put them in a proper political context. But the problem here is far deeper than that of mere terminology.

The following example is instructive. In 1993 the people of Lithuania, the first truly breakaway republic in the former USSR elected to the parliament and the presidency a traditional left-wing party composed of reformist leaders of the former Communist Party. They voted out of power the Popular Front (the 'Sajudis' movement) and its leader who had achieved the secession of Lithuania and its liberation from communism. If we take into account the anti-popular character of communism — of its ideology, structure and actual practice — it remains to be asked: how was it possible that, through free and democratic elections, people voted back to power the former communists?

Let me put aside explanations evidently inappropriate (such as electoral fraud, communist subversive manoeuvring, etc) and assume that people in these countries also hold the right to 'life liberty and pursuit of happiness' as self-evident truths. If so, there is only one possible explanation for the election of the former communists,[27] namely that the difference between former communist reformers and the new democrats in the post-communist countries is actually less significant than it might seem.

I am aware of the fact that this statement may sound almost unbelievable. How can one say that the difference is insignificant if we keep in mind that democrats fought communists and the communists tried to preserve (although in its modernised and reformed way) the then existing communist socialist system? Is that not a crucial difference?

---

27   And also for several similar political trends in other countries: moderation of reforms in Poland, secession of pro-socialist Slovakia, etc.

The answer is both yes and no. Yes, because the differences between communist and democratic values contradict each other in a number of ways, for example, *communalism* versus *individualism*; *subordination* versus *human rights*; *state ownership* versus *private property*. But that does not entail a vast difference in terms of actual economic policies. If we take another criterion — the attitude towards the state's involvement in the economic life of the nation — both communist and non-communist parties in the post-communist world start to look more similar. Consider the following examples. The anti-communist government of Lithuania (in power until 1993) actually did not liberalise monetary policy. The socialist rouble was replaced by another socialist or even 'communist' tender-coupon (called a talona). The first step by the nationalist Estonian government was to cancel the program of privatisation of state property. All post-communist governments in Russia have continued to control prices, and have had a policy of high taxation and tariffs. In this case, it appears that on the political-economic level the communist-reformist and democratic-liberal governments, although ideologically different, have remained within the framework of leftist economic policies. In these countries, nationalism, patriotism, and anti-communism appear to give way to another sort of left-wing policy when it comes to the regulation or non-regulation of the economy. The real opposition, actual liberalism (or libertarianism) was represented by the forces outside the official constitutional structures of state power. For example, it was the national Bank of Estonia (and not the parliament or government) that introduced convertible currency. The mercantile and commodity exchanges and stock markets in Moscow actually started privatisation well before the governmental program was approved.

The right-wing eastern European governments that pursued a shift from state control over the economy to free market principles, had to leave some controls in place (like Gaidar's in Russia that started the voucher-privatisation in 1992 or Mazoviecki's in Poland that implemented market-orientated 'shock therapy' of price-liberalisation) or risk serious political disturbances. For example, the privatisation scheme of the Czechoslovakian Prime Minister Vaclav Klaus finally caused the secession of left-led Slovakia from the federation.

I do not claim that in every case the shift from left to right was really possible during this period of time, or even politically desirable. The point that I want to make is that *political ideas bring about real changes if and only if post-communist 'democratic' governments reassess the role of the state in economic regulation.* The replacement of communist reformers by anti-communists is not in itself a guarantee that meaningful and substantial changes will occur in the post-communist economies of eastern Europe.

Subject to the validity of my point, the new non-communist governments, in many cases, use the label 'right wing' for themselves without proper justification. Political issues like national statehood, political loyalty, ethnic composition of the state, differentiation in legal status of the residents and citizens, among other issues, may be relevant for the anti-communist and post-communist policies, but they are absolutely irrelevant from the point of view of liberalism. To use a trivial liberal truth, for a salesman a customer is a customer, if he or she is able and willing to pay the price; his or her ethnic origins, political convictions and so on have not the slightest importance.

The economic effects of bureaucratic administrativism on the United States, in the period of McCarthyism, was brilliantly described by Milton Friedman in the context of the economic effects of McCarthy's blacklist on Hollywood. (The MacCarthy blacklist was a semi-official list of persons suspected of having ties with the United States Communist Party who were excluded from public office as well as from many jobs in the private sector.) After an Academy Award had been (mistakenly) granted to an author on that blacklist (ie the author had produced a screen-script that was a very marketable one) it became evident to the public that the political coercion could not 'work precisely because the market made it costly for people to preserve the blacklist'.[28] In other words, the blacklist was an administrative anti-market phenomenon just like the whole set of socialist ideas it was supposed to fight. The actual result of the anti-communist witch-hunt was economic loss caused by the implementation of non-economic administrative measures and in this sense McCarthy was quite a radical left-wing politician like his foes from the real and imaginary United States Communist Party. This remains the case despite the fact that recent disclosures from Soviet archives have vindicated Joe McCarthy's suspicions. They have shown that the United States Communist Party's network was much more extensive than previously thought and that the party was completely controlled by the Stalinists in the USSR.

'Left' as an intermediary

If we take liberalism in its classical sense[29] back to its origins, we discover that it is ideologically neutral on the level of value-orientated political phraseology. As Bentham put it: 'each man [is] the sole competent judge as to what is most conducive to his aggregate and ultimate interest'.[30] The following comment by Bentham on the normativity of political ideology (or normative ethics) as imposed on people from outside is especially instructive:

> As often as, speaking of any man, I say he ought to do so and so or he ought not to do so and so, what accordingly I know and acknowledge myself to be doing is neither more nor less than endeavor[ing] to bring to view the state of my own mind, of my own opinion, of my own affections in relation to the line of conduct which on the occasion in question is stated as pursued by him — this much and nothing more.[31]

---

28 M Friedman, *Capitalism and Freedom*, University of Chicago Press, Chicago, 1982, p 20.
29 The term 'liberalism' in its classical sense refers to the ideology which aims at the promotion of free markets, individual freedoms and the minimisation of state interference in economic and social life. The adjective 'right-wing' is used to designate the place of liberalism within the spectrum of all political parties.
30 *The Collected Works of Jeremy Bentham. Philosophy* (ed J R Dinwiddy), Clarendon Press, Oxford, 1983, p 192.
31 J R Dinwiddy, 1983, p 149.

It was in their general ideological sense that Bentham declared that the words 'ought' and 'ought not' *ought* to be banished from the vocabulary of Ethics.[32] As Ludwig von Mises pointed out, for liberalism in the classical sense of the word, 'such questions as whether the capitalist system is good or bad ... and whether it ought to be rejected on certain philosophic or metaphysical grounds are entirely irrelevant'.[33]

So, if we consider that the state is not only an actual power-structure (an *Is*) but is also an institution able to impose an order of actions based on certain ideologies that lie outside the individual (an *Ought*), then the one crucial feature of liberal ideology which can influence political and economic change is its insistence upon the minimisation of state involvement in individual lives and economic structures.

At the same time it would be evidently wrong to say that all that stands to the left of the centre in the political spectrum — communism, social-democracy, McCarthyism, social rationalism, welfare state ideology, 'paying a fair share' doctrine and dozens of other similar doctrines — are conceptually equivalent from the point of view of liberal ideals; not at all. Evidently, there are leftisms that are, to some extent, compatible with right-wing perspectives, as there are also those that are not. 'Fair share' and welfare state ideologies at their worst, when implemented, may cause or deepen economic crises (in the United States, the years of the Carter administration are an example), whereas communism is able to destroy the whole economy as the USSR was able to prove so conclusively. The welfare state in Sweden was compatible with individual freedoms, democracy and private property, whereas state socialism in Russia destroyed them all.

In a way, it could be said that certain types of left-wing ideologies (social-democracies or even some sorts of non-chauvinistic nationalisms) may serve as intermediaries between freedom and totalitarianism. But in which direction is society heading: to democracy or to totalitarianism? An attractive social policy (the aim of achieving economic security for all) was the pretext for the establishment of a totalitarian socialist regime in Russia.[34] The same social policy balanced by increasing marketisation may also serve as a transition to economic freedom and prosperity.[35]

---

32   J R Dinwiddy, 1983, p 253.
33   L von Mises, 1985, note 3 above, p 87.
34   To quote an excellent passage from Hayek: 'Either both the choice and the risk rest with the individual or he is relieved of both ... [The army-type organization] is the only system in which the individual can be conceded full economic security ... this security is, however, inseparable from the restrictions on liberty and the hierarchical order of military life — it is the security of the barracks.' F A Hayek, 1958, note 23 above, pp 126–7.
35   It is worthwhile to mention that this political and ideological question — whether to move from the moderate 'left center' to freedom or to totalitarianism has its equivalent in economics also. Russian analyst Maxim Sokolov demonstrated brilliantly that the immediate economic results of strong monetarism and of its opposite, hyperinflation, are exactly the same: the radical decrease of investments and productivity, impoverishment of population, etc. But there is a crucial difference in the long run: monetary discipline leads to the sanitation of the economy whereas hyperinflation causes its further degradation. *Commersant Weekly*, Russian edition, No 9, 1993, p 3.

Keeping this in mind, we should reassess the changes in the post-communist political ideologies. Although they still remained politically on the left, they replaced doctrines incompatible with liberalism with ones that made moving towards it possible. The welfare state ideology (strong economic safety net, gross redistribution of profits, etc) that replaced communism is able to admit liberal values and economic mechanisms and thus makes the move towards market and freedom feasible.[36]

The same is true about Christianity. Christianity may be interpreted in a collectivistic way, but in its basic essence it is not such a phenomenon Insistence upon true personal human values serves the purposes of our liberation. In March, 1992, Philip Dimitrov of Bulgaria, then at 36 the youngest Prime Minister in Europe noted that:

> As Dostoyevski knew, and the whole history of mankind has proven, without God ... the things most precious to us humans are often denied to us. Because it is our nature as humans that for true achievement, emotional fulfillment and spiritual attainment, we need higher intensity of purpose than everyday concerns can provide.[37]

This 'higher intensity of purpose', Dimitrov said, has to create 'a new and higher moral imperative' in former communist countries that had accomplished 'a revolt of the soul against the soullessness of communism'.[38] It means that Christianity was and is the ideology of individual freedom in post-communist countries. Christianity does not impose any specific models of economic and political development but adds the ethical and metaphysical dimension to the ideologically relatively neutral liberalism. Liberalism is aimed at making people free; Christianity is the imperative that restrains the misuse of this freedom. And even more — once it has been conceded that people are spiritually (and then

---

36   The counterposition between a vulgar and primitive vision, on the one hand, and a more analytical and adequate vision of post-communist-left on the other, is a fact of the realities of today's political studies. Let me quote just one example. What is under discussion in both cases here is whether Yeltsin is a true democrat, or a new sort of undercover communist plotter? Donald S McAlvany (who describes himself as 'a paranoid nut leftover from the Cold War') wrote on 5 October 1991 in his *The McAlvany Intelligence Advisor* that Yeltsin 'is totally dedicated to ... a restructuring and reorganization' of the Communist Party and the Soviet Union from top to bottom', that he 'is not against Gorbachev nor against communism and that he wants to create a party that is 'anti-free enterprise, anti-capitalist, and hard-core Marxist-Leninist' (pp 1 and 8). Another analyst, former US President Richard Nixon states just the opposite: 'President Yeltsin shares our values ... he has repudiated both socialism and communism, believes in a free market and supports the private ownership of property.' *New York Times*, 5 March 1993, p A 17. The sources of McAlvany's mistakes are: (a) his inability to see the existence of certain internal structures within the political left; and (b) more particularly his assumption that the intellectual development of Yeltsin had stopped for some reasons in 1985.

37   'Freeing the Soul from Communism', *The Wall Street Journal*, 23 March 1992. I owe these quotes to Dr Frank Potenziani.

38   *The Wall Street Journal*, 23 March 1992.

politically) free, it is hard to say to them later that they must remain enslaved economically. (The final blow to the Soviet economic system was given by the liberalisation of the press!)

Economic policy based on the assumption of individual freedom cannot remain communist any more because individual freedom and the denial of private property cannot coexist for a very long period.[39] 'Just as capitalism looks to the individual choice of consumers as the keystone for ordering the economy, democracy depends on individual initiative and choice as the source of political decision making', writes Professor Owen Fiss.[40] In countries where these freedoms were denied and where individual property was confiscated and nationalised, this principle has created a new set of problems — problems of re-privatisation. Unfortunately we know quite well how to destroy private property but we do not know how to restore it. The problems are obvious: they include the lack of capital, the lack of market value of many formerly state-owned enterprises and inertia. These are, most probably, the reasons why the policies that were based on the radical shift to the right did not work very well initially and why the supposedly right-wing governments were removed. Instead, change compatible with a liberal democratic order involves a gradual, piecemeal movement through popular privatisation (voucher-privatisation)[41] and partial restructuring of ownership relations in the existing formerly state-owned corporations. This swing backwards — from the radical right-wing policies to right-left ones was sometimes misinterpreted in the west as a giving up of marketisation of post-communist economies. So, for instance, the replacement of 'shock therapist' Prime Minister of Russia, Yegor Gaidar by industrialist Victor Chernomyrdin in December 1992 was interpreted widely as the surrender to communism. It was overlooked that Chernomyrdin had, since 1989, created one of the biggest gas-producing concerns in the world and was

---

39 There are examples of another kind — those of non-democratic political regimes that still did not violate individual property rights. Though they existed for a considerable period of time — in South Korea and Chile, for instance — they could not maintain their stability for long. The same changes occur today, though somewhat more slowly, in China. In these cases, the relation is turned around: once you have said to a person that he or she is free economically it becomes harder and harder to tell that person that he or she is not free politically.

40 O Fiss, 'Capitalism and Democracy', (1992) 13 *Michigan Journal of International Law* 911.

41 The mechanism of this type of privatisation proposed (as far as I know) by the Czechoslovakian Prime Minister Vaclav Klaus is based on the free distribution by the state to the people of some kind of securities (vouchers) that represent a share in all national assets and that can be exchanged for actual shares in privatised enterprises. These securities (having some nominal cash value) may also be traded on the securities markets at their market value. Russia embarked on a similar experiment with the so-called Chubais model of privatisation. Although the privatisation securities issued under this scheme became low-value junk bonds, the primary goal, that of privatising some important state assests, was nevertheless achieved.

rightfully called in the Russian business paper *Commersant-Weekly*: a 'Rockefeller today'.[42]

What actually occurred was the replacement of the program for the immediate introduction of a free-market economy by a system of state capitalism. And in spite of several apparent similarities (the dominance of government controls over a substantial portion of the economy), the difference between state capitalism and socialism is significant. The point here is that the rules of the game are different. In socialism the state executes its control through administrative means and political power. Under state capitalism the rules are those of the market economy and the state is simply the largest shareholder and the strongest player on the field. The state under state capitalism is an owner among other (actual and potential) owners, and is legally equal to them. It means that the state does not, at least in theory, prevent the entry into the market of other economic agents and forces, but rather competes with them in the same market place.

As Professor Fiss puts it: 'The capitalist state [as a sort of capitalist itself] is not allowed to pursue the public interest in a way understood to be independent of consumer satisfaction; the state's function is still defined in market terms'.[43] State capitalism or piecemeal privatisation of state property may actually serve the purposes of restoration of market freedom and economic efficiency provided by fair competition.

Thatcherism is an economic policy that may provide us with an example of how state control (a leftist legacy from labour predecessors) may be used to promote market freedom. Sir Alan Walters remarked that 'under Thatcher the reform of the nationalized corporation was carried through while ... in the public sector ... privatization occurred only after the hard work of reform [termination of public subsidies, monopoly privileges and cheap capital] had been completed'.[44]

In these situations, it is the state itself that must cure the evils produced by it. But this can be done only under one condition — if and only if leaders oppose the state's temptations to expand and preserve its role. This requires a strong ideological belief in libertarian right-wing goals and values capable of meaningfully changing the modern world.

---

42 *Commersant-Weekly*, Russian edition, No 46, 1992, p 4. GASPROM created by Chernomyrdin controls more than 20 gas-producing enterprises, also nine stock markets, eight joint ventures with large western firms (Freeport McMoran, Ost-West Handelsbank, FN6 among them), seven commercial banks, one foreign bank, one foreign banking consortium, two interbank clearing centers, and two offshore companies in Lichtenstein. Joint operations with 'Witershall' will give GASPROM a 35% stake in all new gaslines in Germany. Keeping this in mind it would be hard to imagine Chernomyrdin as a communist leader. It is much easier to imagine that in the case of the restoration of the communist system Chernomyrdin and his 'empire' would be its first victims.

43 O Fiss, 1992, note 40 above, p 90.

44 Sir Alan Walters, 'The Transition to a Market Economy', in (eds) C Clague and G C Rauser, 1992, note 18 above, p 103.

CHAPTER 13

Rule of Law and the Democratic World Order

Geoffrey de Q Walker*

We are living in exhilarating times. The threat of global war has receded almost to vanishing point for the first time this century. Totalitarian regimes in eastern and central Europe and west Asia have collapsed, apartheid has ended in South Africa and liberalisation is unmistakably under way in South America, Burma and Vietnam. For the first time, democracies represent a majority of the world's 171 nations.[1] It is nothing less than a worldwide democratic revolution, which is also spilling over into the established democracies in the form of demands for constitutional reform through such means as the adoption of the initiative and referendum system, administrative law reform and the introduction of bills of rights.

While the hopes held earlier in the 1990s for a new world order under international law and the United Nations peace enforcement have dimmed, the UN has found a new role in the active promotion of democracy throughout the world. The Secretary-General, Dr Boutros-Ghali, acknowledges that the organisation is shifting away from the neutral position it took during the Cold War and is responding to a worldwide demand for democracy. 'Democracy supports stability within societies by mediating between competing points of view', he declares, 'it fosters respect between states, reducing the chances of war'.[2] Indeed, there is no historical instance in which two established democracies have gone to war with each other.[3] It is also clear that the death toll from violence by

*   Professor of Law and Dean, T C Beirne School of Law, University of Queensland.
1   T Mathews, 'Decade of Democracy', *Newsweek*, 30 December 1991, p 32.
2   'UN chief pushes spread of democracy', *The Australian*, 28 April 1994, p 4.
3   R Rummel, *Death by Government*, Transaction Publishers, New Brunswick, New Jersey, 1994, Chapter 1.

undemocratic governments against their own peoples far exceeds the loss of life by military action in war.[4]

One thing we have learned about democracy, however, especially from the experience of the African nations when they first became independent, is that unless a democratic system is based on the rule of law, it will not survive. Unless those in authority abide by the rules of law laid down for the exercise of power, there is no constitution; and unless all parties accept the results of political processes undergone in accordance with law, there is no democracy. The rule of law is also historically anterior to democracy: it existed in colonial America and colonial Australia, and it exists in Hong Kong, in the absence of established organs of political democracy.

Conversely, establishing the rule of law at the domestic level will tend to reinforce it at the international level. Governments of democratic nations do not always comply with international law in their dealings, but when they stray from the path they can, by means of arguments based on law, be embarrassed into mending their ways. Totalitarian governments feel no such embarrassment and use international law mainly for manipulative purposes.

Relevance of the rule of law concept in the United States and Australia

In American and Australian legal education, the rule of law is not normally taught as a separate topic, though its precepts permeate law study. In the United States, the Bill of Rights embodies many of the principles of the rule of law and makes these principles more powerful by making them directly enforceable in court. In Australia, where there is no Bill of Rights, the ideal of the rule of law nevertheless constantly informs judicial development of constitutional and administrative law.

The rule of law doctrine repays study even in the American context for at least two reasons. First, because it is anterior to the constitutional order, not only historically as already mentioned, but also logically. For when we contemplate the legal order and the constitution, we may feel impelled to ask where this elaborate system comes from. Why should the *courts* be the ones to decide which rule applies and whether or not it has been breached? For that matter, why should we have laws at all? Unless we have some concept that enables us to answer such questions, all the institutions and processes of the law, all our constitutional doctrines, would lack an organising principle and a basis for action.[5] The great constitutional cases would become a mere collection of disconnected instances with nothing to explain why the court should have had the right to take jurisdiction over these matters in the first place.

---

4   R Rummel, 1994, Chapter 1.
5   L Jaffe and E Henderson, 'Judicial Review and the Rule of Law' (1956), 72 *Law Quarterly Review* 345, 347.

If such an organising principle does exist, then plainly it must be the basis for our whole legal and governmental system. It must be the most important concept for a lawyer to know.

Second, in the American setting, an understanding of the rule of law concept may help in the interpretation of state and federal constitutions and bills of rights and may suggest desirable changes or additions to them. In Australia, the absence of constitutionally guaranteed fundamental freedoms makes the rule of law ideal even more critical to liberty.

Law and power: maintaining an equilibrium

If we accept that the subject is worthy of study, we should start by noting that one of the main currents that can be observed in the history of human government is the antinomy between two conflicting forces, power and law. In their pure form, power and law are polar opposites. Power stands for arbitrary and unchecked might — the Saddam Hussein model of government. Law stands for a system in which power is checked and restrained by institutions or individual rights and channelled in such a way as to conform with people's values and established patterns of expectation.

Neither law nor power in their pure form can by themselves found a stable system of government. Power is too capricious, coercive and unpredictable, and law, in practice, can become inflexible and may have difficulty in adapting to changing conditions and attitudes. Unless law leaves some scope for power or discretion (in relation to sentencing for example), it can, like power, lead to the build-up of pressures that produce its own downfall.

The rule of law is a legal and constitutional doctrine that reconciles these two antagonistic drives. The doctrine was not invented by the Anglo-American common law system, nor do we have a monopoly of it. It is expressly mentioned in the European Convention for the Protection of Human Rights and Fundamental Freedoms and in the Universal Declaration of Human Rights. A concept rather like it can be found among the Barotse tribes of southern Africa.[6] But while there is broad similarity in what is understood by the doctrine in various countries, it is undeniable that the rule of law has acquired distinct connotations and a special significance in the Anglo-American world. Although we take the doctrine for granted, the degree to which it has been developed by the common law, as well as the manner in which its precepts and principles have in practice pervaded legal and constitutional institutions, has probably been unique and may well be the greatest contribution of Anglo-American culture to western civilisation.

I have mentioned the 'precepts' and 'principles' embodied in the rule of law doctrine. These can be collected and distilled from such sources as international conventions, the leading cases in domestic courts, the judgments at Nuremberg, the deliberations of associations of jurists, and

---

6   M Gluckman, *The Judicial Process Among the Barotse of Northern Rhodesia*, 2nd ed, Manchester University Press, Manchester, 1967.

the learned writings of legal and constitutional scholars. The main principles are, in my view, 12 in number.[7] I will not enumerate them in the abstract, but will give practical examples of them as possible guidelines for the development of democratic government. At the outset, one could sum up the content of the rule of law in two basic propositions:

(a) the conduct of persons and governments should be guided by law; and

(b) the law should possess such properties that people are able to obey it[8] and usually will.

It is not the same thing as mere law and order, which can effectively be maintained by the most tyrannical government, though there is obviously some overlap.

Some guidelines for emerging democracies

As early as 1988, the reformers in the Soviet Union were outspoken in declaring their wish to establish the rule of law in what they then thought would be a reformed Soviet Union.[9] A similar spirit of constitutional inquiry can be seen in other countries that are moving toward democracy, especially those that have been the most shut off from the international current of liberal ideas. If they were to ask us how they should go about establishing the rule of law, what suggestions would we make to them? There are a number of guidelines that I would suggest, not in any spirit of preaching or condescension (as our own governments have quite often strayed from the rule of law ideal and will still do so unless they are continually watched), but as practical distillations of the legal experience of the human race. They are as follows.

Laws against private violence

There must be substantive laws prohibiting private violence and coercion that will protect people from general lawlessness and anarchy. The rule of law must mean this before it can mean anything else. It is hard to think of any legal system that lacks such laws, though in some countries the laws on those subjects may conflict with other guidelines mentioned later.

Government under substantative law

The government itself must be bound by substantive law, not only by the constitution, but as far as possible by the same laws as those that bind other people. We should be very wary when we find governments giving themselves the power to do things to people that people may not do to one another. In some instances such laws will be necessary, but they merit close scrutiny.

---

7 See generally G de Q Walker, *The Rule of Law: Foundation of Constitutional Democracy*, Melbourne University Press, Melbourne, 1988, Chapter 1.

8 See generally J Raz, 'The Rule of Law as a Virtue' (1977) 93 *Law Quarterly Review* 195, especially 198.

9 'Rule of law next aim of Soviet reformers', *The Australian*, 16 May 1988.

In our legal tradition, this principle emerged in its present form in the famous 1765 English case *Entick v Carrington*,[10] which arose out of a raid by government officials, without a warrant, on the house of a citizen for the purpose of searching for certain documents. Lord Chief Justice Camden held that the same principles of law applied to an unauthorised search by a government agent as would apply to a forcible trespass by a private citizen. As Justice Bradley of the US Supreme Court said: 'The principles laid down in this opinion affect the very essence of constitutional liberty and security'.[11] They ensure that a citizen may not be punished or coerced except for a breach of the law, or in other words that there can be no penalty without a law. Police and other agencies should have no power to arrest or imprison people without lawful warrant.

Normativism of substantive law

The *Entick* principle is an essential first step, but it is not enough by itself to ensure government under law. The *substantive* laws of the nation must reflect the principle of 'normativism'. This means, in the first place, that the substantive law should possess the characteristic of certainty. This precept condemns excessively vague laws such as Article 16 of the Soviet Criminal Code which prohibited all 'socially dangerous acts', or the similar provision in Nazi Germany that made punishable 'acts deserving of punishment ... according to the healthy instincts of the race'. This rule also condemns laws that are retroactive, for a law obviously cannot be known in advance if it is not prospective. In this context there may be some ground for uneasiness about the trials of former East German borderguards who killed people attempting to escape to the west. The law under which they have been convicted is the modern German (formerly West German) law of homicide, with natural law and international human rights concepts being invoked to invalidate defenses available to the accused under the then applicable East German law. As Gabriël Moens argues in this volume, the reasoning adopted by the German courts in these cases erodes the certainty of the law and, therefore, contravenes our principle of normativism.

On moral grounds it is hard to symphathise with the defendants. The evidence showed that the guards were opportunists who volunteered for border units for the pay, which was 80% higher than normal army conscript rates, and a good salary by any standard in East Germany. Borderguard service was a fast track to better careers, including postings abroad. Shootings were rewarded with pay bonuses and decorations, but most guards did not wear their medals for fear of abuse from members of the public. Reports of border shootings were suppressed.[12] Plainly, the guards knew that what they were doing was regarded as wrongful by most people, but accepted moral opprobrium in exchange for material benefits.

---

10   19 St Tr 1031 (1765).
11   *Boyd v United States* 116 US 616 at 630 (1886).
12   '"Ambition" drove E German guards', *The Weekend Australian*, 7–8 September 1991; G Moens, 'The German Borderguard Cases: Natural Law and the Duty to Disobey Immoral Laws', Chapter 8 above.

The sentences imposed following conviction have been very light. Nevertheless, an important rule of law concept has been compromised by criminal convictions resting on the reasoning used by the German courts. It would have been preferable if the courts had either found a firmer legal basis for liability, if necessary on lesser charges, or had simply faced the result that criminal proceedings did not lie and had left the victims or their families to whatever civil remedies might be available to them.

The second aspect of normativism is the requirement of legal generality, which is the mirror image of the certainty element. On the one hand, laws should be specific about what they prohibit, but on the other hand, they should not be specific about the persons to whom they apply. Otherwise, law ceases to be a system of norms. Citizens cannot orient their conduct by law if anyone is liable to be targeted by a specific regulation aimed at them. This is the principle behind the ban in Article 1, s 9 of the United States Constitution on bills of attainder as well as ex post facto laws.

The third aspect of normativism is equality before the law. In the west, this principle has sometimes been infringed through the activities of pressure groups and other special interests seeking legislation designed to serve their own private agendas. More serious infringements in other countries have involved the imposition of sanctions on designated classes, whether they be Jews, or bourgeois or landowners or (as in the case of Cambodia), intellectuals. People are more likely to obey and respect the law if they know it is essentially the same for everybody. The equality principle does not, however, preclude unequal treatment when there are genuine reasons for so doing, for example infancy.

The normativism principle counsels some caution in the legal treatment of persons closely associated with fallen totalitarian regimes. A law proscribing and punishing members of the former Communist Party in general, or even members of the Soviet KGB or the East German Stasi as such, might infringe all three aspects of this principle. In the interests of normativism, any such sanctions should be imposed only on those who ordered, or committed, or were knowingly concerned in acts that would constitute crimes under ordinary law, such as murder, aggravated assault, blackmail and the like. This was basically the criterion applied in the West German de-Nazification program.[13] At stake here is the future respect of the population for the law.

At this stage we should notice that many of the points in our guidelines are not absolute rules. They are relative concepts in a legal context. We want legal certainty, but not so much that the law becomes too rigid and moves too far out of line with public opinion. We want equality before the law, but not to the extent of treating children in the same way as adults, the mentally sick in the same way as the sane, or the handicapped in the same way as the whole. The value of these principles is that they force the law-maker to justify any departures from them by reference to an accepted scale of moral values.

---

13   The categories of liability were, however, progressively contracted over time: see I Müller, *Hitler's Justice: The Courts of the Third Reich*, Harvard University Press, Cambridge, Massachusetts, 1991, Chapter 27.

One consequence of this principle is that the statute books will need to be cleared of totalitarian legislation that offends the normativism rule. A process like that under the de-Nazification program in post-war West Germany will be required, though it ought to be more thorough. A good deal of harsh legislation in the Nazi era, such as the law permitting preventive detention, is still in force in Germany, with only the most offensive phrases removed. Hitler's Law for the Prevention of Hereditary Diseases, which led under the Reich to the forced sterilisation of 350,000 people, lay on the statute book until 1974.[14]

Law and public opinion

There must be some mechanism for ensuring that the law is, and remains, reasonably in accordance with public opinion. Otherwise, there may be widespread disrespect for law and the pressures for violent change may build up and ultimately explode. This is ensured by a system of democracy which is capable of aligning the law to moral consciousness of the community.

Enforcement of law

There must also be machinery capable of implementing and enforcing the law, especially the substantive laws against private violence, coercion, general lawlessness and anarchy. This will normally, though not inevitably, require an organised police force. Unless these core areas of law are enforced, people will resort to self-help and private revenge, thereby undermining the first ingredient for a society under law.

Government under procedural law

Similarly, there must be effective procedures and institutions to ensure that government action is also in accordance with law. This ensures what Ihering called the 'two-sidedly binding force of the law'[15] that empowers the ordinary courts to rule on disputes between governments and citizen. Without this enforceable reciprocity, law cannot operate as a restraint on power. With the great advances that have been made in western countries in recent years in the judicial review of executive action, there should be a great number of possible models to choose from here.

Judicial independence

An independent judiciary is an indispensable requirement of the rule of law and indeed of all known methods of controlling power. Unless the law is applied by a body that does not take sides in the dispute, the law has no hope of commanding voluntary obedience from the majority of people. Conversely, the mere survival of an independent judiciary can in itself do much to prevent a final slide into tyranny, as happened in India under the period of 'emergency' rule between 1975 and 1977. In South

---

14   I Müller, 1991, p 227.
15   F Burin, 'The Theory of the Rule of Law and the Structure of the Constitutional State' (1966) 15 *Am U L Rev* 313, 316.

Africa, a relatively independent judiciary succeeded in keeping alive under apartheid significant portions of the rule of law. This was demonstrated, for example, by the Natal Supreme Court's striking down of key aspects of the government's 1986 emergency legislation.[16]

Senior judges in countries that lack a recent tradition of judicial independence and who had close links with the old regime will probably need to be sent into retirement, as happened in West Germany after the Second World War and as is currently being done in united Germany with respect to the judges of the old East German state. Some recent German critics argue, however, that the purging process after 1945 did not go far enough. While the Constitutional Court has been made up of judges with no ties to the Hitler regime, the other courts, including the Supreme Court, for some time largely comprised former Third Reich judges. This, it is said, has done lasting damage to the climate of German jurisprudence.[17]

As so much emphasis is placed on the independence of the judiciary, an observer could fairly ask, as was foreshadowed earlier, why the courts are so particularly suited to administering justice according to law? Why not some other institution? A number of reasons can be given, including professional habit and training, the authoritative publication of reasons for decisions (eg precedents) in law reports, the system of appeals for correcting errors, the openness of the court system and its respect for fairness and impartiality. This respect is partly the result of sheer tradition, but also probably of methods designed to reinforce that tradition, such as the provisions for tenure, for remuneration and removal. Other factors are the intelligence, sound legal training and experience of those appointed to the bench.

Of course, while the courts have to be independent, they must also be bound by law. Their function is to interpret the law and the fundamental principles that underlie it, and apply it to proven facts. If there are no limits to the power of judges to make law, if judges are given, or give themselves, wide discretionary powers, society can become subject to the rule of judges rather than the rule of law. As Lord Camden, Lord Devlin and Justice Learned Hand have pointed out, there is such a thing as judicial tyranny.[18]

Independent legal representation

An independent legal profession can remind the bench of its duty and generally keep rule of law ideals alive. The conduct of the Indian legal profession under the 1975–1977 period of emergency rule is a good example. During those years, lawyers continued to press for *habeas corpus* on behalf of thousands of detainees, despite increasingly obvious risks to

---

16   G de Q Walker, 1988, note 7 above, p 14.
17   I Müller, 1991, note 13 above, p 297. Nevertheless, as early as 1961, the German court system emerged in first position in a comparative study: see S Bedford, *The Faces of Justice*, Collins, London, 1961, Part 2.
18   G de Q Walker, 1988, note 7 above, pp 31, 399.

the lawyers themselves. The courage of the Indian legal profession during that period, though little remarked in the west, shows how an independent legal profession inspired by the rule of law ideal can be a bastion of civilised values that even dictators cannot ignore. The lawyers took their stand at a time when most other people had come to accept the destruction of Indian democracy as irreversible and had begun to make their peace with the regime.

Natural justice

The principles of natural justice or due process must be observed in all trials. In domestic law we define these principles as:

(a) the judge must not be judge in his or her own cause (in other words the courts must be unbiased); and

(b) the court must hear both sides of the case.

These principles are closely related to the requirement for judicial independence. Their function is to ensure that courts remain acceptable as dispute-settling mechanisms. A court that is not seen to be unbiased, like a court that does not seem to be independent, has no significant role in society. In the case of the courts of Russia and the other new Slavic republics, this principle will call for extensive personnel changes. The former Moscow lawyer Konstantin Simis has described how pervasive and habitual bribery permeated the Soviet judicial system from top to bottom.[19] Although the full extent of that corruption was not widely known among the general population, respect for judicial impartiality will require the replacement of many judges with others who are not tainted in this way.

Accessibility of courts

The courts should be accessible to all so that a person's legal rights are not made illusory. Various methods have been adopted or experimented with in order to overcome the high cost of litigation. Legal aid has been introduced on a large scale, but this has produced some problems of its own. Contingent fees likewise raise difficult issues. Another approach has been to adopt procedures that permit parties to handle their matters themselves, as in the Australian Family Court and the Australian Administrative Appeals Tribunals. One of the reasons for the rapid growth of alternative dispute resolution is the desire to find a cheaper means of dispute settlement.

Impartial enforcement

There must be impartial and honest enforcement. The discretion of law enforcement agencies or other government officials or of political office holders should not be allowed to pervert the law. Nor should perjury or other forms of dishonesty by police in criminal proceedings. This will be a

---

19 K Simis, *USSR: The Corrupt Society*, Simon & Schuster, New York, 1982, Chapter 4.

major challenge for the newly democratising countries, as even in the west we have much room for improvement in this area. Perjury by police has been a serious problem in Australia, which is only gradually being overcome by the spread of compulsory taping and videotaping of interviews with suspects.

A Geist of legality

Finally, there must be an attitude of legality. This guideline is essentially a reminder that the other 11 must be observed in spirit as well as in letter. That is more likely to happen if there is a tradition of legality in the society in question. That is certainly the case in the United States, where all citizens are strongly aware of their constitutional rights, or in Australia where people who know nothing else about law are quite conscious of the presumption that a person accused of a crime is innocent until proven guilty (though unfortunately legislation has eroded that presumption in a number of cases).

This attitude will take time to develop in countries that are just coming to the rule of law. People there have been accustomed to thinking of the courts and the legal system, not as protectors, but as forces from which they need protection. They will need to overcome long-standing attitudes of passivity and cynicism, for maintaining the rule of law is not just a task for lawyers, judges, and police. It is an enterprise of which all must be part. As one German law professor has said of his Eastern compatriots, they must learn to be citizens again.[20]

The zeal of the converted — a recharge for the west?

As was emphasised at the outset, these guidelines are not put forward in any magisterial spirit, for even in the established democracies we must be constantly vigilant to ensure that we and our governments do not lose sight of them. Indeed, we may find that the founders of these new democracies, precisely because they know exactly what it means to lack the protection of the rule of law, may embrace its precepts with more intensity and creativity than we currently do in the west. We may therefore receive some valuable feedback and innovative ideas from them. Such a partnership between old and new democracies would be an auspicious beginning for a new chapter in human history.

---

20   N Reich, quoted in 'German Professor Lays Down the Law', *The Australian*, 25 August 1991.

CHAPTER  14

Connecting the Hohfeldian Boxes: Towards a Technical Definition of Liberty

Ben Brazil*

'Liberty' is a powerful word. Much blood has been spilt in the pursuit of liberty, and much suffering endured in its name. It has become the catchcry of nations, of revolutions and of generations. It is, perhaps, surpassed in its political power only by that other much exploited word, 'right'.

But what does this term 'liberty' really mean — surely more than a coronated statue bearing a flame. In popular terminology, liberty can be used to mean just about anything. When cast in the same breath as equality and fraternity, it is clear that the term is being used very loosely indeed. Isaiah Berlin managed to describe the ability to participate in a democratic political process as a liberty. More controversially, liberty is also used by social welfare theorists to describe a state of freedom from material deprivation. The argument is that liberty should encompass not only freedom from restriction, but also freedom from want: for example it is useless to have a liberty to act in one's own individual way if one is incapacitated by starvation.

The defining of words is notoriously difficult, as the multifarious dictionary definitions of almost any term demonstrate. If however, meaningful discussion of liberty is to take place, its definition must be limited to something more tangible and concrete than the chameleon concept described above, which changes its meaning to suit the purpose of the speaker.

Specifically, we must ask, what is the legal meaning of liberty? Ultimately, the extent of liberty is dependent upon whether we can or

---

* Solicitor of the Supreme Court of Queensland. The author thanks Dr Suri Ratnapala for his comments and encouragement.

cannot do something. In our society, the most obvious determinant of this capacity, and the determinant with which this book is concerned, is the law.

So what is the technical, legal, definition of liberty? Certainly it means freedom from legal constraints. But how does this fit into the overall framework of legal statuses, and can this absence of legal constraints be expressed in positive terms?

Hohfeld

The term liberty was used by Wesley Newcomb Hohfeld as one of his basic building blocks of legal statuses. It was one of the terms that he thought was often confused with the term 'right'. In seeking technical definitions of the terms liberty and right, and the relationship between the two, Hohfeld developed his celebrated boxes theory. Ever since its publication in 1913, this theory has been a source of fascination for lawyers.[1]

In this chapter, I endeavour to provide several new insights into Hohfeld's theory, which I believe will eliminate some of the confusion which surrounds aspects of it and which will reveal aspects of the definition of liberty which have not to date been appreciated fully. Specifically, I intend to argue for three propositions:

(a) that, contrary to the widely held view, the two sets or 'boxes' of terms which figure in Hohfeld's system are connected;

(b) that the jural relations identified by Hohfeld are reducible to one fundamental relation involving the liberty/duty (or more accurately, duty/no-duty) dichotomy;

(c) that such reduction yields a positive definition of the concept of liberty; and

(d) that, contrary to the popular view, there can be no liberty without a corresponding right for its protection.

Although touched upon by other writers, these matters have not elsewhere been developed to the conclusions reached herein.

Hohfeld's theory is traditionally explained with the aid of a diagrammatic portrayal of the jural interrelationships within two sets of legal concepts. The first set features the concepts of *right, liberty, duty* and *no-right* and the second set involves the concepts of *power, disability, immunity* and *liability* (see Diagram 1).[2] It is generally thought that the two sets of interrelated concepts, represented in the two boxes, are unconnected in the sense that there is no conceptual identity between the two sets.[3] In the first part of this chapter, I will endeavour to demonstrate that the two sets or 'boxes' are logically connected and that the second

---

1   W N Hohfeld, 'Fundamental Legal Conceptions as Applied to Judicial Reasoning', (1913–1914) 28 *Yale Law Journal* 16–59.
2   Hohfeld used the terms 'privilege' and 'liberty' interchangeably. In this paper, liberty will be used to encompass Hohfeld's privilege.
3   See for example, M Radin, 'A Restatement of Hohfeld', (1938) 51 *Harv L R* 1157.

box is, fundamentally, the application of the first box to itself! (Thus, a power is a liberty to impose a duty.)

In the second part of the chapter, I will use the link between the two boxes to demonstrate that the Hohfeldian scheme, in the final analysis, is the outgrowth of one basic legal relation, namely that between liberty and duty. It will be seen that this re-interpretation allows the extension of the theory, and helps overcome a number of difficulties that have vexed lawyers for many years. I hope, by this re-interpretation, to propose an integrated and coherent theory that provides both a complete description of the universe of legal discourse and a positive definition of liberty. In the final part of the chapter, I will argue that the prevalent view that a liberty can exist without a right for its protection is fundamentally flawed.

Hohfeld's original theory

Hohfeld's analysis of jural relations and the varying criticisms of it have been standard fare in law school curriculums for a long time. Hence it might seem unnecessary to spell out this material. However, it would be convenient to the reader if the theory is briefly set out in its original form before I proceed to introduce the new angles of inquiry undertaken in this chapter. In the first instance, I will set out the theory without the glosses placed upon it by commentators. The glosses, however will not be ignored, but will figure in my later discussions.

In 'Fundamental Legal Conceptions as Applied to Judicial Reasoning', Hohfeld sought to identify the basic building blocks upon which all our legal relations are based. He made no attempt to identify the requirements that must be satisfied before a legal relation comes into existence. Hohfeld merely classified existing legal relations according to their characteristics, and used this classification to break down complex legal relationships into what he described as the lowest common denominators of all legal relations.

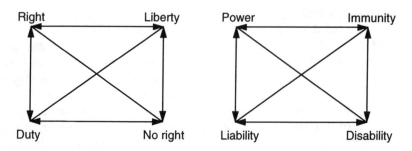

Diagram 1

Hohfeld identified eight terms which he asserted could describe a person's legal status with respect to any given situation. Professor Williams later demonstrated the interrelationship of the concepts with the aid of his 'boxes' diagram (Diagram 1).[4]

---

4   G L Williams, 'The Concept of Legal Liberty', (1956) 56 *Columbia L R* 1129.

Each Hohfeldian status is a three-term relation between one person, one act description and one other person.[5] Thus, where A has a **right** to payment under a contract with B, A and B are the two persons involved, and the payment is the act description. *Right* is the Hohfeldian status linking the three together.

In Diagram 1, vertical pairings represent the totality of the Hohfeldian statuses between two people and one act description. If one person has a right to payment under a contract, the other has a duty, and so on. Vertically paired terms are called *correlatives*. Thus where one term exists, its correlative will always exist in the other person making up the Hohfeldian relation.

The characteristics of the various terms have to date been mostly explained by example. The 'classic' examples are as follows:

(a) A has a right to payment under a contract. B has a duty to pay.

(b) A has a liberty to walk on his land. B has no right that A not walk on his land.

(c) A has a power to make a contract with B if B has sent her an offer capable of acceptance. B then has a liability to have the contract with A made.

(d) A has an immunity from suit for defamation under parliamentary privilege. B has a disability with respect to suing A for defamation.

Thus, duty is the situation where one is required to do or refrain from doing an act, with right being the status of the person the duty is owed to. Liberty exists where the holder of that status can say 'I may' or 'I may not', in relation to an act with the other person having no-right that the holder do or not do the specified act. If a person is able to alter the legal situation of another person, he is said to have a power, and the person who is subject to the power has the correlative liability. If that person has an immunity, however, the first person cannot change the immune party's legal position, and hence has a disability.

The terms diagonal to each other within each box are described by Hohfeld as jural opposites. If A has a duty, she cannot have a liberty with respect to that same transaction. Similarly, a person with a disability cannot have a power with respect to the same situation. Further, the terms are not only mutually exclusive, but also collectively exhaustive. If A does not have a duty, she must have a liberty, and so on.

Williams' diagram allows the identification of a third type of relationship between horizontal terms in the same box, the terms being called contradictories. The existence of a right in A results in the absence of a liberty in B. This relationship can be derived from the two previous relations. Since the existence of a term always implies the existence of its correlative, it also implies the non-existence of the opposite of the correlative, which is in fact the contradictory.

5   J Finnis, *Natural Law and Natural Rights*, Clarendon Press, Oxford, 1980, p 200.

As already mentioned, one of the basic assertions in all interpretations of Hohfeld is that there is no relationship between the two boxes. It is the challenging of this claim which represents the basis of this chapter.

Connecting the boxes

In order to clearly perceive the conceptual connection between the two boxes, we need to understand the nature of power. Hohfeldian power is exercised when a change in legal relations occurs from some fact which is under the volitional control of a human being. He gives as a synonym 'ability'. Dias expresses power as the ability to alter any person's legal position.[6] Harris refers to a relation-regarding voluntary act of a person.[7] Kamba states that '[p]ower expresses the relation of A to B when A's own voluntary act will cause new legal relations'.[8] From this and other definitions, the two vital elements of a power can be identified.

Firstly, a power involves an ability, and its exercise amounts to a voluntary act. There is no duty or imperative involved in the exercise of a power. In fact, a power always involves the exercise of a liberty. Dias states that the liberty to perform or not applies to all types of actions, while only those actions that result in the alteration of existing legal relations amount to powers.[9] Thus it can be seen that power is really a subset of liberty, a special case that deals with existing legal relations.

The second element relates to the consequence of the resort to ability. A power is the ability to alter legal relations. Radin states that powers take us to a level of facts exactly one step higher than that with which we have been dealing.[10] Bentham describes his version of Hohfeld's power as investitive or divestitive of legal rights and duties. The acts which exercise the power are recognised by the law as having certain legal consequences.[11] Whether a right exists often depends upon a purposive human act, ie the exercise of a power. Finnis states that the acts to which powers, immunities etc apply are juridical acts defined at least partly by reference to their effect upon juridical relationships, ie on rights, duties, liberties and no-rights. Thus powers deal with the creation by humans of the legal statuses set out in the first box. Finnis goes on to say that the first box, in contrast, relates to natural acts and these elements are fully definable without reference to their effect upon juridical relationships.[12]

Bringing the two together then, a power is the ability to alter existing legal relations. In fact, a power is a liberty to impose a Hohfeldian duty as shown in the first box. Thus, whereas in the first box I have a liberty to

---

6   R W Dias, *Jurisprudence*, 4th ed, Butterworths, London, 1976, p 33.
7   J W Harris, *Legal Philosophies*, Butterworths, London, 1980, p 77.
8   W J Kamba, 'Legal theory and Hohfeld's analysis of a legal right', (1974) *Juridical Review* 249.
9   R W Dias, 1976, note 6 above, p 36.
10   M Radin, 1938, note 3 above, p 1157.
11   The Bentham analysis is fully discussed in H L A Hart, *Essays on Bentham*, Clarendon Press, Oxford, 1982, p 170.
12   J Finnis, 1980, note 5 above, p 200.

walk on a piece of land, in the second box the basic act 'walk on a piece of land' is replaced by 'impose a Hohfeldian duty', and amounts to a power. Liberty is defined by its effect upon natural acts, power by reference to its effect upon first box duties (Finnis' juridical relations).

The connection that we see here is essentially the first pattern operating upon itself to produce a higher level version of itself. The concept of a pattern repeating upon itself has many analogies in the world of science. Perhaps the closest is the concept of squaring a given number. Take the transformation of five multiplied by any number. It could be 5×3, or 5×7, or 5×152. The number five can be equated to a liberty to do an act. It could be a liberty to walk upon land, to sue and so on. However, if the number five is substituted for the number being multiplied by five, the result is 5×5, or 5^2. This is analogous to a liberty to impose a liberty (which is a sufficient condition for liberty to impose a duty, as a duty is everything a liberty is not).

The other terms of the second box can also be re-interpreted by using the terms in the first box and replacing the basic act they relate to with the imposition of a Hohfeldian duty. Liability is the correlative of a power. Therefore, it can be characterised as a no-right that a Hohfeldian duty not be imposed. Similarly, a disability, as the opposite of a power (a liberty to impose a Hohfeldian duty), is a duty not to impose a Hohfeldian duty, and an immunity is a right that a Hohfeldian duty not be imposed.

Sumner identified this symmetry between the two boxes in *The Moral Foundation of Rights*.[13] However, he did not limit the concept of power to a liberty to impose a duty. Instead, he stated that power is the second order counterpart of liberty. This effectively makes power encompass the imposition of both liberty and duty. The separation of the two concepts which I propose allows further reduction of the legal statuses involved, and leads eventually to the repeating dichotomy outlined below. The attractive nature of this pattern would indicate that the reduction of power into its component parts is a worthwhile exercise.

Thus, it can be seen that the second box is really the first box in relation to Hohfeldian duties. The first box identifies a person's legal status in relation to a basic natural act, ie whether a person can or cannot do it, and the second box identifies a person's capacity to change the legal status identified by the first box. Thus, if I am licensee of some land, I have a liberty to walk upon it. However, the landowner has a power to take away this liberty, thus imposing upon me a duty not to walk upon the land. The terms within the boxes exhaust a person's status in each of the situations that they deal with, making the boxes a complete description of the universe of discourse.

The above re-interpretation of Hohfeld's analysis leads to the conclusion that the boxes are connected, with the second really being the first repeated upon itself.

Once this connection is established, a number of further avenues of investigation and extension arise.

---

13   L W Sumner, *The Moral Foundation of Rights*, Clarendon Press, Oxford, 1987, pp 29–31.

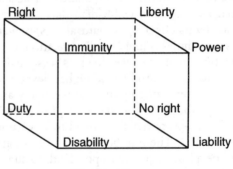

Diagram 2

Extension of Hohfeld's analysis

If the second box is the first repeated upon itself, further repetition will result in a third box and so on ad infinitum. This third box will be characterised by a liberty to impose a power, that is, a liberty to impose a liberty to impose a duty. We can compare this process to the mathematical sequence considered above. The analogous progression of that sequence will be: $5^2 \times 5^2 = 5^3$, $5^3 \times 5 = 5^4$ and so on ad infinitum. A practical example is a minister of state who has power to delegate authority to an official to make determinations imposing a fee payable by a licence holder. The other terms in each extended box will be identified by the standard correlative and jural opposite relationships read mutatis mutandis. The subsequent boxes will result from similar extensions.

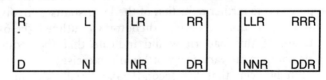

Diagram 3

Bentham states that there is no species of law which confers powers, only imperfect mandates where a law imposing a duty is partly blank and therefore must be filled up by holders of a power.[14] Such a distinction between an imperfect mandate and a higher order power would seem, however, to be overly sophisticated.

The first extension is derived only from the first box in relation to Hohfeldian duties. It is also possible to construct a second series of boxes on the other side of the original box by imposing the first box upon Hohfeldian liberties, as opposed to duties. For example, a public servant has a liberty to give an individual a driver's licence, and thereby the liberty to drive. This extension also repeats infinitely, in a similar fashion to the first extension. Thus there is a liberty to impose a liberty, and so on.

---

14   H L A Hart, 1982, note 11 above, p 170.

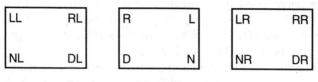

Diagram 4

This second series of boxes is ignored by the Sumner approach outlined above, and is subsumed under the general concept of power.

The liberty/duty dichotomy

Closer investigation of the second box of Hohfeld's original theory reveals that it is not an exact replica of the first box. Although power and liability relate easily to liberty and no-right, immunity and disability relate not to right and duty, but to **duty-not** and **right-not**. A disability is a duty not to impose a Hohfeldian duty, and an immunity is a right that no duty be imposed or a right not to have a duty imposed. The true opposite of a power, (when interpreted as a liberty to impose a duty), cannot be a duty to impose a duty. It is a duty-not to impose a duty (a disability).

This discrepancy is in fact a derivation of an imprecision in the first box which was first identified, albeit partially, by Williams.[15] Each of the four Hohfeldian terms in the first box can be expressed in both the positive and the negative versions of the status it denotes. Let us consider the following cases.

(a) I have a **right-to** be paid under the contract. (R+)
(b) I have a **right-not** to be assaulted. (I have a right that you not assault me.) (R-)
(c) I have a **duty-to** pay under the contract. (D+)
(d) I have a **duty-not** to assault you. (D-)
(e) I have a **liberty-to** walk on my land. (L+)
(f) I have a **liberty-not** to attend the jurisprudence class. (L-)
(g) I have **no-right** that you attend the jurisprudence class. (N+)
(h) I have **no-right** that you not walk upon your land. For convenience, I shall call this status **no-right-not**. (N-)

Thus, when we ask the question: 'what is the opposite of liberty?' we need to clarify whether we mean **liberty-to** (L+) or **liberty-not** (L-). Depending on which we mean, we will get a different answer. If I have a **liberty-to** (L+) walk on my land, it means that I have no **duty-not** (D-) to walk on my land. If I have a **liberty-not** (L-) to walk on my land, I have no **duty-to** (D+) walk on my land. Conversely, my **duty-to** (D+) walk on my land is not the opposite of a **liberty-to** (L+) walk on my land but is the opposite of **liberty-not** (L-) to walk on my land. From this viewpoint, it is observed that a **duty-to** (D+) can co-exist with **liberty-to** (L+). Hohfeld himself identified this fact by giving the example of a landowner contracting with

15   G L Williams, 1956, note 4 above, p 1135.

an outside party to go upon his own land.[16] In that case the landowner will have both a **duty-to** (D+) and a **liberty-to** (L+) enter his land. Therefore **duty-to** (D+) and **liberty-to** (L+) cannot be opposites. The opposites are **liberty-to** (L+) and **duty-not** (D-).

Thus, to deploy the Hohfeldian scheme in a manner which satisfies the correlative and opposite relationships, we need to indicate whether we are using the relevant Hohfeldian term in the positive or negative sense. This means that we have to recognise the fact that there are in fact two editions of the first box of Hohfeldian relations. These two editions are displayed in Diagram 5.

Right to	Liberty not		Right not	Liberty to
Duty to	No right to		Duty not	No right not

Diagram 5

Hohfeld in fact pre-empted Williams' restatement of the liberty/duty dichotomy.[17] He stated that privilege (liberty) is only the negation of duty where the duty has a content precisely opposite to the privilege. Thus a **duty** to *pay money* is the opposite of a **liberty** to *not pay the money*. In effect, Hohfeld incorporated the negation into the subject matter of the terms, instead of into the terms themselves, as Williams did. The latter approach is preferable, as the object is to identify the relationships between the various terms when the subject matter of the terms remains constant. Changing subject matter merely confuses the issue.

Once the second box and subsequent repetitions are identified as relating to **liberty-to** (L+) and **duty-not** (D-), the next question is whether a further extension can be engineered with **liberty-not** (L-) and **duty-to** (D+) as the starting points. In other words, could such an extension be constructed using the second 'edition' of the first box set out in Diagram 5. If so, the second extension could also be replicated in a similar manner, leading to four extensions in total.

At first glance it would appear that such an extension is strictly not necessary. The terms in one edition of the box are easily converted to the terms of the other edition. For example, the phrase 'the **duty-to** (D+) pay money' can be rephrased as 'the **duty-not** (D-) to not pay money'.

However, the same cannot be said of the second box. Superficially, it would seem that the process used in the first box can be replicated. Thus:

(a) The phrase 'the **liberty-not** (L-) to impose a duty' may be rephrased as 'the **liberty-to** (L+) not impose a duty'.

(b) The phrase 'the **duty-to** (D+) impose a duty' may be rephrased as 'the **duty-not** (D-) to not impose a duty'.

---

16   W N Hohfeld, 1913–1914, note 1 above, p 32.

17   W N Hohfeld, 1913–1914, p 32.

However, the second box, when dealing with the basic liberty/duty dichotomy, applies to the positive concepts of duty and liberty only. This dichotomy is the starting point for both original extensions outlined above. The original extensions relate only to the positive elements of the above statuses, and so cannot include extensions based upon the negative versions of the basic dichotomy. Thus the terms of the basic dichotomy cannot easily be amended to 'not impose a duty' and 'not impose a liberty' in the same way as the basic acts dealt with by the first box. **Duty-not** *to impose a duty* cannot be described as a **duty** to *not impose a duty*, because it would no longer be a repetition of the first box, which deals with *impose a duty*, and not *not impose a duty*. Thus the conversion of one repetition to the other by shifting the 'not' cannot take place without taking the legal statuses outside the fundamental repetition of the concepts liberty and duty upon themselves.

For full description of legal statuses, it would appear necessary to have a separate set of extensions encompassing **liberty-not** and **duty-to** imposed upon the basic liberty/duty dichotomy (see Diagram 6).

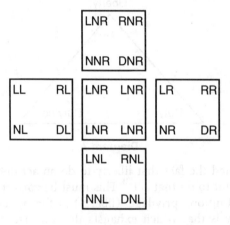

Diagram 6

However, it will later be shown that, by analysing the concept of liberty more closely, it can be seen that a group of extensions such as the second does in fact represent duplication. This duplication is of a different nature to that discussed, and rejected, above.

'Liberty' as 'no-duty' — further thoughts on the meaning of 'liberty'

Despite receiving almost universal approval for his incorporation of a negation into the liberty/duty dichotomy,[18] Williams' gloss on the Hohfeldian theory has been misinterpreted or disregarded on a number of occasions. Dias[19] states that Hohfeld's privilege is the freedom to do or not

---

18   J W Harris, 1980, note 7 above, p 81; R W Dias, 1976, note 6 above, p 28;
      Lord Lloyd, *Introduction to Jurisprudence*, 4th ed, Stevens, London, 1985,
      p 444.

19   R W Dias, 1976, note 6 above, p 28.

to do something, while Lloyd[20] characterises the situation where a person is free to do or not to do something as a privilege or a liberty. For this reason, it is useful to examine ways of restating the concept of liberty in a manner which will help ease the confusion which surrounds it.

The majority of examples used to describe liberty, eg the liberty to walk on one's land, involve freedom of choice. In popular parlance, the word 'liberty' is used to mean the freedom of choice. This usage is perfectly reasonable in most contexts. However, in some legal contexts, and certainly in relation to Hohfeld's scheme, the use of the word liberty in the sense of freedom of choice can lead to serious difficulties. If full freedom of choice is denoted by the term liberty, it would encompass the conditions of both **liberty-to** and **liberty-not**, as defined by Williams. Further, it would make liberty the opposite of both **duty-to** and **duty-not**. This would lead to a three-sided diagram of the possible states of a person's legal condition (see Diagram 7).

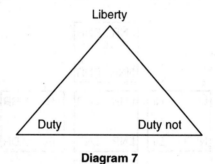

Diagram 7

Williams identified the fact that liberty-to do an act does not necessarily imply a liberty-not to do that act.[21] This must be correct, since, according to Hohfeld's definition, 'privilege' (liberty) is the opposite of duty. The opposite of duty is that which exhausts the universe of discourse apart from duty, and must simply be no duty. This concept is not equal to freedom of choice to act or not to act. A liberty in the sense of the freedom to choose consists of both no **duty-to** act, and no **duty-not** to act. The opposite of duty only comprises half of this combination. As stated previously, it is possible for both **duty-to** and **liberty-to** (no **duty-not** to) to exist concurrently. Thus, there is a subset of no duty that does not amount to full freedom of choice, ie where there is no **duty-to** act but there is a **duty-not** to act. It can be seen that a liberty in the sense of freedom of choice is in fact the combination of no **duty-to** and no **duty-not** to in the one person at the same time. The use of the terms **no duty-to** and **no duty-not** to is preferable to the terms **liberty-to** and **liberty-not** because of the inevitable association of the term liberty with full freedom of choice. The entire situation is illustrated in Diagram 8.

20   Lord Lloyd, 1985, note 18 above, p 444.
21   G L Williams, 1956, note 4 above, p 1140.

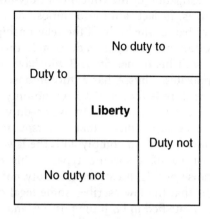

Diagram 8

In this diagram, the horizontal axis represents the entire universe of discourse with respect to a given basic act. At any point on the horizontal axis, a person will have all of the legal statuses described by the zones intersected by a vertical perpendicular at that point. Thus if I have a **duty-to** do an act, I will have no **duty-not** to do that act. If I have **no duty-to** do an act, I may have either a **duty-not** to do the act, or **no duty-not** to do the act, with the latter amounting to a full liberty when combined with the no **duty-to** act. Thus the entire set of legal statuses is represented by the horizontal axis.

The dichotomy of duty/no-duty is therefore the irreducible element of the entire Hohfeldian scheme. The correlative rights and no-rights are not essential to the basic structure of the analysis, as they merely reflect the effect of the duty or no-duty status on another person. The correlative terms are entirely dependent upon the basic dichotomy. A right can only exist if a duty exists, and so on. Thus the boxes can be reduced to the single dichotomy of duty/no-duty.

The horizontal extensions outlined previously result from the repetition of this dichotomy upon itself, and upon each of the elements of the subsequent extensions, *ad infinitum*. The vertical extensions result from the repetition of the duty-not/no duty-not dichotomy upon the basic duty no-duty dichotomy. The entire Hohfeldian analysis can therefore be diagrammatically illustrated as follows:

Diagram 9

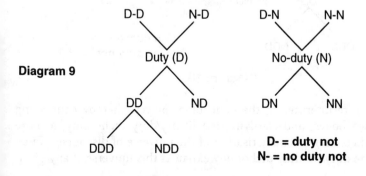

However, closer investigation of the concept of duty-not to impose a duty (D-D) reveals that it is, in fact, a duty to impose no-duty, and therefore covered by the lower half of the 'web'. If the relationship between A and B is such that A has a duty not to impose a duty on B, this necessarily means that, if A complies with his or her duty, B will have no-duty, since duty and no-duty are opposites. Thus A has a duty imposed upon him or her, and the effect of this duty is that B will have no-duty. This is effectively the same as saying that A has a duty to impose no-duty upon B.

Duty does not necessarily mean that a person must do something positive. It merely means that, to comply with the law in a given area, his or her actions must be of a specific type, ie his or her conduct is circumscribed. Because of this, it can include duty not to as well as duty to. The vital point is that the law ascribes some legal consequence to his or her act, and this is satisfied in both the positive and negative aspects of duty. Thus a duty on A to act in a way that gives rise to a no-duty in B (a duty not to impose a duty) is just as much a duty as a duty on A to act in a way that does give rise to a duty in B. The duty relates to the legal restriction on the freedom to act, not to whether the practical consequences of that act are of a positive or negative character.

The translation is clearer when the word 'impose' is replaced with a less restrictive term. In the case of the 'imposition' of a no-duty, the word 'allow' would seem to be more appropriate. In fact, it is most appropriate to describe a duty to impose a duty as a legal restriction on freedom of action which, if complied with, gives rise to a duty in another person. Such a description will apply equally to the 'imposition' of a no-duty. Thus the relationship is not so much a question of imposition, which implies creation of something positive through dominance, as a question of inevitable causation through compliance with the legal duty.

In the same way that a duty not to impose a duty can be described as a duty to impose no-duty, no-duty not to impose a no-duty can be described as no-duty to impose a duty, and so on with all of the terms in the upper half of the web. Thus, there is no need for a duty not and a no duty not — they do not add to the descriptive capacity of the model. The repetition of the basic dichotomy duty/no-duty upon itself is all that is required for a complete description of the universe of discourse.

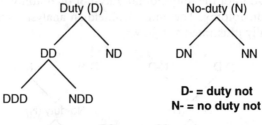

Diagram 10

Therefore, by re-interpreting the concept of power, thereby connecting Hohfeld's two boxes, and clarifying the liberty/duty dichotomy, a more rigorous and coherent characterisation of the universe of discourse can be achieved. The duty/no-duty dichotomy exhausts this universe at any given level, and repetition of the dichotomy allows the analysis to cover all levels. Thus the full potential of Hohfeld's analysis is attained, with any legal status able to be easily classified. Even if the re-interpretation outlined in this chapter is not directly in line with Hohfeld's original definition of terms, I would assert the new analysis as a competing interpretation, as its internal logical consistency and fundamental aesthetic appeal must give it some attraction as a description of the universe of discourse.

Definition of duty and no-duty as the premise of a syllogism

The concept of liberty, then, can be defined as the combination of a no duty to, and a no duty not to. How then, is a no duty to be defined? The obvious answer of an absence of duty is accurate but unhelpful. For a meaningful definition of liberty to be reached, it is necessary to formulate a positive definition of no-duty.

In essence, a no-duty identifies a method of conduct which is *sufficient* for compliance with the law. If I have a no-duty to X, I will satisfy the law by not acting 'X' ie if I have a no-duty to go to the shop it is sufficient to satisfy the law if I do not go to the shop. I cannot have a duty to go to the shop (which I would then breach by not doing so) because I have a no-duty to go to the shop, ie its opposite. It is important to note that the way of 'complying'[22] with a no-duty is by doing the opposite of what seems to be its content; therefore, I 'comply' with a **no-duty-not** to go to the shop by going **to** the shop, and I 'comply' with a **no-duty to** go to the shop by **not** going to the shop.

A no-duty, however, does not identify whether such conduct is *necessary* for compliance with the law. If I have a no-duty to go to the shop, and therefore comply with the law by not going to the shop, it remains unknown whether I may also comply with the law by going to the shop, ie whether I have a duty-not to go to the shop, or no-duty-not to do so. Thus a no duty specifies only a *sufficient* condition, not a *necessary* condition.

A duty, on the other hand, identifies a sufficient and necessary condition of compliance with the law. If I have a duty to go to the shop, the one and only way that I can comply with the law is to go to the shop. It is a final status. Conduct required by law is fully identified by a duty. In contrast, conduct required by law (ie necessary) is not fully determined by a no-duty, and is dependent upon the further legal status of duty-not/no-duty-not.

This dichotomy between necessary and sufficient conditions has a parallel in the field of pure logic and syllogisms. The classic example of the syllogism is as follows:

1   All philosophers are intelligent.
2   Aristotle is a philosopher.
3   Therefore, Aristotle is intelligent.

---

22   Note that 'comply' is used imprecisely here as a no-duty is not finally prescriptive — it is not possible to comply with something that does not finally prescribe anything. *Comply* is used to mean something akin to *follow*.

From the major premise that all philosophers are intelligent, the following conclusions can be drawn.

1   It is sufficient (but not necessary) for intelligence that you be a philosopher. (It is not sufficient for the status of being a philosopher that you be intelligent — hence, if Aristotle is intelligent, it does not necessarily follow that he is a philosopher.)

2   It is necessary to be a philosopher that you are intelligent.

Thus, if we have the statement 'If X, then Y', it means that the existence of X is sufficient for the existence of Y, and the existence of Y is necessary for the existence of X. Thus the 'forward' relationship is one of sufficiency, and the 'backward' relationship is one of necessity.

Since we have identified duty as a necessary condition, and no-duty as a sufficient condition, we can incorporate the conditions they deal with into a syllogism. Duty and no-duty relate the conditions of a given act (say act X) and compliance with the law as it applies to that act. Thus to get a relationship of sufficiency (a no-duty) a 'forward' relationship is called for, and so the order is:

1   If X exists, then compliance exists.

Thus, X is a sufficient but not necessary condition of compliance with the law. This also demonstrates that it is necessary for act X to exist, that compliance with the law also exists (one cannot act X without also complying with the law). However, X is not a necessary condition of compliance with the law (you can comply with the law in other ways), nor is compliance with the law a sufficient condition of X.

In contrast, to get a relationship of necessity (a duty), a backward relationship is needed, and so the terms are reversed:

2   If compliance exists, then X exists.

Thus, X is necessary for the existence of compliance, and compliance is a sufficient condition for the existence of X. However, this premise alone would also mean that compliance is not necessary for the existence of X, and that the existence of X would not be sufficient for the existence of compliance, ie that there is some way of complying by doing the act X without complying with the law.

However, the fact is that in the case of a duty, if you comply with the duty (ie act X), then you inevitably comply with the law — it is impossible not to. Thus it is necessary for X's existence that compliance also exist, and the existence of X is sufficient for compliance to exist. Hence, a duty also involves the reverse premise: if X exists, then compliance exists, as this implies the two conditions just set out.

A duty then consists of two premises:

1   If compliance, then X.

2   If X then compliance.

The point to note is that the second of these is in fact the premise that exists as a no-duty. If X then compliance is simply a way of saying no-duty-not to X. A duty always consists of a no-duty, with a further premise tacked on to the top. This explains the way that in Diagram 8, it seemed that if a duty exists, then a no-duty-not also exists. This can now be explained by the demonstration that a no-duty-not represents half of the premises that a duty consists of.

Hence, we finally have, in the most basic of logical components, namely the major premise of a syllogism, the constituent parts of a duty and no-duty. Hohfeld's ambition of reducing all legal statuses to their most basic elements has been taken to its ultimate conclusion.

Definition of liberty

Since no-duties can be described as 'If act X, then comply with the law', a number of no-duties can be joined together and built up to create a list of possible acts, the doing of which will comply with the law. The classic example is the way that a no-duty to X can be added to a no-duty-not to X to create a full liberty, whether to X or not.

Accordingly, we could create a model of a person's legal status that consists of a vast array of all the possible acts in a person's universe. Each act would be an atom. An atom that has no-duty painted on it represents acts that the person can engage in without breaching the law. In contrast, atoms that have duty painted on them represent acts that will result in a person breaching the law. Thus, a person's activity is restricted to the no-duty atoms — he or she must choose how to act from amongst those atoms. Without intervention of the law, every atom is a no duty. As the law intervenes, it converts no-duty atoms to duty atoms, and thus restricts the range of possibilities that a person has when choosing how to act. If my no-duty to X (ie I am free to not X) is converted to a duty to X, all of a sudden I am no longer free to not X — that mode of action has been taken away from me. This is an accurate description of the way the law intervenes and effectively turns off the lights of atoms, leaving fewer lit atoms to choose from.

Exactly what these atoms consist of however is an important question. The addition of the atoms relating to X and not X would seem to be fundamentally different to the addition of atoms relating to X and Y. Once you can X and you can not X, you have identified all the possibilities in relation to act X — the two are clearly linked. In contrast, a no duty to Y is not so related to X. This demonstrates the way that duties and no-duties specify the acts required for compliance with the law *as it applies to that act, and that act alone*. Thus a duty to X describes the act (X) necessary for compliance with the law as it applies to act X, and no-duty to X describes an act (not X) that is sufficient to comply with the law as it applies to act X, but neither of these legal statuses prescribe anything about act Y. The extensive relationships between duty and no-duty discussed above hold true only for the one act — X.

It may reasonably be asked, why do the acts X and not X have to be treated as related? A no-duty to X and a no-duty-not to X seem to concern two different acts, each of which, when done, results in compliance with the law. In fact, in their no-duty form, X and not X are not related. A no-duty to X has no effect on one's status with respect to not X — ie it is unknown whether I have a duty to not X or a no-duty to not X; in the same way that a no-duty to X has no effect upon one's status with respect to Y. When I say that I comply with the law by following my no duty with respect to X, it says no more about whether I comply with the law as it applies to not X than it does about whether I comply with the law as it applies to Y.

The situation would, at first glance, seem to be different when we are dealing with a duty to or a duty-not. The point is that a duty always implies a corresponding no-duty. Reading once again from Diagram 8, a duty to implies a no-duty-not, and a duty-not implies a no-duty to. The point is that, if you have a duty to X, you cannot have a duty-not to X at the same time, because it is impossible to both X and not X at the same time. Hence, if you have a duty to X, you must have no-duty-not to X. Although in their no-duty forms, the act X and not X would seem to be quite unrelated, once either of them transforms into a duty, it fixes the other into a duty-not, and finally determines the legal acts status existing for both X and not X. On this basis, it would seem that X and not X should always be taken together, since the law applying to X may determine the law applying to not X.

This interpretation suggests that each atom should be regarded as the combination of the X and not X acts. Since the two acts must be regarded as intertwined, the most basic legal status, ie the atom in our model, should be the combination of the two. We will have an atomic status based upon the combination of X and not X, and will consist of three possibilities — duty to X, duty-not to X, and liberty whether to X or not. This is the basis of the argument that a no-duty is not a real world status. Since a no-duty to X will always have a corresponding duty-not to X or no-duty-not to X, there is no point in analysing it as a separate legal status, since it cannot live without its correspondent. If I have a liberty, I know what effect the law has upon whether I can act or not. If I merely have a no-duty, I do not finally know what my legal status with respect to a given act is.

I will now demonstrate why this reasoning is flawed, why no-duty is just as much a real world status as a full liberty, why the atom should be split into X and not X, and why the status of having a duty with respect to X in fact has no impact upon whether I have a duty or no-duty with respect to not X.

As discussed above, no-duties with respect to X and not X can be regarded as logically independent. Thus the combination of X and not X into the one atom is based upon the way that a duty to X seems to prescribe a corresponding no-duty-not to X, and does not allow free determination of duty or no-duty with respect to not X. However, this is in fact not the case. In fact, the existence of a duty to X says nothing about whether there is a duty not to X or no duty not to X. This can be ascertained from the premises that make up duties and no duties.

A no duty not to X can be described as the premise 'if X, then comply with the law'. This is the most basic element that has been ascertained with respect to legal statuses. As shown above, duty not seems in fact to be a compound status — if not X then Y, and if Y then not X. Thus we should start with a no duty as the most basic, irreducible legal status. From there we should identify what a duty really consists of. The answer is quite remarkable.

Imagine we have the atom no duty not to X floating about in space. The law intervenes and converts it to a duty atom — what really happens? The no duty is the premise 'if X then comply with the law' (I will substitute Y for 'comply with the law' — so 'if X then Y'). What the law does by intervening is to say that 'if X then Y' is not true. This is in fact the transformation that takes place between Hohfeld's opposites. A no duty no longer exists — the premise is not true. The question is, exactly what can be implied from this assertion?

If 'if X then Y' is not true, there are two possibilities:

1   If X then not Y.
2   If X, then maybe Y.

Both of these relationships are exclusive of 'if X then Y'. It would seem that which one is the case cannot be specified. However, if we recall that Y stands for 'comply with the law', the second possibility is removed.

This is because it is impossible for an act to have an uncertain legal status. It is not plausible to say that if you go to the shop, you may or may not break the law. The legal system is fundamentally binary; it operates by saying yes or no to the question 'is the law broken'. It is impossible that I could do the same act, under the same law, and not suffer the same consequence. Even in a situation where an administrative discretion is involved, it cannot be said that it is unknown what legal status a given act possesses. The nature of the exercise of the discretion becomes part of the fact in question, and once the discretion is exercised, the legal status becomes certain.

Hence, 'if X then maybe Y' is not a plausible relationship in the case of Y being compliance with the law. Thus when 'if X then Y is not true', the only other alternative — 'if X then not Y' must be true.

Therefore, whatever a duty, as the opposite of a no duty, consists of, it must be able to be found in the premise 'if X then not Y'.

'If X then not Y' has two implications:

1   X is sufficient for not Y.
2   Not Y is necessary for X.

If *X is sufficient for not Y*, then *not X is necessary for Y*. This is a basic transformation of a premise. If X inevitably causes not Y, if Y exists, then X cannot exist, ie not X exists.

Similarly, if not Y is necessary for X, Y is sufficient for not X. Once Y exists, X can no longer exist, so not X must exist.

Thus we have created the following two situations:

1   Not X is necessary for Y.
2   Y is sufficient for not X.

These are the implications of the premise 'if Y then not X', or 'if comply with the law, then not X'.

From our definition above of duty, it can be seen that this is only part of what seemed to be the constituent parts of duty. Certainly 'if Y then not X' is part of a duty not to X. However, it seemed that a duty not also consisted of an underlying no duty to X, ie 'if not X then Y'. What the above discussion illustrates is that the mere absence of a no duty not does not necessarily imply the existence of a no duty to. So if 'if X then Y' is not true, 'if Y then not X' is true, but 'if not X then Y' is not necessarily true.

Therefore, the real, technical definition of a duty not (when defined as the opposite of a no-duty-not) is only the syllogism 'if Y then not X', or in other words, if you comply with the law, you must have done the act not X. The above discussion illustrates the fact that it does not imply the further syllogism 'if not X then Y', ie that you also have no duty to X. If no duty is defined by the syllogism 'if X then Y', its opposite is only part of what constitutes a duty in the classical sense.

Hence a duty in the classical sense is in fact a composite status, comprising two syllogisms. The most basic, irreducible legal status is only one of these syllogisms. This single syllogism is what can now be described as a no-duty in the positive sense, where it is defined not as the opposite of a duty, but in a positive manner as the basic syllogism. A duty as classically defined is not the opposite of this concept, but a composite status including as one of its constituent parts that opposite. The basic 'no-duty' syllogism, as the most basic status, represents the true building block of duties, liberties, and all other 'real world' legal statuses.

One of the impacts of this analysis is that the opposite of a no-duty is not a full duty in the classical sense, and hence is in fact independent of whether there is a coexisting no duty not. This means that the atom dealing with the act 'to X', operates independently of the atom 'to not X'. The existence of the opposite of the basic status 'to X means compliance with the law' is not predicated upon the existence of the corresponding 'to not X means compliance with the law'. So the conclusion arises that there are in fact two separate atoms, relating to the positive and negative versions of an act. These atoms toggle between, respectively, 'duty to' and 'no-duty to' (for the positive atom), and 'duty-not' and 'no-duty-not' (for the negative atom — although duty is being used here not in the classical sense, but as a description of the opposite status to the single syllogism no duty). The above analysis indicates that these two atoms are as independent as two atoms which relate to entirely different acts. So the acts 'X' and 'not X' should be regarded as unrelated, in the same way that the acts X and B are unrelated. Or, to use common terms, the acts of going to the shop and not going to the shop are as legally unrelated as going to the shop and murdering your mother-in-law.

Thus there are two independent atoms floating around in the space that is a person's legal position. The base condition is for every imaginable act to be in the no-duty condition. The intrusion of the law can be seen as the conversion of the no-duty condition into a duty condition, and the subsequent removal of that act from the realm of possible acts a person can perform without breaching the law. The conversion of one atom to a duty does not affect any other atom. Thus we have a broad reaching liberty, which is taken away, piece by piece, by the intrusion of law converting no-duties to duties.

This atomic model also demonstrates the fact that the status of liberty to act or not to act is inherently a conglomerate, and is in no way basic. The underlying statuses of no-duty to and no-duty-not to are legitimate, real world, statuses, which can be added up in the same way as dissimilar acts to form a range of possible legal acts.

It is this range or field of no-duty atoms which truly constitutes the definition of a person's liberty. A liberty is, in truth, the sum of all the acts represented by no-duty atoms, and excludes the duty atoms. It is inappropriate to speak of liberty as a basic status with respect to any act — it is the no-duty attached to the specific act which plays that role. The liberty is essentially the sum of possibilities represented by those no-duty atoms and from which a person has liberty to choose.

Does a liberty involve a protective right not to be interfered with?

One of the most consistent assertions made about Hohfeld's scheme is that a liberty to do an act is quite separate from a right not to be interfered with in the enjoyment of the liberty.[23] It has been suggested that although the two often coincide, with duties not to interfere protecting the liberty, this coincidence is not a logical necessity. The assertion is sought to be justified on the basis that a number of situations exist where a liberty is not supported by an associated right. I will use the new definition of power as the liberty to impose a duty to explain these situations in terms that demonstrate that liberties, by their very nature, are protected by rights.

The most comprehensive list of examples of liberties not protected by duties is given by Williams.[24] One of the examples he gives concerns the situation of a licence to use land given by the landowner. It is said that in such a case, the licensee has a liberty to go upon the land, but the landowner has a corresponding liberty to prevent him, and therefore has no duty not to interfere. This situation can, however, be more accurately described as follows:

(a) The landowner has a duty not to interfere with the licensee's liberty during the subsistence of the licence.

(b) The landowner has a power to take away the licensee's liberty by revoking the licence, thereby imposing a duty not to walk upon the land. Until such power is exercised, however, the duty not to interfere exists.

This analysis reflects the legal position in most jurisdictions. When a licensee enters a piece of land, he or she commits no trespass. The landowner violates the law by forcibly evicting a licensee contrary to the licence. The landowner may perform the juridical act which terminates the licence while the licensee is on the land. The required juridical act may be simply the verbal communication of the fact of revoking the licence, by words such as: 'I ask you not to re-enter this land'. Upon such revocation, the ex-licensee would have a duty to leave the land. But until the performance of the juridical act, he or she enjoys the liberty and also a right that the landowner not interfere with his or her entry.

---

23   See eg, J Finnis, 'Some Professorial Fallacies about Rights', (1972) *Adelaide Law Review* 377; W N Hohfeld, 1913–1914, note 1 above, p 35; G L Williams, 1956, note 4 above, p 1143; W J Kamba, 1974, note 8 above, p 252.
24   G L Williams, 1956, note 4 above, p 1144.

The conventional argument is more poignantly illustrated by Gray's shrimp salad affair, discussed by Hohfeld, Stone, Finnis, and effectively by Dias and Williams who give examples that are substantially similar. In this illustration, A gives B a licence to eat a shrimp salad, but does not agree not to interfere. Thus, the argument goes, B has a liberty to eat the salad, and A also has a liberty to interfere. Whether B succeeds in eating the salad depends upon whether A is physically successful in interfering. The law has little to say in this situation, success being purely a question of physical pre-eminence, there being no duties on either party to refrain from eating or to refrain from interfering. However, it is my view that even in this situation, it is possible to demonstrate that the liberty is accompanied by a protecting right.

If A succeeds in preventing B from eating the salad, the law will do nothing about it. It seems very difficult, then, to assert that B truly has a legal liberty to eat the salad. B cannot eat the salad, and the law has acquiesced in this situation. This can hardly be suggested as being different to the situation where the law imposes a duty on B not to eat the salad. It is illogical to create a distinction between directly imposing a duty not to act in a given way, and indirectly preventing that act, since the eventual legal effect is identical, even though the means used are very different. The important thing is that the law's acquiescence in physical prevention of an act has exactly the same legal effect as the direct imposition of a duty. If A intervenes, B cannot eat the salad, and has no legal remedy. If B has a duty not to eat the salad, this has exactly the same legal effect, ie B cannot eat the salad.

The situation is, of course, quite different where B does succeed in eating the salad. Here, B's liberty to eat the salad remains. A is unable to stop B eating the salad, and has no legal redress for that situation. Thus, under the same principle as outlined above, A really has a duty not to interfere. Thus the point at which the relations change is that of successful interference by A. It would therefore be better to interpret the situation as an original liberty in B to eat the salad, with a corresponding duty in A not to interfere, and a power in A to impose a duty on B not to eat the salad if he succeeds in physically interfering. Thus the interference, although the breach of a duty, is also the exercise of a power which renders the duty obsolete, and removes the liberty of the other person.

A is unable to interfere until he does physically stop B. Thus (using the logic outlined above), he effectively has a duty not to interfere until that time. After being stopped, B cannot eat the salad and therefore has a duty not to. The conversion between these two situations is the exercise of a power, at the point when A successfully interferes.

It may be argued that it is impossible for A to have a duty not to interfere when the law allows him to interfere, and so seems to give him a liberty. It is axiomatic that a liberty and a duty cannot co-exist. However, it is not duty and liberty that co-exist, but duty and power. Since these two concepts originate from different Hohfeldian boxes, they can legitimately co-exist. A can interfere, notwithstanding his duty not to do so, because he is empowered to interfere and remove the duty, not because he ever had a liberty to do so. A does not breach the duty when he interferes because he simultaneously exercises a power, thereby removing the duty.

The key to this puzzle is the fact that the law permits A to bring to an end B's liberty to eat the shrimp salad by a successful act of physical interference. This is not an unusual provision of law. The laws of football (which have legal status owing, *inter alia*, to implications of the law of contract and the law of torts) provides a very similar example. A player in possession of the ball has the liberty to keep moving towards the opponents' try line until such time as he is effectively pinned to the ground by opponents. The successful interference by the defenders brings to an end the offensive player's liberty to move with the ball. Similarly, in the unusual situation presented by Gray's shrimp salad affair, the successful interference by A in the eating of the shrimp brings to an end B's liberty to eat the salad. Thus the point at which the legal relations change is that of successful physical interference by A. Interference, whether it be on the part of A in Gray's shrimp salad affair or on the part of the defender in the football game does not amount to a breach of duty. In each case, the successful projection of physical power (sanctioned by law) is the juridical act which brings to an end the other party's liberty. In other words, in each case the projection of the physical power amounts to the exercise of a power in the Hohfeldian sense.

The example Williams uses that equates to Gray's shrimp salad affair is that of two people seeing a gold watch lying on the road.[25] He asserts that both individuals have a liberty to run and pick up the watch, and neither have a duty not to interfere with the other. I believe this is better interpreted as both parties having a duty not to interfere, but whichever one physically succeeds in picking up the watch first exercises a power removing his duty not to interfere and imposing a duty on the other not to pick up the watch.

The question arises immediately whether every act of physical interference with liberty is an exercise of Hohfeldian power. After all, if I assault you, I create in you a liberty to sue me and, if the court agrees with your version of events, even a right that I pay you damages. This case is clearly distinguishable from Gray's shrimp salad affair, the football game and the case of the gold watch. In the case of the straightforward assault I have acted in breach of a subsisting duty. In the shrimp salad affair and the football game, the law sanctions the assault. In the case of the gold watch, the law legitimates a different type of conflict, but a conflict all the same. In the case of the straightforward assault, the law did not permit or condone the assault and my success in assaulting you does not change that position. My duty not to assault you was not extinguished by my act of assault. I have merely created a factual situation where the law grants you the liberty to sue me.

The conclusion to be drawn from this analysis is that a physical act can amount to an exercise of Hohfeldian power only if it is a 'juridical act' as the term is used by Finnis.[26] Not all those physical acts that create legal

---

25 G L Williams, 1956, p 1143.
26 J Finnis, 1980, note 5 above, p 200.

rights and duties can be described as exercises of power. The act must be one that is sanctioned by law. Thus a bare assault, although it gives rise to a liberty to sue could never be regarded as the exercise of a power. Although the interference in the eating of the salad breaches an original duty, the physical act is a power because it brings the duty to an end. The duty is not rendered obsolete, however, with a simple assault. The law does not then step in and protect the assaulter, as it does the person who exercises a power by physical act. Thus the definition of power must be limited to acts authorised by law.

If the foregoing analysis is valid, it fatally undermines the assertion that a liberty can exist without a duty on the part of someone not to interfere with it. The analysis compels the conclusion that there are just two irreducible legal statuses. One is where the law permits a person to do an act. The other is where the law does not permit a person to do an act. This conclusion is consistent with the layman's commonsense view that under the law, you either can or cannot do an act. The analysis renders unnecessary a third category where you are allowed to do something, but someone else can stop you doing it. By utilising the new definition of power, and identifying a legally sanctioned inability to act as a duty, the innately appealing interpretation of all liberties being protected by duties not to interfere can be adopted.

Essentially, whether this analysis or the classical approach outlined by Williams is adopted is merely a question of semantics. The substance of the legal status remains unchanged, regardless of whether a liberty is protected by a duty or not. As a result, my nomenclature can only really claim to be superior on the basis that it is more inherently appealing. As regards the assertion that all liberties are protected by duties, that claim can probably be justified. However, in making this assertion, it is necessary to state that a person running to collect a gold watch effectively has a duty not to do so, until he does succeed, in which case his duty is removed. Unfortunately, this interpretation must also be said to lack some inherent appeal.

A possible alternative analysis of the problem that allows all liberties to be protected by duties not to interfere is as follows. B (who has the salad) never had a liberty to eat the salad. All he had was a liberty to try to eat the salad, to eat it in accordance with the rules of the 'game' which allow A to interfere. A has a duty not to interfere outside the rules of the game. Thus he cannot shoot B to stop him eating the salad. Similarly, the football player never had a full liberty to carry the ball unopposed. He only had a liberty to carry the ball in accordance with the rules of the game, which allow the opposition to stop him.

The question then arises — what is the legal status of B with respect to the actual eating of the salad, without any conditions imposed upon that eating? It could be argued that B has no legal status regarding this act. The law does not impinge upon this scenario. It provides no duty upon A not to interfere. Thus there is a 'lawless' situation, in which A and B can effectively do what they will. This is outside the universe of discourse. Hart indicates that a completely naked or unprotected liberty should not be thought of as a 'right' (as the term is loosely used), and that a true legal liberty only exists where there is a perimeter of protecting obligations or duties.[27]

The earlier portion of this essay is based upon the assumption that as liberty is defined merely as the opposite of duty, it will encompass everything that is not duty, even if it is an extra-legal status like the one outlined above. However, it could be argued that the liberty/duty dichotomy is fundamentally normative, and therefore the dividing line between liberty and duty is a normative and essentially legal one. Hence it could be optimistic to suggest that a concept that is fundamentally legal in nature (ie liberty) can be used to describe a non-legal concept such as the lawless scenario described above.

Thus it is arguable that the legal status of liberty can only be used to describe a situation where the law has some impact. This is essentially a situation where duties and rights are imposed. If there is no duty to protect a liberty, a lawless situation arises. The classic example of this is where two people are on a desert island, beyond the jurisdiction of any legal system, and can therefore do what they will to each other. Williams would say that they both have absolute liberties, but the analysis above shows that it is better to say that they are in a situation that is beyond the universe of legal discourse, and so the term liberty is not suitable. Thus, we may come to the conclusion that if a liberty is not protected by a duty, it should in reality fall outside the universe of discourse, and not be called a liberty at all.

Conclusion

The second 'box' of terms which figure in Hohfeld's analysis has often been ignored.[28] However, close inquiry reveals that it is analogous to, and is essentially a repetition of the first box. This link between the two boxes reveals the possibility of reducing Hohfeld's scheme to a single repeating dichotomy. An appreciation of the link between the two boxes helps us to define more precisely the idea of liberty. The end result is that there are only two irreducible legal statuses: duty and no-duty, and one irreducible legal relationship between duty and no-duty. The effect is that Hohfeld is taken from being a source of continual consternation to a simple, straightforward yet rigorous and coherent method of describing and distinguishing between all the various legal statuses that a person may have. The basic dichotomy between no-duty and duty can be used to describe the concept of liberty as the addition of all acts in the world with the label 'no duty' attached to them. The intrusion of law is simply the conversion of no duty 'atoms' into duty atoms. Thus the term 'liberty' can at last be tied down and given a technical meaning. Its potency to influence and inflame matters beyond its technical application, however, is unlikely to be dimmed.

---

27   H L A Hart, 1982, note 11 above, p 173.
28   See eg, J Finnis, 1972, note 23 above, p 377.

CHAPTER 15

The Historical and Anthropological Tradition in Jurisprudence

R C Van Caenegem*

Legal history is an indispensable part of modern jurisprudence. Medieval jurists believed, according to Guillaume Budé's famous quip, that 'the Corpus Juris Civilis had fallen from heaven', and asked no further questions. Similarly, some people in past centuries thought that the English common law and constitution were born in the ancient forests of Germany. But today the critical jurist wants to know exactly where law came from, by whom it was created and developed, and for what purpose. It is to satisfy this curiosity that legal history arose and became an established discipline. It occupies a place on the curriculum of university law faculties and inspires the research of numerous scholars, who organise congresses and publish their findings in specialised periodicals and a vast number of monographs and textbooks throughout the world.

Beginnings of legal history

To note the present state of affairs is easy enough, but it is not so straightforward to find out how far it goes back. I for one was surprised that the existing literature had no ready answer to the question of when legal history originated as a distinct discipline. I thought that I would find a brief answer to my question (plus the relevant bibliography) in that useful work of reference, the *Handwörterbuch zur deutschen Rechtsgeschichte*, under the entry *Rechtsgeschichte*, but I was amazed and disappointed to find that there was no such entry, although there were entries for *Rechtsaltertümer*, *Rechtsarchäologie*, *Rechtsvergleichung* and *Vergleichende Rechtsgeschichte*. Thereupon, I began to consult various authorities, only to find, again to my surprise, that there was a considerable variety of

---

*   Emeritus Professor of Law, University of Gent, Belgium.

opinion as to when 'legal history' began. The issue was complicated further by the not always obvious distinction between real legal historians and mere antiquarians. It should be clear, for example, that the study of old law texts does not, in itself, amount to the study of legal history. The medieval glossators and commentators of the *Corpus Juris* spent all their time on a sixth century lawbook, but they were not legal historians: the *Corpus Juris* was studied not as a source of information on the ancient world, but as inspiration for a better legal system in late medieval Europe.

So when was legal history born? Some authorities place this event in the recent past. Karl Kroeschell calls legal history 'a relatively young discipline', a child of the early nineteenth century.[1] Hans Erich Feine, one of the leading historians of canon law of his time, maintained that Ulrich Stutz, a Swiss scholar who taught at Berlin and died in 1938, was the first to have really elevated the history of ecclesiastical law to the rank of an autonomous legal discipline.[2] These claims for the nineteenth century or even the twentieth century are, I believe, based on the narrow view that only history pursued by modern critical methods is worthy of the name. This is unfair to such great scholars as Hermann Conring (1606–1689), who published his *De Origine Juris Germanici* in 1643 and is often referred to as the founder of German legal history, or Sir Matthew Hale (1609–1676), Chief Justice of the King's Bench, whose *History of the Common Law* was posthumously published in 1713. It is true that the trained academic legal historian is a recent phenomenon, but the fact that past scholars took an active part in the political or judicial life of their countries does not diminish their merits as legal historians.

So where do we look for the pioneers? Not to the medieval civilians, as already mentioned, nor to their own great model, classical Roman law. It is generally known that legal history occupies a very modest place in the *Corpus Juris*. Digest, I, 2 devotes a brief passage of about seven columns in Mommsen's edition to the theme *De origine iuris et omnium magistratuum et successione prudentium*. The first of the 53 paragraphs is borrowed from Gaius, the others from Sextus Pomponius, who lived in the second century AD. Gaius explains that legal history is necessary because the origins of things are important. As he puts it, 'this is perfect which consists of all its parts, and surely the beginning is the most potent part of every thing'. Then follows Pomponius' narrative, which is essentially a list of magistrates and jurists and their works (the *iuris civilis scientia*), besides some information on the main constitutional changes in Rome since the time of the kings and the law of the 12 tables. It is noteworthy that nothing was added to Pomponius at the time of Justinian, so that Roman legal history between the second and the sixth century was a blank in the *Corpus*: the last emperor mentioned there is Vespasian (69–79 AD), and the last school of jurists is that of the Proculiani, who flourished under Hadrian (117–138 AD), Proculus himself having lived under Tiberius (14–37 AD).

---

1   K Kroeschell, *Deutsche Rechtsgeschichte*, vol I, Rowohlt, Hamburg, 1972, p 9.
2   H E Feine, *Kirchliche Rechtsgeschichte. Die Katholische Kirche*, Bohlau, Cologne, 1969, p vii. Feine is followed by A Erler, *Handwörterbuch zur deutschen Rechtsgeschichte*, fasc 33, E Schmidt, Berlin, 1971, col 68.

The humanist school of Roman law seems to have a solid claim to the title of founding fathers of European legal history. They were lawyers first and foremost and the *Corpus Juris* remained their polar star, but they saw it as the historical product of a particular civilisation. They used historical and philological methods to understand its meaning and saw the text of Justinian as a source of information for the study of antiquity, which was the overriding ambition of all humanists. Alciatus (1492–1550) and Cujas (1522–1590) were interested in the laws of antiquity, but some of their contemporaries devoted their attention to the laws of the Middle Ages. They studied the *leges nationum Germanicarum* and, in the sixteenth century, provided scholarly editions of, for example, the Salic Law, edited around 1550 by Bishop Jean du Tillet (d 1570) and in 1557 by the Basle scholar Johann Herold (d 1566).[3] In Hungary the *Registrum Varadinense* was first published in 1550,[4] whereas in Spain Lorenzo de Padilla (d 1540) published his *Leyes y fueros antiguos de España* and F de Espinosa (d 1551) his *Leyes y fueros de España.*[5] The civilians were similarly preparing scholarly editions of Roman law texts, either of the whole *Corpus* or of fragments. We think of Dionysius Gothofredus' edition of Justinian's laws in 1583, the best until Mommsen,[6] and of Viglius van Aytta's *editio princeps* of Theophilus' *Paraphrasis*, a Greek adaptation of Justinian's *Institutes* (1534).[7]

Others were concerned with a less remote past and pursued their historical research with political considerations in mind. Their work on the medieval records, however scholarly, had a practical purpose: they wanted to prove something of actual concern. One such scholar was Philip Wielant (1441–1520), jurist, judge and politician, who wrote the first book of legal history in the Low Countries, the *Recueil des Antiquités de Flandre.*[8] This constitutional and legal history of Flanders was written at a moment when the ancient conflict about sovereignty between the kings of France and the counts of Flanders was coming to a head. It was solved by the treaties of Madrid of 1526 and Cambrai of 1529 which severed the centuries-old feudal links between France and Flanders. Wielant pays great attention to this problem and notably to the appeals from Flemish law courts to the Parlement of Paris, which were the clearest manifestation of the country's jurisdictional subjection to the French Crown. Later in the same century, Sir Edward Coke (1552–1634), the most learned common lawyer of all time, began perusing hundreds of medieval court rolls in

---

3 *Pactus Legis Salicae* (ed K A Eckhardt), Impensis Bibliopolii Hahniani, Hanover, 1962, p xxvii (M G H LL Sectio I, t IV, pars 1).

4 Modern edition by J Karacsonyi and S Borovszky for the Hungarian Academy of Sciences, Budapest, 1903.

5 A Garcia-Gallo, *Manual de historia del derecho español*, vol I, V Suarez, Madrid, 1967, p 8.

6 E Spangenberg, *Einleitung in das Römisch-Justinianeische Rechtsbuch*, Hahn, Hanover, 1817, pp 839 ff.

7 Modern edition by C Ferrini, 2 vols, apud S Calvary eiusque socios, Berlin, 1884–1887.

8 *Recueil des chroniques de Flandre*, vol IV (ed J J de Smet), Commission Royale d'Histoire, Brussels, 1865.

order to ascertain the origin and growth of English law and to prepare his *Institutes* (1628-1641), a massive compilation and exposition of 400 years of common law. Modern scholars still peruse the same plea rolls[9] and they are undoubtedly legal historians, but this does not automatically mean that the same epithet applies to Coke — a point to which we shall return later. In the sixteenth century other English scholars were at work who justify Baker's remark: 'If ever the history of English legal history comes to be written the story will begin in the Elizabethan age: Lambard, Dodderidge, Tate, Owen, these legal antiquaries preoccupied with dark and distant problems about the origins of the common law.'[10]

The seventeenth century was a great age for medieval erudition, and legal historians in several countries turned their attention to the national past. Conring's previously mentioned *De Origine Juris Germanici* of 1643 has been called the first pragmatic history of the 'reception' of Roman law in Germany: the Thirty-Years War destroyed the old German Reich and with it the universal validity of Roman law.[11] In England Sir Henry Spelman (c 1564-1641), author of *The Ancient Government of England* and considered the earliest English historian of feudal law, traced the origin of English law to the ancient Germans, whom he called a 'most prime and potent people'.[12] Sir Matthew Hale (1609–1676) was one of the great characters of his age, deeply involved in politics and the law, and Chief Justice of the King's Bench. He not only wrote the first *History of the Common Law* but also the *Jurisdiction of the Lords' House* and, more importantly, a *History of the Pleas of the Crown*, the first history of English criminal law, a notoriously difficult field.[13]

It is less well known that even Hugo Grotius (1583–1645), famous as a civilian and humanist and one of the founders of modern natural law, was greatly interested in ancient Germanic laws. He too, in his *De antiquitate reipublicae batavicae* (1610), traced the Constitution of his country back to that distant past and praised the Batavi, who had lived in

9   See, for an outstanding example, S F C Milsom, *Historical Foundations of the Common Law*, 2nd ed, Butterworths, London, 1981.

10 J H Baker, 'The Dark Age of English Legal History', in *Legal History Studies 1972* (ed D Jenkins), University of Wales Press, Cardiff, 1975, p 1.

11 F Wieacker, *Privatrechtsgeschichte der Neuzeit*, Vandenhoeck u Reprecht, Göttingen, 1967, p 206.

12 D R Kelley, 'History, English Law and the Renaissance', (1974) 65 *Past and Present* 48. Compare G Burgess, *The Politics of the Ancient Constitution*, Macmillan, Basingstoke, 1992, pp 69 ff. Spelman's *Ancient Government* was published by Bishop Gibson in 1698 in a collection of posthumous works on the laws and antiquities of England entitled *Reliquise Spelmanniae*, Awnsham & John English, London. Spelman's book on feudalism, *Origin, Growth, Propagation, and Condition of Tenures by Knight Service,* was published in London in 1641. He also wrote treatises on ecclesiastical matters and compiled a glossary of Anglo-Saxon law terms, as well as a collection of the law of English Church councils of the period before 1066.

13 See T F T Plucknett, *A Concise History of the Common Law*, 5th ed, Butterworths, London, 1956, p 285; J H Baker, *An Introduction to English Legal History*, 3rd ed, Butterworths, London, 1990, pp 218–19; G Burgess, 1992, p 231.

the northern Netherlands in Roman times and were seen as the precursors of the liberties of the Dutch republic.[14]

Legal historians could not fail to notice the importance of medieval canon law. Thus Etienne Baluze (1630–1718), professor of canon law in Paris, edited canons of historic Church councils[15] and his collection of the Frankish capitularies, published in two volumes in Paris in 1677 under the title *Capitularia Regum Francorum*, opened a new path. The seventeenth century also produced the first historical study of the impact of Roman law on modern Europe, by the English lawyer Arthur Duck (1580–1648). Duck, author of *De Usu et Authoritate Juris Civilis Romanorum in Dominiis Principum Christianorum Libri Duo* (1648), also devoted numerous pages to the history of English law. His book was of importance for all of Europe, as it demonstrated the common Roman element in the laws of various countries.[16] John Selden (1584–1654), a leading politician and most learned jurist in the turbulent days of the Puritan revolt, cast his net even wider and may be called the pioneer of universal legal history. His research concerned not only English, but also ecclesiastical law, and encompassed biblical and other ancient legal systems.[17]

The eighteenth century had less interest in and even less respect for Roman law, but legal history was popular. The critical search for the basic axioms of a 'natural law of nations' led to questions about the origins of such fundamental institutions as private property[18] or a free constitution. Some authors dealt with them in philosophical essays, such as Montesquieu, who admired the British Constitution and remarked, with

---

14   See H Grotius, 'De Legibus Gothorum ... sive de veteri jure Germanico ... commentariolum', the prologue to his *Historia Gothorum, Vandalorum & Langobardorum*, apud Ludovicum Elzeverium, Amsterdam, 1655, and the modern edition *Hugo de Groot* (eds F Dovring, H F W D Fischer and E M Meijers), Inleidinge, Leiden, 1952, Appendix V, pp 395–9; A E M Janssen, 'Grotius als Geschichtsschreiber', in *The World of Hugo Grotius*, Holland University Press, Amsterdam and Maarssen, 1984, pp 161 ff; R Feenstra, 'Ius Commune et droit comparé chez Grotius', (1992) 3 *Rivista Internazionale di diritto comune* 11.

15   See, *inter alia*, his *Concilia Galliae Narbonensis*, Paris, 1668 and *Collectio Nova Conciliorum*, vol I, E typographia Franc Muguet, Paris, 1683.

16   N Horn, 'Römisches Recht als Gemeineuropäisches Recht bei Arthur Duck', in *Studien zur Europäischen Rechtsgeschichte* (ed W Wilhelm), Vittorio Klostermann, Frankfurt, 1972, pp 170–80.

17   See in the field of legal history the following works: J Selden, *Titles of Honour*, William Stansby, London, 1614; J Selden, *De Dis Syris syntagmata*, Ex officina Bonaventurae & Abrahami Elsevir, Lugduni Batavorum, Leiden, 1629; J Selden, *The Historie of Tithes*, London, 1618, and J Selden, *Uxor Hebraica*, Typis Richardi Bishopii, London, 1646; on contemporary issues, J Selden, *Mare Clausum*, Excudebat Willelmus Stanesbeius, pro Meighen, London, 1635 and *De Jure Naturali*, William Stansby, London, 1640. Selden's collection of oriental manuscripts went to the Bodleian library in Oxford.

18   See the recent observations in P Stein, 'The Four Stage Theory of Development of Societies' in P Stein, *The Character and Influence of the Roman Civil Law. Historical Essays*, Hambledon Press, London, 1988, pp 395–409.

his tongue in his cheek, that '*ce beau système a été trouvé dans les bois*' (that beautiful system was found in the [ancient Germanic] forests).[19] Others went about their task in a more solid and erudite way and produced early histories of German law. Justus Möser (1720–1794), for example, who studied law at Jena and Göttingen, was very much a man of the Enlightenment and natural law. He was particularly interested in the history of the German Constitution and its democratic components. His *Osnabrückische Geschichte* (1768–1780) was both an erudite piece of legal history and an inspiration for the German national movement of the nineteenth century. One leitmotiv of his work was the notion of a primeval contract between government and people and the importance of liberty and property in the life of the nation. These largely mystical ideas were attractive to the bourgeoisie in general and to Möser in particular, even though he was an enemy of the French Revolution.[20]

The breakthrough of modern critical legal history was achieved in the nineteenth century by the *Historische Rechtsschule* of Friedrich Carl von Savigny (1779–1861) and K F Eichhorn (1781–1854)[21] and by the editors of the *Monumenta Germaniae Historica*, where legal source material occupied an important place.[22] The German impulse eventually reached all of Europe. English legal history attained the best European level with F W Maitland (1850–1906), previous to whom the history of English law consisted of 'the trivial annals of an insular system'.[23] In Spain the breakthrough came with the school of Eduardo de Hinojosa y Naveros (1852–1919), legal historian and medievalist at the University of Madrid and author of the *Historia general del derecho español* I (1887) and the *Estudios sobre la historia del derecho español* of 1903.[24] At various dates, courses in legal history were organised by university law faculties. In Belgium, for example, legal history was taught from the early nineteenth century onwards (Regulations of 1816), while a law of 1835 provided for the history of Roman law, and in 1849 a course called Historical

19 Quoted in T F T Plucknett, 1956, note 13 above, p 71.
20 K Epstein, *The Genesis of German Conservatism*, Princeton University Press, Princeton, 1966.
21 See H Thieme, *Handbuch der Deutschen Rechtsgeschichte*, sub verbo *Historische Rechtsschule*, vol II, Erich Schmidt, Berlin, 1978, cols 170–2. K F Eichhorn, a colleague of Savigny in Berlin, published his *Deutsche Staats — und Rechtsgeschichte* in 4 volumes in Berlin in 1823–1844. See also H Kantorowicz, *Rechtshistorische Schriften*, C F Müller, Karlsruhe, 1970, pp 419–34 and P Koschaker, *Europa und das Römische Recht*, Biederstein, Munich, 1947, pp 254 ff.
22 R C Van Caenegem, *Guide to the Sources of Medieval History*, North Holland Publishing Co, Amsterdam, 1978, pp 189–92, 220–3.
23 T F T Plucknett, *Early English Legal Literature*, Cambridge University Press, Cambridge, 1958, p 17. The reader may also consult the recent biography by G R Elton, *F W Maitland*, Weidenfeld & Nicolson, London, 1985 in the series *Historians on Historians*.
24 See the chapter 'La recepción de la escuela historica del derecho' in J M Perez-Prendes, *Curso de Historia del Derecho Español*, Universidad Complutense de Madrid, Madrid, 1978, pp 232–7. See also A Garcia-Gallo, 1967, note 5 above, vol I, pp 14–15.

Introduction to Civil Law was introduced.[25] In Spain such courses were introduced in 1883.[26]

The sketchy nature of this outline can hopefully be excused by the lack of a comprehensive monograph on the rise and development of European legal history. Indeed, Baker's line previously quoted, 'if ever the history of English legal history comes to be written' could be applied to European as well as English legal history. In Cambridge in 1888 F W Maitland gave his famous inaugural lecture entitled 'Why the history of English law is not written'.[27] Today we might similarly wonder 'why the history of European legal history is not written', although there is no lack of works on the history of European historiography in general.[28]

Legal history: 'the handmaid of the law'?

The legal historians mentioned so far pursued a variety of interests and were inspired by diverse motives. Is it nevertheless possible to come to an agreement about the use of legal history and its essential character? The discussion has gone on for a long time and seems to have often turned on the difference between 'legal history' and 'retrospective law', the essential question being whether our discipline is historical or legal. In other words, is the study of the law of bygone centuries an autonomous pursuit which focuses on the past for its own sake and in all its aspects, or is it a handmaid of legal science, which aims to show how present-day rules and institutions originated[29] and is therefore primarily interested in the law as

---

25   R Verstegen, 'L'enseignement du droit en Belgique. Evolution de la législation aux XIXe et XXe siècles' in *Xenia iuris historiae G van Dievoet oblata* (eds F Stevens and D Van den Auweele), Faculty of Law, University of Leuwen, Leuwen, 1990, pp 173–4.

26   A Garcia-Gallo, 1967, note 5 above, p 13.

27   T F T Plucknett, 1958, note 23 above, p 5. See the reflections in I Fletcher, 'An English Tragedy: the Academic Lawyer as Jurist', in *Lawyers and Laymen* (eds T M Charles-Edwards et al), University of Wales Press, Cardiff, 1986, pp 316–35, and Cocks R, 'History in Eclipse? The Role of the Past in Books on the English Legal System', in *The Life of the Law. Proceedings Tenth British Legal History Conference Oxford 1991* (ed P Birks), Hambledon Press, London, 1993, pp 257–67.

28   See, *inter alia*, J Westfall Thompson, *A History of Historical Writing*, 2 volumes, Macmillan, New York, 1942 and the other works referred to in R C Van Caenegem, 1978, note 22 above, p 159, note 1.

29   It is interesting to see how Professor Meijers found the way to legal history, on which he became a world authority. He started as a follower of 'dogmatic legal science' and a practising barrister in Amsterdam for whom legal history was irrelevant, but soon discovered that certain problems posed by the Code could only be solved through history. Thus one of his earliest studies was devoted to the puzzling enumeration of five real rights in the Dutch Civil Code of 1838, for which he found no logical or dogmatic explanation. Working back from 1838 he discovered that the peculiar list had been copied down the ages and ultimately went back to an obscure dissertation of 1639 by a certain H Hahn in the University of Helmstadt. E M Meijers, 'Art 584 B W en de Zakelijke Rechten', (1907) *Rechtsgeleerd Magazijn* 272 ff. See on this E I Strubbe, 'E M Meijers en de Rechtsgeschiedenis', (1955) 23 *Tijdschrift voor Rechtsgeschiedenis* 401–3.

we now know it? In the former case, legal history facilitates an understanding of the past; in the latter it assists in an understanding of the present law. The distinction is made sharply and consciously by Sir James Holt, for example. In his well-known book on the Magna Carta, Holt points out that his approach 'is different from McKechnie's, for it is the work of a historian not a lawyer'.[30] Hence also Plucknett's apodictic pronouncement that 'legal history is not law, but history'[31] or Baker's warning that Sir Matthew Hale, author of the previously mentioned history of the common law, 'made considerable use of history, but was not truly a historian'[32] and that Coke's 'antiquities' were a guide not to the past but to the present.[33] Equally sharp is Fifoot's different characterisation of the authors of the famous *History of English Law before the Time of Edward I*: 'To Pollock history was the handmaid of the law. To Maitland law was one aspect of history'.[34] W S Holdsworth distinguishes 'sheer antiquarianism' from 'effective legal history', which 'should only give us so much of the history of procedure as will enable us to understand the manner in which our modern rules have been evolved'. And he goes on to quote Justice Oliver Wendell Holmes who warned his readers against 'the pitfall of antiquarianism' and asked them to 'remember that for our purpose our only interest in the past is for the light it throws upon the present'. The legal historian is told to 'avoid what Selden called the sterile part of antiquity' and ordered 'to have his eye on the end of the story'[35] — a straightforward way of preaching teleology. This attitude, by the way, explains why Holdsworth deemed the Puritan interlude and its legal experiments not worthy of his attention because, as he put it, 'the legal historian must pass briefly over the period of the civil war and he cannot describe in any great detail the legislation of the Commonwealth as that legislation was all swept away at the Restoration'.[36]

The concept of legal history as a 'handmaid of the law' (reminiscent of medieval ideas about philosophy as *ancilla theologiae*) deserves some attention. Sir Edward Coke, whom we mentioned before, often scrutinised ancient court rolls and yearbooks in order to underpin his own convictions about what the law was or ought to be, and his search for precedents in *Bonham*'s case is a good illustration of this approach. *Bonham* was not about a legal technicality, but about the burning political issue between those who claimed the predominance of the fundamental

---

30   J C Holt, *Magna Carta*, 2nd ed, Cambridge University Press, Cambridge, 1992, p xi.
31   T F T Plucknett, 1958, note 23 above, p 16.
32   J H Baker, 1990, note 13 above, p 219.
33   J H Baker, 1972, note 10 above, p 2.
34   C M S Fifoot, *Pollock and Maitland*, David Murray Foundation lecture, University of Glasgow, Glasgow, 1971, p 17.
35   W S Holdsworth, *Some Lessons from our Legal History*, Macmillan, New York, 1928, p 6.
36   W S Holdsworth, *History of English Law*, vol VI, Methuen, London, 1937, p 142. T F T Plucknett, 1956, note 13 above, p 54, uses the phrase 'premature advances' for various attempts at modernization at the time of the interregnum, which he also describes as 'anticipations of modern legal reforms'.

principles of the common law as interpreted by the judges and those who maintained the omnipotence of the law-giver, ie the king in parliament[37] — a dispute that was still reverberating around the halls of Westminster in 1993, when the Union (Maastricht) Treaty was the centre of a political storm. Similarly, Wielant was concerned with the political issue of the sovereignty of the Burgundian Netherlands:[38] the 'handmaid of the law' easily turned into a handmaid of politics. In the same vein readers familiar with seventeenth century English history will recall the Norman Yoke theory, which condemned the feudal monarchy as resulting from foreign conquest, and extolled the ancient freedoms of the Anglo-Saxons.[39]

Some readers might think that this sort of 'political history' has been superseded by the strictly scientific methods of our own time, but this could well be an illusion. Anyone familiar with German legal history in the nineteenth and twentieth centuries will be aware of the great political currents and debates which divided learned authors on such topics as the merits of Germanic and Roman law, or the role of feudalism.[40] It is fascinating to see Heinrich Mitteis (1889-1952) for example, a legal historian, debating the merits of German and Roman law and reproaching the latter for being liberal, individualistic and capitalistic, as against the ancient Germanic social sense of warm *Genossenschaft*. He apparently failed to notice that the most liberal and capitalistic society of the nineteenth century was England, where Roman law was largely ignored.[41]

---

37   See on this most famous case T F T Plucknett, 'Bonham's Case and Judicial Review', (1926) 40 *Harvard Law Review* 35–46; S E Thorne, 'Dr Bonham's Case', (1938) 54 *Law Quarterly Review* 543–52; R Berger, 'Doctor Bonham's Case: Statutory Construction or Constitutional Theory', (1969) 117 *University of Pennsylvania Law Review* 521-45; C M Gray, 'Bonham's Case Reviewed', (1972) 116 *Proceedings American Philosophical Society* 35–58; H J Cook, 'Against Common Right and Reason: The College of Physicians Against Dr Thomas Bonham', (1985) 29 *American Journal of Legal History* 301–22.

38   S Dauchy, 'Les appels flamands au Parlement de Paris 1320–1520', in *Vorträge zur Justizforschung. Geschichte und Theorie*, vol I (eds H Mohnhaupt and D Simon), V Klostermann, Frankfurt, 1992, pp 45–77.

39   See the remarks in R Boutruche, *Seigneurie et Féodalité. Le premier âge des liens d'homme à homme*, Aubier, Paris, 1968, pp 12–18; G Burgess, 1992, note 12 above, pp 90–4.

40   See on this vast subject, *inter alia*, H Thieme, *Handwörterbuch*, vol I, sub verbo *Deutsches Privatrecht (German private law)*, Erich Schmidt, Berlin, 1971, cols 702–9; H Thieme, 'Le "droit commun germanique" du moyen âge. Fantaisie des professeurs du XIXe siècle ou réalité?' in *Droit privé et institutions régionales. Etudes historiques J Yves*, Presses universitaires de France, Paris, 1976, pp 663–70; H Thieme, 'Die Germanistische Rechtsgeschichte in Freiburg', in H Thieme, *Ideengeschichte und Rechtsgeschichte: Gesammelte Schriften*, vol II, Böhlau, Cologne, Vienna, 1986, pp 1138–53; K Luig, 'Die sozial-ethischen Werte des Römischen und Germanischen Rechts in der Privatrechtswissenschaft des 19. Jahrhunderts' in *Wege Europäischer Rechtsgeschichte*, P Lang, Frankfurt, 1987, pp 281–307; R C Van Caenegem, *An Historical Introduction to Private Law*, 2nd ed, Cambridge University Press, Cambridge, 1992, pp 155–9.

41   *Heinrich Mitteis nach Hundert Jahren (1889–1989)* (eds P Landau, H Nehlsen and D W Willoweit), Verlag der Bayerischen Akademie der Wissenschaften, Munich, 1991 (Bayer Akad Wiss, Philos Hist Kl, Abh NF 106).

Savigny: 'a disaster for Germany'?

Any legal history which transcends the mere description of antiquarian detail will necessarily be confronted with the great issues of the day and have to address them in some way. In so doing it can play a liberating role by guarding against dogmatism,[42] widening the lawyer's horizon and dispelling national myths. Nationalism is notoriously out of place in legal history, as for many centuries Europe ignored national legal systems and lived either by the cosmopolitan Roman and canon law or by local or regional custom; even the seeming exception, the English common law, was rooted in twelfth century Norman feudalism.[43] Also, the fact that the *Bürgerliches Gesetzbuch* is more Roman than the *Code civil* illustrates the transnational movements in the genesis of the great European codes.

. On the other hand, when harnessed to serve national or racial myths, legal history can play an obscurantist role, and by extolling the existing order it can obstruct change and modernisation. The school of Savigny was profoundly conservative and detested the French Revolution and all its works.[44] Hans Thieme has remarked on the 'considerable damage' caused by the *Historische Rechtsschule*, ie by its unbridled historicism which rejected all timeless norms and by subjecting all law to the contingent, time-bound commands of the state, provided the basis of legal positivism and its total rejection of natural law.[45] In the nineteenth century the latter came to be seen as abstract and cosmopolitan, whereas legal history was solidly steeped in the fatherland and the time-hallowed tradition of the ordinary people.

It is therefore understandable that the French Revolution, rooted in Enlightenment and natural law, was averse to legal history, as was Napoleon who classed its followers among the *idéologues*. It was said in 1789 that the Revolution refused 'to ask the past centuries of barbarism to provide laws for the civilized nations',[46] or, as Rabaut-Saint-Etienne put it in 1792, 'History is not our lawbook'.[47] It was precisely because the study of the past might turn students away from the Code that in 1822 the chair of legal history in Paris was abolished by the government, because, as the Grand Master of the University, Monseigneur Frayssinous put it, these

---

42 H Conrad, *Deutsche Rechtsgeschichte*, vol I, C F Müller, Karlsruhe, 1962, p xvii.

43 R C Van Caenegem, *The Birth of the English Common Law*, 2nd ed, Cambridge University Press, Cambridge, 1988, pp 85–110.

44 R C Van Caenegem, 1992, note 40 above, pp 173–4; F Wieacker, 1967, note 11 above, pp 381–99.

45 H Thieme, 1971, note 40 above, vol II, cols 170–2.

46 M Thomann, 'Lehrfächer an den Universitäten in Deutschland und in Frankreich. Die elsässischen Juristen des 19. Jahrhunderts im Kamp für die Rechtsgeschichte' in *Festschrift für Hans Thieme* (ed K Kroeschell), J Thorbecke, Sigmaringen, 1986, pp 353-362.

47 M Thomann, 1986, p 356.

lectures 'might lead the youth to discuss dangerous questions'[48] — dangerous, presumably, to the newly established *paix bourgeoise*.[49]

Hermann Conrad, for many years professor at Bonn University and a much respected scholar not given to wild statements, called Savigny's School 'a disaster for Germany'. This sort of value judgment is, however, rejected by other scholars as inappropriate and unscientific. Thus Professor Peter Rassow said equally apodictically: 'We historians know no happy history'.[50] But then, if legal historians are denied value judgments, 'will they not deserve the reproach of having failed to guide men toward more intelligent, realistic and just objectives?'[51]

Whether we like it or not, everything significant is in some way political. Napoleon, as we have seen, needed technicians of the law without culture. The Nazis wanted technicians with (historical) culture, but their history was imposed and dogmatic. For a long time the English ideal was to produce lawyers who were first and foremost cultured gentlemen to whom the law came as an afterthought. On the continent the ancient regime produced lawyers who were university trained in the *Corpus Juris*, but also steeped in classical literature: the Dutch 'Elegant School' combined the technical know-how of the Bartolists with the cultural pursuits and tastes of the Humanists.[52] The glossators of the twelfth and thirteenth centuries had been legal technicians without much knowledge of ancient civilisation, and were much derided for it by Alciatus, Budé and their followers.

Legal anthropology and the Enlightenment

Legal anthropology came into its own in the nineteenth century. It was an extension of the time-frame of legal history reaching back to the periods and peoples who ignored writing, and was soon followed by legal archaeology, where dumb objects (non literary) are often the only

---

48 M Thomann, 1986, p 357.
49 The expression has been borrowed from the title of the book by A J Arnaud, *Essai d'Analyse Structurale du Code Civil Français. La Règle du Jeu dans la Paix Bourgeoise*, Librairie générale de droit et de jurisprudence, Paris, 1973.
50 The quote is from the interventions by Conrad and Rassow after a lecture given by Sir Ivor Jennings in Düsseldorf on 16 March 1960. I Jennings, *Die Umwandlung von Geschichte in Gesetz*, Westdeutcher Verlag, Cologne and Opladen, 1965, pp 33–6 (*Arbeitsgemeinschaft für Forschung des Landes Nordrhein-Westfalen, Geisteswissenschaften*, 101). The full quotation of Conrad's phrase on p 36 is as follows: '*Ich möchte sagen, daß die unglückliche Entwicklung unseres modernen bürgerlichen Rechtes zum Teil auf diese Entwicklung der historischen Rechtsschule zurückzuführen ist, ja man kann sogar sagen, daß die historische Rechtsschule in dieser Richtung in etwa ein Unglück für Deutschland gewesen ist.*' Rassow was an authority on German political history from the Middle Ages to the twentieth century.
51 B Lyon, *A Constitutional and Legal History of Medieval England*, Norton, New York, 1980, p xi.
52 See the classic work by R W Lee, *An Introduction to Roman-Dutch Law*, 4th ed, Clarendon Press, Oxford, 1946.

available witnesses.[53] Legal ethnology is mainly interested in the remote, often hypothetical origins of basic institutions. Ever since the ancient Greeks, there has been speculation about the earliest roots of private property, criminal justice and liberal organisation,[54] and the European Enlightenment took the theme up again with great avidity. Nevertheless, it was in the nineteenth century that modern organised and scholarly research was launched by authors such as Bachofen, Maine and Kohler. Johann Jakob Bachofen (1815–1887) was a Swiss legal historian who studied in Berlin and came under Savigny's influence. He extended his research beyond the traditional confines of Roman and Germanic law and became a champion of universal legal history and ethnology, particularly with the publication, in 1861, of his pioneering study on matriarchy, entitled *Das Mutterrecht. Eine Untersuchung über die Gynaikokratie aller Welt nach ihrer religiösen und rechtlichen Natur.* During his lifetime he enjoyed little success. This was not the case with his English contemporary Sir Henry Sumner Maine (1822–1888), whose *Ancient Law, its Connection With the Early History of Society and its Relations to Modern Ideals,* also published in 1861, became a classic and went through numerous reprints. He also wrote *Village Communities in the East and West* (1871) and a *Lecture on the Early History of Institutions* (1875). Maine spent some time in India and returned to England to teach jurisprudence at Oxford University from 1870 to 1878. He described several stages in the development from primitive tribalism to modern statehood seen in a universal comparative framework. Josef Kohler (1849–1919) was a lawyer with universal interests, who taught for more than thirty years in Berlin. He published important work on legal history, legal ethnology and comparative law, passing from late medieval Italian borough charters to Charles V's *Carolina,* Assyrian title deeds and the law codes of King Hammurabi and of the city of Gortyn. As his sphere of interest was much wider than the traditional legal history, in 1878 he became co-founder of (and was frequently published in) the *Zeitschrift für Vergleichende Rechtswissenschaft,* where legal ethnology was given free rein.

The well-known and much deplored fragmentation of scholarly disciplines has meant that legal history, ethnology and archaeology have gone their own ways. This may be beneficial for the thoroughness of detailed research, but tends, regrettably, to reduce communication and exchange of results and ideas. Fortunately, they all tend to widen the lawyer's horizon and illustrate that the concern with and the search for good laws is one of the oldest preoccupations of mankind.

---

53   See on the unsatisfactory relationship between legal anthropology and legal history the remarks by A Erler in *Handwörterbuch,* Erich Schmidt, Berlin, 1971, vol I, cols 1022–5, sub verbo *Ethnologie.* For a brief survey of the rise of legal anthropology see L Carlen in *Handwörterbuch,* vol I, 1990, cols 268–72, sub verbo *Rechtsarchäologie.*

54   P Stein, 1988, note 18 above, pp 396–7.

INDEX

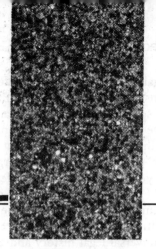